Water, Culture, and Power

Water, Culture, and Power

Local Struggles in a Global Context

Edited by John M. Donahue and
Barbara Rose Johnston

ISLAND PRESS
Washington, D.C. • Covelo, California

Library of Congress Cataloging in Publication Data

Water, culture and power : local struggles in a global context /
  John M. Donahue and Barbara Rose Johnston, editors.
     p. cm.
       Includes bibliographical references and index.
       ISBN 1-55963-521-5 (cloth.) — ISBN 1-55963-522-3 (paper)
       1. Water resources development—Case studies. 2. Water
  resources development—Government policy—International
  cooperation. 3. Water-supply—Political aspects. 4. Water-
  supply—Social aspects.
  I. Donahue, John M.   II. Johnson, Barbara Rose.
  HD1691.W323 1998
  333.91—dc21   97-41051
                                                                    CIP

Printed on recycled, acid-free paper ∞

Manufactured in the United States of America

10 9 8 7 6 5 4 3 2 1

*Dedicated to our children as they enter
the twenty-first century*

Edward Donahue

Bernadette Donahue

Roberto Alejandro Donahue

Benjamin Johnston Edwards

Christopher Johnston Edwards

*whose lives and futures depend
on decisions made in the here and now.*

Contents

List of Illustrations and Tables xi

1. Introduction   1
   Barbara Rose Johnston and John M. Donahue

━━━━━━━━━━━━━━➤ PART I ◄━━━━━━━━━━━

Rights and Resources
Water, Development, and Cultural Survival

2. The Use and Abuse of Aquifers: Can the Hopi Indians   9
   Survive Multinational Mining?
   Peter Whiteley and Vernon Masayesva

3. Water Rights in the Pacific Northwest   35
   Tom Greaves

4. "A River That Was Once So Strong and Deep": Local   47
   Reflections on the Eastmain Diversion, James Bay
   Hydroelectric Project
   Kreg Ettenger

5. Balancing the Waters: Development and Hydropolitics in   73
   Contemporary Zimbabwe
   Bill Derman

6. Water, Rights, and the El Cajón Dam, Honduras   95
   William M. Loker

━━━━━━━━━━━━━━➤ PART II ◄━━━━━━━━━━

Project Culture and Hydropolitics
The Making and Unmaking of Water Development Projects

7. Water Resource Development and Its Effects on the Human   123
   Community: The Tennessee-Tombigbee Waterway, South-
   eastern United States
   Claudia M. Rogers

8. Transacting a Commons: The Lake Biwa Comprehensive   141
    Development Plan, Shiga Prefecture, Japan
    James E. Nickum and Daniel Greenstadt

9. The Big Canal: The Political Ecology of the Central   163
    Arizona Project
    Thomas E. Sheridan

10. Water Wars in South Texas: Managing the Edwards Aquifer   187
    John M. Donahue

11. Gender and Society in Bangladesh's Flood Action Plan   209
    Suzanne Hanchett, Jesmin Akhter, and Kazi Rozana Akhter

PART III

The Culture and Power Dimensions
of Water Scarcity

12. A Reversal of Tides: Drinking Water Quality in   237
    Oaxaca de Juárez, Mexico
    M. Brian Riley, Arthur D. Murphy, and
    Miguel Angel Méndez Rosado

13. Water, Power, and Environmental Health in Tourism   263
    Development: The Bay Islands, Honduras
    Susan C. Stonich, Jerrel H. Sorensen, and Gus W. Salbador

14. Culture, Power, and the Hydrological Cycle: Creating and 285
    Responding to Water Scarcity on St. Thomas, Virgin Islands
    Barbara Rose Johnston

15. Water Between Arabs and Israelis: Researching Twice-   313
    Promised Resources
    Rosina Hassoun

16. Conclusion   339
    John M. Donahue and Barbara Rose Johnston

References   347

Contributors   377

Index   383

Illustrations and Tables

Chapter 2

Figure 2.1. Navajo and Hopi reservations relative to the Peabody   11
Western Coal Company mine
Photo 2.1. Hopi gardens   14
Figure 2.2. Black Mesa and the Peabody Western Coal Company's   20
lease areas
Figure 2.3. Groundwater flow in the N-Aquifer   21

Chapter 3

Figure 3.1. The Lummi Indian Reservation, Bellingham area, and   37
Nooksack River watershed

Chapter 4

Figure 4.1. The lower Eastmain River in Quebec and the Cree Indian   49
village of Eastmain
Figure 4.2. The James Bay region of northern Quebec   50
Photo 4.1. The Mantuwataw Rapids on the Eastmain River   55

Chapter 5

Figure 5.1. Communal areas and natural regions in Zimbabwe   79

Chapter 6

Figure 6.1. The Republic of Honduras and the El Cajón Dam and   98
Reservoir
Photo 6.1. Typical landscape in the El Cajón region   99
Photo 6.2. A view of the streets of Montañuelas   100
Photo 6.3. Residents of the El Cajón region on a veranda in El Mango   103

Chapter 7

Photo 7.1. An eight-barge tow on the Tennessee-Tombigbee Waterway   125
Figure 7.1. Vicinity of the Tennessee-Tombigbee Waterway   127
Figure 7.2. Area of the Tennessee-Tombigbee Corridor Study   129

Chapter 8

Figure 8.1. Japan and Lake Biwa   143
Figure 8.2. The Yodo River Basin   144
Photo 8.1. Development along the Otsu shore of Lake Biwa   152

Chapter 9

Figure 9.1. Water in Arizona: major rivers and dams and the Central   165
            Arizona Project canal
Photo 9.1. President Lyndon Johnson signing the Colorado River Basin   178
            Project Act
Figure 9.2. Route of the Central Arizona Project with the proposed   179
            Orme Dam

Chapter 10

Figure 10.1. The Edwards Aquifer region   190
Figure 10.2. Cross section of the Edwards Aquifer   191

Chapter 11

Figure 11.1. Bangladesh   211
Figure 11.2. Village topography in Bangladesh   212
Figure 11.3. Comparison of average and extreme flooding in Bangladesh   213
Photo 11.1. Bangladesh family in front of their flooded home   217

Chapter 12

Figure 12.1. The Oaxaca Valley, Mexico   240
Figure 12.2. Major water distribution zones in Oaxaca de Juárez   242
Figure 12.3. Neighborhood types and sampling locations in   245
            Oaxaca de Juárez
Table 12.1. Water Facilities in Oaxaca de Juárez, by Neighborhood   246
            Type
Table 12.2. Neighborhood Types in Oaxaca de Juárez, by Socio-   252
            economic Status
Table 12.3. Neighborhoods in Oaxaca de Juárez, by Socioeconomic   258
            Status and Water Quality

Chapter 13

Figure 13.1. Bay Islands, Republic of Honduras   266
Photo 13.1. Home of a middle-class Islander, Bay Islands   273
Photo 13.2. Ladino ghetto, Bay Islands   274

Chapter 14

Figure 14.1. St. Thomas, Virgin Islands   286
Photo 14.1. Water and Power Authority (WAPA) desalination facility,   297
            St. Thomas
Photo 14.2. Private delivery trucks filling their tanks with desalinated 301
            water, St. Thomas

Chapter 15

Figure 15.1. Israeli water projects   327

Water, Culture, and Power

Introduction

Barbara Rose Johnston and John M. Donahue

Water

Water is essential to life. The earth is a world of water, yet it is also a world where freshwater is relatively scarce. Only some 2.5 percent of the total volume of water on earth is freshwater, and large portions of · the global supply are inaccessible.

The water cycle, driven by the sun, lifts purified water from oceans and land and releases it as rain and snow—some 10 percent of this over land and the remainder over seas. A bit more than two-thirds of the global freshwater supply is frozen in glaciers and polar ice caps. The remaining freshwater (0.77 percent of all water) is held in aquifers, soil pores, lakes, swamps, rivers, plant life, and the atmosphere. Thanks to seasonal and geographic variabilities, that which is accessible for human use is an even smaller figure. For example, the Amazon River alone accounts for some 15 percent of global runoff, and an estimated 95 percent of its flow is inaccessible (Czaya 1981).

Of all the water on earth, only one one-hundredth of 1 percent is available for human use as fresh, drinkable water, provided by stable runoff from rivers and lakes and a small amount stored in dams (Postel et al. 1996). Even so, this supply would support many times our present population if it all could be exploited (Meyers 1993, 102–103). However, both the water and the world's peoples are unevenly distributed (Middleton et al. 1994, 141–143).

According to estimates by the United Nations Environment Programme, at least 1.7 billion people living on earth do not have an adequate supply of drinking water, and an estimated 40 percent of the world's population faces chronic shortages. Many of these people live in arid regions, water-stressed countries where rain is limited and they must rely on rivers and groundwater for their freshwater needs. Nine of the fourteen countries of the Middle East, for example, face water scarcity (Postel 1992, 287). Population growth in water-scarce regions exacerbates the problem. By the year 2000, some 300 million people living in fifteen countries in Africa—one-third of the continent's population—will struggle with water scarcity (Postel 1993, 106). Many of those facing water shortages live in degraded watersheds where deforestation, erosion, increased runoff, and microclimatic change contribute to water scarcity. And across the world, in all zones and settings, people are becoming increasingly vulnerable to the forces of global climate change as weather becomes increasingly chaotic and unpredictable and crops freeze, rot, or wither on the vine (Ohlsson 1995).

Water scarcity, however, is more than a matter of disturbed terrain, increased population, and climate change. Water scarcity can also be a by-product of water management projects: the building of dams, canals, and complicated delivery systems may provide water for some at the cost of others, with short-term gains that wreak long-term ecological havoc (Gleick 1993; McCully 1996; Postel 1992; Reisner 1986). Moreover, water scarcity can be a product of the social systems. Many of those facing water shortages live in the world's cities, where water is often supplied to the rich by municipal systems while the urban poor, living on the fringes of cities, are forced to purchase water from vendors at rates as much as forty times higher (Meyers 1993, 103). Many people have access only to water that is unfit for consumption— contaminated by sewage, agricultural runoff, and industrial waste (Hu and Kim 1993).

Finally, the artificial nature of geopolitical borders influences water quality and water scarcity. Many of the important water basins of the world straddle political borders. Water containment and diversion schemes in one country affect supply and quality in other countries. The Nile River basin, for example, embraces parts of nine countries; conflict results as sovereign nations claim competing rights to use, store, divert, and pollute (Homer-Dixon 1996; Lowi 1996; Ohlsson 1995). Water allocations based on political and economic interests often exceed actual water availability, leaving downstream (or less powerful) users with a trickle of salty, contaminated water (Reisner 1986).

In short, water scarcity is more than a matter of decreased supply or increased demand. Water scarcity is influenced by a variety of factors, including topography, climate, economic activities, population growth, cultural beliefs, perceptions and traditions, and power relationships.

Culture and Power

The Chinese word for crisis is written with two characters, one that suggests danger and another that suggests opportunity. In many ways, the story of water at the end of the millennium is a story of the tension between danger and opportunity. The dangers of flood and drought can be transformed into economic opportunities as rivers are dammed, waters are diverted into distant fields, and power is generated to feed factories and towns. Yet such transformations imply other changes as well. Nature is dominated and turned into a commodity, complex bioregions are destroyed (Abramovitz 1995), and human social and cultural systems are dramatically, sometimes drastically, altered. Thus, the story of water is all too often a story of conflict and struggle between the forces of self-interest and opportunities associated with "progress" and the community-based values and needs of traditional ways of life.

In every community, people value water for different reasons and use water in different ways. The quest to capture, store, and distribute a reliable supply of water (or energy) implies the capture of a commons resource and the building of structures and institutions to enclose, commodify, and control it. This process of politicizing and commodifying nature requires centralized institutions of power and a reliance on technology to conquer natural forces. Systems for controlling resource access and use typically reflect the ways in which society is organized and thus recreate and reproduce the inequities in society (*The Ecologist* 1993).

In this book, we present a series of case studies that examine these complex cultural and power dimensions of water resources and water resource management. Contributors to this volume examine the origins, the anatomy, and at times the resolution of water conflicts in the United States, Canada, Mexico, Honduras, the Virgin Islands, Japan, Zimbabwe, Bangladesh, and the Middle East. Case studies span the continuum of water management contexts: dam construction, hydroelectric power generation, irrigation, transportation, water quality, and cogeneration (desalination). Attention is focused on the various actors in water debates, including historical actors and events but also the varied stakeholders: indigenous peoples, politicians, government agencies, environmentalists, agriculture and other industry-specific users, and citizen groups. The chapters present highly contested and contentious cases such as hydroelectric development at James Bay in Quebec, water management in the Colorado River basin, and the role of water access and control in the Arab-Israeli conflict. Cases also explore the cultural and power dynamics of water management in international (e.g., South Texas), national (e.g., Israel), regional (e.g., James Bay), and local (e.g., Virgin Islands) settings.

The book is organized into three parts dealing broadly with the issues of culture, power, and water. Part I (Rights and Resources: Water, Development, and Cultural Survival) explores some of the varied cultural meanings of water and water resources by examining the impact of water resource development on indigenous peoples. These chapters describe how water is the lifeblood of reproductive systems that maintain and support biological and cultural existence and how watersheds are the situational backdrop for cultural meaning, experience, history, and future. Thus, contested rights to use, constrain, and control water often involve contested rights to land and to the loci of power in resource decision making, both factors that sustain cultural identity.

Part II (Project Culture and Hydropolitics: The Making and Unmaking of Water Development Projects) focuses more explicitly on the political process of funding and building water resource projects. These chapters explore the varied reasons for initiating water development projects, describe the political and economic factors that shape these hugely expensive activities, and provide some sense of the promise that sustains the dream of water resource development over the long years between genesis and completion. Because these cases examine the intersection of culture and power, they also illustrate how different cultural notions, needs, and agendas intersect at a conflict axis, challenging the construction and viability of proposed projects and occasionally bringing a halt to the development process. Water resource crises and conflicts present opportunities to contest existing power relations; indeed, the power to declare a crisis in itself is contingent on possession of power (cf. Lees 1995).

Water is power, and the politics of water are such that dead projects can continually be brought back to life, carrying with them the baggage of outmoded dreams. The initial funding of projects creates momentum in itself, and despite changing times and needs, efforts to "fix" nature or protect human investment may continue to be funded for reasons of political capital rather than the actual viability of the project. Efforts to change or transform the focus of projects continually confront the entrenched "project culture," which may find its institutional power threatened.

The contradictions between dreams and reality, between hydro-development and reproductive strategies, and between those who

stand to gain and those who stand to lose result in inevitable conflict—
conflict that presents adverse consequences in both the biophysical
and cultural realms. Thus, part III (The Culture and Power Dimensions
of Water Scarcity) examines the tensions between culture and power as
they structure perceptions and experiences of water scarcity and,
indeed, as they have transformed the very nature of water.

There is growing awareness that water scarcity plays an increasingly significant role in local, national, and international conflicts.
Thomas Homer-Dixon and members of his Environmental Change
and Security Project define three types of scarcity: demand-induced
scarcity, caused by population growth or increased per capita activity;
supply-induced scarcity, marked by a drop in renewable resource
supply because the resource is degraded or depleted faster than it is
replenished; and structural scarcity, which arises from inequitable distribution of resources (Homer-Dixon et al. 1994, 391–400).

It is our contention that an adequate understanding of resource
scarcity must also include an understanding of the process by which
scarcity (or the perception of scarcity) is created—what motivates
people to act in the way they do, to define resources and resource
crises, and to devise responses. Thus, although places and cases vary,
all chapters address the values and meanings associated with water in
a given context, the power to attribute a certain cultural meaning to
water, and different how changes in power result in different definitions of meaning and different patterns of water resource use, access,
and control. Cultural notions, histories, economies, environmental
conditions, and power relations all play a role in establishing differential resource relations, and this differential is a significant factor in
ensuing conflicts and crises.

PART I

Rights and Resources

Water, Development, and Cultural Survival

The Use and Abuse of Aquifers
Can the Hopi Indians Survive Multinational Mining?

Peter Whiteley and Vernon Masayesva

Author Summary

Three actors play significant roles in water use in northeastern Arizona: the Hopi, the Navajo, and the Peabody Western Coal Company. The Hopi cultural and religious understanding of springs (*paavahu*) is contrasted with Peabody's use of water to transport its coal to Nevada by slurry. The company's wells are depleting the springs, and the springs are drying up. Hopi religious concerns with springs and *paanaqso'a* (deathly thirst) are metaphorical of larger issues of global development and natural resource management.

A very long time ago there was nothing but water. In the east Hurúing Wuhti, the deity of all hard substances, lived in the ocean. . . . The Sun also existed at that time. . . . By and by these two deities caused some dry land to appear in the midst of the water, the waters receding eastward and westward.

("Origin Myth" recorded by H. R. Voth [1905b])

This is . . . one of the most arid countries in the world, and we need that water. That is why we do Kachina dances in the summer, just to get a drop of rain. And to us, this water is worth more than gold, or the money. Maybe we cannot stop the mining of the coal, but we sure would like to stop the use of water.

(Dennis Tewa, Munqapi village)[1]

Hopi Society and Environmental Adaptation

The Hopi Indians of northeastern Arizona are an epitome of human endurance: they are farmers without water. According to their genesis narrative, the Hopi emerged from a layer under the earth into this, the fourth, world by climbing up inside a reed. On their arrival, they met a deity, Maasaw, who presented them with a philosophy of life based on three elements: maize seeds, a planting stick, and a gourd full of water. *Qa'ö*, maize, was the soul of the Hopi people, representing their very identity. *Sooya,* the planting stick, represented the simple technology they should depend on: there was an explicit warning against over-dependency on technology, which had taken on a life of its own in the third world below, producing destruction through materialism, greed, and egotism. *Wikoro,* the gourd filled with water, represented the environment—the land and all its life-forms—as well as the sign of the Creator's blessing, if the Hopis would uphold Maasaw's covenant and live right. Maasaw told them that life in this place would be arduous and daunting, but through resolute perseverance and industry, they would live long and be spiritually rich.[2]

The twelve Hopi villages lie on a generally southeast-northwest axis stretching roughly one hundred kilometers (sixty-two miles) as the crow flies (see figure 2.1).[3] The villages cluster in groups around the tips of three fingerlike promontories, known as the Hopi mesas, that form the southwesternmost extensions of Black Mesa, an upthrust plate of the Colorado Plateau (see figure 2.2 on page 20). Black Mesa is bisected by four principal southwest-trending washes, Moenkopi, Dinnebito, Oraibi, and Polacca; all but Moenkopi are ephemeral and flow only after significant precipitation. Smaller washes, Jeddito and Wepo, near First Mesa, are also locally important. The Wepo and Oraibi Washes separate the Hopi mesas from one another, cutting arroyo channels in valleys some 90 to 120 meters (300 to 400 feet) below the mesa tops, on which the villages perch. The washes and their tributary fans are main areas of Hopi floodwater farming. Only the Moenkopi Wash (far removed from the central area of Hopi villages) supports irrigation, in farmlands below the villages of Upper and Lower Munqapi, which remain the most productive areas for Hopi crops (the name *Munqapi,* anglicized to *Moenkopi,* means "continuously flowing water place"—an index of its social importance). The Moenkopi Wash is fed by tributary stream flows and springs but also is fed directly by an aquifer in a layer of sandstone called "Navajo" that sits below the surface of Black Mesa within the hydrological province known as the Black Mesa Basin.[4]

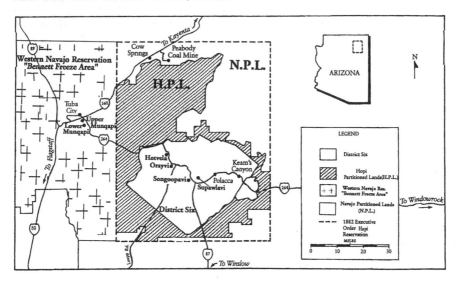

FIGURE 2.1.NAVAJO AND HOPI RESERVATIONS RELATIVE
TO THE PEABODY WESTERN COAL COMPANY MINE

The 1882 Executive Order Hopi Reservation encompassed District Six, origi-
nally a grazing district, which included most of the Hopi village sites; the Hopi
Partitioned Lands (HPL); and the Navajo Partitioned Lands (NPL), which were
created as a result of the Navajo-Hopi Indian Land Settlement Act of 1974.
The Black Mesa mine straddles the north-central border of the HPL and the
NPL. The villages of Upper and Lower Munqapi fall within the Western
Navajo Reservation "Bennett Freeze Area," which currently is also in process
of partition between the Hopi Tribe and the Navajo Nation. Courtesy of the
University of Arizona Press (modified from Whiteley 1988b).

The Hopi's principal supply of drinking water is traditionally found
in springs—indeed, Hopi history, which focuses on centripetal migrations by independent clans from all points of the compass, specifically
remarks on the abundance and reliability of the springs that stud the
walls of First, Second, and Third Mesas.[5] The springs have determined
Hopi settlement patterns and uses of natural resources. As geologist
Herbert Gregory, an early visitor to the Navajo and Hopi Indian Reservations, pointed out:

> One of the surprises . . . is the large number of springs widely
> distributed over the reservation. Tucked away in alcoves in
> the high mesa walls or issuing from crevices in the canyon
> sides or bubbling up through the sands in the long wash
> floors, these tiny supplies of water appear to be distributed in
> haphazard fashion. . . . The ancient cliff dweller was well
> aware of the desirability of these small permanent supplies as

centers for settlement, and many of the present-day Indian
trails owe their position to the location of springs rather than
to topography or to length of route.

(Gregory 1916, 132)

Insofar as the archaeological record confirms traditional history, the
period between 1300 and 1500 C.E. saw a concentric contraction of
more widespread villages—from Mesa Verde, Navajo Mountain, Tsegi
Canyon, the Little Colorado River, and the Hopi Buttes—into such
centers as are still populated by the Hopi today.[6]

Hopi presence in the region and engagement with its particular
environmental exigencies is thus ancient. The Hopi are a Puebloan
people, direct descendants of the Anasazi (an archaeologist's term
from the Navajo word meaning "ancestors of the enemy"; the Hopi,
not surprisingly, prefer Hisatsinom, meaning simply "ancestors"),
who between 800 and 1300 C.E. built some of the most impressive
architectural structures in prehistoric North America. Chaco Canyon
to the east figures in some Hopi migration legends, as do Mesa Verde
to the northeast, Betatakin and Keet Seel to the north, Homol'ovi to
the south, Wupatki to the southwest, and numerous other ruins
throughout the greater Southwest.[7] The common refrain of southwestern archaeologists, "What happened to the Anasazi?," is unequiv-
ocally answered by the Hopi and other modern Pueblos: "Nothing; we
are still here." In Hopi country itself, there is evidence of continuous
occupation by sedentary agriculturalists for a good 1,500 years, and the
Third Mesa town of Orayvi—the oldest continuously inhabited village
in North America—has been dated to at least 1150 C.E. In sum, the
Hopi have learned to live by farming in this semiarid environment
over the course of a long presence.

The persistent occupation of the Hopi mesas for more than a millennium is both remarkable and paradoxical. Unlike the other Pueblos,
the Hopi, with no streams or rivers to support their subsistence
economy's dependence on maize, beans, and squash, must seek their
water elsewhere. The ways in which the Hopi get and use water are a
major part of identity, religious beliefs, ritual practices, and daily en-
gagements and concerns. Much of the complex Hopi religious system
is devoted, in one way or another, to securing necessary blessings of
water—in the form of rainfall, snow, spring replenishment, and so
forth—to sustain living beings, whether humans, animals, or plants.

A calendar of elaborate ritual performances is divided into the kachina season—roughly from December to July—and, from August to
December, a season of more esoteric practices by higher-order religious sodalities—the Snake, Flute, Wuwtsim (Manhood), and Maraw

(Womanhood) societies and the great *Soyalangw* society festival at the winter solstice. All these concentrate in some measure on ensuring beneficial environmental conditions, on keeping the world in balance. The Hopi regard ritual, if performed properly—the cardinal values being pure intentions and good hearts in harmony with one another, sentiments that translate into the philosophical concept of *namitnangwu*—as instrumentally efficacious ipso facto, not as mere symbolic embroidery on a techno-rationalist means of production.

The phrase *Hopi environmentalism* is practically a redundancy.[8] So much of Hopi culture and thought, both religious and secular, revolves around an attention to balance and harmony in the forces of nature that environmental ethics are in many ways critical to the very meaning of the word *Hopi*.[9] Hopi society is organized into clans, the majority of which are named after, and have specific associations with, natural species and elements—Bear, Sun, Spider, Parrot, Badger, Corn, Butterfly, Greasewood, Tobacco, Cloud—indicating the utter centrality of environmental forms and ecological relationships in Hopi thought. Myriad usages of natural species and agents in Hopi religious ritual express the depth and detail of this ecological awareness and concern. A kachina, for example, in appearance, song, and performance, typically embodies and encapsulates key vital principles of the natural world. Even a casual observation of a *Hemis* kachina at *Niman* (the Home Dance, in July), to just take one case, discloses a being festooned with spruce branches, wild wheat, clouds, butterflies, tadpoles, seashells, and so on. The bringing together of these natural symbols is in many instances designed to both evoke and celebrate the life-giving force of water in the world.

Springs, Water, and Rain in Hopi Secular and Religious Philosophy

Paahu, "natural water" or "spring," is absolutely central in Hopi social and environmental thought. Indeed, the identity of the term points to the significance springs hold: they are the prototypical water sources. Supplemented by wells dug by the Bureau of Indian Affairs Agency over the past century, springs supply drinking water and water for livestock. They also feed a series of irrigated terraced gardens on the slopes below the mesa tops, which form another basic site of crop production; the gardens include chilis, beans, a little corn, onions, radishes, and fruit trees (see photo 2.1). The areas around the larger springs are also the only significant wetlands in much of the region. For this reason, they, too, are objects of religious veneration.

PHOTO 2.1. HOPI GARDENS

These terraced gardens below the Third Mesa village of Hotvela are irrigated with water brought by surface pipes and carried by hand from the Hotvela Spring, on the slope below the mesa's edge. Courtesy of the Arizona State Museum, Tuscon.

Even with the introduction of piped water (for the most part, only within the past thirty years), springs remain critical in Hopi philosophy and practice. Springs and their immediate pond life environs serve as the ideal model of life and growth. Such places attract denser presences of life-forms than are found elsewhere in the semiarid landscape. Doves, dragonflies, ducks, cranes, frogs, sand-grass, cattails, reeds, cottonwoods, willows, and numerous other species concentrate at these locations—simultaneously the index and the manifestation of abundant, water-charged life. Such species serve as key symbols of the life-giving force of water in Hopi secular and religious philosophy.

It is hard to imagine anything more sacred—as substance or as symbol—than water in Hopi religious thought and practice. To be sure, some elements may appear more prominent: corn, the staff of life, which is ubiquitous in Hopi religious imagery; rattlesnakes in the spectacular Snake Dance; or performances by masked kachina spirits. But intrinsic to these, and underlying much other symbolism in the panoply of Hopi ritual, is the concern with water. Springs, water, and rain are focal themes in ritual costumes, kiva iconography, mythological narratives, personal names, and many, many songs that call the cloud chiefs from the varicolored directions to bear their fructifying essence back into the cycle of human, animal, and vegetal life. That essence—as clouds, rain, and other water forms—manifests the spirits of the dead. When people die, in part they become clouds; songs call to the clouds as ascendant relatives. Arriving clouds are returning ancestors, their rain both communion with and blessing of the living. The waters of the earth (where kachina spirits live) are, then, transubstantiated human life.

In general, springs and groundwater serve as homes for the deity Paalölöqangw, Plumed Water-Snake, who is a powerful patron of the water sources of the earth and the heavens. Paalölöqangw is appealed to in the Snake and Flute ceremonies, and is religiously portrayed during winter night dances. Springs and their immediate surroundings are places of particular religious worship in some instances, as in the Flute ceremony or during *Powamuy* (the Bean Dance) and *Niman* (the Home Dance). The Flute ceremony is specifically devoted to the consecration and regeneration of major springs; during this ceremony, in an archetypal gesture, the *Lenmongwi*, head of the Flute society, dives to the bottom of a particularly sacred spring to plant prayer sticks for Paalölöqangw.

Resources from spring areas such as water, clay, reeds, and spruce branches are gathered for use in village ceremonies, in which they are deemed to draw in the life-giving power of the springs themselves. Springs as distant as 160 kilometers (100 miles) are visited on a regular basis in order to bring back their sacred water for ceremonies, especially by clan descendants from former settlements adjacent to the springs. Early ethnographers Jesse Walter Fewkes and Walter Hough both remarked on Hopi veneration of springs:

> In a general way every spring is supposed to be sacred and therefore a place for the deposit of prayer sticks and other offerings. . . . Every spring is a place of worship and hence a shrine.
>
> (Fewkes 1906, 370–371)

> No spring in the region is without evidence of many offerings to the deities of water. . . . Sacred Springs may . . . be regarded

as altars, and the offerings as sacrifices, whose essence may be carried by the water.

(Hough 1906, 165)

Since time immemorial, the Hopi have offered blessings of cornmeal and prayers at springs, during specific visits for the purpose or simply while passing through the landscape (say, during herding, hunting, or treks to distant cornfields). When blessing a spring, typically a man also scoops up a handful of water and splashes it back toward his village or fields as a way to encourage the water to transfer some of its power to where humans most need it. Springs attract the rain and snow to themselves and thus serve as powerful foci of value in Hopi thought. Indeed, this is why they are sacred places: if much of Hopi religious thought celebrates life, then springs are self-evident indexes of the dynamic process that produces and sustains life. At the winter solstice ceremonies, feathered prayer sticks are placed over major springs around every Hopi village as both protection and supplication.

Among sources of water, there is a quasi-magnetic relationship: the Pacific Ocean, the Colorado River, rain, underground aquifers, springs, and living plants are mutually attractive—"contagious" in the anthropological sense: "The land is a living organ, it breathes . . . the Hopis say that it is the underground water that sucks in, that breathes the rain" (Vernon Masayesva).[10] *Paatuwaqatsi*, literally "the ocean," is simultaneously a central philosophical principle denoting the universally sustaining water of life. To attract the world's powers of moisture, spring names are used frequently in ritual narrative and song: for example, Talakwavi, Dawn Coming-Up Spring; Tsorspa, Bluebird Spring; Kwaava, Eagle Spring; Paatuwi, Spring on the Rock Shelf; Höwiipa, Dove Spring; Hoonawpa, Bear Spring; Konva, Chipmunk Spring; Kookyangwva, Spider Spring; Tsinngava, Water Droplets Splashing Spring; Söhöpva, Cottonwood Spring. Springwater properly placed in one's field, mud from spring bottoms used as body plaster in kachina costumes, and images of tadpoles or dragonflies decorating kachina spirits—all sympathetically entice the rain.

Springs themselves, like maize in fields, were originally "planted" in the earth by deities or gifted individuals. There was even a special instrument, a *paa'u'uypi* ("spring planter"), known to the elect and used for this purpose. (A spring near Munqapi, for example, is said to have been planted in this way by a man named Kwaavaho—for whom the spring is named—in the late nineteenth century.) Pilgrimages to reconsecrate and draw in regenerative power from especially significant springs at distant points are common in the Hopi religious calendar. Villages may be named for springs, as in the mother village, Songoopavi, "Sand-Grass Spring Place." Some clans have exceptional responsibilities to springs, as does *Patkingyam*, the Water clan, and some springs are sacred to specific clans or religious societies at the different villages. Clan migration routes from former villages are often retraced—both literally in pilgrimages and figuratively in narratives and songs—at certain times of the year. In many instances, clan associations with springs at their ruins or along the route are mentioned as locations of important historical events. Thus, the Water clan has a series of historic points along its migration route from the south that are frequently marked by springs, such as Isva, Coyote Springs, north of Winslow. Similarly, Kiisiwu, Shady Springs, for the Badger and Butterfly clan; Sa'lako, Shalako (a kachina spirit) Spring, for the Bow clan; and Lengyanovi Spring, for the Flute clan, are all memorialized in clan tradition and visited in pilgrimage. In this sense, then, the living springs embody Hopi history: they are cultural landmarks, inscribed with significance, and commemorative reminders of the continuing legitimacy of clan rights and interests in specific areas.

Springs and the life-forms associated with them thus appear in many Hopi stories and sacred traditions, in literary forms such as personal names, and in artistic forms such as basketry, pottery, weaving, and painting. In these intellectual and aesthetic contexts, the substance and forms of springs and wetland life are both described objectively and celebrated with pleasurable appreciation and spiritual gratitude. Personal names, a prime form of Hopi poetic images, often reference springs and water: Paahongva, Water Standing Up (after the tiny columns of water that leap up from raindrops splashing on a pond or puddle); Paanömtiwa, Water Covering Up (perhaps covering a cornfield after a rain); Paatala, Water Light, referring to reflected light on water's surface, particularly in the dark.[11] Many of the species that are totemic emblems of Hopi clans are associated with springs—*paawiki*, the duck; *atoko*, the crane; *paakwa*, the frog; *paaqavi*, reeds; and so on. The celebration of water, its origins or results, forms a major proportion—perhaps half—of all Hopi names. References to flowers—an explicit mark of the Creator's rain blessings—celebrate water as well, such as *Siitala*, "flower light," the reflected sunlight from flowers newly blossomed after a rain, and *Sikyakuku*, literally "yellow foot," which refers to walking along through blossoming flowers while the pollen clings to one's moccasined feet. There are also references to rain, such as Yooyoki "raining," and Yoyvwölö, "rainwater" (there is a priest in one of the ritual orders referred to as the Yoymongwi, "rain chief") as well as lightning, such as Talwiipi, "a single lightning flash," or Talwipta, "lightning in the ongoing process of flashing." Even species that are not so directly associated with water sources are frequently subjects of interest in relation to their behavior toward water.

One name, Sharp Hearer, given by a Spider clan member, refers to the fact that when rain begins to fall, certain spiders secreted inside houses hear the rain and emerge from their cover, running out to drink from the freshly emerging puddles (Voth 1905a). Even here, then, when the species in question has no explicit conceptual link with water, the Hopi denote its significance by its habitual practices in relation to water. The concern with natural water depicted in this name details a precise knowledge of the behavior of the species as well as an aesthetic and creatural delight in the pleasure and happiness that the presence of water affords all beings of the world.

In short, springs are key in Hopi social life, cultural values, and conceptualization of the landscape, all of which form the ground of deeper religious thought and action. The Hopi smoke for rain, dance for it, sing for it, and offer many other forms of prayer for it. In the cycle of life, rainwater and snowmelt nourish the plants, which feed animals and human beings. Thus, prayers for rain are not abstract; they call the clouds to replenish the waters of the earth so that all life-forms will benefit and "be happy." Here, then, is an environment populated not by Western science's instinct-driven organisms without spirit or consciousness but by intentional, spiritual entities that are part and parcel of the same moral system that encompasses human beings. The Hopi have, so to speak, both a moral ecology and an ecological morality. As one Hopi man put it, "We pray for rain so that all the animals, birds, insects, and other life-forms will have enough to drink too." The prolific complexity of Hopi ritual attends to springs specifically and as sources of blessing and vehicles of prayer in general.

Of Coal Mines and Slurries

The springs, however, are drying up, and with them the essential force of Hopi religious life and culture itself. Flows have been progressively declining over the past three decades. Numerous springs and seeps have ceased to produce enough water to sustain crops planted below them. The Moenkopi Wash no longer "continuously flows," and the only major Hopi farming area that depends on irrigation water is in serious jeopardy. In recent years, the Moenkopi Wash has been down to a trickle by late May; not long ago, Munqapi children plunged into swimming holes long into the summer. Even the trickle that does come is supplied by only two upstream tributaries; much of the water from the mainstream itself is channeled into impoundment ponds by the Peabody Western Coal Company.

Peabody, which operates twenty-seven mines in the United States, is the largest private producer of coal in the world. Until recently, the company was part of the British multinational Hanson Industries, which demerged in February 1997. Peabody then became part of a newly formed Hanson spinoff, The Energy Group PLC, but top management remains virtually identical. In 1996, Peabody's total operating profit (including all its mining interests worldwide) was $240 million, and its profit on coal sales was in excess of $2 billion; Hanson's total sales, including its chemical and tobacco interests, exceeded $19 billion, and its total after-tax profit was $2.3 billion (*Hanson Annual Report* 1996).This is no small enterprise.

Peabody's Black Mesa–Kayenta Mine is the only mine in the United States that transports its coal by slurry (see figure 2.2). The strip-mined coal is crushed, mixed with drinking-quality water, and flushed by pipeline to the Mohave Generating Station in Laughlin, Nevada. The cities of Las Vegas and Phoenix—electric oases in the desert—buy some of the power, but most of it goes to the electric toothbrushes, garage door openers, outsize television sets, and other necessities of life in southern California. Most of the slurry water comes directly from the "Navajo" or N-aquifer, 300 to 900 meters (1,000 to 3,000 feet) within the geologic formation of Black Mesa (see figure 2.3).

The pumping, Peabody has claimed, has no effect on the Hopi springs. Those springs, it maintains, are fed not by the N-aquifer but by the overlying "Dakota" or D-aquifer and by snowmelt. The Hopi do not believe Peabody's assertion. But an escalating series of letters from Hopi individuals and officials, both traditional leaders and Tribal Council chairs; petitions signed by several hundred Hopi; protests in public hearings; dissenting interpretations by independent geologists;[12] and repeated refusals by the Tribal Council to sanction the Department of the Interior's renewal of the mining lease have all fallen on deaf ears. Flat rebuttals to Hopi protests continue to be retailed by Peabody and Hanson representatives, and a personal invitation to engage in direct dialogue issued to Lord Hanson, chairman of Hanson PLC, by Tribal Chairman Ferrell Secakuku in June 1994 went ignored. On 30 April 1994, W. Howard Carson, president of Peabody Western Coal Company, voiced the company's party line in a letter to the editor published in the *Los Angeles Times:* "Changes in the flows from their springs may be the result of drought conditions in the region, and perhaps from the increased pumpage from Hopi community wells located near these springs. . . . Peabody Western's pumping from wells that are 2,500–3,000 feet deep does not affect these springs."

Yet Peabody's characterizations of hydrological effects are eminently untrustworthy. Comments and hearings on the U.S. Office of Surface Mining and Reclamation Enforcement's draft environmental

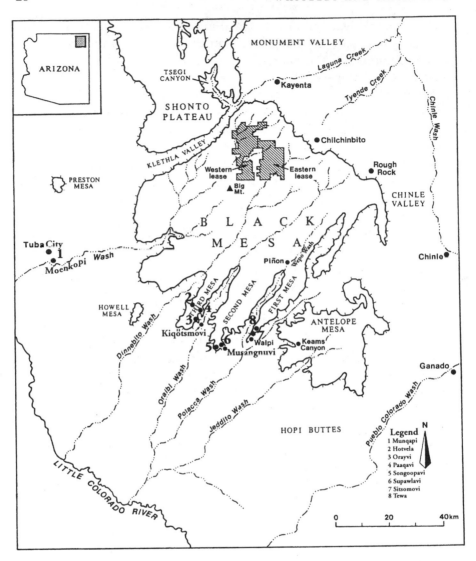

FIGURE 2.2. BLACK MESA AND THE PEABODY
COAL COMPANY'S LEASE AREAS

The geological formation of Black Mesa, with the Hopi mesas and principal washes. The Peabody Western Coal company's two lease areas are marked by hatched lines. Black Mesa tilts downward from north to south. The mining lease areas lie on top of its northern, higher end. The Hopi villages are at the lowest, southern extremity, where the aquifers are significantly closer to the surface. Courtesy of the Center for Archaeological Investigations, Southern Illinois University.

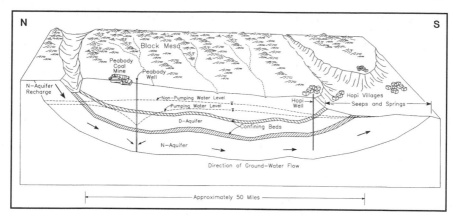

FIGURE 2.3. GROUNDWATER FLOW IN THE N-AQUIFER

The N- or Navajo Aquifer is composed of three layers: from top to bottom, Navajo Sandstone, the Kayenta Formation, and Wingate Sandstone. The N-Aquifer is separated from the overlying D- or Dakota aquifer by the Carmel Formation (indicated by the Confining Beds in the diagram). The D-aquifer also is composed of three layers: from top to bottom, Dakota Sandstone, the Morrison Formation, and Entrada Sandstone. For more on the geologic and hydrological stratigraphy of the aquifers, see Cooley et al. 1969. Courtesy of the Hopi Tribe, Water Resouces Office.

impact statement (DEIS) (U.S. Department of the Interior 1990)[13] produced a welter of objections, both to the sociocultural and environmental effects of the mine and to the shoddy research that produced general ratings of minor or minimal environmental impacts. For example, the Environmental Protection Agency's official response noted:

> We have classified the DEIS as Category EO-2: Environmental Objections—Insufficient Information.[14] . . . We believe the project may result in significant adverse environmental impacts to water resources and air quality that should be avoided. We have also found that the lack of sufficient information on water, air, and biotic resource conditions severely impedes evaluation of impacts, alternatives, and appropriate mitigation measures. We are particularly concerned that the DEIS lacks an alternatives analysis which would enable the Federal agencies and the public to consider less environmentally damaging actions than the preferred alternative [i.e., the slurry].   (U.S. Department of the Interior 1990, 263)

The EPA's more detailed comments on the mine's hydrological compliance with the National Environmental Policy Act noted:

Conclusions based on N-aquifer modelling. While EPA accepts the approach taken in modelling hydrologic baseline conditions and impacts, the conclusiveness of this effort is undermined by lack of data. This limitation, compounded by use of material damage criteria based on thresholds much less sensitive than "significance" under NEPA, leads us to reject the evaluation of hydrologic impacts. EPA believes that the available data do not support statements in the DEIS that the cumulative effects of current and foreseeable mining and related operations (principally the coal transport slurry) are expected to result in only minor hydrological impacts.

(U.S. Department of the Interior 1990, 267)

Six months prior to W. Howard Carson's 1994 statement in the *Los Angeles Times*, top hydrologists with the U.S. Geological Survey (USGS) concluded that Peabody's ongoing analysis of water impacts was based on a wholly inadequate model. Among other shortcomings, "The model is not sufficient to answer the concerns of the Hopi regarding adverse local, short-term impacts on wetlands, riparian wildlife habitat, and spring flow at individual springs" (Nichols 1993). Recent figures (U.S. Geological Survey 1995) suggest that as much as two-thirds of the decline in water level of area wells (ranging from 9.1 to 29.6 meters, or 30 to 97 feet, from 1965 to 1993) is caused by the mine's pumping. Peabody's claim that throughout its thirty-five-year life, the mine would use only one-tenth of 1 percent of N-aquifer water, which would naturally recharge itself, is seriously questioned by a USGS recharge study in 1995 that charted a recharge rate 85 percent less than Peabody's estimate.[15] (It has been suggested that Peabody tried to suppress public release of these discrepant figures because if the figures were verified, the company would be obligated by the terms of the lease to post a bond for aquifer restoration.)

It also seems evident that depletion of the N-aquifer has had serious impacts on the D-aquifer and on the springs themselves; the Moenkopi Wash is directly affected, since it is supplied by N-aquifer seepage and since Peabody impounds surface water at a rate surpassing 2.2 million cubic meters (1,800 acre-feet) per year—water that would otherwise directly supply this wash (U.S. Department of the Interior 1960, 268). Computer simulations by the USGS predict total drying of some major Hopi wells beginning in the year 2011. Upstream Navajo communities are also significantly affected by the drying and by deteriorating water quality; Forest Lake has been particularly hard hit. In recent documents, Peabody has finally acknowledged that it takes water not only from the N-aquifer but also from other aquifers, including the D-aquifer. This has come as no surprise to the Hopi. But as Nat Nutongla, head of the Hopi Tribe's Water Resources Office, puts it, "The elders regard all water as sacred. It doesn't matter whether the springs are supplied directly by the D-aquifer or the N-aquifer or whatever; they represent *all* sources of water."

Peabody's position that declines in Hopi springs derive from increased domestic and municipal consumption, reflecting population growth (principally Navajo) and water development by the Navajo Nation and the Hopi Tribe, is not entirely untrue. Tuba City wells and a significant increase in local population since the 1960s directly impinge on Munqapi area springs. Hopi domestic water use has definitely expanded as newer villages have adopted indoor plumbing over the past thirty years. But these changes, the Hopi argue, are all the more reason not to waste the reserves of N-aquifer water. As co-author and former Tribal Chairman Vernon Masayesva has put it elsewhere:

> I believe there is a water crisis. Peabody Mining Company says that if there is a lowering of the water in the wells, it's because of domestic uses and not as a result of their pumping. And to that, I simply said, "All the more reason why you should not be pumping that water, because the domestic users are already having a significant impact on that N-aquifer water." So why throw away the savings? I see aquifers as money in the bank, in a savings account. So why are we dipping into it?   (BBC Television 1995)

A serious, compromising quandary is that 80 percent of the Hopi Tribe's annual operating revenue is supplied by coal royalties and water lease fees from Peabody. The Hopi Tribal Council (or "Tribe"), a creation of the Indian Reorganization Act of 1934, is formally supported by about half the villages, though even traditionalists opposed to the council rely on numerous benefits it administers. Many people believe they were duped by the council's attorneys when the original leases were signed in the 1960s[16] and that some tribal leaders were co-opted by Peabody. But this is scarcely a factional issue. The Hopi directly involved with the council, including the two most recent chairmen, Ferrell Secakuku and Vernon Masayesva, have strongly opposed renewal of the coal leases in lieu of an alternative means of transporting the coal.

Hopi of all factions, from traditionalist *Kikmongwis* (village chiefs) to modernist technocrats, have been unanimous and clear in their opposition to the use of pristine groundwater to transport coal and in their disbelief of Peabody's denials that the pumping affects the springs. Two examples will suffice. The first is more traditionally inclined. At a public hearing on the environmental impact of the mine held in Munqapi on 8 August 1989, William Garcia recounted a childhood discussion he and his brothers had engaged in with their grandfather, Kyarsyawma, while out herding sheep. Kyarsyawma had first asked for his grandsons' impressions of the land:

> Our response was, "Well, it is just there. It is just there, you know, and we use it now and then, maybe to farm on and to herd our sheep. There is really nothing to it."
>
> He said, "Look at yourself. Look at your body, what do you have? You got some parts there, it looks pretty simple on the outside, but on the inside, inside of you as a person you have a soul, you have a heart. You have some blood running through your body to keep your vital organs going," and he said, "It is the same thing with the land. The land has a soul, the land that we are on has a soul, it has a heart. It also has its own blood. The blood running through it are the streams to keep it alive, to keep us alive."
>
> I always remember that, so to me, after I kind of learned that concept, it wasn't just there anymore. There was a purpose behind it just like there is a purpose here for each and every one of us. We are not just here. . . .
>
> I guarantee you that if we continue to draw this lifeline from mother Earth, then we will no longer exist, just as if someone stuck a needle in your arm and sucked out all the blood, you would be nothing, you would be dead.
>
> (U.S. Department of the Interior 1990, 374–375)

The second example is a petition presented by Mishongnovi village that same year:

> Be advised that we the undersigned members of the village of Mishongnovi are deeply concerned about the effects the mining of coal, by Peabody Coal Company, has had on our water resources. This is most evident in our springs drying up, our farms not producing crops, and our range wells drying up.
>
> Our village leaders have been and are still opposed to use of our water for mining operations. Our water is our life and we

stand firm with our leaders in opposition to future use of our water for this purpose.

(U.S. Department of the Interior 1990, 296)

The Tribal Council favors economic development and does not oppose the mine as such (although some traditionalists do): part of the allure of the mine in the first place was the promise of Hopi employment. But the Hopi say Peabody has aligned itself with the Navajo Nation and ignores Hopi interests, a position borne out in employment figures. Of as many as 900 "Native American"—a useful elision in Peabody's public pronouncements—employees, fewer than 20 are Hopi; the great majority are Navajo, represented by the United Mine Workers Union, which enjoys a special relationship with the Navajo Labor Relations Board.[17] The original leases guaranteed 50 percent of local employment to the Hopi. And Peabody's overall attitude seems to be flagrant disdain for Hopi concerns. In W. Howard Carson's words, "We wouldn't [stop pumping] just to get the Hopi off our backs, because it could create another nightmare. These things snowball" (Gallup (New Mexico) Independent 1993).

Several alternatives to the slurrying of aquifer water have been proposed, and progress has been made on one: the construction of another pipeline from Lake Powell, which would provide domestic water for the Hopi and the Navajo and water for industrial use by Peabody. But Peabody, ever mindful of the bottom line, is evidently using delaying tactics, suspending negotiations and playing the tribes against each other despite support for the project by Secretary of the Interior Bruce Babbitt. Like most negotiations involving the Hopi and the Navajo, the pipeline proposal is subject to the cumulative politics of major land disputes between the tribes, and the Navajo Nation has sought concessions from the Hopi Tribe that it has been unable to gain otherwise. Such disputes affect Hopi interests in other ways, including the Hopi's freedom to conduct religious pilgrimages to some springs. A major sacred spring, Kiisiwu, is on land that was partitioned to the Navajo Nation by Congress in 1974. This spring, associated with principal kachina ceremonies, is visited by ritual-society pilgrims, especially during Powamuy (the Bean Dance) and Niman (the Home Dance). Formerly, local Navajo maintained a respectful distance, but younger generations are impressed less by the ceremonies' religious purpose and more by secular conflict. Recently, there have been physical assaults. If Kiisiwu dries up, this may solve some temporal problems between the Hopi and the Navajo, but at what spiritual cost?

Meanwhile, the Hopi are deeply anxious about all spring declines, for both obvious reasons and deeper metaphysical ones. The Hopi moral philosophy, following a covenant entered into with the deity Maasaw on their emergence into the present world, charges them with the responsibility of taking care of the earth and all its resources; indeed, such behavior is a significant measure of whether one is worthy of the name *Hopi* (see note 9). If the Hopi break the covenant, a cataclysm of cosmic proportions threatens. During the early 1980s, when co-author Whiteley began ethnographic research at Third Mesa, Tsakwani'yma, an older Spider clan man, would sometimes tell me of prophecies he had heard from his uncle, Lomayestiwa (an early twentieth-century leader in the so-called "Hostile" faction at Orayvi). He returned to one such prophecy repeatedly: a time would come when Paalölöqangw, the Water Serpent deity, would turn over and lash his tail deep within the waters of the earth and all land life would tumble back down to the bottom of the ocean. "Can you interpret it?" he would challenge. "It means earthquake. But it's also symbolic of the life we are leading today: *koyaanisqatsi*, a life of chaos." In 1987 and 1988, shortly after Tsakwani'yma passed on, there were two earthquakes on Black Mesa (a rarity), which the Arizona Earthquake Information Center connected to the removal of massive quantities of coal and water. The perception of some elders that this is the result of their souls having been sold out from under them—literally, in the link between groundwater and spirits of the dead—causes profound sadness and a sense of intractable religious desecration.

In addition to long-term Hopi interests, regional economic and demographic patterns make the continued pumping of 4 million cubic meters, or more than a billion gallons of potable water every year for a coal slurry incredibly shortsighted. The twenty-first century will undoubtedly see ever more serious problems of water supply for the rapidly growing conurbations in the West. In this light, Hopi religious concerns with springs become metaphorical of larger issues of global development and natural resource management. But although the Hopi are typically attuned to such universal implications, in the immediate term they are concerned with basic physical, cultural, and spiritual survival. If the springs are to be saved, and with them continued Hopi cultural and religious existence, Peabody's relentless drive toward short-term profits, at the expense of stakeholder concerns, needs a dramatic makeover in line with trends toward local-global balance pursued by more progressive multinationals.[18] In the meantime, the pumps siphon the essence of life from the water roots of Black Mesa and the Hopi springs are withering on the vine.

Food for Thought:
Stakeholders, Shareholders, and Regulators

At the heart of this conflict over resource use is the confrontation between market capitalism and small-scale subsistence economies, or, in other terms, the opposing interests of shareholder and stakeholder. Much talk of sustainable development practices has been grounded in the inexorable logic of rationalist economics, with scant attention paid to different cultural and religious conceptions of the environment and how these might affect practical engagement with the transformation of nature for production.

Regarding stakeholder and shareholder interests, the powers of government to protect the former and regulate resource use are seriously called into question here. The government has a series of trust responsibilities to Indian tribes that surpass its obligations to most other sectors of American society. Specific provisions, such as the Winters Doctrine, could be invoked to protect Hopi and Navajo water resources and life chances. Vernon Masayesva places some of the blame squarely on the government agencies charged with protecting Hopi interests:

> It's a *tragic* chapter in United States–Hopi relations. *Very tragic.* They put our culture at risk, is the way I put it. The reason why Navajo aquifer water is so important is not only because, according to the Hopis, it's what sucks in the rain, but it also feeds the springs where ceremonies are occurring. It also sits in a bowl: *it's the only source of potable water available to the Hopi people* [his emphasis].
>
> (BBC Television 1995)

As a concatenation of powers, the multiplicity of government branches seems to militate against effective stakeholder representation: what the left hand gives, the right will take away. For example, the EPA has been clear in its opposition to the mine's hydrological practices, but it is overridden by the Office of Surface Mining Reclamation and Enforcement (OSMRE), which, not to put too fine a point on it, has seemed to be largely a regulatory surrogate for Peabody's corporate interests. Throughout the public hearings on the DEIS at the Hopi Tribal Headquarters in Kiqötsmovi in August 1989, for example, OSMRE's representative, Peter Rutledge, seemed interested in speaking only on behalf of Peabody; to the Hopi who were present, the difference between the two entities was not clear. I (Whiteley) was sitting next to Stanley Bahnimptewa, then the *Kikmongwi* of Orayvi, who shortly into the hearings grew disgusted, turned to me and said, "Looks like we're going to be here all day," got up, and left.

Recently, the OSMRE renewed Peabody's Black Mesa–Kayenta mine permit. The Kayenta mine itself transports coal by railroad, but the two mines (Black Mesa and Kayenta) are linked administratively and are geographically close, so the renewal demonstrates tacit support (or, at least, benign neglect) of the Black Mesa mine operation, despite widespread public knowledge of the information contained in this chapter.[19] At the annual meeting of Hanson Industries in February 1996, Hopi and Navajo protestors, along with supporters from various environmental groups, succeeded in shutting down the meeting (*Private Eye* 1996). That OSMRE would override the many Hopi protests and renew the mine permit suggests that the rules of the market and the market's control by multinational capital are so entrenched in the thinking of government and industry that even in such a flagrant case, local constructions of environmental interest will not be heard and possible government uses of legal tools to protect stakeholders will go by the board.

If the imbrication of government and corporate interests in water uses seems Orwellian, the bureaucratic labyrinth overseeing regulation is positively Kafkaesque. A series of government agencies have made appearances in this chapter as involved at one level or another with the issues in question, and additional agencies are also involved. All told, the following are included: The Hopi Tribal Council (and various departmental agencies); the Navajo Nation (and various departmental agencies); the U.S. Secretary of the Interior; the U.S. Geological Survey, Water Resources Division; the U.S. Environmental Protection Agency; the U.S. Office of Surface Mining Reclamation and Enforcement; the U.S. Army Corps of Engineers; the U.S. Fish and Wildlife Service; the U.S. Bureau of Land Management; the U.S. Bureau of Indian Affairs; the U.S. Department of Health and Human Services (Indian Health Service); the U.S. Department of Justice; the State of Arizona; the Arizona Department of Health and Human Services; the Arizona Game and Fish Department; and the Arizona Department of Mines and Mineral Resources. This list does not include the municipal interests party to Little Colorado basin water rights adjudications. Multilateral negotiations over the water rights in question—involving the Hopi, the Navajo, Peabody, and municipalities in northern Arizona, and overseen by the U.S. Department of Justice—are ongoing as of this writing. The possibility, say, that the Hopi Tribe could sue Peabody over environmental damage is held in abeyance by these negotiations (in which Peabody is the major player, with most of the wealth) and their attachment to a web of bureaucratic strings. From this governmental quagmire, some Hopi have recently turned to the environmental group the National Resources Defense Council, which is supplying a hydrologist to conduct independent tests of the aquifer.

The key question for the future—how local communities can ensure basic resource needs vis-à-vis the demands of the metropolitan economy—will be played out in many contexts in the American West and in other regions where conflict over resource rights is exacerbated by demographic shifts, increasing urbanization, and absorption of small communities by ever more encompassing forces of market production. Global climate change will be another major factor in the capacity of small-scale indigenous societies to retain control of their environments and resources. It is quite likely that dislocations from climatically marginal areas will produce a significant tide of environmental refugees (see, e.g., Intergovernmental Report on Global Climate Change 1995). In locales like the Hopi Indian Reservation, where water supply is so limited, the threat posed by industrial exploitation of the present sort may well tip the balance prior to changes produced by longer-term impacts.

If we are genuinely committed to sustainability, it is time to expand our understanding of it by listening to members of communities—for example, some Native American communities—that have practiced it for a very long time. If, to be realistic, we do not see an end to global markets as the mainspring of future economic frameworks, the key issue will be how to balance short-term profitability with long-term sustainability. The crux of that, surely, is empowering local stakeholders in the decision-making processes of companies themselves—but that will require corporate willingness to be inclusive, which may be anathema to the current ethos and praxis of the market. Without that will, the only hope for stakeholders is the intervention of government regulatory agencies, but if the actions of the OSMRE and the bureaucratic labyrinth in which decision making is currently trapped in the case presented here are anything to go by, that glimmer of hope offers precious little comfort. During his first campaign for the U.S. presidency, Bill Clinton announced that he would be the "environment president." Perhaps, in the apparent failure of the secretary of the interior to step in here, what is needed to cut through the bureaucracy is an "environment czar" who could respond to stakeholder situations like the Hopi water crisis more effectively. One Hopi commentator, Rebekah Masayesva, summed up the situation with admirable conciseness: "The pumping of pure underground water for slurrying of coal is unconscionable and must stop" (U.S. Department of the Interior

1990:416). Yet eight years after the public hearings, the slurrying persists, and there is still no indication that it will stop soon, no matter how environmentally damaging, socioculturally destructive, economically shortsighted, or, indeed, unconscionable it may be. If we can summon the courage to recognize that in the long term we are all stakeholders, the question for both industry and government is "Why not?"

RESOURCES

The following bibliographic references and internet sites are useful for further study of Hopi and Native American water rights issues.

Lloyd Burton. 1991. *American Indian Water Rights and the Limits of the Law.* Lawrence: University Press of Kansas.

Richard O. Clemmer. 1978. "Black Mesa and the Hopi," in *Native Americans and Energy Development,* edited by Joseph Jorgenson. Boston: Anthropology Resource Center. (Very useful for earlier phases of Hopi resistance to mine.)

Richard O. Clemmer. 1984. "The Effects of the Energy Economy on Pueblo Peoples," in *Native Americans and Energy Development,* Vol. 2, edited by Joseph Jorgenson. Boston: Anthropology Resource Center and the Seventh Generation Fund.

Gallup Independent, 12-20-1993, "Coal Mining May Threaten Hopi Water, Culture." Gallup, NM.

Al Gedicks. 1993. *The New Resource Wars: Native and Environmental Struggles against Multinational Corporations.* Boston: South End Press.

Marianna Guerrero. 1992. "American Indian Water Rights: The Blood of Life in Native North America," in *The State of Native America: Genocide, Colonization, and Resistance,* edited by M. Annette Jaimes. Boston: South End Press. (Includes useful bibliographic references to Native American water issues and conflicts more generally.)

Los Angeles Times, 4-30-1994, "Coal Mining and Hopi Water." Letter to the editor by W. Howard Carson, president, Peabody Western Coal Company.

William D. Nichols (Western Region Groundwater Specialist, U.S.G.S.), 10-28-1993, letter to William M. Alley, chief, Office of Groundwater, Water Resources Division, U.S.G.S.

U.S. Dept. of the Interior, 1990, Proposed Permit Application, "Black Mesa–Kayenta Mine, Navajo and Hopi Indian Reservations, Arizona, 2 vols. Final Environmental Impact Statement OSM-EIS-25. Denver: Office of Surface Mining Reclamation and Enforcement. (Vol. 2, Comments and Responses, includes the full text of numerous Hopi letters, petitions, and oral testimony.)

U.S. Geological Survey. 1995. Results of Groundwater, Surfacewater, and Water-Quality Monitoring, Black Mesa Area, Northeastern Arizona

1992–93. *Water Resources Investigations Report* 95-4156. No. 95-4156. Tucson. U.S.G.S.

Charles F. Wilkinson. 1996. "Home Dance, the Hopi, and Black Mesa Coal: Conquest and Endurance in the American Southwest." *Brigham Young University Law Review*, 1996, no. 2. (A detailed account of the original lease negotiation for the mine, in which Hopi tribal attorney, John Boyden, is clearly shown to have also been working on behalf of the energy companies.)

Hopi Information Network: http://www.infomagic.com/~abyte/hopi.html

Native Americans and the Environment: http://conbio.rice.edu/nae/

ACKNOWLEDGMENTS

Nat Nutongla and Phillip Tuwaletstiwa of the Water Resources Office, Department of Natural Resources, Hopi Tribe, gave indispensable help and comments and were most generous with sources.

We wish to thank *Cultural Survival Quarterly* (1996) for permission to use material that first appeared in "Paavahu and Paanaqawu: The Wellsprings of Life and the Slurry of Death."

NOTES

1. Comments at public hearing on the environmental impact of the Black Mesa–Kayenta Mine, Kykotsmovi, Hopi Indian Reservation, Arizona, 9 August 1989, reprinted in U.S. Department of the Interior 1990, 418

2. See, for example, the accounts of Hopi emergence narratives in H. R. Voth's *Traditions of the Hopi* (1905b) or Armin Geertz's "A Reed Pierced the Sky" (1984). Edmund Nequatewa's *Truth of a Hopi* (1936) contains additional Hopi traditional narratives. Frank Waters's *Book of the Hopi* (1963), the most popular work ever published on the Hopi, is best avoided, however, for its confabulation of the imaginary with the ethnographically accurate.

3. From east to west, the mesa-top villages are arranged as follows:

First Mesa: Walpi, Sitsomovi, Tewa

Second Mesa: Songoopavi, Supawlavi, Musangnuvi

Third Mesa: Orayvi, Kiqötsmovi, Paaqavi, Hotvela

Seventy-two kilometers (forty-five miles) by highway to the west of Third Mesa lie the two villages of Upper and Lower Munqapi, which trace their principal heritage to their mother village, Orayvi. These spellings of village names follow current orthographic conventions established for the Hopi language, which are, as yet, not much used locally—hence the variations between, for example, Munqapi and Moenkopi, Songoopavi and Shungopavi, Hotvela and Hotevilla. Good general accounts of Hopi society, economy, and religion appear in Ortiz 1979.

4. For a description of the area's hydrogeology, see Cooley et al. 1969; Gregory 1916 and Hack 1942 provide more detailed local observations of the Hopi environment.

5. The most comprehensive accounts of these migrations, contested by later generations of archaeologists but still systematically articulated by Hopi clan historians, are found in Mindeleff 1891 and Fewkes 1900.

6. See, for example, Brew 1979, Upham 1982, and Cordell 1989; for more general accounts of Puebloan prehistory, in addition to Ortiz 1979, see Cordell 1984 and Cordell and Gumerman 1989.

7. The other Pueblos—Zuni, Laguna, Acoma, and the Rio Grande Tewa, Tiwa, Towa, and Keres villages—also chart their migrations from some of these ancestral stone and adobe ruins.

8. Hopi attitudes toward the environment accord well with J. Baird Callicott's general meditations on Native American environmental ethics (e.g., 1982, 1996), as contrasted with European conceptions of environment. Amid often uncritical projections of the "ecologically noble savage" by some Western environmentalists, more careful statements on Native American attitudes toward the landscape include Momaday 1974, Vecsey 1980, Brody 1981, White 1984, Brightman 1993, Nelson 1993, and Basso 1996. Although the countervailing position—that Native Americans often despoiled their environments and modified them in major ways (Calvin Martin's well-known *Keepers of the Game* [1978] is an example; see also Redford 1991, Denevan 1992, Alvard 1993, and Buege 1996)—has some validity in specific instances, it must be dismissed in general as motivated by the same tendency toward oppositive projection, but of ecologically ignoble savagery. Any careful ethnographic description of Native American environmental praxis typically discloses fine-grained attention to ecological concerns. For comprehensive discussions of anthropological approaches to environmentalism, see Milton 1993 and Orlove et al. 1996.

9. *Hopi* is more than simply an ethnic identity descriptor; in use, it carries specific implications of ethical engagement—in social action, moral thought, and religious practice. The oft-heard opposite, *qahopi* ("un-Hopi," "badly behaved"), used to chastise transgression of behavioral rules, highlights the ethical dimension of the concept of Hopi-ness.

10. Comments at public hearing on the environmental impact of the Black Mesa–Kayenta Mine, Kykotsmovi, Hopi Indian Reservation, Arizona, 9 August 1989, reprinted in U.S. Department of the Interior 1990, 417. Masayesva, sometime chairman of the Hopi Tribe, elaborated on this perspective in the BBC film *The Hopi Way* (Under the Sun series, 1995), which focuses in part on the Hopi water crisis.

11. For more on the aesthetics, poetics, and natural history aspects of Hopi names, see Whiteley 1992.

12. Examples of all these are found in U.S. Department of the Interior 1990.

One petition, for example, circulated among several villages in August 1989:

> We the members of the Hopi Tribe hereby strongly protest Peabody Coal Company's use of a valuable natural resource, water, to transport coal. We demand that Peabody Coal Company immediately cease the use of water to deliver coal to the generating plant(s) and further demand that the Hopi Tribal Council, the Office of Surface Mining and the Bureau of Indian Affairs put pressure on Peabody to immediately seek alternative means to transport coal.
>
> Water is among our most precious resources and we feel that the millions of gallons pumped to feed the slurry lines are affecting our springs and thus impacting our cultural way of life.
>
> (U.S. Department of the Interior 1990, 261)

13. The permitting procedure for the mine is complex (see Wilkinson 1996 for the original lease history). The lessors are the Navajo Nation and the Hopi Tribe, but mining permits must be approved by a series of regulatory agencies (U.S. Department of the Interior 1990):

    1. The Bureau of Land Management, for a life-of-mining plan (until the year 2023)

    2. The U.S. Army Corps of Engineers, for a Clean Water Act Section 404 permit

    3. The Office of Surface Mining Reclamation and Enforcement, for a permit package that allows renewal of the mining lease, with five-yearly reviews until 2011

14. A source close to the process of EPA review indicated that the DEIS received the EO-2 rating only by the skin of its teeth, and even then with some backstage arm-twisting: the EPA, the source indicated, wanted to rate the DEIS as EO-3 (Environmental Objections—Inadequate), which would have indicated formal failure of the DEIS to satisfy provisions of the National Environmental Policy Act and may well have led to rejection of the permit application without further study.

15. Peabody modeled the recharge rate at 16 million cubic meters (13,000 acre-feet) per year; the USGS study, conducted by an Arizona office, recorded a recharge rate of 2.5 million cubic meters (2,000 acre-feet) per year (figures provided by the Water Resources Office, Department of Natural Resources, Hopi Tribe).

16. Working with Hopi tribal attorney John Boyden's legal files, which were recently made public at the University of Utah, Charles Wilkinson (1996) describes in impressive detail how Boyden was simultaneously working for both the Tribe and the Peabody Western Coal Company regarding water and mineral rights on Black Mesa.

17. Robbie Honani of Supawlavi, then chairman of the Hopi Tribal Council's Resources Committee, noted at the public hearings on the DEIS:

There's less than ten Hopi people working at the Peabody mine
and over 800 Navajos. Peabody has built the town of Kayenta for
the Navajo and for other employees. They have erected a trailer
court for its non-Indian employees and flies their top management
people every day from Flagstaff, and then flies them back again.
Yet there is no trailer court for the Hopi people. And there is no
major road system going up to Peabody.

All taxes in the form of education monies go to the . . . Kayenta
Public School District. Does the Hopi get any of these monies?
No. . . . The State of Arizona receives twice as much money in
taxes than the Hopi Tribe does in actual revenues. The tribe receives approximately $8 million in coal royalty, yet the State of
Arizona receives between $18 to $20 million in taxes a year. Only
a mere drop of that comes back to the Hopi.

(U.S. Department of the Interior 1990, 409)

18. See, for example, *The Economist*'s focus on stakeholders and multinationals, June 24, 1995. In a veritable tide of discussion on stakeholder
questions, see, for example, Altman 1994 and Collins 1995. For excellent
discussions of indigenous stakeholder interests in relation to local and
multinational economic development in different parts of the world, see
any issue of *Cultural Survival Quarterly*.

19. W. Howard Carson marked this event with a two-page letter to the Hopi
tribal newspaper, *Hopi Tutuveni*, published on 30 December 1996,
detailing the benefits the mine had brought to the community, implying
that opposition to the mine was the work of cranks and extremists, and
completely ignoring the widespread Hopi opposition to the slurry.

Water Rights in the Pacific Northwest

Tom Greaves

Author Summary

This chapter examines the struggle over water and water-based resources currently in progress between the Lummi Nation of northwestern Washington State and surrounding communities. Competition over water and its associated resources is increasingly central to the political agendas of countless political units, such as states, cities, and counties, but it poses special threats to the indigenous nations of the United States and Canada, surrounded as they are by a dominant society with a history of appropriating and polluting the water on which Indian communities must depend. This chapter discusses the extent and types of water competition the Lummi currently face and explores how these problems might illumine more widespread patterns.

Back in the 1960s, I did fieldwork in the Virú Valley of coastal Peru, the site of much classic anthropology. Agriculture is the basis of life in Virú, and irrigation is the basis of agriculture. It is easy to identify the boundary between nature and culture in Virú: it is the outermost irrigation ditch. Beyond is nothing but sand. Relative to human and agricultural needs, there is never enough water in Virú. Water is the valley's pivotal scarce resource, and the people grapple with its scarcity every day.

Around the world, water scarcity is spreading. More and more communities, large and small, are discovering how burdensome, even dangerous, it is to have an inadequate and unreliable supply of clean freshwater. My intention here, however, is to focus on a more specific dimension of this larger human problem. I argue that global scarcities of freshwater have a particular relevance to *indigenous* societies, to their futures, and to their universal cultural rights. How are indigenous societies affected? For present purposes a case study will exemplify the more general point. A tense political drama over water is being played out in the northwestern corner of Washington State. For members of the Lummi Nation, their future survival as a culturally distinct people is predicated on the outcome.[1]

A Case in the Pacific Northwest: The Lummi Nation

Just over 1,500 Lummi occupy a modest reservation located west of the growing city of Bellingham, about thirty-six kilometers (16 miles) south of the Canadian border in Washington State[2] (see figure 3.1 on page 37). The Lummi Indian Reservation includes a point of land jutting southward, forming the western side of Bellingham Bay. The reservation's beaches are beautiful, and their shallow tidelands are fine places to seek foods of a saltwater shoreline, such as crabs, clams, and fish. Various roads crosscut the reservation's peninsula and its lands lying to the north. The roads of the reservation interconnect several hamlets with a central administrative site that incorporates the institutions of tribal governance and tribal services, the Lummi Tribal School, and the Northwestern Indian College, one of the twenty-nine existing tribal colleges in the United States.[3] Down the peninsula's western side is a second sizable population center focused on a public ferry landing, a fishing port, a marina, and a modest but locally important Lummi-owned casino.

The Lummi belong to the Coast Salish component of the northwestern Coast cultural area, known worldwide for its unmistakable art styles, maritime culture, and rich ceremonial traditions. The Lummi remain anchored in their traditional culture. At the same time, they are very contemporary, strongly convinced of the value of economic planning, higher education, effective management, environmental research, sovereignty of the Lummi Nation, and maintenance of government-to-government relationships.[4] For the Lummi Nation, what is traditional and what is new need not conflict; indeed, they often interlock. For example, salmon are symbolically and emotionally central to

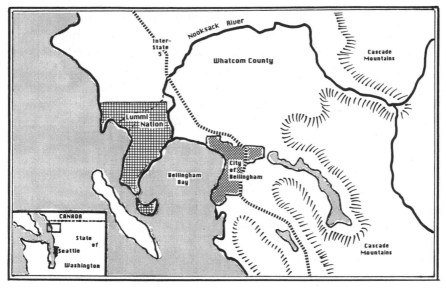

FIGURE 3.1. THE LUMMI INDIAN RESERVATION,
BELLINGHAM AREA, AND NOOKSACK RIVER WATERSHED

The Lummi Indian Reservation is located west of the city of Bellingham, Washington, northwest of Bellingham Bay, and within the lower reaches of the Nooksack River watershed. By the time the Nooksack River reaches the Lummi, it has supported a major farming area, an industrial center, and the urban water needs of the city of Billingham and the densely populated I-5 corridor.

Lummi traditional culture.[5] Yet to maintain the salmon stocks, the Lummi Nation is an active member of regional and international fishing regulatory councils and itself maintains salmon hatcheries generating 4 to 6 million hatchlings each year.[6]

The land in this area is mostly flat and fertile. It was laid down in geologic time as part of the great delta fan of the Fraser River. The Fraser, however, doesn't flow here anymore; instead, it reaches the sea well to the north, at Vancouver, British Columbia. The southwestern corner of the old Fraser delta is now drained by a modest-sized river of its own, the Nooksack. The Nooksack River rises east of Bellingham in the Cascade Range and meanders across the flat agricultural expanse of Whatcom County. Finally, it flows alongside the Lummi Indian Reservation and empties into Bellingham Bay (see figure 3.1).

In terms of elevation, the Nooksack drainage has only modest separation from the delta area to the north, reflecting its common parentage with the Fraser. When the Nooksack floods, water in the middle drainage may flow northward across the border into Canada, exiting via the Fraser River,[7] and in the lower drainage high water sometimes cuts across the Lummi Indian Reservation to its western shore. In its upper reaches, the Nooksack River sustains highly profitable truck farming. When it reaches the developed areas farther south, it is the central water source for major industry; for the dense urban areas associated with Bellingham and the I-5 corridor,[8] and for the Lummi Nation.[9]

The Lummi Nation may be less well known than some larger indigenous nations in the United States, but the Lummi are remarkable. They have an impressive number of committed, insightful leaders. They have nourished and welcomed new talent from among their ranks and given them positions of leadership, departing from the strongly centralized and personalized control that has characterized some other American Indian groups.[10] Further, the Lummi have for years believed in carrying out careful economic planning and acting on opportunities to increase their strength as a people. They believe firmly in their sovereignty, in their treaty rights, and in themselves. They are also acutely conscious of their membership in the worldwide community of indigenous societies and their responsibility to offer effective leadership in that movement.[11]

Bellingham and Whatcom County

Across the bay from the Lummi Indian Reservation is Bellingham, a burgeoning city of 52,000 people. Straddling the I-5 corridor between Seattle and Vancouver, British Columbia, Bellingham has experienced rapid population growth, a boom in retail expansion, and a very active real estate market.[12] Land prices have begun a sharp upward spiral. Attractive, expensive new homes sprout up wherever an ocean or mountain view presents itself. Large public marinas border the bay, berthing a forest of sailboats, fishing boats, and yachts. The good life has come to Bellingham. Latté kiosks and bagel shops abound.

Whatcom County, which surrounds the city of Bellingham and the Lummi Indian Reservation, is mainly rural, but it is also experiencing rapid population growth, especially in the areas nearest Bellingham and along the I-5 corridor leading north to Vancouver. The current population of Whatcom County is 137,000, and estimates of its growth rate in the next decade range from 10 to 30 percent.[13] It is this ongoing and anticipated growth of the city and county that has mobilized the Lummi Nation.

The Importance of Freshwater to the Lummi

On 1 July 1992, the Lummi Nation announced its plans to file, within a year, a federal lawsuit against Whatcom County, the City of Bellingham, the State of Washington, and potentially all other significant public entities regulating or drawing water from the Nooksack River.[14] The planned lawsuit appeared to be predicated on three contentions: (1) because the 1855 treaty establishing the reservation also guaranteed continued access to traditional fishing and marine collecting sites—their livelihood—freshwater to support the Lummi on the reservation is also implied and protected; (2) collectively, the users of the Nooksack have already overtapped the river's output, limiting the current and future ability of the Lummi to provide for their members; and (3) Washington State's Department of Ecology, despite being heavily backlogged by applications for water permits, had actually authorized the use of more water than the river contains and, further, has failed to police widespread unauthorized water appropriation.[15]

The remedial actions sought by the Lummi are three: (1) that the state's Department of Ecology immediately halt all further well and river tap authorizations, including backlogged applications, until it determines the total volume of all previous authorizations and compares that total with the river's capacity; (2) that the Lummi Nation henceforth be recognized as sole authority within its reservation with respect to the management and protection of water sources;[16] and, most important, (3) that the Lummi's share of the Nooksack River's total discharge be fairly determined and fixed for all time. This type of suit is known as a general stream adjudication.

Two interrelated justifications have been reported for the Lummi's threatened lawsuit. First, the Lummi are honoring their cultural link to salmon. Without salmon, they argue, the Lummi culture will be sundered. Regional salmon stocks are now in virtual collapse due to overfishing, disruption of spawning routes, and pollution. To date, the Lummi have sought to ensure their link to the salmon by building and operating hatcheries on the Nooksack River, but if Nooksack water diminishes or becomes further polluted, the hatcheries will be ruined.[17] The second objective is the survival of Lummi culture into the future. The Lummi look at the rapid economic and demographic development of Bellingham and Whatcom County and conclude that the now barely sufficient discharge of the Nooksack River will, if left unchallenged, be increasingly committed to the city, the county, industry, and agriculture. Ipso facto, the Lummi share will decline, and with it, the Lummi's economic and cultural future.

In announcing the planned lawsuit, the late Verne Johnson Jr., chair of the Lummi Nation Water Task Force, asserted that the Lummi Nation's priority over all other water users is secure both in federal case law and under Washington State water rights, the latter because the Lummi are the oldest recognized users of the Nooksack River. Johnson estimated that litigating a general stream adjudication for the Nooksack could require five years of legal proceedings just to sort out who had standing within the lawsuit and another twenty-five to fifty years to reach a resolution. The Lummi have anticipated that in the end, their legal costs for the suit might be millions of dollars.[18]

Since the Lummi announced their plan to sue for a general stream adjudication, they have taken both political and administrative steps toward their objective. First, they wrote and adopted a water code for the reservation, setting up a tribal water authority, policies, and staff so that when the time came, they could demonstrate that they, not outside authorities, were qualified to administer the Lummi's share of Nooksack water.[19] Second, the Lummi Nation announced plans to retain Susan Williams, a Sisseton-Wahpeton Sioux and a nationally known water rights lawyer, to prepare the suit.[20] Third, the Lummi demanded that Washington State's Department of Ecology halt all new water authorizations anywhere in the Nooksack watershed (1) until the Lummi complete a full study of their own water needs[21] and (2) until a full count of all authorized and unauthorized users of the river is completed. The Department of Ecology subsequently agreed to suspend major new water allocations in the lower Nooksack, to the acute distress of developers and public utility commissions all over Whatcom County.[22]

As of this writing (August 1997), the lawsuit has not been filed, and its function seems to be to goad the interested parties to engage in a process of negotiations. Indeed, a succession of consultative and negotiational intiatives has occurred since the Lummi's 1992 announcement. To date none of the various consultations and negotiations has produced a final water allocation, and it is clear that a final solution is years away.[23] The pressure to reach a final settlement builds, however. The state has frozen new authorizations of Nooksack River water and takes no action on more than 500 pending water applications from residents and businesses in the county. Thus, while the Lummi have not yet achieved a guaranteed share of Nooksack water, water allocation is now a high-profile concern in Whatcom County, and the Lummi are an acknowledged central player in whatever resolution will eventuate.

Water Rights as Cultural Rights

In part because water from the Nooksack River is fundamental to the Lummi's connection to salmon, the fight the Lummi Nation is waging over the Nooksack is a fight to protect its culture now and in the future. At present, the salmon stocks on which commercial and sport-fishing depend are severely depleted and the Lummi's own hatcheries can only assist the larger state, federal, and Canadian efforts to sustain the stocks. But the Lummi Nation also looks to the future, taking seriously its obligation to protect its lifeway for the "Seventh Generation." Only about half of the more than 3,000 registered Lummi now live on the reservation. Tribal authorities want to accommodate the eventual return of off-reservation members.[24] An enlarged tribal population on the reservation will require water in excess of what it now consumes. As tribal leaders watch the relentless growth pressures being generated in Bellingham, in Whatcom County as a whole, and along the I-5 corridor, they deduce the obvious: if the Lummi do not act now, more and more of the Nooksack's discharge will be allocated for new developments, inevitably at the expense of the Lummi's current share.

Both of these motives, to conserve salmon and to preserve water for the needs of the Seventh Generation, are aimed squarely at Lummi cultural survival. The Lummi Nation's right to cultural perpetuation is a human right guaranteed not only in United Nations covenants but also in the Point Elliott Treaty of 1855 between the Lummi and the territorial government, which created the Lummi Indian Reservation.[25]

The Lummi Nation's cultural survival is predicated on guaranteeing that river water from the Nooksack will always be there. Other indigenous American groups are engaged in fights over river water, but few present the link between water and cultural survival as clearly as do the Lummi. As in their other initiatives, the Lummi have something to teach other indigenous groups as well as those who are not indigenous: the intimate and permanent connection between the environment, cultural survival, and water.

Food for Thought

A homeland provides a place where a society can function and maintain recognizable interactional boundaries between itself and the cultural systems around it.[26] If an indigenous society can maintain hegemony over some locality, it is in a much better position to resist forces that threaten its integrity and the continuity of its lifeway. Not surprisingly, maintaining, defending, and recouping control over a *place* is an unending preoccupation of most of the world's remaining indigenous societies. Readers exploring the importance of locality for contemporary indigenous peoples might start with John Bodley's classic book *Victims of Progress* (1990) and then begin to look at the long struggle of tribal groups in the United States to retain their lands against the determined expansion of Euro-Americans. Here, James Welch and Paul Stekler's *Killing Custer* (1994) will provide much food for thought.

Place, however, is not just acreage. A homeland must be habitable, and one requirement for habitability is access to freshwater. Where indigenous societies still have legitimized or de facto control of land, it is mostly in small—indeed, shrinking—parcels. As with the Lummi, rivers and streams supplying their lands usually originate outside their enclaves in areas controlled by others. Today, tribal water supplies are often in jeopardy because of upstream water diversion and pollution not only of surface water but also of the groundwater that replenishes wells.[27]

In the long run, the hardest question confronting indigenous peoples is this: How can small, culturally distinct, enclaved societies exercise sufficient leverage over the larger, dominant societies that control the world around them in order to protect the water and other resources that make their homelands habitable? It is already a daunting problem to protect tiny homelands from avaricious outsiders who see timber, grazing lands, or minerals to be had if only those "nuisance" Indians can "just be gotten rid of."[28] Yet even as indigenous peoples combat direct assaults on their homelands, they must also be vigilant of the appropriation of vital natural resources beyond their borders.

RESOURCES

Much can be learned by examining new ways in which indigenous groups are finding levers of political power to assist them in both on-reservation and off-reservation struggles. In addition to the works cited earlier, Fergus Bordewich's book *Killing the White Man's Indian: Reinventing Native Americans at the End of the Twentieth Century* (1996) is a fine place to begin. Indigenous societies' new tools include marshaling the assistance of environmental and human rights organizations, skillfully using the global media, cultivating effective native leaders who understand the external society well enough to exploit its weaknesses, and assembling funds to mount serious campaigns. At the same time, indigenous groups are using modern technologies to communicate with other indigenous groups, sharing knowledge and experience and mobilizing unified initiatives. In recent years, the results have often been surprising.

Those wanting to study these new political capabilities would do well to read Terence Turner's account (1992) of the Amazonian Kayapo's struggle, and triumph, over Brazilian development efforts and to acquaint themselves with the struggle and victory of the Eastern Cree against the hydroelectric project at James Bay, Canada, as described in chapter 4 of this book and in Niezen 1993. More comprehensive overviews are found in Greaves 1993 and 1996.

It is too soon to say that the tables have turned and that indigenous societies are safe. Despite some amazing examples, virtually all of the Amazon's tribal groups are in jeopardy,[29] as are the indigenous peoples of New Guinea and the South Pacific. All of us living in this decade have the opportunity to observe—*and intervene in*—what will be either the final hour of indigenous cultures or the turning point at which indigenous groups become lasting participants in the societies of planet Earth.

NOTES

1. The information on which this chapter is based was obtained primarily from local newspaper coverage of the Lummi, particularly as found in the *Bellingham Herald* from 1990 to 1997, supplemented by discussions with tribal leaders and journalists.

2. For further statistics, including the 27 percent growth rate in the Lummi population between 1980 and 1990, see "Reservation Population Grows," *Bellingham Herald,* 2 August 1991, B1.

3. The Lummi Tribal School is a federally funded private school incorporating kindergarten through eighth grade, emphasizing traditional culture and language ("Lummi Tribal School Teaches Cultural Heritage," *Bellingham Herald,* 27 January 1992, B2).

4. The Lummi were among the first tribal groups in the United States to seek and secure complete self-government, administering federal moneys themselves instead of relying on mediation by the Bureau of Indian Affairs (cf. "Lummis Find New Pride and Power," *Bellingham Herald,* 4 June 1995).

5. See, for example, "Lummi Will Honor Year's First Fish," *Bellingham Herald,* 20 April 1991, B1, and "Fish and Boats Blessed," *Bellingham Herald,* 26 April 1992, B2.

6. See "Lummis Raise Alarm over Low Water Levels," *Bellingham Herald*, 9 April 1992, A1, and "Sockeye Dispute Unites U.S. Fishers," *Bellingham Herald*, 7 July 1992, A1, A2.

7. Indeed, British Columbian authorities have complained vigorously that the United States offices and agencies responsible for the Nooksack need to build sufficient flood control capability to prevent its flooding across to the Fraser, where it has regularly caused major property damage (see KCM, Inc. ca. 1993).

8. The I-5 corridor is the heavily developed north-south interstate highway linking, in this region, Vancouver, B.C., with Seattle.

9. For more a detailed discussion of Nooksack River hydrology, see KCM, Inc. ca. 1993.

10. See "Lummis Chart Government," *Bellingham Herald*, 8 October 1991, B1, B4, for data on current governance structure and recent changes.

11. The Lummi Nation has organized and hosted several meetings of indigenous leaders from societies as far away as Australia and South America, sent a five-member delegation to UNCED in Rio de Janeiro, and has been a significant player in current government-to-government consultations between U.S. indigenous nations and the White House.

12. See, for example, "A Glimpse at Whatcom County's Future," *Bellingham Herald*, 8 November 1992, A1, A6, for a general survey of past and future growth.

13. Growth could, however, be sharply limited if a limited supply of water for urban uses and for job-creating new employers will not permit the expansion. This is a central concern of city and county civic and business leaders. See "A Glimpse at Whatcom County's Future" and "A Look at Tomorrow Today," *Bellingham Herald*, 8 November 1992, A1, A6.

14. The Lummi had been calling for effective regional management and control of unauthorized usage well before the announcement of the planned lawsuit. See, for example, "Lummis Warn of Water Crisis," *Bellingham Herald*, 27 February 1992, B1.

15. Note that the problem involves not only water taken directly from stream channels and impounded reservoirs but also water pumped from wells that tap groundwater. Both sources are part of the same water system for the region. The state had been curtailing new permits in any case as a result of the Growth Management Act; see "Growth Law Leaves Homebuilders . . .," *Bellingham Herald*, 18 August 1991, A1. See also "Tribe to Fight for Water," *Bellingham Herald*, 1 July 1992, A1, A2, and "Lummis Hire Lawyer for Water Fight," *Bellingham Herald*, 21 September 1992, A1, A2.

16. Controlling water use on the reservation is part of another Lummi objective as well. As with so many other reservation lands, nearly half of the 3,147 people residing on the Lummi Indian Reservation are non-Indians. For years, non-Indian residents of Bellingham have owned beachfront homes on the reservation, located along the shore of Bellingham Bay and in several enclavelike developments on the western side of the reserva-

tion, the largest of which is Sandy Point. These developments are almost exclusively populated by non-Indians, who commute to jobs and community life outside the reservation. In nearly every instance, the non-Indian residents collectively refuse to recognize tribal authority. Water politics is one of several hotly contested issues these groups use to resist any Lummi authority over them.

17. See "Governor Joins Effort to Solve County Water Fight," *Bellingham Herald*, 19 January 1994, A1. The Lummi's involvement in regional fish management and conservation efforts also includes active membership in regional, state, and international regulatory bodies. Fishing remains a significant occupation for various Lummi families, but fishing and the cosmological link to salmon are of fundamental symbolic importance to the Lummi Nation as a whole.

18. Although tribal authorities had not earmarked specific funds to cover legal costs, press reports suggested that profits from the Lummi's casino and, possibly, Department of Interior funds would eventually be used. See "Lummis Hire Lawyer for Water Fight," *Bellingham Herald*, 21 September 1992, A2. However, in the summer of 1997 the Lummi closed their casino because an essential part of their customer base, Canadians from Vancouver, now had equivalent gambling opportunities in their own city. The Lummi's casino closure seems likely to increase the financial burdens of financing a protracted legal battle.

19. See "Tribe to Fight for Water," *Bellingham Herald*, 1 July 1992, A1.

20. See "Lummis Hire Lawyer for Water Fight," *Bellingham Herald*, 21 September 1992, A1.

21. The Lummi have been funded by the U.S. Environmental Protection Agency to conduct such a study. See "Lummis Get $45,000 to Protect Water Source," *Bellingham Herald*, 6 September 1992, B1.

22. See "Development Drought: Lack of Water Stunts Industrial Growth in County," *Bellingham Herald*, 5 July 1994, A1, A2, as well as "Lawsuit Suggested as Way to Stimulate Water Talks," *Bellingham Herald*, 26 January 1994, A2, and "Water Permits Fall on Dry Times," *Bellingham Herald*, 16 March 1994, A1. The suspension of new water rights also extended to the Lummi Indian Reservation, where more than half the residents are non-Indians living on properties purchased from individual Lummi. Claiming that the reservation has no jurisdiction over them, many of these non-Indian residents are clustered in developments with their own water companies and systems of wells. The state's restrictions on new wells impose an important constraint on the defiance these associations direct at reservation authorities.

23. Presently the Lummi are participating in a federally sponsored effort to decide the allocation of water between tribal and nontribal residents, an issue that has been extremely bitter in recent years. It is hoped that a settlement in this more limited sphere could lead to a successful, regionwide process (see "Water Talks on Horizon," *Bellingham Herald*, 19 February 1997).

24. See "Lummis Support Code," *Bellingham Herald*, 3 July 1992, A1, and "Lummis Hire Lawyer for Water Fight," *Bellingham Herald*, 21 September 1992, A1, A2.

25. In the viewpoint presented here, cultural rights are a subset of human rights. Whereas most recognized human rights are enjoyed by individuals, such as the right to a fair trial, a few rights are centered in groups, as in the right of an ethnic minority to its own cultural survival. See Greaves 1995 for a discussion of cultural rights and also "Oldest Claims Win Water Fight," *Bellingham Herald*, 26 January 1994, A2.

26. Gypsies (and perhaps certain other groups) are an apparent exception in that kinship, language, and political oppression seem to be greater unifiers than the pursuit of a common homeland.

27. Agriculture, industry, and urban populations in the drier regions of the world have long fought over water, but as urban populations rapidly grow, freshwater is a problem even in traditionally wet areas, as in the Puget Sound region discussed here. Increasingly, the scarcest natural resource worldwide is freshwater. When water is fought over, politically weaker groups usually lose out—and political weakness has traditionally characterized indigenous groups.

28. The disastrous consequences of reducing the land available to indigenous groups, which often rely on low-intensity use of large areas of land to sustain a traditional lifeway, are well illustrated in Richard Reed's study of the Amazonian Guarani (1990). When an external society decides that "the Indians" need only a remote place to live and a few acres to farm, the consequence is often ethnocide, the cultural extermination of a society, and to a large degree genocide, the physical death of most of its people.

29. This is illustrated, for example, by an article in the summer 1996 issue of *Abya Yala News*, the journal of the South and Meso American Indian Rights Center, titled "Confronting Cultural Extinction: Indigenous Cultures Continue to Vanish from the Americas" (*Abya Yala News* 1996). *Abya Yala News* is just one example of the burgeoning number of indigenous-controlled media that share information and experience among groups and interface with the nonindigenous public.

CHAPTER 4

"A River That Was Once So Strong and Deep"
Local Reflections on the Eastmain Diversion, James Bay Hydroelectric Project

Kreg Ettenger

Author Summary

As part of Quebec's massive James Bay Hydroelectric Project, several major rivers were diverted from their natural courses to provide more water for the project's main generating stations. One of these, the Eastmain River, was the lifeblood of the residents of Eastmain, a 300-year-old Cree Indian village that sits on the river's bank not far from James Bay. The disruption of the river's natural flow has had dramatic impacts on its physical and biological characteristics and on its usefulness to local residents, who once depended on it for food, water, transportation, and other needs. These impacts were described forcefully and eloquently by the citizens of Eastmain in recent testimony against the proposed Great Whale River Hydroelectric Project. This chapter presents excerpts from this testimony and offers the author's insights on the long-term effects of major water development projects on downstream communities.

I blame it all on the person who started destroying the land, the river. Now we do not have good drinking water, and a river that was once so strong and deep and that had provided for a lot of families is now all dried up and sad to look at. It's so sad that we have lost all our native source of food and our way of life, and all because he wanted power.

—Alice M., age seventy

This chapter describes how one small community in northern Quebec was affected by a major water development venture: the colossal James Bay Hydroelectric Project. Eastmain is a Cree Indian village of some 400 residents located on the southern bank of the Eastmain River, near where it flows into James Bay (see figure 4.1). In the early 1980s, the river was diverted northward by means of a major dam and a series of dikes about 160 kilometers (100 miles) inland. A major tributary, the Opinaca River, was also dammed; both rivers now feed most of their waters into a huge reservoir complex, increasing the output of several major generating stations along the La Grande River. Besides the obvious environmental impacts caused by the creation of the reservoirs themselves, the loss of flow in the Eastmain and Opinaca Rivers has had major impacts on water level, water quality, and wildlife habitat along the rivers' courses downstream from the diversions. These changes have had significant repercussions for the residents of Eastmain.

For more than 300 years, Eastmain residents have relied on their river for water, food, and transportation. Even before the existence of the community itself, which grew out of a Hudson's Bay Company trading post, residents of the region depended on the Eastmain and other major waterways. As with most northern Native peoples, water was—and still is—the primary resource: it is how one gets around in a land of trackless bogs and dense brush; where beavers build their lodges and muskrats dig burrows; where bears and moose come to drink; where geese and ducks congregate during their spring and fall migrations; where trout, whitefish, and pickerel swim; and where humans go to get them all.

It is this dependence on water and wildlife that so often makes hydroelectric development devastating for northern Native communities (Waldram 1988). Ecological changes associated with reservoirs, new diversion channels, and radically fluctuating water flows can wreak havoc on local wildlife populations as well as make it difficult for hunters to reach them. This means that local economies, which rely heavily on "bush products"—furs, fish, trees, berries, medicinal plants, and the like—can quickly be affected. A scarcity of viable alternatives for employment and income often creates economic dependence and poverty, which in turn may lead to a rash of social problems, such as depression, suicide, and alcohol and drug abuse. These problems have been documented in a number of Native communities throughout Canada that are affected directly or indirectly by hydroelectric development or similarly disruptive events (Waldram 1988; Vecsey 1987; Shkilnyk 1985).[1]

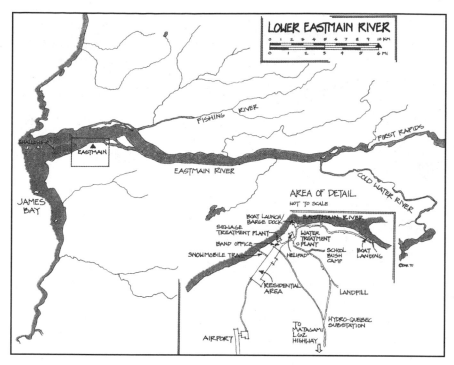

FIGURE 4.1. THE LOWER EASTMAIN RIVER IN QUEBEC
AND THE CREE INDIAN VILLAGE OF EASTMAIN

Eastmain (population 400) is located on the southern bank of the Eastmain
River near where it flows into James Bay. Local use of the river continues but
has been severely affected by damming of the river 160 kilometers (100 miles)
upstream. Map courtesy Dan Reeder.

The James Bay Hydroelectric Project

The James Bay Hydroelectric Project is a vast complex of electricity-
generating stations, reservoirs, transmission lines, roads, and various
other features within an area of some 10,000 square kilometers (4,000
square miles) in mid-northern Quebec province, a region widely
known as James Bay (see figure 4.2). The landscape here consists
mainly of stunted black spruce forest interspersed with large areas of
mossy bog and dotted with low, rounded hills of exposed Precambrian
rock from the Canadian Shield. The harsh climate, in particular the
brutally cold winters, severely limits the type of plants found and their
rates of growth; it also means that recovery of areas damaged by fire or
flooding is painfully slow. Wildlife in the region is well adapted to the
cold and snow, and the furs from such animals as beavers, otters,
minks, lynxes, and martens are world renowned for their quality.

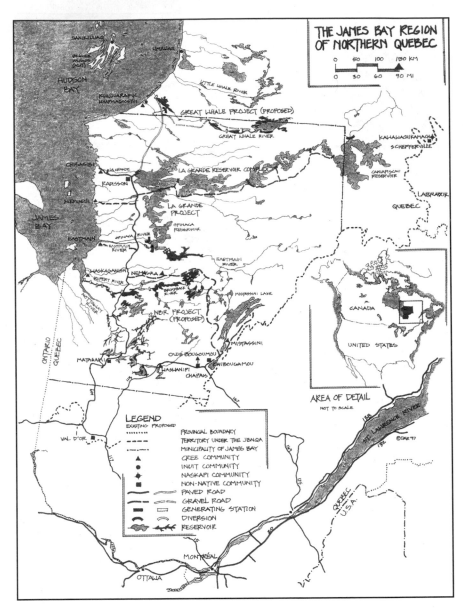

FIGURE 4.2. THE JAMES BAY REGION OF NORTHERN QUEBEC

The James Bay Hydroelectric Project, a vast complex of electricity-generating stations, reservoirs, transmission lines, roads, and various other features, lies within an area of some 10,000 square kilometers (4,000 square miles) in northern Quebec. Map courtesy Dan Reeder.

The Cree people and their ancestors, who have lived in this region as long as there have been fish to catch and animals to hunt, learned to make the most of what they were given, developing over millennia the particular knowledge, skills, and beliefs needed to survive in such an unforgiving place. They used every part of the animals they killed, including meat, fur, sinew, and bone. What they did not eat they wore; what could not be worn was used to make snowshoes or needles or scrapers. What little was left was hung from trees or placed in water, depending on the species, to show respect for the animal and preserve good relations with its spirit guardian, so crucial to a hunter's future success and his family's survival (Tanner 1979). Over the centuries, even as the Cree joined the global economy through the fur trade, this essential relationship between the people and animals of James Bay did not greatly change.

When plans for the James Bay project were announced by Quebec's government in 1971, the Cree were the last to hear of them. Since that time, they have been fighting a battle to preserve their way of life or at least to maintain such traditional activities as hunting and trapping as viable economic options. To some degree, they have been successful, winning financial compensation and protection of key rights while re-taining control over portions of the territory.[2] They have also been able to convert to an economy based largely on wage employment, although hunting, trapping, and fishing remain important activities for most families and the primary source of food and income for some. By and large, the nine Cree communities in Quebec are not completely op-posed to regional development, although most would like to have more control over decisions that ultimately affect them, including plans for future hydroelectric development.

When Hydro-Quebec, the provincially owned utility that developed the James Bay project, announced in the late 1980s that it was moving ahead with plans for the Great Whale River Hydroelectric Project (named for the next major river to be dammed and tapped for energy production), the Cree reaction was understandably negative. There were to be no more hydroelectric projects in the region, Cree leaders said, without their input and approval, as well as a full review of the likely social and environmental impacts of further development. At first Hydro-Quebec resisted, arguing that the Great Whale River pro-ject was not a new development at all but simply another phase of the already approved James Bay project. A federal court disagreed, how-ever, and ultimately Hydro-Quebec was forced to submit the project for review under federal and provincial guidelines for new hydroelec-tric projects in the James Bay region, as specified in the James Bay and Northern Quebec Agreement (see note 2). The document Hydro-Quebec produced in response to these requirements (1993) is on a scale similar to the James Bay project itself: it consists of thirty volumes dealing with everything from mercury contamination in reservoirs to the impact of roads on wildlife movement. Of course, this is what one might expect when considering the effects of transforming an area the size of a small country and creating reservoirs comparable to the Great Lakes.

What the study did not adequately address, however, was how these extensive environmental modifications have affected the Cree residents of the region, who still rely heavily on wildlife harvesting to supplement their incomes and as a vital component of their culture. This gap was due in part to Hydro-Quebec's limited approach to gaining local input: its "community consultation" consisted simply of a set of prepared surveys, one for each affected community, dealing with specific issues and designed to be filled out by a band employee or representative. Cree communities refused to participate in this narrowly focused study. Instead, they demanded a more comprehensive approach based on open interviews with community residents, conducted by social scientists hired by the Cree and with Cree ownership of the data collected. An agreement between the Cree leadership and Hydro-Quebec was reached in early 1994, and research took place in the spring and summer of that year, with a final multivolume report completed in August (Scott and Ettenger 1994, Nakashima and Roué 1994).[3] The report consists mainly of testimony given by local residents about their perceptions of the various impacts of hydroelectric development on Cree lands, organized according to geography (reservoir areas, roads, etc.) and nature of impact (e.g., ecological, economic, social, cultural).

The primary difference between the two reports is not one of empirical observation: both hunters and scientists can see the impacts of the reservoirs and other features of development, although the systems for measuring those impacts can differ considerably. Rather, the main disparity seems to be one of interpretation. What, for example, does the creation of a reservoir mean to a Cree as opposed to what it means to an environmental scientist working for Hydro-Quebec? The latter may interpret the event according to "objective" measures such as biomass production, with the new reservoir simply representing the replacement of one ecological niche with another, as in the following conclusion from the Great Whale River project so-called "feasibility study": "Although the biological diversity of the area would not be jeopardized in any way, the chief effect of the [Great Whale] project would be to reduce the land environment in favor of the aquatic environment" (Hydro-Quebec 1993, 252). To the Cree, however, who live in the region and depend on the land and for whom the rivers, lakes, hills, and streams are part of a personal and cultural history, the losses—whether economic, social, cultural, or even psychological—may be profound.

This chapter is not meant to serve as a full analysis of the social and environmental impacts of the James Bay Hydroelectric Project. The objective here is much more limited: it is simply an attempt to explain how one aspect of the project, the diversion of the Eastmain River, has been so damaging to the residents of Eastmain. It addresses only one location—the river adjacent to the community—and focuses on a few main uses of the river: for transportation, for fishing, and for collecting water. The choice of location and impacts is somewhat arbitrary; other impacts of the project have been equally devastating, and other communities have been deeply affected. But it is hoped that this examination of one particular set of impacts and the ways in which they affect one small community will contribute to a better understanding of the wider implications of hydroelectric development for local populations. The story of the project's effects on Eastmain residents is also pertinent to one of the goals of this book, namely, to show how the element of culture can play a significant role in determining the outcome of water development projects. Hearing the concerns and opinions of affected groups, in their own words, may help us to gain the cross-cultural perspective needed to truly and accurately gauge the impacts of development projects (Curtis 1992).

The River Then and Now

Many Eastmain residents have strong recollections of time spent on the river before the diversion. Their accounts of these events, as well as more general reminiscences of the river and its past uses, are infused with a sense of individual and community well-being. The prediversion period is often viewed as a time of relative calm and security when residents knew what to expect from the river and in the rest of their lives. In terms of local perceptions, at least, the fate of the village seems to be intertwined with the fate of the river: just as the river was irreversibly changed by the James Bay project, so too was the community of Eastmain. Memories of the river "how it was," therefore, are associated with images of the village at a time when Cree society still ran strongly along traditional lines.

> There's a lot of stories and a lot of things to be shared when
> you reflect back to the good use of the river. There is the
> flow; there is the real Indian aspect of being able to paddle on
> a river downstream and upstream. . . . There's also the har-
> vesting that goes with it. There was always good fishing on
> that river no matter where you stopped.
>
> —Willie M., age eighty-one

In contrast, residents now see the river as irrevocably damaged by
the James Bay project. Its lack of flow, decreased depth, and increased
salinity and the disappearance or decline of several fish species indicate to local people the poor condition of the Eastmain River today.
And it is not just the river that is in trouble: the community itself is
seen by many as suffering from a host of problems, as is Cree society
in general. Of course, the links between what happened to the river
and what is happening in the village are not always clear and obvious.
But in many people's minds, the connections are real, if intangible.

> Everything seems to have gone from us. Nothing runs the
> way it used to when there were happy times. Then, even
> though we were hungry and we didn't have everything, we
> were happy as we could be. But nowadays it's all confusing
> and people seem to be very unhappy about something.
>
> —Winnie S., age fifty-five

> We have lost a lot; we've lost everything. We lost our source
> of food and our beautiful river. Even the furbearing animals
> are not near us anymore. I'm saying this because I'm telling
> the truth. Everyone notices our loss, and depression seems to
> have come over us because of our great loss. Nothing tastes
> the same as it did long ago before the dams. So this is my tes-
> timony of how affected we are in everything, the great loss
> we have encountered.   —Daisy C., age eighty-one

Physical Changes and River Travel

The physical changes that resulted from the diversion are obvious to
residents. First, the water level itself decreased considerably. Today,
residents say, one can almost cross the river on foot near the village
during a very low tide, which was unheard of in the past. Essentially,

the water level in the river's estuary now depends on the tides of James Bay, whereas in the past the river's strong flow maintained its level. The loss of current has also meant that sediment is not pushed completely out of the river's mouth, so new sandbars and gravel bars have formed near the village. In general, residents say that the river near the community has become more like a shallow coastal bay: brackish, sluggish, and controlled by tidal currents and storm-driven waves rather than by a strong river's flow (see photo 4.1).

Because of these physical changes, travel on the river today is difficult or impossible during low tide, as rocks and sandbars prevent the use of canoes with outboard motors. This can mean delays as long as half a day while waiting for the tide to come in; at times of extremely low water level in fall, it may be impossible to use the river for days at a time. These delays are more than just an inconvenience; during fall

PHOTO 4.1. THE MANTUWATAW RAPIDS
ON THE EASTMAIN RIVER

Prior to the diversion of the Eastmain River, Mantuwataw was one of the river's most dangerous rapids, requiring a long canoe portage. Now the river struggles to fill its banks here even during late-spring runoff, when this photograph was taken. The view is from the Mantagami-LG2 Highway. Photograph by Kreg Ettenger.

spawning runs and waterfowl migrations, they can have serious effects on fish and wildlife harvests and can make it difficult for a villager to return home for food or medical attention. For groups taking short trips to the bay, an unexpected and prolonged low tide may mean spending one or more nights with few provisions on an island or along the coast of James Bay during cold fall weather. One resident reported being stranded for two days while she and her family waited for the water to rise so they could return to the village.

Several families in Eastmain still travel inland every year to spend the winter trapping beavers, martens, lynxes, and other furbearing animals, as well as hunting for moose and caribou, on their family-owned hunting territories or traplines. For these families, and for others that no longer make the inland journey, the Eastmain and other rivers were highways to the territory's vast interior before there were roads or bush planes to make travel easier. The rivers allowed them to transport gear or furs for long distances while avoiding insect-infested bogs and dense bush; fall travelers also stocked up on fish for the long winter ahead. Although the annual journey was often dangerous and always tiring, those who did it as a way of life, many of whom are in their sixties and older today, have strong and vivid memories of the experience. It is these men and women, born and raised in the bush, who feel most deeply the loss of what the Eastmain River once was.

> It was always a proud moment for me to be able to paddle down the river and show up at the Cree village of Eastmain to share with my people a bear, which is in my culture, in my tradition, one of the most respected animals of the Cree Nation. And that is what I miss the most. My trapline is important, but the river will always be the most important part of my life. . . . On the river you have memories as a little child, as a little boy growing up—memories of your parents, memories of your brothers and sisters, and memories of your friends. You also have graves of your friends. What was written into my knowledge from the river is very important to me, especially at this time, knowing that I will never, ever again be able to paddle up or down that river. I can honestly say that nobody will ever be able to paddle on that river again. How many people that are going to be born in the future, how many of them will believe that was the way it was until the year of the development? How many of those people will question just how important it was? Even our people will eventually question the importance of this river. Because

they themselves will never be able to experience what I experienced, and only the memories will remain with me.

—Willie M., age eighty-one

As a final note with respect to physical changes and travel, residents agree that since the diversion, winter ice conditions on the river have changed noticeably, making travel more difficult and dangerous. One man lost his life when, a year or so after the diversion, his snowmobile broke through what appeared to be safe ice near the mouth of the river. Many residents believe that the higher salinity of the river and increased tidal action, both resulting from the diversion, make it more difficult now than in the past to assess the thickness and condition of ice. As a result, safety precautions have been adopted, such as testing the thickness of the ice daily and closing the river to snowmobile travel earlier in the year. The latter measure has forced the community to charter a helicopter for several weeks each spring to transport hunters and their families to and from coastal goose camps.

When the ice finally melts away, it does so without warning and with none of the power and excitement of its prediversion breakups. This change in itself was noted by several residents as a significant impact of the diversion.

> [Breakup] was an exciting event for everyone in the community, because the current of the river was so strong. The ice looked so beautiful when it broke up. It was so nice to hear the rumble of the ice going. It would pile up and the crystal clear ice would tinkle like bells. It would sound like dishes breaking. This is another thing that is missing because the river is now motionless.
>
> —Florrie M., age sixty

> You could see the ice breaking up in big chunks and big sheets of ice—just like a bulldozer, all the way to the mouth of the Eastmain River. But now it doesn't break up, it just melts away. It just melts, just like a lake with no current.
>
> —Edward G., age seventy-one

According to geographer John Newton (1995, 115), "Break-up and freeze-up are pivotal points in the calendar of northern communities, a significant seasonal transition reflecting a changing relationship with the land." The loss of this important annual event is another painful reminder to Eastmain residents that their lives, like the natural cycles of the river, have been forever changed by hydroelectric development.

Water Quality

A frequently mentioned change in the river since the diversion is a noticeable decline in water quality. This is especially troubling because the past uses of the river—for drinking, bathing, and fishing—were based on its perceived cleanliness and healthfulness.

> The river was healthy long ago because it was always flowing, always throwing out the dirt and pollution, whatever was coming in from inland.   —Charlie M., age sixty-nine

> I remember I used to go down in the wintertime, I would go right onto the ice, drill a hole in the ice, and just start getting water from it.   —Minnie C., age sixty-two

> On calm evenings there would be people getting water from the river and storing water for everyday uses, like for cooking, drinking and washing.   —Daisy C., age eighty-one

Since the diversion, the river has essentially been lost for these purposes. The causes are various: the decline in flow, which has allowed the brackish waters of James Bay to move upstream several miles; a community sewage treatment plant that discharges effluent into the river adjacent to the village; seepage from gas tanks and discarded fuel drums along the river bank; and the perceived threat of mercury contamination and other pollution from upstream. If the river still had its original flow, these might not be major problems in terms of water quality. But when people see objects in the water floating *upstream* as the tide comes in, they know the river near the village is useless for most purposes. Water samples gathered near the community and tested for contaminants confirm these impressions.

The incursion of salt water into the river may also be affecting the local water table, lowering the quality of the municipal water supply (now provided by a well) and making water treatment more difficult and expensive. Despite a new million-dollar water treatment facility, the taste and appearance of the municipal supply is often poor, and many residents refuse to use it for drinking or cooking (a new proposal calls for lakewater to be piped several miles to the village, at a cost of some Can$25 million). Instead, they collect rainwater from roofs, gather it from pools on local islands, or melt snow. Bottled water is purchased in local food stores, although it is expensive, and from a local entrepreneur who distills and sells water from his home. Still, many miss the days when freshwater could be collected directly from the river.

> The water is so dirty it is of no use to us. It is salty and is not even good to use for washing clothes, whereas long ago we got our drinking water from there; the water was good for all uses. Now today, we have no drinking water until we pay for it. Tap water is no good for drinking or cooking. Now that they have taken our waters, they are making us pay for water, when the Creator made these strong, healthy rivers for the Natives to use in good health. . . . Now we are forced to drink rainwater and melted snow.   —Florrie M., age sixty

Water, to the Cree, is a source of life and renewal. A familiar Cree legend explains changes in wildlife populations by stating that at certain times, land animals such as caribou "disappear" into lakes or rivers, to reappear years or decades later. Clean water is usually associated with strong current; stagnant lakes and ponds are seen as unhealthy for humans and animals alike. The spring runoff in particular is an event during which rivers, lakes, and streams cleanse themselves of brush and other debris accumulated over the year. Downstream from the Eastmain dam, however, the river now lacks sufficient current even in spring to carry away fallen logs and brush, creating obstacles to travel and suggesting that the water in the river, like that in the snag-filled reservoirs above, is tainted. Many residents also believe there is a connection between the diversion and observed changes in the quality of lakes and streams in the region. The perception of pollution is widespread, and most residents blame it on tampering with the river upstream.

Local Fishing

Besides providing drinking water, the Eastmain River was extremely important as a source of food. Several species of fish, including trout, whitefish, cisco, burbot, sucker, and pickerel, were caught in large numbers near the village at various times of the year, usually by nets set in channels on either side of the river. Several nearby sites, including a series of falls called the First Rapids about twenty kilometers (twelve miles) upstream, were important for pike, sturgeon, and other species.

> Fishing was very important in the daily lives of the elders and people that hunted and fished and trapped on this land before any store-bought goods were available.
> —Daniel M., age fifty-four

> People used to set nets in front of the community; there was always fishing there. There were always a few nets right in front of the village [and] across the river. . . . And at the mouth of the river there were three or four areas where people used to set summer nets, like right around mid-July. And right up to the First Rapids people used to set nets.
> —Edward G., age seventy-one

Fishing was and is an important economic activity, providing a critical resource at times of the year when other foods can be scarce. In past periods of famine, the availability of fish from lakes and rivers could mean the difference between life and death. Even in relatively good years, fish provided a welcome change in the bush diet, especially after a long winter of beaver, moose, and caribou meat. Many elder Cree in particular have strong feelings about fish for these reasons and also because fishing was often a group activity and thus a bonding force in Cree society. Families would gather to fish at major rapids in fall, during spawning runs of trout and other species. Fish was also an important item of trade between family groups in Eastmain. In early summer, families coming downstream from their traplines would bring smoked fish from inland lakes and streams; these would be exchanged for smoked goose and other foods harvested that spring by coastal families.

The Eastmain River near the village was essentially common property, available for all to use. This was especially important for families that lacked access to productive trapping areas or for some reason could not make the arduous annual trip inland for winter hunting and trapping. Even for families that relied mainly on other areas for food and income, the river provided a reliable alternative source of food, especially during summer and fall months.

Like I said, we weren't rich, we didn't have very much money back then to buy food. And when we used to go fishing we were pretty sure that we would have something to eat all the time. . . . I always felt people were being treated equally with what they could get from the river.

—Minnie C., age sixty-two

I was raised here in Eastmain. As I was growing up, my father passed away when we were very young, so my mother did the hunting for us. . . . I would be the one to go out with my mother to set out nets because that was mostly how we survived, right here on the Eastmain River.

—Daisy C., age eighty-one

Today, there is no fishing activity directly adjacent to the village, and there is little upstream. The increased salinity of the estuary, combined with lower water levels and decreased current, have forced some fish species to relocate or have otherwise thinned their numbers. This is especially true for sensitive species such as sturgeon, which have virtually disappeared from the river.[4] Spawning runs have diminished considerably, possibly due to the loss of critical spawning areas upstream as well as the river's decreased current and increased temperature. Several rapids have experienced severe reductions in flow, especially during late summer and fall, when some fish would be moving upstream. Finally, low water levels make it more difficult for people to set nets in the river, and the shallow water makes ice fishing practically impossible, as thick late-winter ice actually touches the bottom of the river in some spots.

Residents are also concerned about the quality and safety of fish caught in the river. Prior to the diversion, fish caught near the village were considered healthy and good tasting, reflecting the purity of the river at that time.

Back in the old days, when they used to be able to fish by net just across the river here, the fish used to taste so good. . . . I remember that it used to be so good compared to today.

—Alice M., age seventy

Back then the fish was very good, very fresh. And even the [broth] of the fish when it was boiled, people used to drink that, and they even used to eat the livers of the fish. That's how good the fish was.

—Minnie C., age sixty-two

In contrast, many residents now say the fish taste strange or look unhealthy, leading some to decrease their consumption of local fish or stop eating them altogether. For others, however, the desire for traditional foods still outweighs fear about safety or perceptions of changes in appearance and taste.

> It's no good to go fishing in the river anymore. . . . The fish are not as healthy as they used to be, even if there's a few fish here and there. We don't eat off the river anymore.
> —Minnie G., age fifty-two

> Us elders, we know that there's a taste, that the fish is different now. But we still eat it because we want to eat it, because we feel that we need the fish. —Alice M., age seventy

Fear of mercury contamination also affects people's perceptions of the safety of local fish populations.[5] Community residents are aware of warnings from the Cree Health Board about consuming certain species of fish from within or around the reservoirs, where mercury contamination is a serious problem. Many Cree, however, have reduced their consumption of fish from other areas as well, not fully trusting scientists or health officals to tell them where it is safe to fish. Incomplete, inaccurate, and conflicting information from various sources has contributed to this problem.

> People of this community are . . . scared and frightened . . . when it's mentioned that there is existing mercury in fish. I for one have noticed people have decreased their consumption of fish since they've heard of the mercury contamination.
> —Luke T., age sixty-four

> I would say that we do eat less fish now than before, and part of the reason is because of what we were told, that there is mercury in the fish, and we're afraid that we might end up eating fish that has lots of mercury. Even my husband doesn't really want to eat fish anymore because of that.
> —Daisy C., age eighty-one

Such concerns about fish safety and quality, along with the decline in local fish populations, have forced many residents to go farther afield in search of this important food source. In particular, the waters of James Bay are now a favored spot for both setting nets and fishing with rod and reel. Travel on the bay requires a large "freighter canoe" with an outboard motor, however, and such an outfit can cost in excess of Can$10,000 (U.S.$7,000)—not to mention operating costs. Bay fishing also requires more planning and is inherently less safe than river fishing: water conditions are generally rougher on the bay, travel distances are greater, and a broken engine or damaged boat can lead to tragedy. An individual is therefore unlikely to undertake such an excursion alone. These factors have made daily fishing trips difficult or impossible for many, especially elders and low-income residents.

> Today when we want good healthy fish, we have to have great big canoes and strong outboard motors because we now go quite a ways out to the shores of James Bay, away from the once-healthy Eastmain River. . . . We have to spend a lot of money if we want to eat healthy fish and other game, because we now have to go out a long way from the river and all its polluted waters.
> —Alice M., age seventy

Many who depended on local fish in the past have become more reliant on store-bought foods, which are expensive, less nutritious, and often less desirable. This has a significant economic effect on many families, especially those with low incomes. And because many who relied on fish are now in their sixties or older and few have jobs in the community, one segment of the population has been affected disproportionately. To these older community residents, the shift to store-bought foods represents more than just the replacement of a healthy, natural food source with a less desirable and less nutritious substitute, with consequences for health and well-being. It also means the loss of a way of life and of the personal satisfaction of living off the land.

Psychological Impacts of Development

Feelings about the Eastmain River diversion run deep in the community, suggesting that emotional and psychological factors may be one of the most significant, if less evident, long-term impacts of water development projects. Many elders, for example, feel a sense of loss due to the destruction of the local fishery, which means they can no longer contribute fresh food to their families or the community. Setting nets close to the village was an activity that could be engaged in even by those too old or infirm to travel inland or along the coast for hunting and fishing excursions. The river's diversion has contributed to a drastic decline in this activity, leading to a sense of worthlessness among many older village men and women.

> We elders felt we were very useful back in those days because we were able to do something for the community, like by putting out our nets and checking them and bringing back fish and sharing with the community. . . . I do a lot of thinking about it and I do miss it.   —Daisy C., age eighty-one

> Our elders look so sad and confused, and it hurts to see them like that, because their way of living and their dietary source has been taken away from them. Therefore they just sit around looking sad and confused, even if they are healthy. Because now they have no way of going out to the river, because the river is dry, no good for anything.
>   —Alice M., age seventy

Older village residents seem the most saddened by the loss of their cherished river and by the changes occurring in their community. These individuals grew up depending on the river for sustenance, learning from their parents and grandparents how to harvest its rich resources, and experiencing firsthand its many moods and dangers. For the elders of Eastmain, therefore, the damage done to the river is not just aesthetic or even functional. It is a wound to the soul of the river, an offense to its spirit.

> Looking at the river today, seeing that the river is dry—it really hurt me when I saw the river was like that.
>   —Daisy C., age eighty-one

> The last time I saw the river upstream, I hurt so much to see the once-strong river now a very dry one. The passages where we used to paddle are full of pussy willows now, and other shrubs are growing there. It is so sad to see what Hydro has done to our land.   —Florrie M., age sixty

> Especially the old people, I know they're still hurt by it. . . . It's like losing somebody that's very close to you.
>   —Dennis C., age thirty-seven

Although the pain of this wound is felt most keenly by the elders, for whom the river was a source of material sustenance and spiritual regeneration, anguish over the loss of the river transcends any age group.

> I think it is very painful for our elders. Not just them—for my
> age group too. . . . I think it is very painful to see, to live with
> a river that was ruined.   —Rose D., age 35

Besides the loss of their land and water resources, local residents seem to be reacting to what they see as a loss of community control, of personal autonomy, of self-respect, and of traditional values and culture. They are unsure of what the future holds for them as individuals, as a community, and as Native people in Quebec and Canada. This uncertainty contributes to a general sense of anger and frustration that also relates directly to the hydroelectric projects: many residents harbor deep resentment at the way they have been treated by Hydro-Quebec and other provincial development agencies. These agencies and the province in general are often blamed for the "man-made disaster" from which the residents of Eastmain are still recovering today.

> I'm angry about the pollution of the river and everything
> that's polluted on our land. I'm angry about it because I know
> that we'll never ever get back our healthy plants, herbs, and
> the healthy animals that we used to have, the healthy fish,
> that they'll never be as good as we had them before.
>   —Winnie S., age fifty-five

> My general feeling is anger to all the development, all the
> things that have happened to me as an individual or to my
> family or to my community in the last 20 years. . . . For the
> youth [too] I feel that there's an angry process, and I'm not
> too sure that that angry process can be remedied with words,
> although I would never accept seeing violence.
>   —Abraham W., age seventy-four

Finally, many local residents draw strong connections between what has happened to their river and what they see as the future of Cree society. In many ways, the river is their link to a former way of life, that of the full-time hunter and trapper who spent nine or more months of the year in the bush. Today, fewer than one in eight families in Eastmain rely mainly on traditional harvesting activities, and even they are supported by considerable subsidies (CHTISB 1995). The loss of the river, though not the only reason why fewer Eastmain residents are trapping today, represents a turning point in the history of this community. It says to many local people, particularly those old enough to have experienced life as full-time trappers, that there is no turning back.

Conclusion: Local Knowledge and Social Impact Assessment

All resource development, especially when applied on a scale similar to that of the James Bay project, affects those people who live near and have traditionally used the altered resource. An understanding of the ways in which local people are likely to perceive and respond to these impacts is critical when planning such projects, either to improve their design or to better gauge whether they are worth building in the first place. Testimony from people who have already experienced such changes, such as the Cree of James Bay, can be an important source of data for planners and policy makers involved in resource management and development. But exactly how and when this information is to be used, and its ultimate role in such decisions, is a more complicated matter.

The first extensive use of local testimony for impact assessment in Canada took place during the Mackenzie Valley Pipeline Inquiry, a three-year official review of potential environmental and social impacts of a proposed gas pipeline in the Northwest Territories (Berger 1977). Besides detailed testimony from social scientists familiar with the region and its people, the concerns of local Indian and Inuit residents were expressed at community public hearings and other forums. For this and other reasons, the "Berger Inquiry" (named for the chief justice who oversaw the pipeline review and was instrumental in its design) is "widely regarded as a landmark in the public assessment and review of industrial development" (Usher 1993, 116).

The Mackenzie Valley Pipeline, the James Bay Hydroelectric Project, and other controversial resource development projects in northern Canada have helped change the way Native communities are viewed by project advocates while redefining these communities' roles with respect to development planning. Barriers to greater local involvement in development planning persist, however, including a perceived lack of scientific credibility of traditional knowledge, which is often seen as anecdotal or subjective. Even when local knowledge is collected, interpreted, or corroborated by "trained" (i.e., Western) scientists, its credibility is not ensured in the world of policy and law. In the Gitksan and Wet'suwet'en land claims case in British Columbia, for example, testimony given by an anthropologist in support of aboriginal communities was dismissed on the ground that such evidence was biased and unreliable because of the researchers' primary ethical responsibility to their subjects (Monet and Skanu'u 1992, 188).

In the final analysis, the way in which local knowledge is used depends mainly on power relations, a fact that returns us to the theme of this volume. If the developer of a region's water resources does not care about the people who live there—does not value their culture or recognize their right to use and have some control over the resource—and if it has the power to exert its will, then the knowledge and concerns of local people will mean nothing. Those who view acculturation or assimilation as an inevitable result of modernization are not likely to see the value in preserving traditional aspects of a society for their own sake. On the other hand, a growing body of evidence suggests that preserving elements of one's cultural heritage is vital in the face of rapid social and economic change, such as that occurring in many Native communities in Canada and elsewhere. For such communities, protection of traditional resources and activities is often an issue of cultural survival as well as an assertion of their right to continued use of such resources and an essential element in indigenous self-government.

Inadequate attention paid to community needs or cultural values in the course of regional development is not unique to James Bay, as many of the chapters in this volume show. But there is a growing movement to include local people's knowledge, concerns, and even visions for the future when making critical resource decisions. And for their part, local people are often willing to take part in this process as long as there is a chance that what they say will make a difference. Not one resident of Eastmain, for example, refused to be interviewed for the community consultation, even though the residents' past relations with Hydro-Quebec had been less than positive. For many, the chance finally to be heard and to share their experiences with others was greater than their mistrust of Hydro-Quebec or of the development planning process in general. As one trapper expressed it:

> There's a lot of stories, a lot of information, a lot of issues and items and culture to be covered when . . . we start talking about it. There's a lot of information, a lot of unshared information.
> —Daniel M., age fifty-four

Food for Thought: Development and Cultural Change

Resource development ventures such as the James Bay project can significantly affect a community's ability to pass on that body of knowledge and experience that makes it unique and helps it retain its identity while moving forward in ways that suit its needs—in other words, its culture. The loss of critical places, for example, may affect the way people view their past or may even diminish their ability to recall specific events. Stories and myths about the land may not hold true when the landscape itself has been altered, or they may not make sense to the young people, whose lives are quite different from their grandparents'. As one resident of Eastmain put it, flooding a trapline to create a reservoir meant the loss of another "Cree college"—a place where young men and women go to learn the important skills and lessons of traditional bush life. Once development has taken place, the sense of individual and community loss may overwhelm the desire to retain what is left of local culture—or it may drive a community to take steps to preserve it. These issues must be considered when trying to discover the long-term effects of major water development schemes on small communities, especially when these communities possess cultures that are distinct from that of the larger society.

RESOURCES

Several books have been written about Cree culture and about the James Bay Hydroelectric Project, with varying biases and emphases. The most complete description of traditional Cree hunting society is found in Adrian Tanner's *Bringing Home Animals* (1979). For a comprehensive analysis of the economic and social changes occurring in Cree villages, read Richard Salisbury's *A Homeland for the Cree* (1986). A powerful account of the James Bay project and its impacts on traditional Cree life is found in *Strangers Devour the Land* by Boyce Richardson (1991), an experienced ethnographic filmmaker and author. Other books about the project include Sean McCutcheon's *Electric Rivers* (1991), Michael Posluns's battle book *Voices from the Odeyak* (1993), and former Quebec premier Robert Bourassa's blatantly prodevelopment *Power from the North* (1985). Less political and more personal are Roy MacGregor's *Chief* (1989), an illuminating biography of the first Cree Grand Chief, Billy Diamond; anthropologist Regina Flannery's *Ellen Smallboy: Glimpses of a Cree Woman's Life* (1995); and Chisasibi resident Margaret Sam-Cromarty's collection of poems, *James Bay Memoirs* (1992).

Articles on the Cree have appeared in popular magazines ranging from *Audubon* to *National Geographic*. Most of these deal with the traditional lifestyle of the Cree, the James Bay project and its impacts, and threats to the wildlife and environment of the region. Keyword searches of general periodical databases are a good place to start. Many scholarly articles have also been published in fields ranging from anthropology to ecology; some of these can be found in major journals, whereas others appear as "gray literature" (such as reports prepared for specific clients or unpublished conference papers). Notable authors who address contemporary natural resource conflicts include Harvey Feit (1989), Colin Scott (1993), Ignatius La Rusic (1991), and Fikret Berkes (1988).

Films dealing with the Cree and the James Bay project include *Power of the North* (Wild Heart Productions, Montreal) and several by Boyce Richardson, including *Job's Garden, Our Land Is Our Life,* and *The Flooding of Job's Garden* (Tamarack Productions, Toronto). The topic has also been featured in a number of television programs, including *The Nature of Things* with David Suzuki (*James Bay: The Wind That Keeps on Blowing,* Canadian Broadcasting Corporation, 1991).

The nine Cree communities of Quebec are officially represented by the Grand Council of the Crees (of Quebec) (GCCQ), a mainly political and advocative body, and the Cree Regional Authority (CRA), which is primarily an administrative organization. The address for both is 2 Lakeshore Road, Nemaska, Quebec, Canada, J0Y 3B0 (telephone: 819-673-2600, fax: 819 673 2606). Several organizations and coalitions supporting the Cree and opposing further hydroelectric development in James Bay emerged during the fight against the Great Whale River project; the GCCQ/CRA office should have up-to-date information on which of these are still active. Some major environmental organizations, such as the Natural Resources Defense Council, have research and advocacy programs dealing with issues in James Bay. It should be noted that although the Great Whale River project has, at least for the time being, been shelved, other conflicts related to forestry, mining, and wildlife management in the region are ongoing.

The Nation is a biweekly magazine covering Native news, politics, and culture in the James Bay region (the title refers to the Cree Nation). Individual subscriptions are Can$65 per year in Canada and U.S.$70 per year elsewhere (Can$75 and U.S.$85 for institutions), payable to Beesum Communications. Write to P.O. Box 48036, 5678 Parc Avenue, Montreal, Quebec, Canada H2V 4S8 (telephone: 514-272-3077; fax: 514-278-9914; email: beesum@odyssee.net).

Internet resources on the James Bay Cree are growing rapidly. A few World Wide Web sites of note include the Grand Council of the Crees' home page (http://gcc.ca); Creenet, based in Wemindji (http://www.creenet.com); Canada's Department of Indian Affairs and Northern Development (http://www.inac.gc.ca); the Web site of the Cree-Naskapi Commission (http://ppp.atreide.net/cnc); and a Web site called Arctic Circle at the University of Connecticut (http://www.lib.uconn.edu/ArcticCircle). *The Nation* magazine, cited above, also has a Web site (http://nisk.creenet.com/~nation).

ACKNOWLEDGMENTS

This chapter is based on material collected by the author for a study conducted with senior coresearcher Colin Scott on behalf of the Grand Council of
the Crees (of Quebec) and the Cree Regional Authority and funded by Hydro-
Quebec (Scott and Ettenger 1994). Use of the material for publication is with
consent of the Grand Council, which retains ownership of the data for all
other uses. Additional support for the author's continuing research in
Eastmain, which helped shape the ideas in this chapter, was provided by the
Wenner-Gren Foundation for Anthropological Research, the National
Science Foundation's Arctic Social Sciences Program, and the Cree Regional
Authority.

I am grateful to Rick Cuciurean of the Cree Trappers Association and to
Peter Castro of Syracuse University, as well as the editors of this volume, for
their helpful comments. I would also like to thank the residents and the
Band Council of the Cree First Nation of Eastmain for their kind assistance
and support. Special thanks go to Fred Tomatuk, who expertly translated
interviews with local hunters; to Minnie Gilpin, Marjorie Mark, Eva Louttit,
and Isabelle Cheezo, for translation and transcription assistance; and to
Emily Whiskeychan, for help of many kinds.

NOTES

1. Of course, not all communities respond in the same way to environmental changes, and not all economic and social trends in Native communities are due to development. Eastmain and other Cree communities
   were already experiencing profound changes in the years before the James
   Bay project, as studies carried out in the 1960s show (Chance 1968).

2. The James Bay and Northern Quebec Agreement (JBNQA), signed by the
   Cree in 1975 after lengthy negotiations with the governments of Quebec
   and Canada, is essentially a modern treaty that protects vital Cree rights
   and interests while permitting resource development in the James Bay
   region. It guarantees the Cree the right to continue harvesting wildlife
   throughout the region and allows for their input in development decisions
   that could have a negative effect on these activities. It ensures that the
   Cree are provided with certain vital services while reinforcing their
   authority to administer many of their own affairs. The JBNQA also established several programs designed to help the Cree maintain traditional
   activities, including an Income Security Program, which pays a subsidy to
   full-time trappers and their families. Finally, it gave the Cree money to
   compensate them for their loss of land and resources and to help them
   develop their own local and regional economies.

3. On 18 November 1994, Quebec's premier, Jacques Parizeau, announced
   without warning that the Great Whale River Hydroelectric Project was to
   be postponed indefinitely. Many observers, however, saw this action as
   driven by political and economic motives rather than as a response to the

findings of the community consultation or to more general Cree opposition to the project.

4. Few sturgeon are now found in the river below the Eastmain dam, and those caught are described as "skinny" and "unhealthy" and generally are not eaten. The loss of abundance and quality of this species, which is described as a "proud" and "special" fish, has deep cultural as well as economic implications. Perhaps more than with any other species, the decline of the sturgeon seems analogous to the changes in the Eastmain River itself: from something strong, healthy, and pure to something weak, sickly, and deformed—an unnatural abomination of its former self.

5. Mercury is found in the soil and vegetation of the James Bay region, in an inorganic form generally not harmful to wildlife or humans. When flooded, however, plants and soil are decomposed by bacterial processes that convert mercury into a more toxic form called methylmercury, which can be absorbed by animals. As methylmercury moves up the food chain, it becomes more concentrated and thus more harmful. Predatory fish such as pike, which traditionally have been important food sources for the Cree, can accumulate levels of mercury that render them unfit for human consumption.

Balancing the Waters
Development and Hydropolitics in Contemporary Zimbabwe

Bill Derman

A u t h o r   S u m m a r y

In Zimbabwe, the history of colonialism, racism, and dispossession has created a situation in which water rights are tied to land tenure and, as a result, are largely controlled by whites whose commercial enterprises obtain individual title to lands. Rural producers on traditional land have had little opportunity or means to gain title to lands (and thus water rights) for subsistence-oriented communal production. A new water plan promises radical restructuring of water rights. However, the emergence of a more balanced and equitable approach to water resource allocation is dependent on reform of the land tenure system.

What is the meaning of water? One might as well ask, "What does it mean to be human?" The answer may be found in our relation to water, the mother of life. When the waters again run clear and their life is restored we might see ourselves reflected whole.

(David Orr)[1]

The development of Africa has always been driven by outsiders. This is true not simply in the sense that economic power in colonial and independent Africa has lain outside the continent, but also in that power to define goals, to make plans and spend money, indeed power to define the meaning of development itself, was in the hands of strangers. Rural

Africans without formal education lie furthest away from the
center of such power.

(William Adams)[2]

Development is, above all, a way of thinking.

(Wolfgang Sachs)[3]

Introduction

Water, like many other building blocks of life, is absent in the construction of anthropological theories, although being omnipresent, it
has entered into descriptions and analyses of irrigation systems, the
organization of oases, access to drinking water in desert societies, and
the like. Until relatively recently, water in sub-Saharan Africa was a
backdrop, an element of nature that usually was not problematized.
Sub-Saharan Africa lacked the extensive systems of waterworks and
control characterizing parts of Asia and the Middle East.[4] It also lacked
the widespread water scarcity found in North Africa and even the
western United States. Yet water drew explorers to Africa to search for
the source of the Nile, and many of these explorers were able to
explore the inner reaches of the continent by following the courses of
rivers, as did David Livingstone in tracing the Zambezi and Shire
Rivers in southern Africa. Water, like human history itself, was
somehow regarded as having a single origin, a point that could be
determined in the flow of time. Such searches tell us more about the
conceptual models we use than about the processes by which we seek
to understand.

With a few notable exceptions, anthropologists in southern Africa
did not concern themselves with water. Water was, for the most part,
tangential to their research and practice until efforts were made to
build dams and alter water flows.[5] There then emerged rich studies of
river basins, watersheds, and the social and health consequences of
damming rivers. Domestic water use, on the other hand, remained
understudied. For example, although feminist anthropologists' focus
on women's work has led to a wider knowledge of how time-con-
suming and difficult it often is to obtain potable water, the dramatic
consequences of boreholes in arid African lands have often escaped
feminist or gender-specific analysis.[6] In Africa as a whole, numerous
dams were constructed following the independence of various coun-

tries.[7] In addition, the Sahelian drought and famine of 1969–1974, several recent Ethiopian droughts and famines, and processes of desertification, combined with greater knowledge of African rivers, lakes, groundwater, and aquifers, led to a new emphasis on water. In Africa, as in the global environment, water rapidly came to be viewed as a scarce resource that would have to be managed and controlled differently from before. In the words of researchers at the World Bank, "Water resources in Sub-Saharan Africa have become a strategic commodity, with supply limited in terms of quantity and quality, and demand increasing due to population growth and economic development" (Sharma et al. 1996, ix).

Thus, water management, which is subject to the realities of culture, nature, and power, constitutes a critical arena for understanding how scarce resources for development and environmental protection are being contested in the region. The watersheds of Zimbabwe, part of a larger system of water resources in southern Africa, are envisioned as an object of human management: rivers and waters are to be economically and efficiently regulated. In the poignant words of an African engineer, dams must be built because they are "the only way to stop the water running to waste" (Adams 1992, 13). Water management must include the immensely contradictory needs of industrialization, irrigation, direct human consumption, and the layers of organisms dependent on water for their survival as part of what we used to term ecosystems.[8]

In this chapter, I analyze the current state of play in the reformulation of Zimbabwe's water act as a case study of the reconceptualization and management of water at national and global levels. In my estimation, an examination of the history, discourse, economics, politics, and ecology of water is an excellent entry point for exploring the alignment of material interests in water allocation and distribution with the competing discourses about water. Because of its colonial history, dual property regime, and profoundly different cultures, Zimbabwe serves well as a locale in which to explore the different uses and understandings of water.

The chapter is organized into four sections. The first section briefly summarizes current discourses about water, the second reviews the historical background of water law and policy in Zimbabwe, and the third shifts to current efforts to promote a new water act for the country. The fourth section is a brief reflection on water issues in the Zambezi Valley and how they might be affected by the new water law.

Water and the New Environmental Discourses

The dominant motif in the contemporary consideration of water is scarcity. This motif now dominates virtually all disciplines. Within the scarcity framework, two different perspectives coexist. The first emphasizes scarcity from an economic perspective, viewing water as an economic resource that should be subject to appropriate pricing combined with efficient systems of allocation and distribution. In this view, increasing population, urbanization, and industrialization and unpredictable or declining rainfall are leading to major shortfalls in water availability. This is perhaps best expressed in the phrase "managing water as an economic resource,"[9] whereby policy makers and planners act at global, national, and regional levels to determine how and under what conditions water should be made available. The term *economic* remains undefined and unproblematized. The World Bank, partly because it conducts studies and projects in multiple countries, on the one hand emphasizes water as a scarce economic resource and on the other proposes models for water's sustainable and equitable use. The actual historical experiences of different countries in water management remain unexamined for the difficulty of extricating water from concentrations of political and economic power.

The second perspective is reflected in the works of numerous ecologists, who are concerned less with efficient economic use than with the availability of clean water for natural and human purposes. This concern is expressed, for example, in the influential writings of Sandra Postel, who posits:

> Most fundamentally, water scarcity challenges us to adopt a
> new ethic to guide our relationship to the earth's natural sys-
> tems, to other species, and to each other. Recognizing our-
> selves as part of the life support network we depend on and
> learning to live within water's limits are integral aspects of
> creating a society that is sustainable in all respects. (1992, 24)

Similarly, Robin Clarke (1993), using contemporary global discourse, titles her book *Water: The International Crisis*, in which chapter 1 is "Water Scarcity." She focuses particularly on water degradation and emphasizes that the basis of all life is being threatened.[10]

Sometimes linked with this discourse on water, and at other times argued separately, is the decline in water quality that threatens fresh-water fish species and aquatic environments. In this perspective, the emphasis is not on economic management for development but on protection of the remaining rich freshwater systems from "pharaonic projects"—massive public or private works that endanger important ecosystems and ecological restoration.[11] This approach is characteristic of North American literature on that continent's major river and lake systems, as well as opposition to major dam projects throughout the world.[12] The importance of rivers as "natural systems" has not been systematically expressed for sub-Saharan Africa, although most rivers in the United States are best thought of as, in Richard White's felicitous term, organic machines.[13]

It is not surprising that ambitious attempts are being made to calculate the water needs of growing human populations, shifting economies, and biological systems. This work, which is being undertaken at multiple scales, including the global one, is interesting and significant both for its substance and for its discourse (see, for example, Gleick 1993 and Cohen 1995). Arguments about the growing scarcity of water recapitulate the 1970s discussion of limits to growth.

In reviewing these competing perspectives, it is my intent not to argue for one or another but to contribute to an increased understanding of water allocations within and among countries and the discourses used to argue for one or another policy or action. These competing scientific discourses are deployed to enroll policy makers and technicians in specific and exclusive strategies.[14] The policy makers, in turn, represent different, often conflicting, material interests, including industrial and mining, agricultural and irrigation, hydroelectric, and what might broadly be termed environmental interests.

Three of southern Africa's countries presently face inadequate water supplies, and the number is likely to grow in the very near future (SARDC 1994). Possible shifts in the region's climate, two major droughts in the 1990s, and South Africa's apparently insatiable appetite for water have led to a growing focus on water. The Zambezi River constitutes one of the major foci of broad international interest because its waters potentially can be used by a number of countries for development purposes. Here, I focus on Zimbabwe, examining how water issues were considered in colonial Rhodesia, continuities with independent Zimbabwe, and contemporary efforts to break with the past.

Land and Water in Rhodesia

The banal comment that we can't know the present without knowing the past has a living reality in contemporary Zimbabwe, and issues regarding access to water reinforce this view. Zimbabwe, before 1979

Rhodesia or Southern Rhodesia, continues to have two distinct land tenure systems stemming directly from colonial conquest. The first, incorporating what are now known as communal areas (formerly tribal trust lands), is a "customary," nonmarket-based land tenure system, and the second consists of large-scale commercial farms (see figure 5.1).[15] There is a large and excellent body of literature on the inegalitarian distribution of land as a result of the colonial settler state, particularly the creation of huge farms as a rationale for expropriating the property of Africans. This process of expropriation has been magnified by the inequitable distribution of water and water rights (Bratton 1994; Moyo 1995; Palmer 1977a, 1977b).

In Zimbabwe, as was the case in Rhodesia, a combination of English and Roman-Dutch water law prevails. English water law is based on the notion of the riparian principle: an owner of riparian land (land adjacent to a stream) has the right to use the water passing through his or her land. Roman-Dutch water law, on the other hand, is based on a grant of the right to use water, which is regarded as public property. As set out in Rhodesia's Water Act of 1947 (a revision of the Water Act of 1927), the right to use water in Zimbabwe today depends on the type of water in question: a distinction is made between private water and public water. Private water is the sole and exclusive property of the owner of the land on which it is found. Regarding underground water, the owner of the overlying land "may for any purpose abstract [withdraw] and use underground water from any point on the piece of land" (Section 73, p. 536). This provision restates the English common-law doctrine of absolute ownership of underground water by an owner of overlying land. The 1947 Water Act was revised again in 1976. The legislation remains in force until the new Water Act is presented to parliament, discussed, and then passed.

Granting of the right to use public water (surface water), on the other hand, is an exclusive function of the Water Court (now the Administrative Court), created by the Water Act of 1976. The right is dependent on the date on which an appropriation or right to draw is made. In sum, given a fixed quantity of water, those who have the earliest legally recognized rights take precedence over later claimants. An appropriation is effected by filing an application with the registrar of the Administrative Court either to store public water for a stated purpose or to withdraw public water from a public river or stream for a stated purpose. Significantly, even if public water passes through an individual's land, that individual cannot legally use it unless he or she applies for rights, and then only if the rights have not already been allocated. A right to the use of public water, when granted, is a real

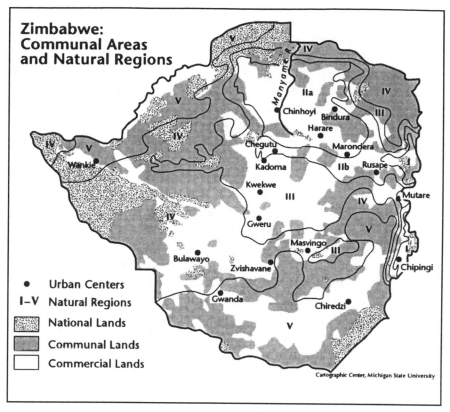

Zimbabwe: Communal Areas and Natural Regions

Legend:
- • Urban Centers
- I–V Natural Regions
- National Lands
- Communal Lands
- Commercial Lands

Cartographic Center, Michigan State University

FIGURE 5.1. COMMUNAL AREAS AND
NATURAL REGIONS IN ZIMBABWE

Shown here are the divisions between Zimbabwe's national parks land and commercial and communal farm areas. The natural regions roughly indicate rainfall areas, with natural region I having the highest and V having the lowest. The commercial farm areas tend to have higher rainfall and therefore greater agricultural potential. The course of the Manyame (Hunyani) River is also indicated.

right that is registered against the title of the property to which it relates. The right attaches in perpetuity.

Two points are of particular salience. First, Africans dispossessed of most of their lands on the high plateau, the area of highest rainfall, were not strategically situated to apply for water rights. Second, because the property regime in the tribal trust lands (now communal areas) is not individual freehold but communal, during colonial years black Zimbabwean farmers had to apply to the Department of Native Affairs, and now they must apply to the Ministry of Local Government and Rural and Urban Development (MLGRUD) or the Ministry of

Agriculture, to obtain water rights. One of the major differences between communal areas and commercial farmland was that because
communal area farmers did not have ultimate ownership of their land,
their requests for water rights were presented by government depart-
ments. European farmers, however, who rapidly obtained water rights,
did so (and, indeed, continue to do so) on their own behalf, not through
intermediaries. In the past, European farmers succeeded because they
knew how to apply for water rights, they were relatively highly capi-
talized and could construct dams and other water conveyances, and the
laws were structured to benefit them. In addition, commercial farmers
were encouraged to form River Boards to manage surface waters. There
were no black Zimbabwean members on the Water Court until independence. Moreover, the River Boards have remained without African
representation from the 1930s until the present. The former president
of the Administrative Court (previously the Water Court), E. T. Matinenga, commented that although he did not believe the water act was
racist in intent, in practice the majority of people were unaware of how
to obtain rights to water (Matinenga 1996, 4).[16] In my estimation, this
is a very generous view.

Another significant part of colonial policy was the delineation of
Rhodesia into six hydrological zones. These zones were created to fa-
cilitate the work of the Hydrological Branch of the Water Department,
which was charged with assessing the annual flow in the country's
rivers. The annual flow in turn determined the number of allocations
that could be made. Although clearly cognizant of annual rainfall vari-
ation and therefore of water flow, the distribution of water rights by the
secretary of water development did not take annual variability into
account.

Finally, the Water Act of 1927 was founded on the notion (repeated
in the legislation of 1976) that wetlands, called *dambos* in Zimbabwe,
play an important role in regulating river flows and, in particular, in
maintaining dry season flows.[17] The act thereby rendered all cultivation on *dambos* illegal (Bullock 1995, 70–71; Matiza 1992). The
Streambank Protection Regulation of 1952 prohibits cultivation on
wetlands and within thirty meters (roughly thirty-three yards) of a
stream bank. These laws were intended to protect Rhodesia's wetlands
and rivers but in fact restricted African farmers' access to the best soils
and lands. Neither law has yet been repealed, despite widespread cultivation of both stream banks and wetlands.[18] Enforcement of these laws
was to be carried out by the Natural Resources Board, a continuously
underfunded and understaffed division of the Ministry of Environment

and Tourism. The degree to which these laws were enforced was determined by the energy and commitment of district commissioners (those responsible for the colonial tribal trust lands) and, since independence, district administrators and District Councils.

The New Water Act

In Rhodesia, as in many other African countries, water policy and law were determined by colonial policy and law. However, unlike the situation elsewhere, the government—first the colonial Rhodesian government and now the Zimbabwean government—has the strength and infrastructure necessary to control the allocation and use of water. The impetus to do so stems from long-standing concerns about land division. Approximately 119,038 hectares (294,148 acres) of land are currently irrigated. Eighty-two percent of this land belongs to large-scale farms, either privately or corporately owned. Virtually all sugar cane and wheat, 50 percent of tea, 70 percent of coffee, and 45 percent of cotton are produced under irrigation. Increasingly, tobacco, the most important agricultural export commodity, is grown under irrigation. As of 1994, only 7 percent of Zimbabwe's irrigable land was in communal and resettlement areas. The remaining 11 percent was in farms run by the government-owned Agricultural and Rural Development Authority (ARDA) (Matiza 1996).

In 1992, the Zimbabwean government passed the Land Acquisition Act (revised in 1996). This act permits the president of Zimbabwe or the minister of lands and water resources (or any other minister to whom the president may, from time to time, assign the administration of this act) to designate any rural land for reorganization or settlement (Zimbabwe 1996). Following the passage of this act, President Robert Mugabe appointed a Commission of Inquiry to examine appropriate agricultural land tenure systems for Zimbabwe. Once again, without going into detail, the commission was directed to examine existing land tenure arrangements in Zimbabwe and to recommend appropriate land tenure systems for sustainable resource management, farm productivity, and investment as well as the most suitable land tenure system for each farming sector. The Land Tenure Commission held hearings and discussions in all of Zimbabwe's districts. The commission's interest in water was primarily from an agricultural standpoint, and it rapidly uncovered the huge disparities between the commercial farm and communal area sectors with regard to water access and rights. As a consequence, the commission recommended revision of Zimbabwe's water act, noting that because communal farmers did not hold title to their land, they had difficulty in obtaining rights to water. The commission recommended that new mechanisms be found to distribute this critical resource equitably among communal and resettlement farmers, but it did not necessarily recommend that the only land tenure regime be private or corporate ownership. In addition, it found that there was no comprehensive master plan for water development in Zimbabwe and recommended that one be written (Zimbabwe 1994, 1:117). Because the commission's mandate was agricultural, it did not consider how to approach the significant ongoing environmental changes stemming from increased withdrawals of river water.[19]

In 1991 and 1992, coincident with the activities of the Land Tenure Commission, Zimbabwe suffered its worst drought of the twentieth century. This disaster, combined with scientific models of global climate change, led the strong central government to begin rewriting the Water Act of 1976. To emphasize the growing importance of water, the Department of Water Development was moved from the Ministry of Lands and Agriculture to the newly separated Ministry of Lands.

According to E. T. Matinenga, one of the key authors of the new draft water act, riparian landowners will be given first priority to the water in rivers contiguous to their land. The on-the-ground situation in Zimbabwe is that the indigenous population, although often riparian, does not have access to public water because of overcommitment of water rights, with none left for communal area residents. In addition, the government has favored its own schemes over those of individual farmers and has been able to do so because of current land tenure law, which rests ownership of communal areas ultimately with the state. The public interest doctrine must therefore be invoked in favor of individual smallholders to reallocate public water, albeit on sound and acceptable grounds (Matinenga 1996, 5). Matinenga and the other authors propose that river catchment/basin authorities replace members of the Administrative Court as the water allocation agency. In the view of its proponents, this action would lead to decentralization of water management entities and the loss of some power by private interests and, therefore, more efficient utilization of water. Current suggestions are to abolish the distinctions among public water, private water, and underground water. For identification purposes only, the distinction between surface water and underground water would be maintained, but all water would fall under public ownership. Matinenga envisions a permit system that would extend for a given time period—the draft water act (not yet available for public comment as of this writing) sug-

gests twenty years—while respecting previous rights. What would happen at the end of this period has not, to date, been specified.

The draft water act also contains important changes in the way in which water is to be understood and managed as a national and local resource. The government of Zimbabwe, under the influence of major donors, proposes to create the Zimbabwe National Water Authority, which will be organized through catchment water management lines and will follow the recommendations of a new secretariat called the Water Resources Management Strategy (WRMS) in the Department of Water Resources Development (DWRD). The WRMS is currently functioning. According to Alex Bolding (1996), who has been studying the Nyanyadzi catchment in the eastern part of the country, Zimbabwe is following World Bank strategies, with emphasis on a greater use of incentives and pricing for water distribution and allocation. This experiment in redesigning water policy and law may well serve as an example for other sub-Saharan countries. The process in Zimbabwe appears to be less transparent and open than a similar effort under way in the Republic of South Africa. There, the Ministry of Water Affairs and Forestry initiated a water law review that resulted in publication of a booklet titled "You and Your Water Rights" (Republic of South Africa 1995). The booklet invited written and oral responses; thus, the ministry sought public agreement of its principles. On 19 November 1996, the cabinet approved a set of fundamental principles and objectives for a new water law. The Ministry of Water Affairs and Forestry is currently drafting a new bill on the basis of these principles; the bill will undergo a lengthy public review. In Zimbabwe, on the other hand, the process to date has been far more concentrated within the central government. Whether, in the end, there will be significant differences in the outcomes of these two processes remains to be seen.

Water Law, Water Rights, Water Discourse, and the Zambezi Valley

As in many communal areas in Zimbabwe, no one in the eastern Zambezi Valley has any right to withdraw water from the major rivers. The only legal water rights are, in fact, those of the Agricultural and Rural Development Authority (ARDA), which runs two large estates, one already irrigated and the other to be irrigated in 1997. It is not clear, however, that lack of water rights per se has blocked small-scale farmers from irrigating their land as much as have the terrain and a lack of capital. Small-scale farmers in other areas (particularly the eastern highlands) irrigate their land without legal water rights simply by digging furrows to divert water.[20] In addition, valley residents hand-irrigate their riverine fields and gardens despite laws barring such stream bank cultivation.

The issues in the eastern valley, however, are, for the moment, quite different. They revolve around large-scale planning exercises and village consolidation that are based on moving people away from the valley's seasonal rivers. I have been studying the largest of these projects, the Mid-Zambezi Valley Rural Development Project (MZP), for several years (Derman 1990, 1997a, 1997b). These processes are, at the end of the day, based on the Streambank Cultivation Act and the water act, which prohibit stream bank or riverine cultivation. In short, national laws meant to prevent erosion in the more accidented high plateau are being used as the basis for development planning in a semi-arid valley environment, where residents regard the scarce riverine land as a critical resource in their effort to cope with both drought and flood years.

It can be argued that the MZP represents a continuation of the colonial mode of planning and conceptualization of nature. Indeed, this mode of planning represents the consequences of radically different cultural approaches toward nature and the apparent triumph of a "scientific" blueprint approach. The establishment of a system of private landownership on the high plateau combined with private appropriation of water represent the cultural basis of European settlers. This cultural model appears to be dominant and will be difficult to effectively resist.

One dramatic change observed by many long-term residents of the Zambezi Valley is the loss of permanent water pools in the larger rivers that flow through the valley. Residents disagree as to its cause, but in general they attribute it to extensive dam construction by commercial farmers and government on the high plateau. Many residents continue to hold the view that water graces the land because of their great ancestral spirits, whereas others are more pragmatic. In general, they regard access to water as a fundamental right, although they wouldn't express the principle in such a direct fashion. Water, usually in the form of rainfall, has become a major focus of residents' lives due to the droughts of 1991–1992 and 1994–1995. Residents disagree as to the causes of these two devastating droughts. Many older people connect them with a loss of respect for the royal ancestral spirits (mhondoros) and the spilling of human blood without proper propitiation.[21]

Currently, there are two proposed irrigation projects in the eastern

Zambezi Valley in addition to the ARDA estates. Residents express complex and varied opinions about irrigation in the valley. Older residents tend to prefer the use of annually flooded riverine fields, whereas migrants tend to favor irrigation schemes of both large and small scale. Irrigable land, however, will be available for only a small percentage of the valley's population. Omitted in this discussion of irrigation projects are women's gardens and fields, which are hand-irrigated and constitute a significant and growing contribution to household nutrition and income. Women's small-scale irrigation goes virtually unnoticed, and as is all too often the case, the assumption is that it can be easily replaced by larger-scale development interventions.[22]

Finally, there is the issue of domestic water supply. Although from a hydrological perspective, domestic water use represents a very small part of withdrawals from major rivers, it is a highly significant issue for local populations in semiarid environments that depend on either dried river beds or boreholes (deep well pumps). Timothy Lynam, in his detailed study of 108 households in six valley villages, found that water accounted for the largest number of hours in the collection and use of common property resources.[23] Thus, access to and distance from water became critical issues when the Mid-Zambezi Valley Rural Development Project moved many residents away from rivers. The developers built some wells (to date, many fewer than were promised), but these wells often have not been properly maintained. Boreholes have become sources of water for livestock during the dry season, and women are also expected to establish vegetable gardens at them. Shallow river wells remain a critical backup in case of failure of boreholes.

Directly to the west of the project zone and planned irrigation scheme are some of the most important sites in the CAMPFIRE (Communal Area Management Programs for Indigenous Resources) project, areas that are highly dependent on riverine environments for both their human and animal populations. The conservation of biological diversity and natural habitats is essential to the continued success of CAMPFIRE programs.

Thus, access and rights to water are critical issues for the Zambezi Valley, but it is not yet clear how these interests will be incorporated into water management planning and law. Historically, valley residents' interests have not been included in planning for dam building, irrigation schemes, and the like. And again, the restrictions on riverine and wetland cultivation do not take into account the valley's semiarid climate.

A brief examination of the Manyame (Hunyani) River watershed illustrates why valley residents' interests and the interests of those in similar environments will most likely take very low priority in the new Zimbabwe National Water Authority. The Manyame River, arguably the most important river in Zimbabwe, originates near the nation's capital, Harare, supplies drinking water for Harare and surrounding areas, flows through major commercial farm areas, descends into the valley, and flows into Mozambique before joining the Zambezi River.[24] Currently, there are five River Boards governing the different sections of the Manyame. The idea is to combine these and have only one Catchment Authority. At present, there is an experimental catchment authority along the length of the Mazoe River, called the Mazoe Catchment Pilot Project, into which the Mazoe's old River Boards have been incorporated. The catchment authority has held an initial meeting, at which all catchment stakeholders were brought to the table. These included representatives from local government and mining and agricultural interests, chiefs, water engineers, and the WRMS's secretariat. How the interests of downstream communal areas are to be integrated remains to be seen, given current allocations, which leave virtually no water unclaimed. It is not specified whether or when other River Boards are to be combined or how decisions are to be made for Zimbabwe's different catchments. To complicate matters further, Zimbabwe, as part of the Southern African Development Community (SADC), must take into account downstream international users of its waters.[25] This proviso assumes great importance for a river like the Manyame, which flows 64.4 kilometers (40 miles) through Mozambique before reaching the Cabora Bassa Reservoir and the Zambezi River.

The most important voices for the Manyame will most likely be commercial farmers; domestic water users in Harare, Chitungwiza, and surrounding cities; and industry representatives. One communal area, Zvimba, lies on the western bank of the Manyame, yet at present it has few water rights. Because of historical injustices and the area's relatively good soils, people here will probably gain greater water rights. In addition, this communal area carries great political weight because it is the home of President Mugabe.

The few case studies that have been conducted (Bolding 1996; Manzungu 1995; Magadlela 1996) indicate that decentralization of water allocation will require a profound rethinking by Zimbabwe's central government and its agricultural ministries of the principles underlying water allocation and distribution. For example, they detail how those without water rights are to use water, but those with water rights, invariably in government irrigation schemes but downstream, are in conflict. The irrigation-scheme farmers believe that since they pay money to grow crops under irrigation, whereas catchment farmers use most of their water without paying for it, catchment farmers should be barred from such utilization. In turn, the catchment farmers assert that they are not illegal users, maintaining that because God and the ancestors bring the rain, the waters belong to everyone. Balancing these competing interests and views will provide multiple challenges for the foreseeable future.

The Zambezi Valley and other semiarid environments will pose particular problems for future water allocation. How and in what ways valley residents will be able to present a powerful voice among stakeholders is difficult to envision under the current circumstances. It is my intent, along with fellow researchers, to examine how this might come about.

Conclusion

The attempt to balance competing interests in Zimbabwe's waters has, as elsewhere in southern Africa, taken on a high profile and high priority. As in south Africa, water in Zimbabwe is enmeshed in debates about land tenure. Competing interests include those of large-scale commercial farmers and smallholders in the communal areas, along with mining, industrial, CAMPFIRE, and domestic interests. The present strategy is to follow World Bank guidelines in the construction of water resource development projects.[26] Zimbabwe, like South Africa, has undertaken a fundamental and profound reexamination of its water use, water rights, and water law. Currently, more than two-thirds of the country's water is consumed by irrigation. In its efforts to introduce new efficiencies by charging more for water and increasing the supply of water to small-scale farmers, Zimbabwe will be faced with complex and difficult political decisions. The strategy is to blend increased centralization, in the form of the Zimbabwe National Water Authority, with decentralization, including the creation of catchment authorities. The new Zimbabwe National Water Authority, whose mandate will be provided by the new water act, will be guided by a new Water Resources Management Strategy group, which will provide new and improved hydrological data on which to base decisions. Although everyone is more than aware of, for lack of a better phrase, different ecosystems' water requirements, specific ways in which these different requirements will be accounted for in water decisions have yet to be established.

In the eastern Zambezi Valley, downstream from some of Zimbabwe's most powerful economic and political interests, it remains unclear how water availability and rights will be allocated. Whether there is political leeway for genuine innovation and decentralization will be the subject of intense and complex political contestation. This will involve the vast network of development donors, environmental organizations, government ministries, and other actors within Zimbabwe. The inextricable bond between the land issue and the water issue leads one to be less than sanguine in anticipating water policy, law, and rights based on fairness, equity, and sound ecology. This will have less to do with the discourse of water management than with the deployment of an array of material interests and cultural constructs in water allocation. In short, alternative schemes of landownership do not appear to be on the immediate agenda. Although water is, indeed, different from land, its essentialness to all life remains at best only partially incorporated into contemporary land and water policy in Zimbabwe.

Among South Africa's twenty-eight principles for a new water law are the absence of private ownership of water, legal recognition of the unity of the water cycle, and the setting aside of a "reserve" for basic human needs and environmental ecological functions on which humans depend. These are combined with a clear recognition of the international nature of many river systems, which frames water as an indivisible national asset. Issues of democracy and representation then become central in asking, Who does the government represent? Water management in Zimbabwe and in southern Africa cannot be separated from basic political issues, which in the end will determine to whom the water flows and for what purposes. The political side of water ecology remains muted in Zimbabwe, however. This is because the dominant party, ZANU-PF, and the government claim to speak for "the people" in insisting that all their actions will be for "development."[27] Under current circumstances, those who argue that existing plans and actions will be for the benefit of narrow or private interests are currently being sidelined, and traditional small-scale farmers who argue that water should not be treated as a private economic commodity are being marginalized. Whether or not the government can contain these important political debates will be determined in the near future.

Food for Thought

To understand the dominance of irrigation for water use in a semi-arid environment such as Zimbabwe or elsewhere, one needs to look at the continued dominance of large-scale commercial farmers at all levels, including water policy formulation. Zimbabwe has few parallels in Africa due to the dominance of white settlers and their command over state resources. This included harnessing the state to create the necessary dams and water conveyances for the successful establishment of a highly commercial agriculture. Due to the dominance of this intensive and successful commercial production based on tobacco, maize, vegetables, livestock, and, increasingly, horticulture, Zimbabwe more closely parallels water policy in parts of the American West and Southwest and Mexico (Sheridan 1995a, 1995b; Enge and Whiteford 1989).

Zimbabwe's current efforts to introduce patterns of equity in water allocations are long overdue, but most likely will fall short because the water policies are not integrated with land policies, and small-scale farmers will not be able to command the state's resources the way the settlers did. In addition, this integration will most likely become more difficult with a recent government reorganization. As of 1 August 1997 a new ministry was created called the Ministry of Rural Resources and Water Development. Water was thus shifted out of the Ministry of Lands. The Ministry of Lands has now been recombined with agriculture. At independence in 1980 it was the Ministry of Lands, Agriculture, and Water. Thus, the Minister for the Department of Water Development changed overnight with, as yet, unknown implications. And the budget, in real dollar terms, is smaller for the department in 1998–99 than it was in 1997. With another drought predicted for this year (due to an already large El Niño), government will move very rapidly toward having water viewed as an economic good, although making exceptions for primary users (e.g., domestic consumption in the communal areas). Thus, while primary use will remain exempt from pricing (except in the cities), the value of water will increasingly be measured in dollars. Efforts to introduce equity will become far more difficult because nonefficient producers will not be able to afford the water, and government does not have the funds to invest in alternative solutions. Government will rely on a few showcase dams, which will be predominantly donor-funded—but that is another important story. Indeed, one major dam project for communal areas has been stopped due to no government funds. Gender and environmental issues, while given high prominence, seem, for the moment, to be add-ons. In making and carrying out water policy, countries such as Zimbabwe seem more concerned with legislative procedures and bureaucratic reorganization than with the definition of new cultural goals whose outcomes might genuinely challenge existing power and economic relations.

ACKNOWLEDGMENTS
The funding for this research was provided by Michigan State University with assistance from the Centre for Applied Social Sciences (CASS) at the University of Zimbabwe. CASS provided me a home and, as I have found for the past decade, a model of collegiality. In particular among its members I would like to thank Dr. Calvin Nhira, Professor Marshall Murphree, and Dr. James Murombedzi for engaging with me in the analysis of water. Dr. Nhira and I have begun a comparative study of the two Catchment Pilot Projects that are to serve as models for the entire nation.

NOTES

1. "Reflections on Water and Oil" (Orr 1994, 59).
2. Adams 1992, 35. Although Adams's book remains the best single work on water in Africa, it is deeply embedded in the separation of local African-rooted knowledge and practice from Western knowledge and practice. This analysis works in considering why and how African views have not been incorporated into the planning and implementation of river basin plans and projects. However, it does not address how these models have been incorporated into contemporary knowledge and practices of African actors.
3. Sachs 1996, 243.
4. Karl Wittfogel's (1957) work, emphasizing the economic, social, and political ramifications of controlling water, is the best known of twentieth-century attempts to address the importance to human societies of control and mastery of nature.
5. The studies of Tonga populations conducted by Elizabeth Colson and Thayer Scudder before and after the construction of Lake Kariba stand out for their consideration of water (Colson 1960; Scudder 1962; Scudder and Colson n.d.).
6. Despite the apparent growing importance of water, three recent feminist books have virtually no discussion of the topic: Braidotti et al. 1994, Harcourt 1994, and Mies and Shiva 1993. On the other hand, Peters 1994 provides a rare study of boreholes in Botswana.
7. The dreams, plans, and projects of water control are well summarized in

Adams 1992. A global look at the ecology and politics of large dams can be found in McCully 1996.

8. Some recent theorists question the utility of the ecosystem concept. See, for example, Norgaard 1994. Others, like Frank Golley (1993), support ecosystem studies that consider energy flows and cycles, which in turn provide a basis for the study of global change and other biospheric problems.

9. This is, in fact, the title of a book by James Winpenny (1994), who argues that it is both one of the largest and one of the most universal problems facing contemporary humankind.

10. For the most complete survey of the state of the world's freshwater resources, see Gleick 1993.

11. In a vast body of literature, Ashworth 1986, Caldwell 1988, Fradkin 1984, Gottlieb 1988, White 1995, and Worster 1985 stand out.

12. William Adams (1992) provides an excellent summary of river-planning efforts in Africa.

13. White (1995) regards the Columbia River as an intersection of human and natural creation. There is no early possibility of its "return to nature"; it will remain partially managed by humans for the foreseeable future.

14. My own bias is toward protecting freshwater quality and freshwater environments. I much prefer free-running rivers and believe that there is growing evidence that we would be better off adapting to them than investing so much in controlling them. My bias may simply stem from my love of canoeing. There is, however, a large and impressive body of literature in the United States supporting this perspective. See, for example, Outwater 1996 and Palmer 1994.

15. The current land distribution is as follows:

Land Distribution in Zimbabwe

	Large-Scale Commercial Farms	Small-Scale Commercial Farms	Communal Areas	National Parks and Safari Areas
Total area (km^2)	157,000	14,200	163,500	56,200
Population	1,713,000[a]		4,662,000[b]	—
Total area (%)	40	4	42	14

[a]There are approximately 4,400 owners of large-scale commercial farms. The remainder are farmworkers.
[b]Includes both small-scale commercial farms and communal areas.

16. The Department of Water Affairs and Forestry of the Republic of South Africa, through its minister, has reached similar conclusions: "The present Act [the Water Act of 1956] is not only difficult to understand, but also difficult to apply in practice. It distinguishes between underground water and surface water, between public streams and private streams, and between normal flow and surplus water. Different rules apply to different categories of water, and it is difficult to allocate water to the different categories of users" (Republic of South Africa 1995, 20).

17. The question of what specifically constitutes a *dambo* has been subject to debate as well as the consequences of wetlands cultivation. The colonial solution of barring cultivation while promoting grazing has led to the transfer of gullying from commercial farms to communal area farms. Overgrazing is the best hypothesis to explain this change, according to McFarlane (1995). For an excellent summary of *dambo*s and their uses, see Matiza 1992.

18. My studies in Zimbabwe have focused on a rural development project in the eastern Zambezi Valley. Part of my interest in water issues stems from efforts by the developers of this project to move valley residents away from riverine areas, in order to prevent them from cultivating land alongside the rivers, while designating these areas for grazing. For a discussion of riverine cultivation and the Mid-Zambezi Valley Rural Development Project, see Derman 1997a and 1997b.

19. The commission's report did have an important chapter on land tenure and its implications for natural resource and environmental management (Zimbabwe 1994, vol. 2, chap. 12).

20. The best descriptions of irrigation in the absence of formal water rights are found in Bolding 1996, Magadlela 1996, and Zaag 1996. Although these case studies were conducted in the eastern highlands, they could be duplicated in many communal areas where there are adequate supplies of water.

21. For a consideration of the contemporary role of royal ancestral spirits, see Spierenburg 1995. These beliefs are widespread and are found in all the case studies included in the Zimwesi volume. For example, C. Vijfhuizen (1996, 7) writes about the Mutema chieftaincy in southeastern Zimbabwe:

People believe that royal ancestral spirits bring rain. Accordingly, they also believe that ancestors are able to keep away the rain or to stop it. People refer to conflicts between chiefs as reason for drought. They argue that these conflicts refrain chiefs from worshiping. Ancestors do not let it rain if they are not being worshiped. Hence, chiefs should solve their conflicts, unite and worship together. Then it will rain.

Although I find a summarization of the Mutema's beliefs in such a unitary fashion problematic, it is clear that very different views continue to persist about rain and ancestors from those of hydrologists, engineers, agricultural economists, and other scientists.

22. Women's gardens are discussed in Heather Holtzclaw and Bill Derman, "Invisible Irrigation: Women and Development Projects in the Eastern Zambezi Valley, Zimbabwe," unpublished paper, 19.

23. Personal communication, January 1997.

24. At present, there is limited information on flow cycles and water quality in the Manyame. For a summary of available information about the flow, see Johansson et al. 1995.

25. The general SARDC perspective on the environment can be found in SARDC 1994.

26. These guidelines are laid out in *A Guide to the Formulation of Water Resources Strategy*, edited by Guy Le Moigne et al. (1994). It is almost as though Zimbabwe were using this document as a text for how to proceed. This is not a judgment about the appropriateness of the World Bank's discourse but only an observation that it has become central. The World Bank attempts to define a process rather than to define substance and results: it sets out the need to develop water rights and legislation but does not state what these should be.

27. For an examination of the tensions between democracy and development in Zimbabwe, see Derman and Murombedzi 1994.

Water, Rights, and the El Cajón Dam, Honduras

William M. Loker

Author Summary

This chapter reviews the social costs of the El Cajón Dam in north-central Honduras, the largest hydroelectric dam in Central America. The chapter critiques the dam both in terms of development strategy in the national social and economic context of Honduras and in terms of its effects on local communities located around its 112-square-kilometer (43.2-square-mile) reservoir. The El Cajón Dam cost more than $800 million, in a country of 5 million people with an estimated per capita income of $590 per year (1990). Despite this massive investment, Honduras faces an acute shortage of electrical energy, due largely to the failure of the El Cajón Dam to generate projected levels of electricity. Proposed explanations for this failure include climate change, mismanagement, environmental degradation of the watershed, and technical problems with the dam's construction. A major flaw of the El Cajón project was mishandling of the resettlement and indemnification of people living near the reservoir. If drastic steps are not taken to provide viable livelihood strategies for these people, the result will be their continued unnecessary suffering and a shortened life span for the most expensive single item of physical infrastructure in the country.

Introduction

Rights, it is said, are the weapons of the weak against the strong. Rights are ethical principles based on the assumption that "all individuals . . .

need protection from injury and degradation, and from unfairness and arbitrariness in the allocation of basic resources and in the operation and rules of social life" (Lukes 1993, 432). However, what constitutes "universal human rights" is a subject of some controversy. Do human beings have a right to basic subsistence? This chapter argues that such a right does exist. Yet rights matter only to the extent that people can enjoy them. How do we know when the right to subsistence has been violated? What duties exist to redress a violation of subsistence rights?

The El Cajón Dam in Honduras is a major hydroelectric facility, the largest in Central America. For various reasons explored in this chapter, most of the people living in the reservoir impact zone had not been relocated when the dam was completed and the waters began rising in 1984. This chapter explores the failed process of resettlement and the continuing effects of the dam on those who remain in the area. The question to be addressed is whether the construction of this dam violated the subsistence rights of the people affected. The chapter argues that the dam did violate these rights and that the relative power of the actors involved—government officials, international financial institutions, engineers, and consultants on one side and poor, marginalized farmers on the other—explains the failure of those who carried out the project to mitigate the negative social and economic consequences of the dam. The chapter also details the ongoing efforts of local people to cope with the radically changed social and natural environment caused by the dam and makes recommendations for restoring the subsistence rights of those affected.

Subsistence Rights

Western liberal philosophy has a history of being somewhat skeptical of, even hostile to, the notion of subsistence rights and economic rights in general. When we think of basic rights, we tend to limit our consideration to such concepts as liberty, freedom of expression, property rights, and a few others. However, a strong argument can be made for a right to basic subsistence. In fact, rights to subsistence and other economic rights are recognized internationally in the United Nations' Universal Declaration of Human Rights and numerous other international covenants.

A particularly clear argument for subsistence rights is made by Henry Shue in his book titled, *Basic Rights: Subsistence, Affluence, and U.S. Foreign Policy*. The book explores the concept of basic, universal human rights, what Shue terms "the moral minimum—the lower limits of tolerable human conduct, individual and institutional" (Shue 1980, ix). A basic right is one that is so fundamental that its enjoyment is essential to the enjoyment of all other rights: "When a right is genuinely basic, any attempt to enjoy any other right by sacrificing the basic right would be self-defeating" (Shue 1980, 19). According to Shue, the list of basic rights is probably not a long one. In fact, he identifies three: rights to physical security (freedom from assault, torture, and the like), rights to subsistence (to be discussed in more detail on the following pages), and rights to participation, principally because the right to participate in the life of society (including, but not limited to, political participation) seems to be a prerequisite to securing rights to subsistence and physical security (Shue 1980, chap. 3).

What exactly are subsistence rights, and how can they be effectively exercised? According to Shue (1980, 23), subsistence rights include "minimal economic security . . . unpolluted air, unpolluted water, adequate food, adequate clothing, adequate shelter, and minimal preventative health care. . . . To have available for consumption what is needed for a decent chance at a reasonably healthy and active life of more or less normal length, barring tragic interventions." Shue leaves open the question of whether all people enjoy economic rights beyond those of subsistence. In singling out subsistence as a basic right, he argues that the enjoyment of these economic basics is essential to the enjoyment of other rights people might have.[1]

In a discussion relevant to the El Cajón case, Shue addresses the issue of "systemic deprivation." In the real world, it is often difficult to assign responsibility for the violation of subsistence rights to a single individual; often, a deprivation of the right to subsistence is systemic in nature. Systemic deprivation results from "the confluence of many contributing factors" (1980, 47). The notion of systemic deprivation is relevant to the El Cajón case because if, in fact, the El Cajón project violated subsistence rights, the ensuing deprivation was caused not by the actions of a single individual but by a complex series of events. Shue also assets that systemic deprivations can be either "accidental" or "inherent." Accidental deprivations are "unpredictable and relatively easily remediable coincidences in an economic system." Inherent deprivations are "predictable . . . elements in a consciously adopted . . . economic plan or policy . . . essential elements in the strategy that produces them. . . . Essential deprivations can be eliminated only by eliminating the strategies that require them. Accidental deprivations can be eliminated by making less fundamental changes while retaining the basic strategy" (1980, 47). In the El Cajón case, this is an important distinction. If the El Cajón project caused deprivation of people's subsistence rights, one must ask whether this was an essential element of the dam's construction or an accidental by-product that could have been avoided with better planning and implementation of the project. This chapter argues that the El Cajón Dam project entailed an essential violation of people's right to subsistence, analyzes the reasons why, and suggests what might be done to amend the situation.

The El Cajón Region: A Brief Overview

The El Cajón region includes the area flooded by the El Cajón Reservoir and adjacent lands, towns, and communities (see figure 6.1). It is an isolated, mountainous, highly rural region in north-central Honduras. The local topography is extremely rugged, ranging from 160 meters (525 feet) above sea level in the now-flooded river bottoms to 2,280 meters (7,480 feet) above sea level at nearby Montaña del Pico Pijol. In 1988, the year of the latest census, the total population of the region was estimated to be 3,500. The predominant settlement pattern is dispersed, with widely scattered individual houses or clusters of houses and some small towns (see photo 6.1). The largest population center in the region is Montañuelas, with a population of 739 in 1988

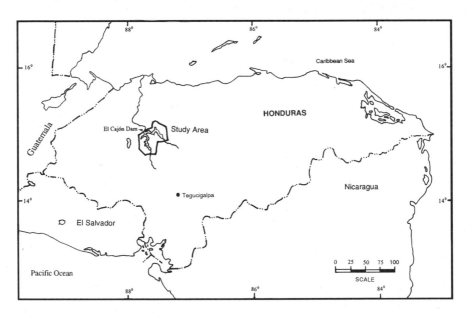

FIGURE 6.1. THE REPUBLIC OF HONDURAS
AND THE EL CAJÓN DAM AND RESERVOIR

Anthropological fieldwork has focused on the study area surrounding the reservoir, as indicated in Figure 6.1. Map courtesy of William M. Loker.

(see photo 6.2). Other significant communities include Ojo de Agua (population 639), Mal Paso or Las Majadas (435), Cabeceras (201), and El Mango (180). However, most of the region's residents live in scattered homesteads. The town of Las Lajas (population 1,972), located near the El Cajón region, received some migrants from the area when the dam was completed.

The El Cajón hydroelectric dam was completed in 1984, after five years of construction and an even longer period of feasibility studies. The dam is a double-curvature concrete arch dam 225 meters (738 feet) high, among the ten highest dams in the world. It impounds a 97-square-kilometer (37.4-square-mile) reservoir that, at capacity, holds 5.7 million cubic meters (4,621 acre-feet, or 1.5 billion gallons) of water. The power station is located 200 meters (656 feet) below ground level and contains four generators, each producing seventy-three megawatts. The cost of these works, including transmission lines and financing charges, was U.S.$785 million. In 1991, the El Cajón Dam generated 1,487 gigawatt-hours of electricity, equivalent to 70 percent of Honduras's total electricity generation. In subsequent years, however, the

PHOTO 6.1. TYPICAL LANDSCAPE IN THE EL CAJÓN REGION

Rugged mountains and narrow river valleys distinguish the terrain of the El Cajón region. Note the deforestation in the foreground for the growing of maize and grazing of cattle. This area of the Humuya River is now underwater, flooded by the reservoir of the El Cajón Dam. Photo courtesy of William M. Loker.

PHOTO 6.2. A VIEW OF THE STREETS OF MONTAÑUELAS

In Motañuelas, the largest town in the immediate vicinity of the El Cajón Reservoir, tile roofs cover rustic wood-frame houses. Note the lack of electrical wires; even with the town's close proximity to the dam and reservoir, it lacks electricity. Photo courtesy of William M. Loker.

dam has consistently operated below capacity because of low reservoir levels, contributing to a crippling energy shortage in the country during 1993–1994.[2] More than U.S.$12 million in additional funds has been invested in the dam to ensure its structural integrity, to stop leaks, and to control flooding in the power station. Thus, the project has cost Honduras at least U.S.$800 million. Most of this was borrowed from the Interamerican Development Bank and the World Bank, contributing to Honduras's onerous national debt.[3]

The dam was built in a narrow gorge on the Humuya River, and it drowned adjacent portions of the Sulaco, Humuya, and Yure Rivers. As is frequently the case, the flooded river bottoms represented the region's prime agricultural land. A study of land use carried out before the dam was finished (Loker 1989) determined that river bottom lands were often under continuous annual cultivation (of maize, beans, and squash), with a brief fallow period during the dry season, when the fields were often used for grazing of cattle. Average yield of maize from these lands was 1,830 kilograms per hectare (4,034 pounds). The surrounding slopes were also planted with maize, with more gently sloping land yielding about 1,165 kilograms per hectare (2,568 pounds) with a 4:5 crop fallow cycle and steeply sloping land yielding about 1,333 kilograms per hectare (2,939 pounds) with a crop fallow cycle of 2:5. Thus, the river bottom lands were more productive in a given year, more productive over the long run (due to their ability to support almost continuous cultivation), and more capable of supporting intensive use. These lands are, of course, no longer available.

The vast majority of local people make their living through small-scale agriculture. I studied the local agricultural economy in 1983–1984 (before the dam was built) and again ten years later, in 1994. In 1994, I carried out thirty-six structured interviews with local residents focused on their economic activities, general welfare, and reactions to the dam. Nearly all those interviewed (97 percent) plant *milpas,* small fields of maize (average field size is about three and a half hectares), sometimes intercropped with beans and squash. About 85 percent of those interviewed indicated that the milpas remain as important to their economic well-being as they were before construction of the dam. By far, the predominant crop grown is maize, both for household consumption and for sale to meet cash needs. Other crops include beans, rice (a dry upland variety), and squash and very small amounts of sugar cane, tomatoes, and yuca. Agricultural technology is fairly simple: maize is planted using a digging stick after clearing a field, either by machete or by a combination of machete and herbicide.[4] Weeding is done manually (by machete) and with herbicide. The most common item of agricultural technology besides the hoe, machete, and digging stick is a backpack sprayer for applying herbicide, owned by 47 percent of respondents. Other farmers borrow or rent sprayers. In terms of chemical inputs, more than 90 percent use herbicide and 56 percent use fertilizer.

Livestock plays an important role in the household economy. Most households raise pigs (66 percent of households interviewed) and chickens (80 percent of households). In addition, about half of those interviewed own some cattle. Two of those interviewed owned more than 150 head, six owned 20–80 head, and nine owned fewer than 20 head. A few families are engaged in cattle raising, and they are relatively powerful as a result of holding and using large tracts of land. As we shall see, one of the indirect effects of the dam was that large landholders involved in cattle ranching expanded and consolidated their hold on large tracts of land after creation of the reservoir.

Agricultural production alone is not enough to sustain many households. About 43 percent of the households interviewed also rely on temporary, seasonal wage labor. Only one-half of the households interviewed grow enough maize to meet household needs; those that do not must purchase maize at some point during the year. About one-half of those interviewed indicated that they own the land they cultivated, with the remainder split between those who borrow land from more fortunate kin or friends (14 percent) and those who rent land (26 percent), with 8 percent claiming to cultivate communal or national lands. Fully 63 percent of those interviewed cultivate steeply sloping land.

In summary, the people who live in the El Cajón region are predominantly small-scale farmers, growing food for home consumption and sale (see photo 6.3). They are what are usually termed *campesinos*, or peasants, in the Latin American context. Although most *campesinos* are poor, the people of the El Cajón region are poorer and more isolated than most Latin American peasants. A few households own extensive tracts of land that they use for raising cattle, though even these households tend to grow some maize for home consumption and sale.

The El Cajón Dam as Development Strategy

The goal of the El Cajón hydroelectric project was to "establish a reliable power supply at the least cost" (World Bank 1992a, 1). Several facts about Honduras dictated the choice of hydroelectric power as the most appropriate strategy: (1) Honduras lacks fossil fuels almost entirely. Planning for the project took place in the mid-1970s. At the time projections were being made regarding future energy needs, it was thought that the cost of petroleum would continue to rise. Honduras was devoting significant amounts of foreign exchange to the purchase of petroleum in order to generate electricity, an expense that hydropower would alleviate. (2) Honduras had, and continues to have, low rates of electrification: only about 38 percent of households had access to electrical power. Lack of electrical power was also thought to be constraining industrial growth. (3) Honduras's Central American neighbors were also deficient in electrical generating capacity yet lacked comparable resources for hydroelectric development. Thus, Honduras was thought to have a "comparative advantage" in generating electricity, which could then be exported to other Central American countries. This would convert the country's power sector from a net drain on foreign exchange to a generator of foreign exchange.

For several reasons, this strategy did not work out as planned. Several of the trends and predictions that contributed to the decision

PHOTO 6.3. RESIDENTS OF THE EL CAJÓN REGION
ON A VERANDA IN EL MANGO

Residents of the El Cajón region gather on the veranda of a house in El Mango to talk, relax, and play guitar. The building to the left is the kitchen, in a separate structure from the main house, on the right. The guitarist sits on a pedal-operated sewing machine. Photo courtesy of William M. Loker.

to construct the dam either were reversed or changed dramatically from projections made in the 1970s. These projections were used in calculating the "internal rate of return" of the El Cajón Dam, which did not perform as expected financially or technically. The price of oil did not continue to rise in the 1980s and 1990s but, in fact, declined in real terms. Thus, the relative costs of hydropower versus thermically generated electricity were not as favorable as projected. Furthermore, Central America was plunged into political turmoil in the 1980s, restricting the market for the export of electricity. Nicaragua was to be the primary purchaser of Honduran electrical power, but an economic crisis there created by political uncertainty—attributable largely to anti-Sandinista U.S. policies—depressed demand for electrical power, and the country was unable to pay for the electricity it did import. The cost of the El Cajón Dam was also higher than anticipated. Originally estimated to cost U.S.$500 million, it has, as described earlier, cost U.S.$800 million to date. Additional financial problems beset the project as well; for example, Honduras's national currency, the lempira, was drastically devalued relative to the dollar in the late 1980s and early 1990s. At the same time, the basket of European currencies on which the debt was calculated appreciated markedly relative to the dollar, raising the dollar costs of the dam. This double devaluation—of the lempira relative to the dollar and of the dollar relative to other foreign currencies—meant that Honduras had to pay much more in terms of lempiras than was anticipated. Currently, the external debt of the National Electrical Energy Company (ENEE) stands at U.S.$690 million, a figure that represents about 21 percent of Honduras's total foreign debt (World Bank 1992a). Most of this is due to the El Cajón Dam.

Clearly, many of these political and financial developments could not have been anticipated or predicted. But several questions come to mind regarding this development strategy, such as the *scale* of the investment relative to Honduras's gross national product. Was it wise to build such a large, expensive item of infrastructure, given Honduras's limited capacity to repay the construction loans? One does not have to adhere to Murphy's Law to question whether all the projections of cost, capacity, and return were realistic. Surely in a project of this magnitude, it could have been anticipated that "things would happen" to upset the projections. The result of these miscalculations is that Honduras is saddled with a massive debt that forecloses other development options. And ironically, due to technical shortcomings, the dam is failing even to meet the country's domestic energy needs.

Ten years after the dam's completion, Honduras still had low rates of residential electrification, especially in rural areas. Eighty to 90 percent of urban households were electrified, whereas only 19 percent of rural households were. Bringing electricity to many of these areas is considered "uneconomical" (World Bank 1992, 25, en passim). There has been a dramatic expansion of low wage, export-oriented, *maquiladora* textile industries in Honduras, due in part to the availability of cheap electricity in the early years of the dam's operation. That development—which has highly questionable social effects in any case—is now imperiled by the lack of electricity.

Social and Ecological Impacts: Villages of the Dam

The principal purpose of this chapter is to examine the effects of the El Cajón Dam project on the local population and to determine whether these effects represent a violation of subsistence rights. This question is independent of any other benefits or costs the dam may have generated. The dam may or may not have been a sound investment from a macroeconomic standpoint, it may or may not have been designed and built in a technically sound manner, and it may or may not be making a significant contribution to the country's development. But if the dam was built at the expense of the basic human rights of a significant number of people, the project must be called into question.

To anticipate the argument, let us assume that the El Cajón project was a sound investment and that any technical problems or economic failures that have occurred were either inadvertent or unforeseeable. Development projects such as the El Cajón Dam serve broad, national interests that are thought to outweigh the harm done to particular individuals. Yet even if it is true that the dam served broader interests, if it was *predictable* that the dam would harm the subsistence rights of some individuals, it was and is the duty and obligation of those involved in its construction to mitigate or minimize these damages. Of course, the El Cajón Dam was not the first ever dam built, and a substantial body of social science knowledge existed that could have predicted some of the project's negative effects (Scudder 1973; Scudder and Colson 1982; Goodland 1978; Partridge, Brown, and Nugent 1982; Hansen and Oliver-Smith 1982). Ignorance is seldom a valid excuse for violation of rights, but clearly, in the El Cajón case, ignorance is not a valid plea.

People living in the reservoir impact zone of any dam are affected in predictable and largely negative ways. Therefore, it was incumbent on the developers of the project to compensate those affected in a timely and fair manner. It would make no sense to argue that because dams (or other forms of development) hurt *someone*, they should not be permitted; that would be an untenable position. However, when a project will harm people in predictable ways, concerted effort and fair compensation to mitigate that impact are necessary. There is widespread agreement on this issue (e.g., World Bank guidelines on involuntary resettlement in Cernea 1988; see also Schorr 1984a). In the case of the El Cajón project, the government of Honduras recognized its obligation to local people, but for various reasons—most directly having to do with the power of the state and the poverty and lack of power of those affected—it failed to provide fair compensation. This neglect was so pervasive and resulted in such harm to the local population that it did indeed constitute a violation of their basic human rights—specifically, their right to subsistence.

Resettlement

Feasibility studies recognized the negative effects the dam would have on the population living in and around the reservoir area (Motor Columbus 1976, chaps. 4, 5). These studies discussed the necessity of offering adequate compensation for the loss of land, houses, and improvements and the need to offer a range of alternatives to those being relocated. The studies included a preliminary survey of possible relocation sites. Twelve sites were evaluated in terms of availability of land, suitability of available land for agriculture, current land use and population, degree of similarity to agro-climatic conditions in the El Cajón region (to minimize the negative effects of dislocation on those affected), and proximity to the relocatees' soon-to-be-inundated homeland. Of all the sites examined, the Bajo Aguán, an agricultural colonization zone along the Aguán River of the Caribbean littoral, was found to be the most problematic because of bad living conditions in the region, including poor health, educational, and sanitary facilities, low-quality housing, and general neglect of the area by government authorities (Motor Columbus 1976, chap. 4, p. 20).

Considerable effort was expended during the initial planning of the resettlement effort to ensure its smooth implementation. Anthropologist Thomas Schorr (1984b) outlines the steps necessary for successful resettlement to take place, with emphasis on the necessity for interinstitutional coordination and a realistic time line for accomplishing such a difficult feat of "social engineering." Schorr points out that relocation presents an opportunity to "maintain or improve the living standards" of those involuntarily displaced by a dam (1984b, 228–229) and presents clear guidelines for successful relocation of displaced people, based on the experiences of multiple hydroelectric projects in Latin America, *including the El Cajón project.*

Of all the elements of the El Cajón project, no single aspect was more important to local residents than the relocation effort. A preconstruction survey estimated that about 1,848 people would be displaced by the dam and 313 houses would be flooded (INA 1979). This is almost certainly an underestimate; in informal interviews carried out in 1983, personnel of the Honduran National Electrical Energy Company (ENEE) estimated that about 3,000 people would lose land or other property to the reservoir. There existed elaborate plans for resettlement, including job training and other social assistance for residents affected by the dam (Motor Columbus 1976; Schorr 1984b), which never materialized as the project proceeded.

Quantitative data on the resettlement process are sparse. A retrospective study carried out in September 1991 indicates the degree of failure of the resettlement effort (ENEE 1991). This report indicates that only about 100 of the 600 families affected by dam construction left the region. Of these, only 47 families were relocated in an organized manner by the government institutions associated with this effort. Preconstruction feasibility studies estimated that relocation costs would be on the order of L 25,000 per family (about U.S.$12,500 at the 1979 exchange rate of two Lempiras to the U.S. dollar), but actual funds spent were only L 4,000 per family (ENEE 1991). The families relocated by the government were taken to the Bajo Aguán, the area judged by the feasibility study to be most problematic for successful resettlement. According to the 1991 study, relocated families encountered problems of inadequate housing and a lack of sanitation facilities and potable water supply, and conflicts over land arose between new arrivals and established residents. When, after numerous petitions by local residents, these conflicts were finally resolved, the relocatees ended up with an average of 2.9 hectares, or about 7 acres, per family—an inadequate amount of land. In addition, relocated families were obliged to form a cooperative and work their lands collectively. This strategy is specifically criticized by Schorr (1984b, 232), who states that if households that are unfamiliar with this means of organizing production are required to adopt it, they will face "a total change in their way of life and as a consequence will experience the socioeconomic disintegration of the domestic group, a decline in the quality of life . . . and a high rate of abandonment of the new settlements." Indeed, of the forty-seven families sent to the Bajo Aguán in the resettlement effort, only twenty-one remained in the area by 1991, a desertion rate of more than 50 percent.

My perspective on the relocation process is decidedly "grassroots": I was in the region in 1983–1984, when resettlement was taking place, and discussed prospects, plans, and reactions to resettlement with local people. From this perspective, the resettlement process was not encouraging. For example, in 1983, thirty families from the town of El Mango, near the upper reaches of the reservoir on the Sulaco River, were taken to the Bajo Aguán for resettlement. Within a month of their resettlement, twenty-nine of these thirty families had returned to El Mango, dissatisfied with conditions in the Bajo Aguán and the treatment they had received. Rumors soon circulated among local residents that the ENEE simply took families to the Bajo Aguán and dropped them off with a month's provisions of rice and beans and building materials for them to construct their new homes.

Indemnification

As stated earlier, planned resettlement accounts for 47 of the approximately 100 families that left the zone when the waters began to rise. The remaining 53 families left for various destinations—some to nearby towns in the immediate area, such as Las Lajas and La Libertad. Others migrated to more distant cities, such as San Pedro Sula and Comayagua. No systematic follow-up has been conducted to investigate their status. But the vast majority—five out of six families—elected to receive cash indemnification and stay in the zone. (Cash indemnification is considered the "least desirable" resettlement option, according to Scudder and Colson 1982, 286.) There is near universal criticism in the region today regarding how cash indemnification was handled. Again, my perspective is decidedly "bottom up." Cash indemnification was received very late in the process of implementing the project. Schorr (1984b, fig. 3) recommends that developers of hydroelectric projects begin providing cash indemnification two years *prior to* filling the reservoir. In the case of the El Cajón project, most people received their indemnification literally as the waters were rising.

In July 1984, I was finishing up my studies in the region. I left the area by way of Montañuelas (the largest nearby town), departing at 4:00 A.M. accompanied by two local men who had assisted me in my fieldwork. After walking for three hours, we reached the main road, a rough dirt track, leading out of the region. We heard the sound of a large truck laboring up the hill. The truck was loaded with local people, many of whom had participated in my land use study, on their way to the capital to collect their indemnification checks. This was in July 1984, when the dam had "closed" and the waters were rising fast in response to one of the rainiest wet seasons in the memory of local residents. Many had planted crops in areas that would be flooded, hoping to eke out one more harvest before the waters rose. They lost their crops and received their checks too late to use them effectively to relocate.

Aside from the delay in receiving indemnification, most were dissatisfied with the amount of compensation they received. Many long-term residents of the region lacked clear legal title to their land and consequently received reduced compensation for the land they cultivated. Others worked the land of absentee landholders, paying nominal or no rent. In general, significant amounts of cash indemnification were received by only a few people, many of whom were absentee owners. Those who worked the land and used it to supply their basic economic needs—their subsistence—received little or nothing.

ENEE records of cash payments illustrate this problem. The ENEE recorded cash compensation on numbered maps, by lot and landowner. The three maps with the largest areas affected by the project (HM 44,

HN 23, and HN 32) accounted for 4,300 hectares (10,625 acres) of the 11,000 hectares (27,181 acres) for which indemnification was provided. Examination of these records reveals that large cash indemnifications were captured by relatively few people. For example, Map HM 44 included twenty lots with a total of 1,383 hectares. A total of L 258,959.18 was paid in indemnification. Ten individuals received L 211, 627 of this compensation for about 1,051 hectares of land. The ten individuals involved owned 76 percent of the land and received 82 percent of the cash indemnification. In area HN 23, a total of sixty-two lots covering 1,799 hectares (4,445 acres) was indemnified at a cost of L 338,753. Eight individuals, who owned 75 percent of the land, received L 231,400, or 68 percent of the total. In area HN 32, a similar pattern prevailed: of the twenty-eight lots adjudicated, nine individuals received 76 percent of the compensation for 69 percent of the total area indemnified. These figures illustrate three relevant points: (1) even before construction of the dam, there was a high degree of concentration of legal title to lands in the hands of a few people; (2) the lion's share of cash indemnification was received by a small minority of people; and (3) most of those affected by the dam received token sums, which were inadequate compensation for their loss of livelihood and left them unable to manage their own relocation successfully or cope with the drastically changed social and natural landscape after the reservoir was filled.

In conclusion, project authorities made inadequate provision for relocation of local residents, violating many of their own guidelines and other well-enunciated principles for effective relocation of those affected. The failure of the relocation effort encouraged people to accept cash indemnification, which was too little and too late to be of much good for most of them, and most of this cash was monopolized by a select few. The vast majority of local residents, including many who had earned their subsistence from affected lands, were deprived of their means of survival and received little or no cash indemnification. Most residents stayed in the region and received little or no compensation for their loss. For all these reasons, the developers of the El Cajón project can be roundly criticized for mismanaging the relocation process and causing significant harm to most of those directly affected by the project.

Effects of the Dam on Local Residents

The construction of the dam and reservoir left a very changed social and natural landscape. How have people adjusted to their new circumstances? It was to begin answering this question that I returned to the area in June 1994, exactly ten years after the reservoir was filled. I traveled widely in the reservoir impact zone, interviewing local residents, many of whom had participated in my earlier study, and observing local conditions firsthand. I asked residents a series of questions about how conditions in the area had changed over the past ten years. When asked about the availability of land compared with the situation ten years before, 87 percent answered that it was more scarce; when asked about problems caused by the dam, slightly more than 68 percent mentioned land scarcity as one of the most serious. Additional problems mentioned were increased illness (malaria) and interference with land use practices by dam authorities. About 17 percent of those questioned claimed the dam had caused no problems for them; generally, these were households living farther from the reservoir. When asked what benefits the dam had provided, 75 percent of respondents reported none. Those who mentioned benefits listed improved fishing (12 percent), improved transportation (6 percent), or some combination of these and other benefits (6 percent).

Perhaps most disturbing was the overall deterioration of economic conditions in the region. Not only was land in short supply, but wages had also declined drastically. Ten years before, the average daily wage had been L 4.00, or U.S.$2.00, before the devaluation in the late 1980s. In 1994, the average wage was L 10.00, or U.S.$1.16, which represented a 42 percent decline in real terms in ten years. A *medida* (4.5 kilograms, or 10 pounds) of maize, the average daily household consumption, cost L 10.00 in June 1994. Thus, a day's work bought only a *medida* of maize—without the beans, salt, cooking oil, and other basics that go into an average peasant's meager diet. People who were unbelievably poor in 1983–1984 were reduced to further poverty ten years later. When asked how their incomes compared with those of ten years before, 24 percent said they had increased, 15 percent said they were about the same, and 61 percent said they had decreased, with almost half of the people whose income had decreased (29 percent) claiming a drastic drop in income.

How much of this deterioration in living standards is attributable to the dam? Some of it is related to an overall decline in standards of living in rural Honduras and is not directly due to the dam. But wages seem to be particularly depressed in this region, at least indirectly as a result of the dam. It would take an extremely sophisticated multivariate analysis using comparative data from a number of similar regions in Honduras to isolate the effect of the dam on declining living standards, and to date this type of analysis has not been pursued. But the decline in wages, when combined with decreased access to land, places local peasants in a double bind. Retreat into the subsistence economy is a classic *campesino* strategy for dealing with bad economic times, but this option has been foreclosed for many by the current squeeze on land availability. The dam reduced access to land at precisely the time when people needed it most.

Changing Land Use Patterns

The scarcity of land is also inducing changes in land use practices; specifically, population pressure on a limited and poorly distributed land base is inducing both expansion and intensification of land use. Regarding expansion, two observations are relevant. First, broadleaf tropical forest is now virtually extinct in the reservoir impact zone. This vegetation type is an indicator of good-quality soils, favored by farmers for cultivation of crops. Formerly found in river bottom areas along the main river courses, along tributary rivers and streams at slightly higher elevations, and in areas of deeper soil some distance from rivers and streams, this vegetation type has disappeared because of inundation of the river bottoms and clearing for agricultural use in other areas. Second, agriculture has expanded into areas of mixed oak-pine forest with shallower soils and, in some cases, into the extensive pine forests characterized by thin, highly acid soils. Both of these vegetation types are usually found on steep slopes, which cover about 86 percent of the study area. At this point, it is not possible to quantify how much formerly forested area was converted to agricultural land in the ten-year period in question, though research on the question is ongoing. However, it is evident that cultivation of these poorer lands on steeper slopes is problematic due to higher rates of erosion and generally lower yields than are typical of less erodible, more fertile soils elsewhere in the region. The increased erosion caused by cultivation of these slopes also threatens the dam through higher-than-expected rates of siltation.

Land use has also changed on existing agricultural lands. Two phenomena are worth noting: (1) the expansion of cattle raising into formerly cultivated lands and (2) the increased use of chemical inputs, particularly herbicide and fertilizer. Regarding the expansion of cattle raising, evidence is largely anecdotal and qualitative at this point, though remote sensing data will help quantify the extent of this process in the future. Several people interviewed claimed that after the reservoir was filled, displaced cattle ranchers purchased more fertile upland areas, formerly used for agriculture. The cattle ranchers had owned much of the land in the now-flooded river bottoms as well as extensive tracts of steeply sloping land with a combination of sparse pine forest and a grass understory, which they used for grazing cattle. When displaced from the river bottoms, these ranchers used their cash indemnifications to buy up remaining unflooded agricultural lands and converted them to pastureland. This displaced the maize farmers, who now are either cultivating steeper slopes or obtaining permission to periodically cultivate the more favored lands now in pasture. In the process of cultivating these lands, the maize farmers both weed the pastures and, to the extent that they use fertilizer, help maintain their fertility.

The expansion of agriculture into more marginal lands and the routine cultivation of pastureland have caused an intensification of agricultural practices. Farmers have markedly increased their use of the broad-spectrum herbicide paraquat and have also begun to use fertilizer. In 1983–1984, 65 percent of farmers used herbicide, a practice started in the late 1970s, whereas in 1994, 94 percent of farmers did so. The use of herbicide represents the largest cost of production for *milpa* farming, both in the purchase of the chemical and in the purchase or rental of a backpack sprayer to apply it (as mentioned earlier, fewer than half of the farmers interviewed own backpack sprayers; the rest must borrow or rent them).[5] Formerly, farmers used herbicide in combination with manual techniques to weed their fields during the growing season. Now, because farmers are cultivating pastures, they use paraquat to clear the land before planting as well as for weeding during the growing season. Undoubtedly, not only has the percentage of farmers using herbicide increased, but rates of application have also gone up.

In 1983–1984, fertilizer was not used by any of the farmers interviewed in their *milpas,* but in 1994, 55 percent of those responding had used it, a remarkable increase. Apparently, the use of fertilizer began in the early 1990s and continues to increase. Fertilizer is applied at the rate of two 50-kilogram (approximately 110-pound) sacks of urea per hectare; each sack costs about L 100. When I asked the farmers why they had begun using fertilizer, the most frequent reply was that "the land is tired" and needs fertilizer to produce. It is the case that plots are being farmed more frequently; that is, fallow periods are being shortened and many plots are being farmed for several years in succession. The overall cultivation system has changed from one based on slash-and-burn agriculture to a kind of rotational grazing-herbicide-maize cultivation system using fertilizer.

It is not clear whether the steps being taken to intensify agriculture are sustainable in either ecological or economic terms. One thing is certain, however: increasing numbers of farmers are dependent on cattle owners for access to land for farming. Since farmers are intensifying production on rented land, there is little incentive for long-term investment in measures to enhance productivity, such as soil conservation techniques that protect the soil from erosion and build up its fertility and structure. From an applied, development point of view, current land use arrangements present a formidable barrier to the innovations necessary to restore and maintain the productive capacity of the land. This latter task is of direct interest to the dam management authority, which is interested in reforesting and otherwise improving natural resource management to protect the reservoir from siltation caused by erosion. Such environmental degradation not only would imperil the useful life of the dam but also would further impoverish local residents.

Conclusion

Did the El Cajón Dam project violate the subsistence rights of people residing in the immediate reservoir impact zone? Clearly, the answer is yes. One difficulty in answering the question, however, is the fact that the subsistence rights of these same people were probably being violated *before* construction of the dam. Their subsistence rights probably would have been violated in the absence of the dam as well. Residents of the region share the same unacceptable living standards found in other rural regions of Honduras, in Central America, and throughout Latin America as a whole—indeed, in many rural areas of the so-called Third World. In many of these areas, large numbers of people are suffering deprivation due to systemic factors that revolve around the distribution of power in their societies: economic policies and social institutions that sacrifice their rights to subsistence and economic strategies that continue to enrich a minority at the expense of the poor majority (see Stonich 1993 for a recent analysis of rural poverty in a similar region of Honduras).

Even given these circumstances, the El Cajón project can be said to have a particular and well-defined role in violating the right to subsistence of many people living in the immediate reservoir impact zone. The dam caused deprivation over and above that which would have been experienced in the same population in the absence of the project. The deprivation the project caused was foreseeable, based on other experiences with large dam projects. The feasibility studies carried out prior to the dam's construction outlined a comprehensive approach for dealing with expected negative impacts, including a plan for resettlement of the population, but the studies' recommendations were not adequately implemented. The procedures followed, in fact, opposed the advice provided by national and international consultants. This neglect is at least partially explained by the skewed distribution of power mentioned in the previous paragraph.

It is inevitable that hydroelectric development will displace some people and that these people will suffer in the process. As one official associated with the dam told me in 1994 when I complained of the deterioration in living conditions of local residents, "The El Cajón project was not made for them. The project screwed them. But the project had other, much bigger objectives." This is a frank assessment, yet it goes against the official rhetoric, which states: "The weak budgetary commitment to resettlement is a clear indicator of the low institutional concern for an adequate treatment of the people who were forced to move for the project. Although the project was justifiable in the overall development of the country, it should not have been achieved at the sacrifice of some Hondurans who, due to the circumstance of living on lands affected by the reservoir, were forced to leave their homes" (ENEE 1991, 31, translated by the author).

The project is a prime example of systemic deprivation: a violation of rights to subsistence based on the confluence of multiple factors. It is difficult to assign responsibility to any one individual for this violation of rights. Clearly, however, the national government and its institutions responsible for approving and implementing the project bear primary responsibility, as do international institutions such as the Interamerican Development Bank and the World Bank, which financed construction of the dam. Individuals and institutions operating at the national and international levels were aware of the projected negative effects yet ignored their own guidelines and procedures for mitigating these effects. The successful examples of resettlement provided by projects carried out in areas similar to the El Cajón region (e.g., Partridge 1993) argue that the harm done to local residents was not an essential aspect of the El Cajón project. Much of the suffering that continues to plague the local population could have been avoided.

The El Cajón project worsened the plight of an already poor people. The negligence of those who planned and constructed the project drove many people from poverty to misery. In the process, it greatly increased the difficulty of pursuing the only form of subsistence available to many—small-scale agriculture—and left local residents unable to provide for their own basic needs. If we accept the concept of subsistence rights, the national and international agencies involved in the El Cajón project have a duty to redress the violations of rights that have occurred. The Honduran government and the international institutions involved in the construction of the El Cajón project should share the costs of restoring the subsistence rights of those affected.

On a positive note, if worsening the plight of the people living in the region was avoidable, it is feasible to redress this injustice and restore a measure of their subsistence rights. Those who financed and built the dam should undertake a concerted, well-coordinated, and well-financed program to repair the ecological, social, and economic damage done. Investment should be made in restoring the productivity of the region, providing access to productive resources and employment for local residents, and establishing basic health care and educational facilities in the region. Because the El Cajón region is relatively small and the number of people involved is not overwhelming, the cost of such an effort would not be prohibitive—certainly much less than the price of the dam. Some of the financing could be derived from revenue from the dam.

The El Cajón experience is not simply a case of harming the interests of one small segment of society in order to obtain a greater social good. The El Cajón Dam is a monument—literally and figuratively—to an outmoded concept of development. This concept views development as a top-down process led by a technocratic and political elite whose primary task is to replicate the social and economic conditions of the wealthy countries in poorer countries (like Honduras) primarily through the transfer of technology. The El Cajón Dam failed in a social sense (and possibly in a technical sense as well) because it was a product of this outmoded way of conceiving and implementing development. The top-down approach cut out most Hondurans from the decision-making process regarding the financial, technical, and social risks associated with the construction of such a grandiose project.

Even though the El Cajón Dam was an extremely costly project, especially by Honduran standards, the planning and implementation of which proceeded with little or no public examination of its costs or consequences, the public is clearly required to bear the project's financial costs as well as the costs of alternative development strategies forgone. Greater public participation in development decision making at the national level may have raised questions about the scope, scale, and technical feasibility of the project. Alternative strategies, such as a series of smaller dams (now viewed as a better alternative by some World Bank personnel in light of the current dam's difficulties), might have been seriously considered. Local residents were also cut out of the decision-making process. It is unlikely that local people would ever have been enthusiastic about losing their homes and fields, yet had they been actively consulted on how best to mitigate the project's negative effects, the prospects for successful relocation and indemnification would have been greatly enhanced. This lack of participation by the local population doomed the relocation and indemnification effort to failure. The El Cajón Dam project points out once again that for development to be truly successful, it must be informed by dialogue, participation, and respect among diverse social sectors within and among different countries and must be guided by a special concern for the effects of development on vulnerable people whose rights to subsistence are constantly at risk.

The concept of rights to subsistence provides an important conceptual tool for orienting development policies and projects, including hydroelectric and irrigation development, in a more general sense. The widespread lack of even the barest subsistence levels among hundreds of millions of people around the world today is the moral scandal of the late twentieth century. Recall that subsistence rights are the "moral minimum." If we cannot fulfill even the moral minimum for many—perhaps most—people in the world, what hope is there for fulfilling other rights and conditions that are also integral to the realization of human potential?

Food for Thought

The case of El Cajón raises a number of questions applicable to large-scale development projects, such as dams, that result in the removal of local inhabitants. For example, are subsistence rights in fact universal human rights? A good starting point for examining this question is the United Nations' Universal Declaration of Human Rights. Further, how do subsistence rights and water rights fit into the larger concept of rights? If rights are the "weapons of the weak" against those more powerful, how do they become established in a society? Under what conditions do the "strong" permit the establishment of rights to restrict their power?

The El Cajón case presents a situation in which the harm done to the local population was foreseen and steps were outlined in the project's planning stage to address potential problems, yet these steps were never properly implemented. This chapter claims that the relative power of the two parties involved—the government, engineers, and international consultants on one hand and the local *campesinos* on the other—explains this failure. What other factors might explain the failure to enact plans to minimize the negative effects of the dam? How could the same mistakes be avoided in the future?

This chapter also proposes that steps be taken to restore the subsistence rights of those affected by the dam. Some would argue that this is impossible or too costly. Others might say that the prospects for such an undertaking are poor because the same government institutions that botched the resettlement program would only fail again. Are these valid arguments? In designing a project to restore the subsistence rights of the people affected, what information would be needed, and what role should the local people play?

Development—of water resources or of other types—always involves trade-offs. Some people benefit, and some are harmed. There are also ecological costs to development. How do we weigh these trade-offs? Who makes the decisions regarding the feasibility and desirability of a particular development strategy? How strong are our analytical tools for predicting the effects of development? A thought-provoking exercise might be to choose a particular development project and examine the process for deciding on its feasibility, its desirability, and the mechanisms to compensate those hurt by the project. What about impacts that are difficult to value in monetary terms (those involving species or lifestyles or those that affect aesthetic, historical, or religious significance)? How are these handled in social and environmental impact statements?

RESOURCES

For more information on the El Cajón Dam, OAS 1992 is an excellent resource; large dam projects in general are critiqued in Goldsmith and Hildyard 1986. The August 1991 issue of *Civil Engineering* (pp. 42–48) presents a debate about the desirability of large dams.

The concept of basic rights in the context of international development is explored in the Oxfam publication *Words into Action: Basic Rights and the Campaign Against World Poverty* (Simmons 1995).

About 10 million people per year undergo the process of "administratively imposed displacement" required by infrastuctural development, about 4 million per year due to hydroelectric and irrigation projects alone. Social scientists have begun to pay more attention to this process. For a good recent summary of ways to minimize the negative effects of involuntary displacement, see *Anthropological Approaches to Involuntary Resettlement: Policy, Practice, and Theory* (Cernea and Guggenheim 1993).

ACKNOWLEDGMENTS

The 1994 research reported here was supported by a Mississippi State University Faculty Research Initiation Grant. Previous research, in 1983–1984, was supported by a National Science Foundation Doctoral Dissertation Improvement

Grant (BNS-82-17706) and the University of Colorado, Boulder. Permission to carry out this research and valuable logistic and intellectual support were provided by the Instituto Hondureño de Antropología e Historia, Dra. Olga Joya, Director. I also wish to thank the people of the El Cajón region for their hospitality and support during all phases of this fieldwork.

NOTES

1. If we identify the right to subsistence as a legitimate, basic, universal human right, then this right must be effectively exercised and guaranteed. Shue points out that guaranteeing any right does not mean ensuring that it can be upheld under any and all contingencies but simply means ensuring that it can be enjoyed and protected from predictable "standard threats." He concludes that subsistence rights are limited in scope: "It is not impractical to expect some level of social organization to protect the . . . minimal supplies of the essentials of life" (1980, 25). "The fulfillment of basic and non-basic moral rights consists of effective, but not infallible, social arrangements to guard against standard threats to . . . subsistence" (1980, 34). But is this truly possible in the real world? Shue examines a number of arguments against the possibility of guaranteeing a right to subsistence, including (1) that the "overpopulation" of the world makes it impossible to fulfill subsistence rights or that attempting to do so would harm significant portions of the present population as well as future generations; (2) that fulfillment of subsistence rights would place an intolerable, if not unlimited, burden on everyone except the poorest—it would violate the rights of others to fulfill these rights; and (3) that there is no moral obligation to help those who are far away and that doing so might even harm the poor closer to home. After careful consideration, Shue rejects each of these arguments.

2. The reasons for the dam's failure to perform to expectations because of low reservoir levels is a matter of some controversy (see Loker 1995). Potential explanations for low reservoir levels include prolonged drought, diversion of water upstream from the reservoir, mismanagement of water in the reservoir, and leaks at the site of the dam and/or elsewhere in the reservoir.

3. In 1990, Honduras's debt was about U.S.$3.5 billion, which works out to U.S.$595 per capita, or more than three times the value of its annual exports, and 40 percent more than its total gross domestic product (World Bank 1992). This represents an exceptional level of indebtedness, even by Latin American standards.

4. The predominant herbicide used is paraquat (trade name Gramoxone, 1,1'-dimethyl-4,4'-bipyridilium dichloride), applied by backpack sprayer. Little or no protective clothing is worn during its application, and the herbicide is usually purchased informally in containers lacking instructions

or warning labels. Widespread use of this herbicide may represent a significant health risk to those who apply it.

5. In 1994, a liter (about 1.06 quarts) of paraquat cost L 50, with an application rate of 2–3 liters (2.1–3.2 quarts) to every hectare (2.47 acres). Rental of a sprayer cost L 10—the same as the daily wage of an agricultural laborer. Purchase price was L 500–700.

PART II

Project Culture and Hydropolitics

The Making and Unmaking of Water Development Projects

Water Resource Development and Its Effects on the Human Community

The Tennessee-Tombigbee Waterway, Southeastern United States

Claudia M. Rogers

Author Summary

Construction of the Tennessee-Tombigbee Waterway was an ambitious engineering feat. It is a 376.6-kilometer (234-mile) "highway for barges" linking the Tennessee River in Kentucky and Tennessee with the Tombigbee River in Mississippi and Alabama. Along with the nearly $2 billion spent to build this waterway, Congress appropriated nearly $7 million more to assist in economic development and social change for some 2.4 million people then residing in the fifty-one counties bordering the project. This chapter examines the record of that assistance and evaluates the consequences to the human community of a project built on the promise of benefits to an impoverished region of the United States.

Introduction

In addition to local and state water management offices, several federal agencies are responsible for managing the water resources of the United States. Those agencies include the U.S. Army Corps of Engineers, a part of the Department of Defense; the Natural Resources Conservation Service, formerly the Soil Conservation Service, of the Department of Agriculture; the National Marine Fisheries Service, of

123

the Department of Commerce; and the Bureau of Reclamation and the U.S. Fish and Wildlife Service, of the Department of the Interior.

In carrying out their respective duties, these agencies spend billions of dollars yearly on new and existing projects to develop or maintain the water resources of the United States. For the most part, citizens and their lawmakers regard this expenditure as a benefit to those people closely affected by the water projects funded. Hence, whether it is a Hoover Dam, which cost $50 million in Depression-era dollars, or a waterway linking the Tennessee River with the Gulf of Mexico at a price of slightly less than $2 billion in 1987 dollars, we continue to think of such massive infusions of money as boons to economic progress.

Anthropologists and other social scientists, however, know that so-called economic progress affects the entire subculture of a given region, including its social system, political organization, community structure, values, and behavior patterns. Such effects can be positive, bringing increased opportunity to a larger number of residents, or negative, solidifying existing patterns of political power and economic dominance. This chapter presents a brief examination of a public work that was justified in large part by the claim of economic development for an impoverished portion of the United States.

The Tennessee-Tombigbee Waterway

The Tennessee-Tombigbee Waterway, linking the Tennessee River in Kentucky and Tennessee with the Tombigbee River in Mississippi and Alabama, is a 376.6-kilometer (234-mile) "highway for barges" and the latest link in some 41,038 kilometers (25,500 miles) of inland and coastal waterways in the United States (see photo 7.1). It is one of the most ambitious waterway development projects in U.S. history and the largest civil works project ever undertaken by the U.S. Army Corps of Engineers.

Waterway transportation offers certain advantages to an industrial society. A modern hopper barge, for example, can carry as much as 1,361 metric tons, or about 1,500 short tons (3 million pounds), of cargo, equaling that carried by fourteen jumbo rail cars or fifty large tractor-trailer trucks. Where a water route can be used, the results to the shipper are lower costs and higher energy savings.

Although the Tennessee-Tombigbee Waterway fits well into the modern transportation network, it was conceived in the early 1800s to provide a shorter, reliable water route to the Gulf of Mexico for citizens

PHOTO 7.1. AN EIGHT-BARGE TOW
ON THE TENNESSEE-TOMBIGBEE WATERWAY

Construction of the Tennessee-Tombigbee Waterway was an ambitious engineering feat. The waterway is a 376.6-kilometer (234-miles) "highway for
barges" linking the Tennessee River in Kentucky and Tennessee with the
Tombigbee River in Mississippi and Alabama. Photograph by Adrien Lamarre,
U.S. Army Corps of Engineers, Mobile District, 1987.

moving to developing eastern states. One hundred eleven years
elapsed, however, from the time the "Tenn-Tom," as it is known in
navigation circles, was first officially studied by the federal government until it became a reality. In the interim, it was alternately shuf-
fled from obscurity to high visibility through twenty-two presidential
administrations—Ulysses S. Grant was president when the waterway
route was studied initially—fifty-five terms of Congress, eight lengthy
studies and revisions, and two major lawsuits.

Construction began on the waterway in 1972 and was completed in
1985, when it was opened to through commercial traffic. This massive
project required the movement of 234.7 million cubic meters (307 million cubic yards) of earth, more than that involved in construction of

the Panama Canal; the pouring of 1.7 million cubic meters (2.2 million cubic yards) of concrete; and the placement of 29,900 metric tons (33,000 short tons) of steel. During its thirteen years of construction, the project employed 75 primary contractors, 1,200 subcontractors, and, at the peak of construction, some 3,000 workers. Overall, the project required more than 25 million hours of labor (Green 1985).

History of the Waterway

As it flows from its headwaters in the Appalachian Mountains to its confluence with the Ohio River, the Tennessee River makes a deep southward loop, into the states of Alabama and Mississippi (see figure 7.1). At the southernmost point on this loop, there are fewer than 483 kilometer (300 miles) in a direct line to the Gulf of Mexico and even fewer to the headwaters of three other rivers, the Black Warrior, the Alabama, and the Tombigbee, which merge and flow southward to join the gulf via Mobile Bay at Mobile, Alabama. Before 1985, the water route to the gulf via the Tennessee River and its connection to the Ohio and Mississippi Rivers was more then 1,931 kilometers (1,200 miles) long.

In October 1970, President Richard Nixon signed the Public Works Bill of Fiscal Year 1971, which authorized the expenditure of $1 million to begin construction of the Tennessee-Tombigbee Waterway. It had been ninety-six years since Congress first authorized a study of the project. At the beginning of construction, the cost was estimated at $323 million (in 1963 dollars). Total cost of the project on completion, however, was $1.993 billion, including costs borne by the states of Alabama and Mississippi. Roughly 80 percent of the increase in cost was attributed to inflation over the thirteen-year construction period; the remaining 20 percent was a result of design changes. To construct the waterway, 34,633 hectares (85,579 acres) of land were acquired outright and easements were taken on an additional 10,198 hectares (25,200 acres) for a total of 44,831 hectares (110,779 acres). The project encompasses just more than 1,600 kilometers (1,000 miles) of shoreline.

Project Economics and Benefits

The total estimated construction cost of the Tennessee-Tombigbee Waterway was $1.993 billion in federal costs and $153 million in local

FIGURE 7.1. VICINITY OF THE
TENNESSEE-TOMBIGBEE WATERWAY

As the Tennessee River makes a deep southward loop into the states of Alabama and Mississippi, there are fewer than 483 kilometers (300 miles) in a direct line to the Gulf of Mexico and even fewer to the headwaters of three other rivers, the Black Warrior, the Alabama, and the Tombigbee, which merge and flow southward to join the gulf via Mobile Bay at Mobile, Alabama. In October 1970, President Richard Nixion authorized the expenditure of $1 million to begin construction of the Tennessee-Tombigbee Waterway, which would eliminate the 1,931-kilometer (1,200-mile) water route to the Gulf via the Tennessee River and its connection to the Ohio and Mississippi Rivers. Map from U.S. Army Corps of Engineers, *Project Maps* (Mobile, Ala.: U.S. Army Corps of Engineers, Mobile District, 1992), R36.

costs borne by the states of Alabama and Mississippi, and the U.S. Army Corps of Engineers estimates operating and maintenance costs at $17 million per year. Construction of the waterway was authorized on the basis of economic projections indicating it would return more in national benefits over the first fifty years of its life than would be spent on construction and operating costs.

The *recognized* economic benefits projected were virtually all national transportation savings, although some other categories were included; for example, dollar values were assigned for recreational benefits and for benefits to local areas during construction. The Tenn-Tom is generally described as a "throughput" waterway; that is, more than 75 percent of the commodities shipped on it transit the entire waterway rather than originating or terminating at some point on it. Total tonnages of all commodities shipped have ranged from 1,543 metric tons (1,701 short tons) in 1985 to 7,171 metric tons (7,905 short tons) in 1994 and 7,898 metric tons (8,706 short tons) in 1995. The largest amount of commodities shipped on this waterway to date was 8,999 metric tons (9,920 short tons) in 1988, an anomaly resulting from drought conditions on the Mississippi River (U.S. Army Corps of Engineers 1996).

Bulk shipments on the waterway include, in order of tonnage amounts, wood products, crushed rock, coal, chemicals, and fuel. Much of the waterway's usage derives from import and export of goods within the inland United States. Although regional development was not calculated into the official benefits justifying the Tenn-Tom, many areas along its route are undertaking new development, from wood- and grain-handling facilities to large new industrial plants. A handful of such facilities already exist, and three more are under construction.

Recognizing the opportunities created by the waterway, Congress passed three resolutions during the 1970s that, taken together, authorized the Tennessee-Tombigbee Corridor Study to examine the region's capacity for future growth. Unique in its geographic and substantive scope, the study included fifty-one counties in four states between the Ohio River and the Gulf of Mexico (see figure 7.2). These counties are home to nearly 3 million people spread out over almost 82,880 square kilometers, or 32,000 square miles. The region boasts three urban centers, Birmingham, Mobile, and Tuscaloosa, all in Alabama, where about one-third of the population of the fifty-one counties lives. Seventeen percent of the residents of the study area are concentrated in small towns such as Amory and Aberdeen in Mississippi and Demopolis in Alabama, which typically have populations of 7,000 to 8,000. The rest of the corridor residents live in rural areas. Ethnic and racial diversity are limited. Little more than one-quarter of corridor residents are black, and fewer than 1 percent consider themselves Native American; the latter are principally members of the Choctaw Tribe in east-central Mississippi.

Local economies are dominated by manufacturing, principally of textiles, lumber and wood products, paper, chemicals, and metals; by household and other personal services; by agriculture; and, to a lesser degree, by contract construction. Textile manufacturing, personal

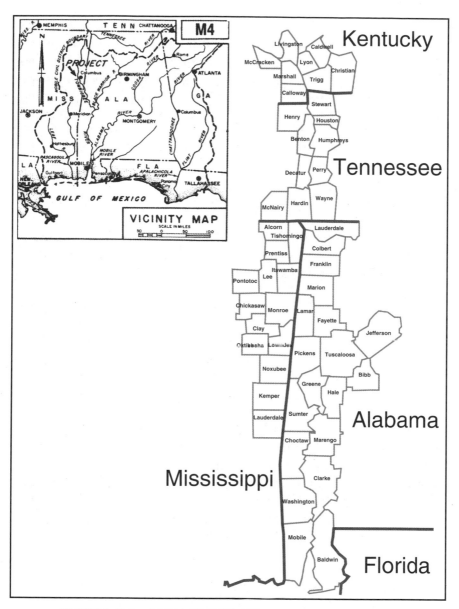

FIGURE 7.2. AREA OF THE TENNESSEE-TOMBIGBEE
CORRIDOR STUDY

Recognizing the opportunities created by the waterway, Congress passed three resolutions during the 1970s that, taken together, authorized the Tennessee-Tombigbee Corridor Study, unique in both its geographic and substantive scope. The study area included fifty-one counties in four states between the Ohio River and the Gulf of Mexico. Maps from U.S. Army Corps of Engineers, *Project Maps* (Mobile, Ala.: U.S. Army Corps of Engineers, Mobile District, 1992), M4.

services, and agriculture are examples of low-wage, low-security industries and are sensitive to the health of the national economy. Hence, employment rates and income levels vary widely and often dramatically. Indeed, in 1985, when the Tennessee-Tombigbee Waterway was completed, the unemployment rates throughout the corridor ranged from 7.3 percent in Hardin County, Tennessee, to 15 percent in coastal Alabama. Corridor residents consistently receive only 70 to 85 percent of the national average per capita income of $18,696 determined by the 1990 census.

Given the characteristics just described—a nonurban settlement pattern, fragile economies subject to forces beyond local control, high rates of unemployment, and low levels of personal wealth relative to the national average—it is not surprising that expectations would be high that a project such as the Tennessee-Tombigbee Waterway might provide the stimulus necessary to attract social change in the guise of economic development.

The Corps responded to Congress by developing a study whose goals were "the identification of water, related land, environmental, and human resources as they pertain to expected growth, and the development of plans for the utilization of these resources to best support future growth" (Galdis 1985, syllabus). To meet these goals, the Tennessee-Tombigbee Corridor Study was intended to become an aid for local officials in planning for future growth and development of communities adjacent to the waterway. Conducted from 1977 to 1986 at a total cost of $6.9 million, this effort was based on the extensive and continuous involvement of residents in the corridor counties in each phase of the study, including design, data collection, analysis, and plans for local use of the study results.

Study Outputs

The Tennessee-Tombigbee Corridor Study addressed four categories: economic development, human resources development, environmental quality, and water resources development. As the study progressed and large volumes of data were collected, it became obvious that some of the data should be computerized to make the information both easily accessible to users and responsive to updating requirements. Two computer systems were developed: an economic impact assessment model that computed and analyzed social and economic information and a geographic information system that provided sophisticated visual data display and analysis. Both systems provided information needed to determine whether the effects of growth would be beneficial.

Ninety volumes of written reports were also produced to give local planners and officials a preview of the region's future (Galdis 1985). The report covered an impressive array of subjects, including listings of criteria a county should meet to attract manufacturing industries; basic agricultural production and future transportation needs; counties with high levels of poverty, unemployment, and illiteracy; education and vocational training needed to attract new companies; an inventory of housing and community and social services, in conjunction with an evaluation of how to provide basic housing and services; and listings of environmental factors such as physiography, locations and types of minerals, natural and recreational areas, endangered species, state records of historic and archaeological sites, air and water quality, and maps delineating wetlands and water supplies, including groundwater, surface water, rates of consumption, and projected availability of potable water correlated with estimated population growth. The same breadth and depth of information was collected and categorized for each of the fifty-one counties within the corridor. The two-part product—the large and detailed information base and the computerized delivery systems—allowed each community or special interest group to "try on" any type of economic development to see how it might affect the community economically, socially, and environmentally.

Study products, then, were designed to be predictive tools, "technological crystal balls" to assist and clarify the decision-making process for local officials. Indeed, the emphasis on regional development so integral to the continued funding of the Tennessee-Tombigbee Waterway was echoed clearly in the focus of the corridor study products. Studies in support of economic development—the economic impact assessment model, an industrial location analysis, a transportation linkage evaluation, and a guide to waterfront development activities—were the centerpiece around which all other parts of the study were created. Regardless of their potential, however, the study products were underutilized. How best, then, can the effects of the Tennessee-Tombigbee Waterway on the people along its route be assessed? What indicators can be used to judge the positive and negative consequences of the waterway's construction and operation?

Current Effects

Indicators of the waterway's effects are found in various sources, such as local applications of corridor study products, secondary demographic and economic data from the Bureau of the Census and another computerized economic impact forecasting model the U.S. Army Corps of Engineers developed twenty-five years ago to evaluate proposed military actions.

The two computerized systems of the corridor study—the geographic information system and the economic impact assessment model—are not used. They were not funded after 1986 and hence do not contain current data. The written reports are used only sporadically, if at all. Only two continue to be requested: the industrial location analysis and the guide to waterfront development activities, written by the author of this chapter (Rogers 1985). The lack of continued utilization of the study products does not mean a failure of the study process, however. The reasons for the study products' obscurity include a lack of congressional funding to keep the reports and models current, ready accessibility elsewhere of the information initially presented, a lack of awareness of the study and its results on the part of planners throughout the corridor counties, and a general de-emphasis on regional planning in favor of special interests or specific community-based growth strategies.

Actual development activities directly related to the "highway for barges" are numerous but tend to be clustered in Mississippi. The extent of the development was determined by consulting a list of counties in the corridor in which new economic activities have taken place since 1985. The list begins at the northern end, with McCracken County in Kentucky, where the port of Paducah marks the confluence of the Ohio and Tennessee Rivers, and proceeds south along the Tennessee River through the eight counties studied in Kentucky and the ten in Tennessee to northeastern Mississippi. The list of counties continues south through fourteen counties in Mississippi and nineteen in Alabama and ends in southern Alabama, at the Gulf of Mexico and Mobile and Baldwin Counties. A recent publication by the Tennessee-Tombigbee Waterway Development Authority (1995), based in Columbus, Mississippi, list jobs and moneys new to the area. To gauge a wider effect of such infusions, multipliers from the Economic Impact Forecasting System, a computerized database and forecasting tool of the U.S. Army Corps of Engineers, can be applied to both employment figures and new revenues. This system contains information for the entire United States and gives projections of how much money and how many jobs might result from additions of outside revenues and positions (U.S. Army Corps of Engineers n.d.). The key assumption is the infusion of *outside* money and the dynamic effect it has on local spending and the creation of additional employment.

In Kentucky, eight counties are contiguous with or adjacent to the Tennessee River and therefore were included in the corridor study (see figure 7.2). To date, only one, McCracken County, located at the confluence of the Tennessee and Ohio Rivers, can claim the infusion of new money—some $2.3 million—into its local economy. This is not surprising, as Paducah, the county seat, is also a sizable port for traffic on both river systems. With a multiplier of 1.98, that $2.3 million could become $4.6 million, meaning that for every new dollar, almost one other dollar is generated. No new jobs, however, have been reported.

The situation in Tennessee is just the opposite. Of the ten counties that are part of the corridor, only McNair County had an increase in employment, with eleven jobs created and reported to the Waterway Development Authority between 1985 and 1995. There are no estimates of added moneys. Again, the use of a multiplier—this time, for employment—turns eleven into sixteen. Hence, the eleven new positions generate enough extra economic activity that five more jobs can be created to handle that activity.

Mississippi and Alabama have fared considerably better. In Mississippi, with fourteen counties lining the Tennessee-Tombigbee Waterway, six have received new moneys and new jobs. In Tishomingo County, located at the confluence of the Tennessee River and the Tenn-Tom Waterway, residents claimed 127 new jobs and $8.1 million in new revenues. Applying the multipliers for the county yields some 212 new employment positions and $12.3 million in revenues. Tishomingo County also is the site of the Yellow Creek Port and Marina and the projected home of a nuclear energy plant proposed by the Tennessee Valley Authority. Farther south, Lee County, with its county seat of Tupelo, birthplace of Elvis Presley, had 150 new positions and almost $85 million in new investments from sources outside the county. A calculation of the probable effects of such economic stimuli yields some 314 jobs and $157 million. Both Itawamba and Monroe Counties are directly on the waterway and reportedly have 549 more jobs and $41.3 million in new moneys, or a total of nearly 1,000 new positions and $67.7 million in new revenues. Local spokespersons in Clay County listed additions to the economy of 202 jobs and $77.2 million, or 340 jobs and nearly $11 million dollars in new moneys. In Lowndes County, where the Tennessee-Tombigbee Waterway Development

Authority is located, employment has increased by 470 positions and revenues have grown by $137.7 million, for 991 new jobs and $247.7 million in additional moneys over the first decade since the waterway opened in 1985.

Of the nineteen counties in Alabama included in the corridor study, only six have received new jobs and moneys since 1985, when the waterway opened: Pickens County in western Alabama, with 148 new positions and $12.6 million in additional revenues; Tuscaloosa County, one of five metropolitan areas in the state of Alabama, with 1,700 new jobs and $25 million in new moneys; Sumter and Marengo Counties, both of which are rural and impoverished, with 150 and 1,000 new jobs and $27 million and $250 million in new revenues, respectively; and Mobile and Baldwin Counties, at the Gulf of Mexico, with slightly more than 2,600 new jobs and $1 billion in new revenues.

To date, then, a total of seventeen counties throughout the corridor—one-third of the total of fifty-one—have shown increases in jobs, new private sector investments, or both. Assuming the validity of the multiplier effects, the total number of newly created jobs in counties adjacent to the waterway is just more than 7,100. It is also assumed that the waterway was and is the major impetus for opening each business in each particular county. Using the multipliers for each county brings the total for the region to more than 17,600. In a population of almost 3 million people, 17,600 new jobs in the ten-year period from 1985 to 1995 is not impressive.

Similarly, the moneys invested in new businesses total $2 billion for the same ten-year period. Calculating with the income multipliers brings the total to $4.6 billion for the fifty-one counties in four states. These also are disappointing numbers when compared with the four states' 1994 total personal income of $287.2 billion, as reported in the *Statistical Abstract of the United States* (U.S. Bureau of the Census 1995). The corridor's added income of $4.6 billion—generated over a period of ten years—is just 1.6 percent of the $287 billion in income determined for one year alone.

The addition of employment and revenues to an area often results in population growth: more jobs and more money attract more people. This has not been the case, however, in the four states considered here. Taking the three decennial counts from 1970 to 1990 and calculating the percentage of change shows, at most, population increases of 19.4 percent in Tennessee and 18.3 percent in Mississippi. Kentucky had nearly a 16 percent increase, whereas Alabama changed by 11.3 percent. From the highest percentage to the lowest, the rate of change is less than 1 percent per annum in the twenty-year interval. Again, these figures are not impressive. Similarly, changes in per capita income have not reflected the promise of economic prosperity associated with the waterway. Indeed, in twenty-five of the fifty-one counties in the Tennessee-Tombigbee corridor, per capita incomes decreased between 1979, during construction, and 1987, after completion of the waterway. In Kentucky especially, residents of seven of the eight corridor counties experienced decreases in income ranging from 1 percent to nearly 6 percent, after correcting for inflation. In one-half of the ten corridor counties in Tennessee, residents also reported a drop in per capita income, averaging between 1 and 5 percent for the same period, 1979–1987. The other five counties reported increases of 1 percent and 6 percent, which translate to only $18 to $500 per year.

Mississippi residents have not fared better. In one-half of the fourteen Mississippi counties in the Tenn-Tom corridor, residents saw their incomes drop by 3 percent, 9 percent, 4 percent, or 1 percent. Individuals in the other seven counties claimed a slight rise in income, from 2.5 percent to 7.5 percent. In Tishomingo County, residents had the most noticeable decline, at almost 9 percent, from $8,445 per capita in 1979 to $7,704 in 1987. Much of this shift can be attributed to completion of the Bay Springs Lock and Dam and the divide cut portion of the waterway. These are the major features of the northernmost section of the waterway, a section consisting of a 6-mile-long, dredged channel forming Yellow Creek Embayment of Pickwick Lake on the Tennessee River, and a 27-mile-long cut through the Tennessee Valley Divide, ending at Bay Spring Lake. This lake is a 7-mile-long reservoir impounded by Bay Spring Lock and Dam. Both the divide cut and the dam required huge but temporary infusions of construction workers and managers into rural northeastern Mississippi. Neighboring Colbert County in Alabama also had a drop of nearly 9 percent, probably for the same reasons. As for the remaining corridor counties in Alabama, five others reported annual decreases, but only of 1 percent to 5 percent, or $67 to $353 per person per year. Income rates for thirteen counties rose, from slightly more than 8 percent in Choctaw County, in the southwestern part of the state, to 4.7 percent in Baldwin County, on the Gulf of Mexico. Neither of these increases, however, can be attributed to the Tenn-Tom, as waterway-related activities were not the basis for the increases. Rather, service and retail sectors expanded to meet population growth.

Conclusion

Construction of the Tennessee-Tombigbee Waterway rearranged the topography of northeastern Mississippi; disrupted the lives of thousands of people for fifteen years; was the focus of fierce, though legislatively and judicially contained, enmity; cost southern legislators nearly all their political chits just to keep it funded; and raised the expectations during the 1960s and 1970s of nearly 2.5 million people in four states that its completion would bring affluence to their isolated and impoverished lives. The Tennessee-Tombigbee Waterway is a good example of how water—or the control of water—can be a political tool. In this case, the joining of the Tennessee and Tombigbee Rivers was the tool of the politically powerful. And it became a promise to the politically marginal—a promise that millions of dollars in federal moneys would be spent in their communities and counties to buy their goods and services and to provide their labor force with well-paying jobs. Economic and social benefits were promised for all. Moreover, the economic development resulting from this federal spending was to give the region the boost it needed for long-term prosperity. Hence, the expectations of the residents living along the waterway were high during the planning, design, and construction of the project—and, as indicated on the foregoing pages, those expectations were not met. What was held out as a promise of social justice became, as historian Jeffrey Stine claims, a "cruel hoax" (1993; 176).

Did the project warrant such expenditures? Select southern governors, county commissioners, and landowners, as well as minimal majorities in Congress, thought so. Is the nation as a whole the better for its construction? Probably not. Compared with the $75 billion corporate welfare burden estimated by the Cato Institute (1996), the nearly $2 billion spent between 1972 and 1985 for both the Tennessee-Tombigbee Waterway and its companion corridor study was a small drop in a large bucket.

At annual Waterway Development Conferences held in late summer every year, speakers from both state governments and private sector companies express their active endorsement of any additional revenue-producing and employment activities along the Tenn-Tom. The current claim is the creation of 42,000 new jobs and annual payrolls totaling some $1.1 billion (Eastman 1996, 8). Indeed, from 1983 to the present, the generation of any new jobs or increases in local income has been attributed to the waterway. This is boosterism—x number of jobs and millions or billions of dollars in salaries, all attributable to one phenomenon. Such claims can be easily inflated and just as easily refuted. Let us focus instead on the ethnographic context of public–private investments. What standards for business investment should exist in regions where the impetus of that investment is the infusion of public moneys? In formulating such standards for investments, let us look beyond the number of projected jobs and ask instead: What kinds of jobs are these? What will be the salary levels, and what skills will be needed? "Coordinating" the french-frying of potatoes at a fast-food franchise is qualitatively and quantitatively different from smelting pig iron at a new steel-manufacturing plant. Will the companies train their respective workforces? Will there be opportunities for promotion or for advancement within job categories? Will day care be provided? What about family leave for parents? Are the security, growth potential, and stability of the new businesses high? How committed are these new businesses to supporting their local communities and to cooperating with local interests beyond the chamber of commerce, city hall, and the state development office? Furthermore, how much of the profits earned and supplies and services purchased stays in the region? Business behavior based on positive responses to these standards would benefit a large number of individuals and lead to basic cultural change in social interaction, in major institutions such as education, and in political participation. Then, the confluence of water, culture, and power would be an achievement.

Food for Thought

A more detailed analysis of the environmental politics involved in planning and building the Tennessee-Tombigbee Waterway can be found in Jeffrey Stine's *Mixing the Waters: Environment, Politics, and the Building of the Tennessee-Tombigbee Waterway* (1993). Stine has done a thorough job of researching documents and interviewing the myriad individuals in the organizations and agencies involved in the controversial water project. He chronicles clearly and concisely the complexities that make the Tenn-Tom a milestone in political, judicial, and engineering circles. Marc Reisner takes a national view of water, culture, and power in his *Cadillac Desert: The American West and Its Disappearing Water* (1986). His documentation is exhaustive, his insight is impressive, and his evaluation of the settlement of western states *and* the role of federal water projects in that settlement is both satirical and intriguing.

For insight into the role of government funding in hydropower development, *Rivers at Risk* (1989) primer is a good place to start.

Subtitled *The Concerned Citizen's Guide to Hydropower*, it is a publication of American Rivers, Inc., a nonprofit conservation organization founded in 1973 to preserve rivers and their associated landscapes
in the United States. The guide lives up to its name; it is a how-to
book about dealing with the Federal Energy Regulatory Commission,
delineating the procedures and regulations involved in assessing new
projects and deciding whether to relicense existing ones.

Among the journals that regularly treat the subjects of applied
research and findings are the anthropological standards *Human Organization*, published by the Society for Applied Anthropology, and
Practicing Anthropology, issued by the American Anthropological
Association. *Impact Assessment*, the journal of the International
Association of Impact Assessment, contains articles by practicing professionals from throughout the world who make their living, or much
of it, from evaluating the potential effects on people and/or places of
proposed water projects and other massive construction activities.

On a cross-cultural note, the book *Anthropological Praxis*, edited by
Shirley J. Fiske and Robert M. Wulff, is useful. Of particular interest is
the description of how residents on a Paiute reservation near the Grand
Canyon in Arizona became active participants in a water-related development project. The author of this chapter, Allen C. Turner, used
anthropological methods to restore a lost cultural practice to the tribe
and at the same time ensure that federal assistance—in this case from
the U.S. Department of Housing and Urban Development—brought
about physical improvements that benefited the local Paiute. A
broader look at the value of anthropology in evaluating the potential
effects of any large developmental effort can be found in Kevin
Preister's chapter on issue-centered social impact assessment. It is a
good example of how an anthropological focus can shift the emphasis
of impact assessment from mere compliance with federal law to the insightful resolution of controversies.

The question of how to recognize and resolve issues of power and allocation of water and other resources in the public domain is also addressed in the growing literature on sustainable development. One
might begin with the report of the President's Council on Sustainable
Development (1996) titled *Sustainable America: A New Consensus*
and then search the World Wide Web, beginning with the U.S. Department of Energy's home page (http://www.doe.gov/), for additional reports from federal agencies and from communities across the United
States on local efforts to define and solve problems cooperatively. Paul
Hawken's treatise *The Ecology of Commerce: A Declaration of Sustainability* (1993) is an attempt to lure business and industry away

from the "us-versus-them" mind-set that characterizes so much of the debate about water allocations, land use, and the ownership of forests and timber holdings. Hawken's book leads the reader to further discussions of power, people, and culture.

ACKNOWLEDGMENTS

While writing this chapter, I was employed by the Mobile District of the U.S. Army Corps of Engineers. I owe special thanks to all my fellow employees for their ready assistance in finding and providing obscure references to the construction of the Tennessee-Tombigbee Waterway; the conduct and products of the Corridor Study; and the results, ten years later, of these two efforts at an engineered control of the physical and social environment.

C H A P T E R   8

Transacting a Commons
The Lake Biwa Comprehensive Development Plan, Shiga Prefecture, Japan

James E. Nickum and Daniel Greenstadt

Author Summary

The history of Lake Biwa, Japan's largest lake, illustrates many of the collective choice problems that arise from the lack of clear property rights, or more broadly, the difficulty of adjusting human institutions such as property rights to the needs of a large and complex ecosystem such as a lake and its watershed. The recently completed Lake Biwa Comprehensive Development Plan (1972–1997) accentuated the problem by operating within a project-oriented bureaucratic culture. After a brief historical review, this chapter discusses the complex power relationships between the different bureaucratic actors as reflected in the development plan and in the project plans that preceded it.

Introduction

The Lake Biwa Comprehensive Development Plan, in effect from 1972 to 1997, governed the rights of downstream users in Osaka to additional waters from Lake Biwa, Japan's largest lake, and the right to compensation of Shiga Prefecture, where Lake Biwa is located. The plan reflected negotiations of power among bureaucratic agents, none of whom had full control over the quantity or quality of the resource. This chapter explores some critical contested terrains, both historically and over the quarter-century life of the plan. These include competing and shifting constructions of national and local development interests, of rights to water and to compensation, of whether and how

141

to divide the lake by use of engineering projects to satisfy different sectoral interests, and of the responsibility for arresting deterioration in lake water quality. The situation is complicated by the absence of clearly negotiable and transferable rights, leading the protagonists to resort to constructs such as development and cultural restoration to bolster their negotiating positions.

Lake Biwa is by far the largest lake in Japan, covering an area of 673.8 square kilometers (260 square miles); it is a bit smaller than San Francisco Bay but much deeper, reaching a maximum depth of 104 meters (341 feet), roughly the length of an American football field or an international soccer field (see figure 8.1). The lake is divided into two distinct subunits, each itself called a lake, joined and separated by a narrows that is 1.35 kilometers (0.8 mile) wide. The deep Northern Lake, with a surface area of 616 square kilometers, or 238 square miles, has by far most of the water, which is relatively clean and circulates in three separate complex patterns, creating a variety of ecosystems. The narrow Southern Lake has less than one-tenth the surface area of the Northern Lake and is much shallower. Nowhere is it more than 10 meters (33 feet) deep, yet its shores harbor the greatest concentration of people and industries in the area, particularly in the prefectural capital of Otsu (population 270,000). The Southern Lake is in effect the upper drain for all of Lake Biwa into the only outlet, the Seta River. The Seta flows from the outskirts of Otsu, changes its name to the Uji River at the Kyoto border, and eventually provides nearly two-thirds of the water for the Yodo River, which flows through Osaka (see figure 8.2).

Lake Biwa is insignificant in size compared with the largest lakes of continental countries such as the United States and Canada, which share Lake Superior, with an area of 82,360 square kilometers (31,799 square miles) and a maximum depth of 406 meters (1,332 feet). Yet its location in the center of Japan imbues it with an economic, historical, and symbolic significance that far exceeds that of its counterparts in other countries. Separated by a thin ridge of mountains from the ancient capital of Kyoto and located upstream from the country's second largest conurbation, with more than 10 million inhabitants, Lake Biwa's leading status in Japan is more than just an interesting statistic.

The very name of the lake, taken from that of a classical musical instrument (a four- or five-stringed lute, called a *pipa* in Chinese) that its shape resembles, resonates with culture and history. It evokes the complex harmonies that no doubt ran through the mind of the legendary Prince Genji as he, or the historical royalty he was modeled after, sat high on the hills a millennium ago, the evening sun at his

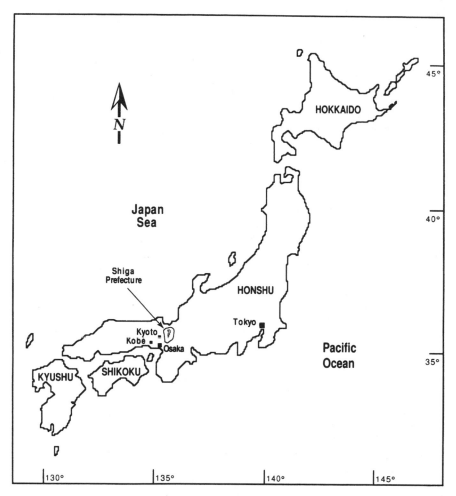

FIGURE 8.1. JAPAN AND LAKE BIWA

Lake Biwa is by far the largest lake in Japan, covering an area of 673.8 square kilometers (260 square miles); it is a bit smaller than San Francisco Bay but much deeper, reaching a maximum depth of 104 meters (341 feet). Its location in the center of Japan imbues it with an economic, historical, and symbolic significance that far exceeds that of its counterparts in other countries. Map courtesy Daniel Greenstadt.

back casting an orange glow on the lake as it stretched into the mists and mountains on the northern horizon.

Throughout Japan's history, Lake Biwa's watershed has tended to correspond nearly exactly with a single region, once called the land of Omi. In 1871–1872 the newly established Meiji government formed Shiga Prefecture out of the multiplicity of Omi's feudal domains,

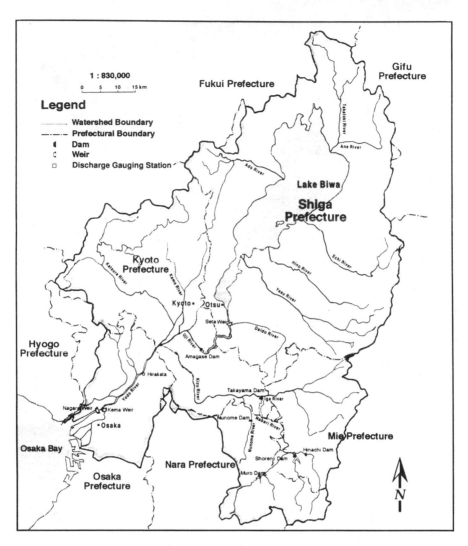

FIGURE 8.2. THE YODO RIVER BASIN

Lake Biwa is actually two lakes, joined and separated by a narrows that is 1.35 kilometers (0.8 mile) wide. The deep Northern Lake, with a surface area of 616 square kilometers (238 square miles), has by far the most water. The narrow Southern Lake has less than one-tenth the surface area of the Northern Lake and is much shallower. Nowhere is it more than 10 meters (33 feet) deep, yet its shores harbor the greatest concentration of people and industries in the area, particularly in the prefectural capital of Otsu (population 270,000). The Southern Lake is in effect the upper drainpipe for all of Lake Biwa, feeding into the only outlet, the Seta River. The Seta flows from the outskirts of Otsu, changes its name to the Uji River at the Kyoto border, and eventually provides nearly two-thirds of the water for the Yodo River, which flows through Osaka. Map courtesy Daniel Greenstadt.

called *han*, that had made both central control and collective action difficult to implement.

History

Lake Biwa is steeped in historical tradition. Azuchi, the first of the great stone castles that followed the introduction of the gun into Japanese warfare, was built overlooking the eastern shore of the lake by the great warlord Oda Nobunaga in the 1570s. At that time, and for most of history, the principal role of Lake Biwa and its surrounding littoral plain was as a gateway to and from the capital region. Many of Japan's most famous battles were fought in this region. In more peaceful times, travelers came both by land from the eastern realms, which are now the urban corridor stretching from Nagoya to Tokyo, and by water and land from the regions lying north of Lake Biwa along the Sea of Japan.

As often happens at crossroads and entry points, a thriving merchant class developed in Omi that sold products such as mosquito nets, jute yarn, herbal medicines, and kimonos throughout Japan. These merchants were rewarded for their business acumen, and their peripheral status vis-à-vis the established merchant classes of Osaka and Tokyo, by being branded in popular parlance as "Omi bandits" (Okura 1990, 11).

Nonetheless, until very recent times, Shiga Prefecture remained a lightly populated backwater. Historically, virtually all uses of the water of the lake by residents were instream, primarily for fisheries and secondarily for transporation. Water for the fields and for domestic uses came from inflowing streams, ponds, and aquifers. Until the present century, the main water concern of shoreline residents was that there was sometimes too much of it. The narrow, shallow, gently sloped Seta River discharged a maximum flow of only 50 cubic meters per second (cms) (13,000 gallons per second (gps)), far from enough to drain away floodwaters quickly (a cubic meter is 264 gallons). Hence, when the floods came, Lake Biwa would turn into a detention basin, its littorals, remaining soaked for long periods of time, making shoreline agriculture a very risky business.

Repeated requests from Biwa's farmers to the shogun's government during the Tokugawa Period (1603–1867) to dredge the Seta River yielded limited results. Besides the technical difficulty of enlarging the river's capacity in any lasting way, the security-obsessed shogunate was reluctant to allow dredging near an adjacent secret military crossing. In addition, problems of burden sharing led to conflicts among villages around Lake Biwa, and the more populous downstream areas fought to keep the excess floodwaters from winding up in *their* fields, shops, and courtyards (Kada and Furukawa, 1984, 31–32). At this time, local autonomy was very strong, both at the village level and in the dozens of feudal domains (*han*), making upstream-downstream co-operation extremely difficult. The concept of one's belonging to a "place" *(ba)* that is in rivalry with other "places" has persisted in the corporate and bureaucratic cultures of twentieth-century Japan.

With the Meiji Restoration in 1868 came a number of political, economic, and conceptual shifts, both nationally and regionally. Japan was seen as a unified nation that needed to strengthen itself to avoid being consumed by the imperialism and colonialization that had begun to sweep over the rest of Asia. To get a strong army, the Meiji leaders recognized that it was necessary to create a "rich country." This in turn set the ideological backdrop for appropriating the resources of some areas, usually rural, to support the economic development of urban-industrial others, now identified with the development and survival of the nation as a whole. In the case of Lake Biwa, this appropriation was played out under the rhetorical cloak of developing water resources. At the same time, appropriation was not entirely expropriation, as Shiga Prefecture's de facto right to compensation has been established and acknowledged early on.

With the relocation of the nation's capital to Tokyo following the Meiji Restoration, Kyoto turned to industrialization in order to maintain its viability. For this it needed water and power, both of which it was able to obtain through two diversions from Lake Biwa (8.35 cms, from 1890, and 15.30 cms, from 1912). Beginning in 1914, the city of Kyoto paid Shiga Prefecture a "power generation water use fee," setting a precedent for compensation between downstream administrations and Shiga. From 1938 to 1946, this monetary transfer was referred to as a "donation" rather than a fee, and since then it has been termed "gratitude money."

The level of financial gratuity is adjusted periodically and was given legal form in 1976 by a contract between Kyoto and Shiga. The latest agreement, in the form of an official memorandum, was made in 1995, providing an annual payment of ¥220 million (U.S.$20 million) for a period of ten years (*Kyoto Shimbun*, 19 March 1996). Shiga uses this money for projects related to the transfer of water, such as watershed protection through tree planting and other forms of erosion control.

No doubt one reason for the change in terminology for this financial transfer is that the River Law of 1896, amended in 1964, declares the water in rivers to be public property. According to the amended law, water use rights are allocated on behalf of the public by the river administrator. Under the old River Law, the builder of a structure such as a dam or weir was responsible for allocating use rights. Water use rights in Japan are a very complex blend of tradition, regulation, and pragmatic adjustments. In general, they tend to be grandfathered—pre-existing rights, usually agricultural, are not taken away unless they are no longer used. Transfers are allowed but only within the same use category (e.g., agriculture, industry, municipal) and only with the approval of the administrator (Nakashima 1993, 55–57).

Thus, in terms of existing rights, the role of administrator involves the not-too-enviable duties of registration, adjudication, and occasional crisis management. The payoff comes in the control of new rights. Since agriculture already claims virtually all the base flow of Japan's rivers, new rights usually come from creating new storage facilities through structures such as dams and weirs. Once downstream interest groups began to see Lake Biwa as a reservoir rather than a flood hazard, contention began over control of the amount and allocation of a huge infusion of new water use rights.

For the most important rivers (Class A), the administrator is the minister of construction, who also designates which rivers are Class A. The Seta River is a Class A river and falls under Ministry of Construction (MOC) jurisdiction, but Lake Biwa is under the jurisdiction of Shiga Prefecture even though the minister of construction has designated it a Class A river. The predominant view in Shiga is that "water belongs to the state, but Lake Biwa belongs to Shiga" (*Kyoto Shimbun*, 12 March 1996). The MOC tends to view the lake as part of one river basin that should have a single administrator.

Shiga has perceived itself as under seige from the MOC as the latter has tried to extend its direct management powers over the lake itself on numerous occasions over the past fifty years. As we shall see, the tension created by this jurisdictional separation has underlain relationships between Shiga on the one hand and the MOC, downstream governments, and the central government on the other.

From Flood Control Structure to Water Source

With the exception of the diversions to Kyoto, development of Lake Biwa's water resources initially involved making use of the water downstream to generate hydroelectric power, largely an instream use. But with the construction of a control weir near the head of the Seta

River in 1905 (renovated in 1961) and the enlargement of the river's discharge capacity from 50 cms to 200 cms (53,000 gps) in 1908, to 400 cms (110,000 gps) in 1953, to 600 cms (160,000 gps) in 1967, and to 800 cms (210,000 gps) in 1987, it became possible to consider using Lake Biwa as a giant water source.

As early as 1940, a plan was initiated to tap the lake's water for downstream transportation, irrigation, tap water, and industrial use, and additional water rights were allocated for these purposes. Moreover, in the economic reconstruction that followed World War II, the lake's power generation potential was nearly fully "developed." People migrated from upstream areas such as Shiga to the coastal urban complexes such as Osaka-Kobe-Kyoto that were the centers of industrialization and economic growth. The population growth, increased production, and higher incomes that accompanied double-digit economic growth in the lower reaches also produced double-digit increases in the demand for water and other resources.

Hence, downstream users could argue that transferring water from a lagging region to a leading one was of benefit to the economy and therefore to the nation as a whole. Shiga countered that its chances to participate in the development process should not be hindered by a transfer it regarded as inevitable—hence, "comprehensive development" of the lake was necessary, benefiting upstream as well as downstream areas. The stylized exchange between the downstream and upstream administrations, as told by Shiga, went as follows:

> *Downstream:* Lake Biwa has more than enough water. Why not let a little more of it flow down to us in the lower reaches?
>
> *Shiga:* Lake Biwa is more than just a reservoir for the lower reaches. Many people live around the lake whose lives are deeply connected to its water. So when you talk about using Lake Biwa's water you also have to consider the impacts of lowering the water and the livelihoods of the people along its shores. That in itself is a constraint. But also, the development of Lake Biwa means more than simply supplying more water to downstream. It has to include some projects that are useful to the residents around its shores. (Shiga Ken 1983, 36)

Dividing the Lake

As Japan's economy barreled along in the 1960s, a number of grandiose plans were proposed to build structures within the lake to tap its water. These proposals reflected different attempts to divide the lake commons in ways that would allow the inevitable transfer downstream while protecting or enhancing different interests in Shiga. Since none of them was adopted, they are usually relegated in the telling to the status of interesting historical asides. They are worth considering here, however, because they highlight in physical form the negotiation of power among different interest groups in the Lake Biwa–Yodo River area.

The Cutoff Plan

The first plan, proposed in 1960 by a group composed of downstream interests and the MOC, was the Katata-Moriyama Cutoff (*shimekiri*) Plan, which proposed building a dam across the lake at the narrows.[1] This dam would have allowed as much as 3 m of water to be pumped from the water-abundant Northern Lake without altering the level of the Southern Lake. Hence, the developmental node of Shiga around Otsu would in effect be incorporated into the downstream.

The idea of dividing the lake into its two components was anathema to Shiga. The desire to maintain the integrity of the lake was no doubt reinforced by the reluctance of the 70 percent of the prefecture's population, including voters, who lived around the Northern Lake to bear the costs of modernization for Otsu and Osaka. The population around the Northern Lake was 600,000 in 1972, compared with 240,000 around the Southern Lake. Since that time, both parts of Shiga have grown; the population of the Northern Lake area is still dominant, at roughly 800,000, compared with 400,000 for the Southern Lake area (Shiga Ken 1996, 34). An additional factor was that allowing the MOC to build a structure in the lake would have given it the right to allocate the water going over it, in effect eliminating the prefectural government's custodial rights over the waters of the Southern Lake. Moreover, the River Law was in the process of being revived at this time, and the MOC was seeking to extend its control over entire basins.

The Pipeline Plan

The prefectural government countered the MOC's plan with a plan to build a pipeline from the interior of the Northern Lake directly to the lower reaches. A pipeline would have given the prefecture a stronger argument for retaining its prerogatives (Sanbongi 1988, 74). Although it would have had some effect on the shorelines of the Southern Lake, the pipeline would have kept the lakes connected and thereby maintained the symbolic as well as political integrity of Shiga. The pipeline project also involved a much more modest transfer of water (20 cms) than did the cutoff plan, and it would have been cleaner.[2] It also would have set an upper bound on future extractions, something that was not guaranteed by the Cutoff Plan.

Another, somewhat more subtle, point is that the pipeline would have measured the volume of transfer at the site of its withdrawal in Shiga Prefecture. Later MOC proposals involved measuring volume downstream at Hirakata, after the other tributaries had flown into the Yodo River. This would have allowed the MOC to withdraw additional water from Lake Biwa if the flow from other tributaries declined due to upstream development.

The Submerged Dam Plan

The MOC's response to the Pipeline Plan was to alter the design of the cutoff dam so that its top would be 1.4 meters (4.6 feet) below the surface. This would have kept the lakes joined and allowed the shorelines of the Southern Lake to share some of the pain of withdrawal with those of the Northern Lake. At the same time, the 3-meter (9.8-foot) drawdown of the Northern Lake was not modified. In effect, then, the Submerged Dam Plan involved an additional 1.4-meter (4.6 ft.) drawdown from the Southern Lake. Downstream water allocations would have increased by 48 cms (12,700 gps). To ease the discomfort, the MOC offered, as a side payment to Shiga, to build some development projects such as roads, river control structures, and lakeshore works.

Doughnut Plans

The most intriguing yet fanciful proposal was made by the Ministry of Agriculture. Its Doughnut Plan entailed constructing an embankment at a depth of 5 meters (16.4 feet) almost all the way around the inside of the lake, with a road on top of it and twenty-one bridges connecting it to the shore. This plan would have divided Biwa into an outer (shoreline) lake with a stable water level and an inner lake that would have provided water to the downstream area and served as a drain for floodwaters from onshore. Although the doughnut in the lake was not quite pie in the sky, it did not provoke much enthusiasm from those who looked at the price tag (¥70 billion or U.S.$200 million, in 1960s prices) or the focus on agricultural protection to the neglect of development-oriented compensation works. A second, more modest Doughnut Plan that would have allowed all the transfer water to be taken from the middle of the Southern Lake sank like soggy pastry.

In sum, these various plans represented a clash of bureaucratic interests and cultures that to some extent reflected their different clienteles. The MOC is divided into regional bureaus and claims the right to manage river systems in their entireties. Hence, at the time, it was a natural ally of the downstream users, who sought to have Lake Biwa "managed" to benefit their own economic growth sectors. At the same time, the principal business of the MOC is the construction of public works, linking it into a "concrete triangle" in which the ministry, general contractors with nationwide operations, and the ruling Liberal Democratic Party (LDP) support one another in building projects and political careers (Woodall 1996). Hence, the MOC was more than willing to offer "compensation" to Shiga Prefecture—in the form of development projects (see photo 8.1).

The Ministry of Agriculture represents primary producers: farmers, fishers, and foresters. These occupations also form a power base for the LDP, in exchange for which they too have been protected from international competition and heavily subsidized with price supports and projects. Unlike the construction sector, however, agriculture is much more territorially based, and it appropriates the rhetoric of cultural preservation and food security to protect its privileged position. The message communicated by the Doughnut Plans, which had little hope of being adopted, was that the interests of the farmers and fishers should be protected at all costs.

The position of Shiga Prefecture was much more complex, and conflicted. In protecting the perceived interests of its existing population (and electorate), it needed to maintain its claim over the MOC to be custodian of the waters of the lake without being antidevelopment. Indeed, the Shiga government itself has been very prodevelopment and project oriented and was particularly so in the early 1970s. At that time, the maintenance of water quality, especially in ways that required stepping outside the project culture, was not a primary concern to the prefectural government, although the issue was raised by the press.

The Lake Biwa Comprehensive Development Plan

The idea of dividing the lake by means of grandiose projects ended when the Ministry of Construction withdrew its Submerged Dam Plan in July 1968. New water releases were to be carried out through changes in the operation of the Seta River weir, which was operated by the MOC and lay clearly within its undisputed management domain. Yet pressures on the water supply caused by rapid economic growth continued to build, and the contested terrain shifted to such questions

PHOTO 8.1. DEVELOPMENT ALONG THE OTSU SHORE
OF LAKE BIWA

Development is greatest along the southern Otsu shore of Lake Biwa. In this photograph, the former Lake Biwa Aquarium is seen in the foreground, and a new opera house, under construction, is visible in the background. Photo courtesy of James E. Nickum.

as how much water was to be withdrawn, what the nature of compensation works would be, and who would pay for them. The MOC proposed that a maximum drawdown of lake water be set at 2 meters (6.6 feet) below the standardized normal level and that water rights be established to an additional 40 cms (11,000 gps), not at the Seta River weir but at the downstream station of Hirakata. Shiga Prefecture held out for a maximum drawdown to –1.5 meters (4.9 feet).

A group was formed within the policy-making group of the ruling Liberal Democratic Party dedicated to brokering the "comprehensive development of Lake Biwa." Finally, in March 1972, the ministers of construction and of other relevant ministries, together with the governors of Osaka, Hyogo, and Shiga, signed an agreement providing for the 40-cms increment in water rights sought by the MOC but setting a maximum "utilization" drawdown of 1.5 meters. On the surface, this agreement met Shiga's demands but with a crucial and nearly nullifying proviso: in cases of severe drought, the minister of construction was empowered to reduce the drawdown further, to a "compensation level" of up to 2 meters.

The Diet, Japan's parliament, quickly passed the 1972 Special Measures Act to enable the Lake Biwa Comprehensive Development Plan (LBCDP), which was to run for ten years. Befitting the largely urban-based antipollution mood then sweeping the country, the Diet added a proviso that one objective of the plan was to ensure the quality of the lake's water. For the most part, however, the LBCDP was drawn up by the concerned parties with development and compensation, rather than environmental conservation, in mind. The LBCDP provided for a large number of projects under the broad categories of conservation, flood control, and water utilization. About one-sixth of the total cost was devoted to projects to deliver water downstream.

The 1972 Diet act called for three "special financing measures" to supplement the normal levels of funding available to Shiga Prefecture for such public works. One was an increase in the subsidies to Shiga from the national government, both by making minor adjustments in the cost-sharing ratios and by having the MOC or its parastatal affiliate, the Water Resources Development Public Corporation, take on the bulk of major development projects. The other two measures were more pathbreaking, involving the provision to Shiga of direct financing and low-interest loans by the downstream beneficiaries, in particular Osaka Prefecture (50 percent) and the city of Osaka (23 percent) (Shiga Ken 1983, 184–185). Although a precedent had been set with the Kyoto diversions, it was extremely unusual for one prefecture to provide funds for construction projects in another's territory.

It is worth noting that the amount involved was only a small percentage of the total project cost or of Shiga's obligations. Using cost-sharing ratios fixed by law, the central government would have paid 48.4 percent of the 1972–1992 costs (totaling ¥1,524.9 billion); Shiga, 39.3 percent; the lower reaches, 9.6 percent; and "other" sources, 2.7 percent. The special financing measures changed these to 49.9 percent, 34.0 percent, 13.4 percent, and 2.7 percent, respectively. Hence, the net subsidy to Shiga was ¥81.4 billion, 5.3 percent of total costs or 13.6 percent of the prefecture's share. More than two-thirds of this transfer came from the downstream prefectures (Shiga Ken 1983, 178–179).

Thus, in the end, Shiga was able to win commitments to compensatory projects and downstream users could look forward to having their projected water shortages alleviated. An equally important result of the LBCDP was that it fixed the rules governing the lake's development over the following decade, together with firming up the roles and bargaining positions of upstream and downstream interests and central government. The irony is that once the institutions were in place, the world changed.

Phase One: 1972–1982
The two worldwide oil shocks of 1973–1974 and 1978–1979 brought an abrupt end to nearly two decades of rapid economic growth in Japan. The resulting slowdown in provision of public investment funds was a major reason why only about 40 percent of the project's original goals had been completed by the end of the first phase of the LBCDP in 1982. At the same time, the projected increase in downstream water demand failed to materialize.

Instead, overall water consumption declined as municipal (including domestic) uses stabilized and industrial withdrawals fell to nearly half their 1972 level. With escalating energy costs and tightened water emission controls, also imposed in the early 1970s, factories became more careful about resource use in general and increased their reuse rates of water in particular. Even MOC planners were forecasting that it might never be necessary to draw the full 40-cms allotment through the Seta weir.

A citizens' lawsuit filed in 1976 sought to halt many of the LBCDP's projects, notably a centralized sewage treatment plant on an artificial island within the lake, as well as projects to increase control over the flow to downstream areas. The grounds for the complaint were that much of the plan addressed one problem that no longer existed, downstream water demand, to the neglect of one that was very much present, water quality.

WATER QUALITY
There is an apocryphal Chinese curse, "May you get what you want." Shiga got its economic development. Even at the time the LBCDP was initiated, Shiga was already in the midst of an economic boom because of its incorporation into the suburban periphery of the Keihanshin (Kyoto-Osaka-Kobe) metropolis. The consequent haphazard influx of people and industries, especially into the southeastern part of the prefecture, together with an intensification of rice production practices, increased the burden of pollutants flowing into the lake (Nakamura 1995, 17–18). The additional infrastructure provided under the plan, such as a "management road," served only to accelerate these tendencies.

Even in the decade before the LBCDP, there were some warning signs that the ecology of the lake was being disturbed. In particular, tap water occasionally began to emit a musty odor that has since become associated with Lake Biwa water. In the 1970s, the Southern Lake began to exhibit more visible signs of eutrophication, the excessive nutrient load that comes from high concentrations of phosphorus in combination with nitrogen and often leads to outbreaks of sometimes rather noxious aquatic plant growth. In particular, a freshwater red tide of a flagellate plankton (*Uroglena americana*) has appeared almost annually from 1977 onward, killing fish, fouling tap water, and imparting to the Southern Lake a most unappetizing fragrance.

When the red tide first appeared, an extremely vocal and well-organized citizen movement launched a campaign to clean up the water, focusing on reducing household use of synthetic detergents containing phosphorus. Shortly thereafter, in 1979, the prefectural government passed the Ordinance for the Prevention of Eutrophication of Lake Biwa, which banned the sale and use of laundry products containing phosphorus. The ordinance also addressed industrial, agricultural, and livestock-breeding sources of pollution by regulating the treatment of wastewater containing phosphorus and other offending chemicals. This was the first legislation in Japan on lake water quality, and it provided the impetus for the Diet's enacting a nationwide act on the subject in 1984.

Unlike other legislative arenas in Japan, environmental protection has historically tended to be an area in which local governments are more likely than the national government to initiate new regulations. It is also one of the few areas in which they have the authority to innovate, provided them by the Diet in the Revised Basic Law for Pollution Control Measures of 1970. The prefectural government went on in 1980 to enact the New Lake Biwa Environmental Preservation Measures Act. This legislation called for more scientific research, the incorporation of environmental education into the public school curriculum, and the inclusion of water-quality conservation as an item in the prefectural budget.

The success of all these efforts depends on how one looks at it. Levels of phosphorus and, to a lesser degree, nitrogen in the Southern Lake did fall quickly from the peak levels they had reached in the late 1970s. Nonetheless, concentrations of three of the key water quality indicators—total phosphorus (T-P), total nitrogen (T-N), and chemical oxygen demand (COD)—have remained more or less constant in both lakes since the early 1980s. Only phosphorus in the Northern Lake has remained at or near the admittedly strict environmental standard set by Shiga Prefecture. T-N and COD have remained well above the standard in both lakes, although higher in the Southern Lake, and T-P in the

Southern Lake has been more than double that in the Northern Lake (Shiga Ken 1996, 33).

Water quality in the lake has remained consistently poor. The duration of the red tide has declined from seventeen or eighteen days per year to less than a week, but another abnormal plankton growth, the bluish *aoko*, or "water bloom" (*Anabaena* sp. with *Microcystis* sp.), has increased in severity in recent years; in 1994, it even invaded the Northern Lake. Given that the population and economy of Shiga have continued to grow, however, it may be considered a measure of modest success that the water has not become markedly worse.

Phases Two and Three: 1982–1997
As noted, in 1982 the LBCDP was far from complete. More than half the construction work set out a decade earlier remained to be done. Even the resource development projects aimed at allowing the release of an additional 40 cms were far from complete, although by and large they were further along than were the projects intended to benefit lake area residents. With this in mind, and with the deteroriating quality of the lake water continuing to attract intense public concern, the Shiga prefectural government requested that the downstream and national governments extend the term of the plan, including all special financial measures, for another ten years. Shiga also asked that four new, but relatively small, project categories—livestock waste management, rural wastewater treatment, refuse disposal, and water quality monitoring—be added to protect water quality. All parties agreed, and a revised agreement was approved by the Diet in March 1982.

Although the Shiga prefectural government was responsive to citizen pressure to act against eutrophication, in particular through the banning of synthetic detergents, it was more resistant to the court case to stop some of the key projects on environmental grounds. Like most such cases, the litigation dragged on for more than a decade, with the number of plaintiffs falling from 1,000 to fewer than 10 because of costs and discouragement. Nonetheless, while it was in play, the litigation did cast a cloud over the plan. By the time the Otsu District Court held against the plaintiffs in 1989, however, citizen activism had died down and the builders could proceed without concern about an unpredictable court decision.

By 1992, the completion rate for LBCDP projects had neared 90 percent and the downstream prefectures had become more insistent that Shiga allow the release of the full additional water allocation. Shiga, however, was able to make a case for extending the special financial arrangement for an additional five years, on the ground that it would not have the funding to complete the remaining 10 percent on its own. It was implied that those projects would otherwise be abandoned. In return, an allocation of 27 cms, which downstream users had already been drawing from the Yodo River since 1972 with MOC approval, was officially assigned to those users as water rights.

Preparing for Post-LBCDP

With the final five-year reprieve, Shiga Prefecture began looking ahead to life after the plan. In summing up the results of the past quarter century, all could agree that the projects had succeeded marvelously in "water resource development" for downstream users, either in times of emergency or in the case that overall water use demands were to grow again, and in "water control" to protect Shiga's shoreline. Regrettably, most could also agree that water quality was, if anything, degraded by those very same projects.

The record 1994 summer drought tested the water delivery system as the lake, already low because of reduced inflows, was drawn down to a record 1.23 meters (4 feet), still quite a bit less than the 2 meters permitted by the LBCDP. A simulation exercise released in July 1996 by the Shiga prefectural government estimated that downstream Osaka had thereby been spared an economic loss of ¥200 billion, and Hyogo Prefecture (where Kobe is) had been spared ¥50 billion, a total of a bit more than U.S.$2 billion (*Chunichi Shimbun Nagoya*, 10 July 1996).

From the standpoint of the downstream administrators, this probably indicated a reasonable return on their twenty-five-year contributions. However, whether the project as a whole would stand up to a rigorous financial cost-benefit test, including the money spent by Shiga and the national government, is another matter altogether.

Still, there were benefits to Shiga as well. In May 1995, the water level went the other way, reaching a peak of +0.93 meter. Yet the area of rice fields that were flooded, 742 hectares (1,833.5 acres), was less than one-fourth of the 3,377 hectares (8,345 acres) that had been swamped by a similar flood in July 1972. Even more dramatic was the drop in the number of dwellings affected, from 755 to only 7 (Shiga Ken 1996, 29).

Blessings have been more mixed in other areas. The stagnation and probable deterioration in water quality have already been noted. Fish catches have plummeted. Reed beds, useful for purifying the lake's water and providing habitat for fish and fowl, have fallen victim to shoreline construction. The sewage system remains underdeveloped.

And the lake is increasingly being tapped as a water source by Shiga residents themselves.

The Shiga prefectural government believed that it had to pull out all stops to protect its interests once the LBCDP expired in early 1997. In particular, it lobbied the national government either to extend the part of the Special Measures Act that applied to water quality or to establish a new law that would both continue the subsidy for costly projects such as sewerage and recognize the decision-making rights of the prefecture, especially vis-à-vis the MOC. Such a law would also provide Shiga with a firmer legal foundation for issuing regulations.

Shiga Prefecture began a publicity campaign in the newspapers and on television in fall 1995 to "save the lake," hoping to use the force of public opinion, as one observer put it, "to fill in the outer moat of the state," with its well-entrenched ministerial interests (*Kyoto Shimbun*, 12 March 1996). It prepared beautiful posters showing the fish and fowl of the lake, accompanied by text that stressed that the clean waters of the lake are a legacy of coexistence between people and nature that comes from past generations and that should be passed on to the future. Using the ancient name for the region, written with the Chinese characters for "freshwater sea," the posters called for the creation of a "New Omi Culture."

The government responded coolly to Shiga's overtures, arguing that it did not want to single out Lake Biwa for special treatment when there were so many deserving places and that the MOC and other ministries already had plans and laws governing water quality protection. Shiga continued to press. Arguing that cleaning up the lake's water would benefit as many as 14 million people in the region that makes use of it, it was able, after intense negotiation, to get the governors of downstream Osaka Prefecture, Kyoto, and Hyogo to join it in signing a letter to the national government requesting that the requisite legislation be passed and additional project funds be provided. The coalition unraveled quickly, however, when the state remained adamant in its position. An attempt by Shiga to activate a water-quality protection fund with contributions from downstream jurisdictions, which was provided for in the earliest LBCDP but never put into practice, struggled on but with uncertain prospects.

Shiga put together a proposal for a new long-term (to the year 2010) program of twenty-seven construction projects with a price tag of ¥1.88 trillion (U.S.$17 billion), aimed primarily at improving water quality. The state countered that everyone recognized that water quality was a problem in Lake Biwa, but that not all agreed it was a crisis demanding action on the government's part.

In July 1996, Shiga enacted three prefectural ordinances aimed at improving water quality. But the national government holds most of the cards, including the ability to authorize (or fail to authorize) increases in local taxes. As the old options come to a close, Shiga is left looking for a new legal, financial, cultural, and institutional framework with which to approach the ecological and water-quality issues that the former bureaucratic approach failed to address.

Food for Thought

The history of Lake Biwa and of the LBCDP illustrates most of the "collective choice" problems that beset water use conflicts. We can see clashes between upstream and downstream interests, between locality and nation, between development and preservation, between bureaucracies and the citizenry at large, between government agencies themselves, between different parts of Shiga, and between different categories of users whose relative power changes over time. No side ever wins completely, and coalitions of various interests are fragile and rarely endure, especially at the local level. In this light, the rigidity of the LBCDP indicates the difficulty of negotiating such an agreement. As it passes into history, it may prove to have been a temporary, though restless, respite in a longer-term battle. And looming behind this drama is an even larger conflict between human institutions and complex ecological processes, which, even after years of intensive research, remain imperfectly understood in critical areas such as the specific mechanisms leading to algal growth.

The essential human institution in this narrative is the property right, and with it the consequent distribution of risks and obligations it involves. In its premodern state of more than a century ago, Lake Biwa was an open-access resource regarding which the interests of different users (fishers and transporters) rarely conflicted, and those who inhabited the shores bore the brunt of floods. At that time, establishing an explicit, complex system of rights over the water would not have been worth the effort. With modernization, development, and national strengthening, however, came new, offstream demands on the lake's waters. The River Law asserted the prerogative of the national government, embodied (literally as well as figuratively) in concrete form in the development-oriented Ministry of Construction, to distribute water use rights over major surface flows. Shiga has been able to assert a de facto right over the waters of Lake Biwa, but not a strong enough one to prevent the transfer of water rights to downstream prefectures.

It has been quite common during the twentieth century for states to declare that waters are essentially public and, in particular, that rights are not freely transferable among private parties, including local government entities. In the United States, this view has come under increasing criticism as leading to various perverse outcomes. For example, established users are accused of wasting water in order to avoid loss of rights. Also, environmental problems, or "externalities," may be aggravated if property rights are too narrowly defined or do not provide those affected with the power and incentive to identify and take action against polluters.

In addition, where water rights are held by the government, they become the property of specific agencies, each with its own bureaucratic culture. The mobility and multiple uses of water inevitably mean that numerous government bodies will claim rights over it at one point or another in the hydrological cycle. Attempts to "unify" management of water under one umbrella, such as the MOC, usually fall far short in practice and lead only to further uncertainties.

Many economists these days claim that environmental problems are caused by a lack of clear and transferable property rights. The course and outcome of the LBCDP clearly reflect the lack of "clear property rights" over the waters of Lake Biwa by either Shiga Prefecture or the MOC. The history of the plan might have been quite different—indeed, the plan might never even have existed—had either Shiga or the MOC had clear and transferable rights to the water.

Yet it also must be considered that the major contenders, that is, those with an established right to contend, were operating in a project-oriented bureaucratic culture that posited the desirability of economic development and the budgetary increases such development brings. Now that the ecological problems created by the compensation projects have become a bargaining chip and the imperatives of postindustrial economic development are demanding a cleaner lake, the question for the foreseeable future is whether Shiga can replace or retrofit the project culture with one that is broader based, perhaps even environmentalist.

Shiga's prospects of making a change are perilous given the even lower likelihood that the rival MOC will succeed in engineering the necessary changes in its orientation. Still, there is hope, as witnessed by the transformation of the U.S. Bureau of Reclamation from a builder of dams to a friend of the environment. Indeed, the MOC is not opposed to water quality and other environmental concerns as long as they can be addressed by public works. Like the Ministry of Agriculture, it has embraced the rhetoric of environmentalism to promote its interests. The problem is whether a project approach can work.

The way in which Japan approaches the problem of "transacting the commons" of Lake Biwa and its success or failure in reversing the damage done to its complex ecology have implications that go well beyond the bounds of a relatively small but significant lake. They will indicate whether the current configuration of hydropolitical interests, largely project oriented and relatively closed to the public, can break down the institutional barriers that have prevented many of Japan's most important waters, not just Lake Biwa, from showing significant improvement in quality over the past decade. On a wider scale, Japan's success or failure in reorienting its project culture will speak volumes about the prospects for using the world's political institutions to come to grips with the environmental problems besetting our global commons, such as our overfished oceans and our carbonating atmosphere.

RESOURCES

Readers wishing to pursue this topic further may consult Michiyo Akiyama and Masahisa Nakamura, "Water Resource Management in a Metropolitan Region Downstream of a Large Lake: Osaka, Japan" (1994); Masahisa Nakamura, "Lake Biwa: Have Sustainable Development Objectives Been Met?" (1995); G. E. Petts, "Water Management: The Case of Lake Biwa, Japan" (1988); and the Lake Biwa Research Institute, 1-10 Uchidehama, Shiga 520, Japan (http://www.lbri.go.jp).

ACKNOWLEDGMENTS

We would like to acknowledge the invaluable assistance of the Lake Biwa Research Institute and in particular its director, Dr. Masahisa Nakamura, who, among other things, provided the senior author with the latest materials on Lake Biwa.

NOTES

1. Katata Cho and Moriyama Shi are the political subunits of Shiga Prefecture on the western and eastern sides of the narrows, respectively.
2. The relationship between drawdown levels (in meters) and volume (in cms) is very complex. The subsequent association of a 2-meter drawdown with a 40-cms withdrawal indicates that the Pipeline Plan offered considerably less water than did the Cutoff Plan.

CHAPTER 9

The Big Canal
The Political Ecology
of the Central Arizona Project

Thomas E. Sheridan

Author Summary

Desire for control of the Colorado River has run like a drug through the veins of Arizonans throughout the twentieth century. Until the 1950s, Arizona watched California wrest that control away as Arizona refused to ratify the Colorado River Compact, which apportioned the Colorado's flow among the seven upper and lower basin states. Arizona also opposed the construction of Hoover Dam, which made the Imperial Valley bloom. In place of pragmatism or compromise, the state embarked on a quest for its own Holy Grail— Colorado River water impounded in a huge dam and transported 300–500 miles to farmland in central and southern Arizona. The reasons why Arizonans supported the "High-Line Canal" ranged from California envy and a desire to make the desert an agricultural oasis to racist fears of a "great Asiatic city and state" arising in the Colorado River delta. Arizona finally ratified the compact in 1944 and formed the Central Arizona Project (CAP) to lobby for the scheme. By the time Congress finally authorized the CAP in 1968, however, agricultural economists were demonstrating that Arizona farmers could not afford CAP water and Native Americans and environmentalists were contesting the route of the big canal and the location of its dams.

Introduction

In his provocative book *Rivers of Empire: Water, Aridity, and the Growth of the American West,* historian Donald Worster resurrects

Asian scholar Karl Wittfogel's hydraulic hypothesis to characterize the undeniably vital relationships between water, culture, and power in the modern western United States. According to Worster:

> The American West can best be described as a modern hydraulic society, which is to say, a social order based on the intensive, large-scale manipulation of water and its products in an arid setting. That order is not at all what Thoreau had in mind for the region. What he desired was a society of free association, of self-defining and self-managing individuals and communities, more or less equal to one another in power and authority. The hydraulic society of the West, in contrast, is increasingly a coercive, monolithic, and hierarchical system, ruled by a power elite based on the ownership of capital and expertise.   (Worster 1985, 7)

Anyone familiar with the modern history of Arizona realizes that part of Worster's characterization is true. As this chapter reveals, Arizona politics in the twentieth century have been dominated by the quest for the Central Arizona Project—the Big Canal that carries water 335 miles uphill from the Colorado River to Phoenix, Tucson, and the cotton fields in between, not to mention numerous Indian reservations (see figure 9.1). Arizona's fascination with big water projects began even before the Central Arizona Project, however. During the late nineteenth and early twentieth centuries, farmers and land speculators in the Salt River valley—the largest and most fertile conjunction of arable land and available surface water in the entire Southwest—watched helplessly as floods alternated with droughts and drove many of them out of business. One conservative report estimated that there were 127,512 acres being farmed in the Salt River valley in 1896 and 96,863 acres in cultivation nine years later, a decline of 24 percent (Sheridan 1995a).

In desperation, members of the Salt River Valley Water Users' Association turned to the federal Reclamation Service, founded in 1902. Inflamed with the conservationist "gospel of efficiency," federal engineers adopted the Salt River Project as their first major experiment in reclaiming the "great American desert" (Hays 1975). Sixty miles northeast of Mesa, the easternmost of the Salt River valley's farming communities, they built Roosevelt Dam, the largest masonry dam in the world at that time (Smith 1986; Rogge et al. 1995).

Roosevelt and the dams that followed tamed the Salt and allowed the long-staple cotton boom of World War I to industrialize Arizona

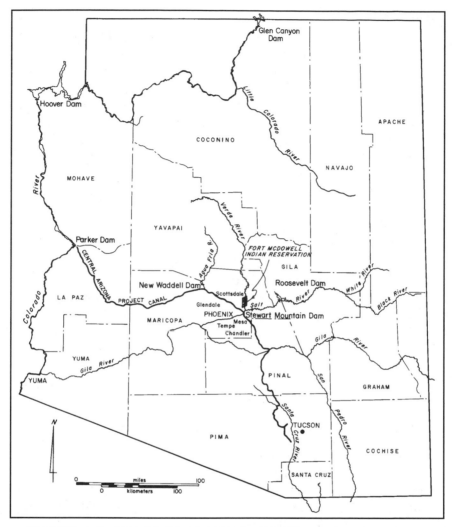

FIGURE 9.1. WATER IN ARIZONA: MAJOR RIVERS AND DAMS
AND THE CENTRAL ARIZONA PROJECT CANAL

Arizona politics in the twentieth century have been dominated by the quest
for the Central Arizona Project—the Big Canal that carries water 335 miles
uphill from the Colorado River to Phoenix, Tucson, and the cotton fields in
between, not to mention numerous Indian reservations. Figure courtesy of
Tom Sheridan.

agriculture (Sheridan 1995a). During and after World War II, the hydroelectric power those dams provided transformed Phoenix and its satel-
lites into the largest metropolitan area between Los Angeles and
Dallas–Fort Worth (Luckingham 1989). Big government financed and
built the hydraulic system that permitted big business to flourish in

Arizona. Modern Arizona is, without question, "a social order based on the intensive, large-scale manipulation of water and its products in an arid setting" (Worster 1985, 7).

But is it "increasingly a coercive, monolithic, and hierarchical system, ruled by a power elite based on the ownership of capital and expertise" (Worster 1985, 7)? Historian Donald Pisani provides a sharp critique, contending that Worster grossly overestimates the amount of control exercised by his two-headed elite (Pisani 1989). The early history of the Salt River Project is a case in point. The federal Reclamation Service may have constructed Roosevelt Dam and its waterworks, but the Salt River Valley Water Users' Association bought the project back. The farmers who belonged to the association, not federal bureaucrats, were running the Salt River Project within seven years of the dam's completion (Sheridan 1995a).

In my book *Arizona: A History* and elsewhere, I have suggested that a better metaphor for the politics of resource control in modern Arizona is that of a feudal society of competing warlords—copper companies, railroads, ranchers, farmers, utility companies, real estate developers, municipal governments—held together by a weak state (Sheridan 1995a, 1995b). In Arizona, business, big or otherwise, is not necessarily a monolithic force, and neither is the federal government. Different federal agencies compete for jurisdiction and appropriations and even sue one another over Indian water rights. But even the feudal warlord model implies too much concentrated authority because it ignores the messy and convoluted impact of consumer demand for cheap water, cheap power, and all the benefits they produce, including the "Sun Belt lifestyle." It also fails to account for another shifting source of power in the struggle over water in Arizona—transient political coalitions of consumers, environmentalists, and Indians—that form and dissolve depending on the issue at hand. All these forces have shaped the development of the Central Arizona Project. No other water project in Arizona better reflects the changing realities of water, culture, and power in a society in which one generation's vision of the future becomes the next generation's discarded past (Sheridan 1986).

California Envy and the Imperial Valley

In a sense, the vision of the Central Arizona Project began in the mid-nineteenth century, when thousands of forty-niners crossed Arizona during the California gold rush. "What this God-forsaken country was made for," one forty-niner wailed, "I am at a loss to discover." The Southern Pacific and the Atlantic & Pacific (later the Santa Fe) Railroads drove their crews and dragged their construction cars across Arizona's deserts and plateaus not because they had any interest in Arizona but because they wanted to suckle in the land of milk and honey on the Pacific coast. Arizona was little more than an unpleasant obstacle—hot, parched, and desolate. California was always the prize (Sheridan 1995a).

This created a bad case of California envy in the minds of many Arizonans. Even after thousands of settlers put down roots in Arizona and the Salt River Project made Phoenix rise from the ashes of the pre-Columbian Hohokam, California was always bigger, richer, more famous. And the biggest prize of all was the Colorado River, which ran like a drug through the veins of Arizonans for most of the twentieth century. By the 1920s, the Salt River had been tamed and the Gila River was being broken and maimed (McNamee 1994). The San Pedro, Santa Cruz, and Little Colorado Rivers had never amounted to much in the first place. The Colorado, on the other hand, taunted Arizona farmers as it roared down out of the Rockies on its 1,440-mile journey to the Gulf of California. The river deposited 140,000 acre-feet of silt per year in an enormous delta where roving jaguars and mythical alligators stalked the fantasies of the few explorers who ventured there. It also poured millions of acre-feet of runoff into an arm of the ocean that belonged to Mexico. Arizona farmers and politicians figured there had to be a way to channel that water onto the desert and make it bloom.

That put Arizona on a collision course with California, which had already been diverting the Colorado for a generation to irrigate a hallucination called the Imperial Valley. In 1849, a heat-crazed physician named Oliver Wozencraft fell off his horse in the Mojave Desert on his way to the California gold fields. Crawling to the edge of the Alamo Barranca, he stared into the Salton Sink, a vast, shimmering depression 300 feet below sea level. It was one of the hottest, most desolate areas in North America, but what Wozencraft saw there were not sand dunes and salt flats but an oasis of green fields and flowing water. He spent the rest of his life trying to convince others of his vision, dying in 1887 after a congressional committee dismissed it as the "fantastic folly of an old man" (Stevens 1988).

Ten years later, however, engineer Charles Rockwood and investor George Chaffey formed the California Development Company and turned folly into profit, at least for a time. In a land where sandstorms lashed across the desert in blinding sheets, Rockwood dug the sixty-mile-long Alamo Canal from the Colorado River to the Salton Sink while Chaffey was changing the sink's name to the Imperial Valley. "Water is king: here is its kingdom," he proclaimed, and people believed him. By 1904, more than 7,000 people were growing 75,000 acres of alfalfa and barley in the sink's rich alluvial soil. Wozencraft's hallucination had become real (Stevens 1988).

That vision became a nightmare the following year. When their first canal silted up, Rockwood and Chaffey breached the Colorado's banks and dug another canal. But the partners had no money to put a headgate on it, so they gambled that the Colorado would remain as tranquil as it had been during their development's first four years. They were wrong, not just on a human scale but on a geologic scale. The first floods surged out of the mountains in March 1905, driving an uprooted oak tree into the mouth of the intake and creating a whirlpool that sucked floodwater into the canal. Within days, the channel was sixty feet wide, and the floods kept seething off and on for the next sixteen months. By the time they subsided, the Salton Sink had been transformed into the Salton Sea, a briny lake that was seventy-two feet deep in places and stretched for 150 square miles (Stevens 1988).

Then the Colorado began to backtrack like a predator stalking its hunter. Because the sink was below sea level, the floodwaters of the Colorado plunged nearly 300 feet in elevation as they rushed down the steep grade of the canal. So after filling the Salton Sink, the river cut back through the loose alluvial soil, creating a small waterfall that grew larger and larger as it chewed its way upstream. By 1907, the waterfall was 100 feet tall. If the Southern Pacific Railroad, which took over the California Development Company after it went bankrupt, had not spent $3 million to throw a rock dam across the intake, the waterfall would have created a channel so deep the Colorado never could have flowed back into the gulf. Through greed and blundering, Rockwood and Chaffey almost reshaped the topography of the lower Colorado River basin (Stevens 1988).

The farmers of the Imperial Valley spent the next two decades erecting a series of levees to keep the Colorado at bay. But the levees were only a temporary barricade, so the Reclamation Service, under Arthur Davis, John Wesley Powell's nephew, decided to tame the river once and for all. In 1917, when California interests went to Washington to win support for their proposed All-American Canal, Davis shot the proposal down. He was not opposed to the canal itself, but he envisioned it as part of a much more sweeping program, one controlled and financed by the federal government, not private corporations. Irrigation, flood control, water storage, the generation of hydroelectric power—Davis wanted it all. But the cornerstone of his scheme was the construction of the biggest dam in the world "at or near Boulder Canyon" between Nevada and Arizona. The "Great Pyramid of the American Desert" had been conceived (Stevens 1988; Hundley 1975; Reisner 1986; Fradkin 1984).

The Colorado River Compact and the Anticompact Crusade

Before that pyramid could be built, however, the waters of the Colorado had to be divided among the seven states it drained. Those states—Wyoming, Colorado, Utah, New Mexico, Nevada, Arizona, and California—had very different economies with very different needs. Moreover, the political ecology of the Colorado River basin bore little resemblance to the flow of its rivers and streams. Most of the runoff originated in the upper basin states, yet the greatest water demand and political power resided in southern California, which contributed next to nothing to the river. As a result, the single most powerful coalition that emerged was between California and the Reclamation Service. After initial resistance, the Californians realized they had to buy Davis's whole package to get their ditch. They therefore submitted a series of bills to construct both Boulder Dam and the All-American Canal. The other states, in contrast, opposed the legislation at first because they believed that the dam would benefit only California. They also advanced their own schemes to utilize the river, with Colorado arguing that it had the right to all water arising within its boundaries. The fight was long, intense, and complicated, and for several years it seemed that no consensus would be achieved (Hundley 1975; Reisner 1986).

But then the U.S. Supreme Court upheld the doctrine of prior appropriation in *Wyoming v. Colorado* (1922), dismissing Colorado's contention. That decision caused upper basin leaders to reassess their opposition to Boulder Dam. Delph Carpenter of Colorado came up with the compromise that eventually prevailed. He proposed that the Colorado River basin be cut in two at Lee's Ferry, with half the river's flow (7.5 million acre-feet per year) going to the upper basin (Wyoming, Colorado, and parts of Utah, New Mexico, and Arizona) and half going to the lower basin (California, Nevada, and parts of Arizona, Utah, and New Mexico). After months of debate presided over by Secretary of the

Interior Herbert Hoover, Carpenter's proposal was accepted. The water commissioners of all seven states signed the Colorado River Compact in Santa Fe, New Mexico, on 25 November 1922 (Hundley 1975).

Now they had to convince their state legislatures to ratify the agreement. Bitter battles broke out in all the states, but the bitterest of them all took place in Arizona, which would have to compete with California for the lower basin allotment. Many Arizona leaders, including Congressman Carl Hayden, initially supported the compact. Hayden did not believe that the upper basin states would ever use their share of the water and figured there would be plenty of the Colorado left over for Arizona. But George W. P. Hunt did not see it that way. Reelected to his fourth term as governor two days before the compact was signed, Hunt believed that Arizona was entitled to the lion's share of the Colorado because the river flowed through or along the state for almost half its length (580 miles). "Arizona cannot afford to give away her greatest natural resource, with millions of acres awaiting development, and she cannot afford to plunge blindly into a contract that may be unfair to her," he warned the Arizona legislature in his inaugural address in January 1923. Colorado River water for irrigation and hydroelectric power was the lifeblood of Arizona's future prosperity (Parsons 1947; Rusinek 1984; Goff 1973; Fradkin 1984).

Over the next few years, Hunt's opposition to the compact hardened, and as it did, his flamboyant rhetoric heated up. In a jab against Mexico's rights to the river, he muttered about "Asiatic colonies in Mexico just across our border." He also damned American speculators like Harry Chandler, publisher of the *Los Angeles Times*, who headed a syndicate that owned 840,000 acres in northwestern Mexico and rented the land to Japanese, Chinese, and Mexican farmers. Anti-Oriental and anti-Mexican racism was the subtext—and a powerful rallying cry—for anticompact forces (Hundley 1975; Rusinek 1984).

Because of his rhetorical excesses and enormous size, Hunt was as easy to caricature as he was to criticize. Hoover dismissed him as that "blunderbuss of a governor in Arizona, who knew nothing of engineering." Arizonans joked that whereas Jesus may have walked on water, their state had a governor who ran on the Colorado River. But Hunt touched a chord that reverberated not only among his populist followers but also among some of his worst enemies. State congressman Lewis Douglas, the son of James S. Douglas of the Phelps Dodge and United Verde copper companies, led the fight to amend the compact in the Arizona legislature. Douglas asserted that Colorado River water was a resource that belonged to the state of Arizona, not the federal government, and that Arizona had the right to levy a tax on power generated by its hydroelectric plants. He did so because executives of the copper companies believed that royalties from the sale of power would reduce their own state tax burden. Douglas later attacked Hunt on other issues, but the two men and their supporters made state control of the Colorado River the canon that dominated Arizona politics for the next two decades (Hundley 1975; Rusinek 1984; Smith 1980).

Other Arizona leaders such as Carl Hayden quickly came around, especially after William Mulholland, the man who seized the water of the Owens Valley for Los Angeles, announced that his city wanted 1,500 cubic feet per second of Colorado water for its domestic supply. Arizona now had a new villain: Los Angeles, "the West's most notorious water hustler," according to historian Norris Hundley. The anti-compact coalition soon included the copper companies, private utilities, and the Salt River Valley Water Users' Association, which derived most of its revenue from the sale of hydroelectric power. California was stealing Arizona's river with the full support of the federal government, and that made Arizonans mad (Hundley 1975; Smith 1980; Rusinek 1984).

Because of such opposition, ratification of the compact died in the Arizona legislature. The battle then shifted to Washington, where Arizona's congressional delegation led the fight to block the Boulder Canyon Dam Act, which was reintroduced for the fourth time in 1926. Under both the bill and the compact, California would receive 4,400,000 acre-feet of the Colorado, whereas Arizona's share would be only 2,800,000 acre-feet (Nevada received the remaining 300,000 acre-feet). An amendment granted Arizona exclusive rights to the Gila River and stipulated that those rights "shall never be subject to any diminution whatever by any . . . treaty" with Mexico. But by then, anti-California sentiment was so strong that compromise would have been political suicide for any Arizona politician (Hundley 1975).

By 1928, however, California support had overwhelmed Arizona opposition. In May, the House passed the Boulder Canyon Project Act even though the dam site had been shifted to Black Canyon twenty miles downstream. Carl Hayden and Henry Ashurst, Arizona's senior senator, led a filibuster that stalled it in the Senate that spring, but at the opening of the second session, the Senate invoked cloture and passed an amended bill on December 14. The margin was overwhelming—64 to 11. By the following spring, six of the seven states had ratified the Colorado River Compact, and President Herbert

Hoover, one of the pact's architects, declared that both it and the Boulder Canyon Project would now take effect. Two years later, the construction of Boulder, then Hoover, then Boulder, then Hoover Dam—the name changed back and forth for seventeen years—began (Hundley 1975).

The Beginnings of the Central Arizona Project

To the rest of the United States, Hoover Dam symbolized the mastery of humankind over nature at a time when many men and women did not have steady jobs or enough to eat. White concrete against black rock, the structure curved upward for 726 feet, making it the highest dam in the world. It was the New West's most ambitious sculpture, public art that prevented floods and produced hydroelectric power. More than 5,000 workers braved heat and isolation and risked death to build it, and it was the first major stage in the transformation of the Colorado from a wild river to a tame ditch (Stevens 1988). To many Arizonans, however, the dam was a bitter symbol of defeat, a monument to Arizona's powerlessness and California's greed. The state's water politics therefore became increasingly defiant during the 1930s.

That defiance reached its comic-opera climax in 1934, when Governor Benjamin Moeur called out the Arizona National Guard to prevent the construction of Parker Dam. One hundred fifty miles downstream from the "American Pyramid," Parker Dam was much more prosaic—a utilitarian structure designed to divert Colorado River water into an aqueduct leading to Los Angeles. It was not going to make another oasis like the Imperial Valley bloom in the desert; it was simply going to water the lawns and wash down the throats of Arizona's insatiable urban neighbor on the Pacific coast. So Moeur summoned about a hundred of his troops and marched them off to the heat-scorched, dust-tormented dam site eighteen miles from Parker, Arizona. There, the guardsmen commandeered a ferryboat, which became Arizona's "navy," and one of them caught pneumonia and died (Fradkin 1984).

The press treated the whole affair as a joke, and in most respects it was. Moeur's proclamation "To repel an invasion," his declaration of martial law, the very idea of one state taking up arms to halt a construction project—all smacked of eccentric lunacy. But the stunt did delay construction of the dam for more than a year, and Moeur did wring approval of the Gila Irrigation Project east of Yuma out of the Department of the Interior in return for recalling his "machine-gunners" and "infantrymen" (Fradkin 1984). Meanwhile, Arizona lost a series of Colorado River water cases in the U.S. Supreme Court because of its failure to ratify the Colorado River Compact.

What the state did in place of embracing pragmatism or compromise was to embark on a quest for its own Holy Grail. The grail, of course, was water—Colorado River water impounded by a huge dam and transported 300–500 miles to the farmlands of central and southern Arizona. In the 1940s, the grail became known as the Central Arizona Project, but in the 1920s, it was called everything from the Arizona High-Line Canal to a madman's dream. Regardless of how quixotic it was, however, the quest burrowed deep into Arizona's collective political psyche. When Congressman Morris Udall was fighting President Jimmy Carter to keep the Central Arizona Project from being abolished fifty years later, he said, "The Central Arizona Project is a very old dream. I first heard it from my grandfather" (Fradkin 1984, 10).

One of the first of the dream spinners was George Maxwell, founder and executive secretary of the National Reclamation Association. Maxwell had been involved in Arizona water politics since the 1890s, when he proclaimed the virtues of the Salt River Project across the nation. After that project became a reality, he turned his attention to the Colorado, arguing that a dam should be built in Boulder or Black Canyon to divert water to irrigate 2.5 million acres in Arizona. W. S. Norviel, Arizona's water commissioner, appointed a former member of the U.S. Geological Survey named Harry Blake to make a study of the proposal. "Diverting and carrying water across a hot, arid country without crossing any large bodies of irrigable land until a point 470 miles south of its diversion is reached would be a very precarious undertaking," Blake concluded (Hundley 1975, 159).

Other experts, including Arthur Davis, agreed with Blake's assessment, but Maxwell was not deterred. He called for another study to investigate a "high-line canal" leading from a 700-foot-high rock-fill dam at Glen Canyon upriver from Lee's Ferry. Davis retorted that the route would wind through mountainous terrain for much of its 400- to 450-mile course and would be "a waste of our money and time" (Hundley 1975, 162). G. E. P. Smith, a professor at the University of Arizona, concurred, dismissing the canal as an absurdity. When asked to comment on a rock-fill Glen Canyon Dam, he could only mutter, "My engineering instincts rebel when I try to contemplate it" (Hundley 1975, 161).

But Maxwell's real obsession became the "Asiatic" menace swelling like a tick on Arizona water just south of the border. After the Colorado River Compact was signed, Maxwell ranted to President Warren

Harding that the agreement was "a carefully camouflaged effort to hamstring Arizona and . . . to establish a great Asiatic city and state in [the] Colorado River delta." He went on to say that the compact would inevitably result "in a war with Asia in which Arizona and California would be the shock country as was Belgium in the World War" (Hundley 1975, 233). With his white beard and ruddy face, the great crusader for reclamation had become a racist crackpot.

Another, more influential knight of the quest was Fred T. Colter, a rancher and state senator from Apache County. In 1923, Colter founded the Arizona Highline Reclamation Assocation to champion Maxwell's scheme. Then, in behalf of the state, he filed on all Colorado water that flowed through Arizona, proposing a series of forty projects to dam, pump, and channel that water to the Salt River valley and Pinal County. More than anyone else, Colter kept the dream alive in the 1920s and 1930s. He organized public meetings. He ground out propaganda. He published maps showing the routes of his improbable canals. And even though Colter himself failed to win the governorship on several tries, he terrorized any candidate or elected official who dared to suggest that Arizona ratify the compact. That did not happen until after Colter's death in January 1944 (Hundley 1975).

For more than two decades, then, Arizona went its contrary way, fighting and losing—in Congress, in the Supreme Court, in just about every political arena except its own voting booths. Farmers expanded their acreage by pumping groundwater aquifers, not by diverting the Colorado. Beneath the grandiose schemes and grotesque racism, however, the ultimate irony of all lurked on the pages of the hydrological reports. The Colorado River Compact was based on the assumption that the average annual flow of the river was 16.4 million acre-feet at Lee's Ferry, the dividing line between the upper and lower basins. Hydrologists derived that figure from Reclamation Service measurements made at a gauging station at Laguna Dam just north of Yuma between 1899 and 1920. The dam was hundreds of miles south of Lee's Ferry, but the agency figured that losses from evaporation were offset by the flow of tributaries in between. Furthermore, the measurements did not include discharge from the Gila, which emptied its waters— supposedly 1.07 million acre-feet per year—into the Colorado below Laguna Dam. Under pressure from the politicians, the engineers made the Colorado swell (Hundley 1975; Fradkin 1984; Reisner 1986).

Their calculations turned out to be scientific wishful thinking, a bad case of hydrological myopia based on two of the wettest decades on record. During the drought years of the 1930s, the average annual flow of the Colorado was 11.8 million acre-feet, nearly 5 million acre-feet shy of the 7.5 million acre-feet apiece promised to the upper and lower basins and the 1.5 million acre-feet ceded to Mexico under an international treaty in 1944. A number of scientists suspected as much in the 1920s, when the compact was being debated. In 1928, Major General William L. Sibert's Colorado River Board of geologists and hydrologists issued a report that recommended the construction of Boulder Dam but concluded that the flow of the Colorado was probably about 15 million acre-feet per year. Even that figure was too optimistic; between 1922 and 1972, when more accurate gauging equipment was employed along the river, the average annual flow was 13.8 million acre-feet (Hundley 1975; Fradkin 1984; Welsh 1985; Reisner 1986.)

By then, however, the die was cast. Arizona wanted the grail even if the grail was tarnished and the Colorado was not quite the river the commissioners thought it was back in 1922. Science took a back seat to politics, and men like Carl Hayden spent the rest of their careers fighting for their state's fair share of a pipe dream. They saw the state change. They saw the old extractive order recede into the countryside as a new urban order arose. But the cities needed water to grow, and the competition with California intensified as Arizona attracted its own urban industry and commerce during and after World War II. Besides, Hayden and others remembered the bad years—the floods, the droughts—and wanted to guarantee a future for Arizona free of those fears.

Legal Victory: *Arizona v. California*

The crusade was little more than a gleam in Arizona's eye until the Arizona legislature finally ratified the Colorado River Compact in 1944. Two years later, farmers, bankers, utility companies, and urban planners formed the Central Arizona Project Association to lobby for the scheme. Dominated by agricultural interests, the association joined forces with the Bureau of Reclamation and Arizona's congressional delegation to win authorization for the Central Arizona Project in Congress, where Arizona's two powerful senators—Ernest McFarland and Carl Hayden—introduced a series of bills beginning in 1947. Three years later, the Senate approved one of those bills—S.R. 75—by a substantial margin (55–28). Because of the enormous California delegation, however, opposition in the House was considerably more formidable (Hundley 1975; Johnson 1977). In the end, the House Committee on Public Lands sidestepped a showdown by delaying action until the U.S. Supreme Court resolved the quarrel over water rights between Arizona and California.

Arizona had tried to bring its case to the Court on three different occasions during the 1930s, but the Court had dismissed the suits because the state had not ratified the Colorado River Compact. In 1953, however, the Court agreed to hear Arizona's complaint. Because the case was so complex, it also appointed a special master to weigh the legal, economic, and hydrological issues presented by the two states. *Arizona v. California* began before Special Master Simon Rifkind on 14 June 1956. It ended on 28 August 1958. During the 132 trial days, Rifkind heard from 105 scientific experts, examined 4,000 exhibits, and plowed through 22,593 pages of testimony. Nearly two years later, he issued his draft report (Johnson 1977; Hundley 1975).

Rifkind upheld Article III(a) of the compact, which allocated 2.8 million acre-feet per year of the Colorado to Arizona and limited California to 4.4 million acre-feet per year. If there was not enough flow to meet the allocation of 7.5 million acre-feet to the lower basin states, flow would be apportioned according to allocation percentages: 44/75 for California, 28/75 for Arizona, and 3/75 for Nevada. Rifkind also determined that the tributaries emptying into the river below Lee's Ferry (the dividing line between upper basin and lower basin states) were not included in the compact. The amount of water Arizona removed from those drainages therefore could not be subtracted from its mainstream allocation. On 3 June 1963, the Supreme Court adopted most of Rifkind's recommendations by a vote of 5 to 3. After ten years of courtroom sparring, Arizona had finally triumphed over its archenemy, California (Johnson 1977; Hundley 1975).

Legislative Compromises

But legal victory did not ensure congressional appropriations. During the next five years, the fight over the Central Arizona Project degenerated into blatant pork barrel politics. On one side were Secretary of the Interior Stewart Udall; Arizona's five-member congressional delegation, led by Carl Hayden, chairman of the Senate Appropriations Committee; and Hayden's close friend Floyd Dominy, the cigar-chomping, woman-chasing head of the Bureau of Reclamation. On the other were the forty-two-member California delegation, Congressman Wayne Aspinall (D-Colorado), Senator Henry Jackson (D-Washington), and a growing army of environmentalists marshaled by David Brower and the Sierra Club (Reisner 1986; Johnson 1977; Fradkin 1984; Berkman and Viscusi 1973; Welsh 1985).

Aspinall, chairman of the House Committee on Interior and Insular Affairs, wanted to ensure that the upper basin states, particularly Colorado, got their share of the compact's allocations. In return for his support, Hayden tacked five water projects in Aspinall's Colorado district (Animas–La Plata, Dallas Creek, Dolores, San Miguel, and West Divide) onto the Central Arizona Project bill. Jackson feared that the bill's authorization of studies on transbasin water transfers would eventually siphon water from the Pacific Northwest's Columbia River system, so he obtained a ten-year moratorium on such research. The environmentalists opposed two dams—Bridge Canyon and Marble Canyon—that would have flooded both ends of the Grand Canyon to provide hydroelectric power to pump Central Arizona Project water 1,200 feet uphill to Phoenix and 2,100 feet uphill to Tucson. Udall killed both dams and suggested instead that the bureau purchase a share of the coal-fired Navajo Generating Plant at Page, Arizona. And finally, California demanded the deliverance of all its annual allocation of 4.4 million acre-feet of water, even during years of low flow. That was the hardest compromise of all because the Colorado had averaged only 13 million acre-feet of flow per year since 1930. But Arizona finally bit the bullet and accepted the California Guarantee. On 30 September 1968, President Lyndon Johnson signed the Colorado River Basin Project Act, which included authorization of the Central Arizona Project (Reisner 1986; Johnson 1977; Fradkin 1984; Berkman and Viscusi 1973; Welsh 1985; Wilson n.d.) (see photo 9.1).

Local Resistance and Coalition Politics

In Phoenix, the movers and shakers gathered in the venerable Westward Ho Hotel to celebrate the bill's passage. Nevertheless, the battle over the Central Arizona Project continued on two fronts. The first was over the route of the system itself, particularly the location of its dams. The 1968 bill authorized more than 300 miles of pipelines and aqueducts, the consumption of 547,000 kilowatts of energy from the Navajo Power Plant, and the construction of four dams to impound Central Arizona Project flow or the flow of other Arizona rivers. The proposed Buttes Dam was located on the middle Gila River; Charleston Dam, along the San Pedro; and Hooker Dam, along the upper Gila, where it would have flooded portions of the massive Gila Wilderness, the first wilderness area set aside in the United States (Reisner 1986; Welsh 1985; Wiley and Gottlieb 1982).

But the dam that generated the most controversy was Orme Dam, at the confluence of the Salt and Verde Rivers northeast of Phoenix (see figure 9.2). Promoted as a flood control structure, the dam was

PHOTO 9.1. PRESIDENT LYNDON JOHNSON SIGNING
THE COLORADO RIVER BASIN PROJECT ACT

On 30 September 1968, President Lyndon Johnson signed the Colorado River Basin Project Act, which included authorization of the Central Arizona Project, as members of Arizona's congressional delegation looked on: (standing, left to right) Congressman John Rhodes, Senator Carl Hayden, Congressman Sam Steiger, Secretary of the Interior Stewart Udall, Senator Paul Fannin, and Lady Bird Johnson. Photo courtesy of Special Collections, University of Arizona Library.

designed primarily to store Central Arizona Project water during winter so it could be released during the summer peak demand season in the Salt River valley. The dam also would have inundated twenty-five miles of floodplain along the Verde—a stretch that contained the nesting grounds of three of the seven pairs of endangered southern bald eagles along the river as well as two-thirds of the Fort McDowell Indian Reservation. The Yavapai of Fort McDowell were being called on to sacrifice their reservation so the Salt River valley could have more water (Reisner 1986; Welsh 1985).

Many Yavapai objected. So did the Maricopa Audubon Society and a newly formed group called Citizens Concerned About the Project, which brought environmentalists and Indians together to protest the dam site. The federal government tried to splinter the opposition by

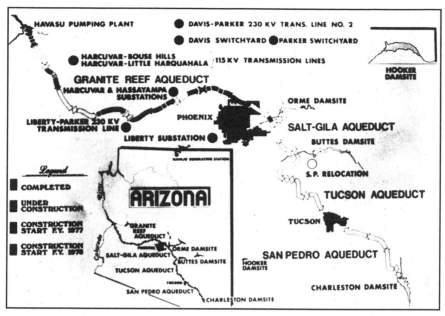

FIGURE 9.2. ROUTE OF THE CENTRAL ARIZONA PROJECT WITH
THE PROPOSED ORME DAM

Proposed route of the Central Arizona Project prior to the defeat of Orme Dam and the adoption of the Bureau of Reclamation's Plan 6. Photo courtesy of Special Collections, University of Arizona Library.

offering the Fort McDowell Yavapai $30 million for their land, about $70,000 per member. Tribal leaders polled Yavapai living on the reservation and found that 140 opposed the sale, 8 had no opinion, and only 1 supported relocation. The Bureau of Reclamation and the Central Arizona Project Association then decided to "educate" the Indians by sponsoring five seminars and forcing a second vote, which lowered the voting age to eighteen and included tribal members living off the reservation. The margin was narrower—144 to 57—but once again, the Yavapai turned the government down. Invoking the spirit of Wassaja (Dr. Carlos Montezuma, a Yavapai who became one of the first American Indian physicians in the United States), who had warned them not to surrender the "sweet waters of the Verde" more than five decades earlier, the Yavapai educated the government, teaching it that land had more than a dollar value and that cost-benefit analysis was not the only worldview (Reisner 1986; Welsh 1985; Wiley and Gottlieb 1982).

After hearing their testimony, the Carter administration cut the funding for Orme Dam in 1977. Proponents tried to resurrect the structure three years later, when huge floods surged down the Salt River and forced the Salt River Project to release massive amounts of water, washing out eleven bridges in Phoenix. But the escalating costs of the dam finally doomed the project: $38 million in 1968, $350 million in 1981, and a whopping $700 million a year later, after geologists revealed that the dam site was on a fault zone subject to earthquakes (Reisner 1986; Welsh 1985; Wiley and Gottlieb 1982).

The Bureau of Reclamation came up with its $746 million Plan 6 instead, which called for the strengthening of Stewart Mountain Dam on Saguaro Lake and the raising of Roosevelt Dam by seventy feet. Plan 6 also proposed two new dams—the relatively noncontroversial New Waddell on the Agua Fria River, to enlarge the storage capacity of Lake Pleasant, and the Cliff Dam on the Verde, upriver from the Fort McDowell Indian Reservation. Because Cliff Dam would have created a six-mile-long reservoir where two pairs of bald eagles nested, environmentalists and dam builders squared off a second time, and bald eagles once again became a symbol of the resistance. But opponents also charged that the only real reason for the dam was to protect a stretch of the Salt River floodplain through Phoenix, where the Rio Salado Project was being planned. The Rio Salado Project—a riverfront development of homes, factories, businesses, and hotels—was the largest real estate scheme in Arizona, one that would have cost the state's taxpayers at least $600 million. When voters rejected it, the rationale for Cliff Dam disappeared, and the bureau settled for New Waddell and a bigger Roosevelt Dam (Welsh 1985).

Paying for the Big Canal

But even though the bureau lost several battles over the Central Arizona Project's route, it won the war to fund the project itself. And victory on that second front turned out to be increasingly expensive for Central Arizona Project beneficiaries as well as for the American taxpayers. In 1968, the estimated price tag of the Central Arizona Project was $1.5 billion, which Arizona pledged to repay over a fifty-year period after construction was completed. There was a huge federal subsidy hidden in that repayment schedule, however, because farmers utilizing Central Arizona Project water were exempt from interest payments and municipal and industrial water users had to pay an interest rate of only 3.3 percent. As interest rates soared into double digits a decade later, President Jimmy Carter put the Central Arizona Project on his famous hit list of eighteen water projects he wanted to eliminate in 1977. But as author Marc Reisner points out in *Cadillac Desert*, "Water projects are the grease gun that lubricates the nation's legislative machinery. Congress without water projects would be like an engine without oil; it would simply seize up" (Reisner 1986, 319). Arizona congressman Morris Udall labeled the hit list the "George Washington's Birthday massacre," even though he later admitted that "one man's vital water resource project is another man's boondoggle" (Reisner 1986, 326–327). After both the House and Senate passed bills restoring all but one of the projects, Carter threatened to veto them until congressional and public pressure cracked his resolve. Seventeen chambers of commerce and 104 public utilities, irrigation districts, and water companies voiced their vociferous support for the Central Arizona Project alone (Wilson n.d.).

Meanwhile, the Central Arizona Project began to bulldoze its way across the desert, chewing up federal money and threatening the solvency of the people it was supposed to help. Congress appropriated $1.5 billion in 1971, but the Office of Management and Budget impounded those funds until Arizona came up with a workable repayment plan. In response, the state legislature created the Central Arizona Water Conservancy District consisting of Maricopa, Pinal, and Pima Counties. The district was given the power to levy an ad valorem property tax to repay the costs of constructing the Central Arizona Project, but irrigation districts still had to bear the costs of building the canals that would deliver Central Arizona Project water to individual fields. In 1967, the year before Congress authorized the project, a group of agricultural economists from the University of Arizona including William Martin and Robert Young had predicted that farmers would never be able to afford Central Arizona Project water after paying for the delivery systems. They argued that instead farmers should offset the growing costs of groundwater pumping by conserving water and shifting to higher-value crops (Young and Martin 1967; Kelso, Martin, and Mack 1973; Bush and Martin 1986). It was outright heresy, akin to suggesting that the Holy Grail was filled with vinegar. Arizona agricultural interests denounced Martin and Young as traitors. Politicians and the press raked them over the coals (Volante 1992; Reisner 1986; Wiley and Gottlieb 1982; Kelso, Martin, and Young 1973; Bush and Martin 1986; Welsh 1985).

But as Central Arizona Project costs skyrocketed, the economists' predictions took on the force of prophecy. In 1980, the Carter administration mandated that Arizona's 2.8 million acre-feet of Central Arizona Project water would be allocated in the following fashion: 309,828 acre-feet for Indian reservations, 640,000 acre-feet for municipal and industrial users, 1.5 million acre-feet for non-Indian farmers, and the remainder for other uses (Wilson n.d.). That year, Central

Arizona Project water cost about $30 per acre-foot before the costs of the distribution systems were factored into the equation. When they were, the costs were astronomical. In the Maricopa-Stanfield irrigation district alone, Martin and political scientist Helen Ingram discovered that farmers would have to spend an additional $160 million to channel Central Arizona Project water onto their crops. That would tack another $100 per acre-foot each year to the price of Central Arizona Project water, exceeding the costs of groundwater pumping ($39 per acre-foot in 1980) by $91. "In 1980," according to Marc Reisner, "about the only crop you could raise with water that cost $130 per acre-foot was marijuana" (Reisner 1986, 311).

The scenario grew even grimmer a decade later. By then, the projected costs of the $1.5 billion project had swollen to $3.6 billion. Non-Indian farmers were supposed to buy the 1.5 million acre-feet set aside for them during the first thirty years of delivery, but sales to the non-Indian agricultural sector crested at 501,000 acre-feet in 1989 and then plummeted to 260,000 acre-feet in 1991. By 1992, farmers were planting only 49 percent of the land eligible for Central Arizona Project water. Their reasons were simple: pumping water from the Colorado River required about twice as much energy as pumping water from subsurface aquifers. Even when power was heavily subsidized, Central Arizona Project water cost more than groundwater. Many irrigation districts contemplated bankruptcy despite the interest-free loans Congress had begun granting them in 1984 (Wilson 1992).

Escalating costs were not restricted to the agricultural sector; non-Indian farmers' unwillingness or inability to buy more Central Arizona Project water threatened the financial viability of the project itself. A study by agricultural economist Paul Wilson of the University of Arizona concluded that property taxes would increase and costs would rise to $150 to $200 per acre-foot if agricultural demand continued to plunge (Wilson 1992, 31). As Wilson put it:

> "I see CAP agriculture attempting to shift as much of its CAP water allocation and associated debt as is legally and economically possible to other CAP water users, i.e. M&I [municipal and industrial users] and Native Americans. Without these changes in CAP contracts, a majority of the CAP districts, and a significant portion of the growers, will declare bankruptcy and surrender their economic fate to the bankruptcy courts. In either case, the districts/growers will return to their deep water wells as their primary, if not sole, source of water for irrigation."   (Wilson 1992, 54)

True to form, the Bureau of Reclamation and the Central Arizona Water Conservation District began a financial restructuring of the project. As former Arizona congressman Sam Stiger had predicted seven years earlier, "They'll skin the cat twenty ways if they have to, but they're going to make the water affordable. Congress will go along, because it will be goddamned embarrassing for Congress to have authorized a multibillion-dollar water project when there's no demand for the water because no one can afford it. The CAP belongs to a holy order of inevitability" (Reisner 1986, 315–316).

Meanwhile, individual irrigation districts, such as the Harquahala Irrigation District, west of Phoenix—the first irrigation district in Arizona to accept Central Arizona Project water in 1985—freed itself of debt by selling its Central Arizona Project water rights back to the federal government. It then bought Central Arizona Project water on the spot market as needed (Wilson n.d.). In Wilson's words:

> As the federal government and the CAWCD [Central Arizona Water Conservation District] negotiate the "final" repayment obligations of the State of Arizona, all current economic evidence validates the prophetic analysis of William Martin and colleagues who questioned the economic wisdom of investing in the CAP for non-Indian agriculture. Districts with low cost ground water and surface water supplies did not contract for CAP water. Districts with relatively higher cost ground water supplies contracted for water but were uanable to afford the water. Eight of the nine original subcontractors have waived their rights to CAP water. M&I [municipal and industrial users] now subsidize non-Indian agriculture and finance recharge projects (e.g. Arizona Water Bank) to increase the utilization of Arizona's Colorado River allotment, protecting the allotment from California and Nevada interests. As predicted by Barr and Pingry, the sale of surplus electric power has become a critical source of funds for project repayment. And even M&I users (e.g. Tucson) have discovered that CAP water is significantly more expensive than alternative sources of water.
>
> (Wilson n.d., 18)

Conclusion

The ironies involving the Central Arizona Project never end. What began as a farmer's dream in the 1920s became a largely urban endeavor by the 1970s. When Central Arizona Project water finally reached Tucson in 1993, however, its high salinity and the chemicals used to treat it corroded pipes, damaged plumbing fixtures, and enraged Tucson consumers. To people used to drinking groundwater, it also smelled and tasted bad. After city officials denied there was a problem, a group called Citizens for Quality Water sponsored an initiative—Proposition 200—to prevent the City of Tucson from delivering Central Arizona Project water to homes and businesses until it met the standards of one of the city's groundwater well fields. Fifty-seven percent of the voters agreed, even though the City of Tucson and all the major developers opposed the initiative. After a half century of political struggle and economic manipulation, Arizona's second largest metropolitan center refused to drink the water coming out of the 335-mile-long big canal (Juliani 1996).

Food for Thought

The history of the Central Arizona Project raises many questions about the relationships between water, culture, and power in the American West. First, of course, is the question, Who pays? Western farmers, western cities, western industries, and western consumers have all benefited enormously from federal water and power subsidies, a fact that makes western political conservatism and the cultural pose of rugged individualism all the more contradictory. But there are deeper questions as well—about the nature of water and about the relationships between humans and the landscape. Is water simply a commodity to be bought, sold, and swapped among its many users as western rivers are dammed and destroyed and the western landscape is transformed? Or does the integrity of those rivers need to be preserved in order to protect other resources, such as wildlife and riparian vegetation communities? The resolution of those questions will involve a profound reexamination of cultural values as well as cost-benefit analyses.

And culture is perhaps the least understood part of the political equation. The original cultural logic driving the Central Arizona Project was that water flowing down a river undiverted was water wasted. Judeo-Christian values, capitalist ethos, and the gospel of efficiency demanded that the great American desert be "reclaimed" from wilderness and waste by taming western rivers. As long as Arizona and the West were dominated by extractive industries like mining, ranching, and agriculture, there were great debates about how to apportion water and land. But no one except a few visionaries such as John C. Van Dyke, author of *The Desert* (Scribner, 1901), questioned the underlying cultural logic itself. Both the desert and the wild rivers had to be subdued and made productive. In Arizona, this agrarian vision was sharpened by fears that the people of California and Asian farmers in Mexico were scheming to steal Arizona's fair share of the Colorado River.

As the era of extraction waned and the West was transformed into an overwhelmingly urban society with an economy based on service and manufacturing, however, the debate became more complex. Proponents of the Central Arizona Project and other big western water projects continued to invoke the logic of agrarian production, but the ideology of endless and unrestricted urban (and suburban) growth muscled its way into the political ecology of water control as well. During the postwar boom, construction became one of Arizona's major industries as Phoenix and Tucson sprawled across the desert. The millions of newcomers wanted such desert amenities as sunshine and warm weather, but they rejected desert constraints. Federally subsidized water and power projects provided cheap water and energy to thousands of housing developments financed by Federal Housing Administration and Veterans Administration loans. According to *Arizona Tomorrow*, a report prepared by Herman Kahn's Hudson Institute in 1979, Arizona had redefined "the very term desert." The report went on to say, "Desert living with air conditioning, water fountains, swimming pools—getting back to nature with a motorized houseboat on Lake Powell (itself a man-made lake), and going for an ocean swim in a man-made ocean are all contemporary examples of the marriage between life-style and technology" (Bracken 1979). As long as Arizonans did not have to pay the full costs of their water and power, why talk about limits?

Twenty years after the report was written, Arizona's "marriage between life-style and technology" had given Phoenix some of the dirtiest air in the nation, with 9.6 smog alert days per year, almost as bad as southern California (*Arizona Daily Star*, 1 January 1997). Meanwhile, water-hungry Las Vegas, the fastest-growing city in the United States, talked about redrafting the Colorado River Compact to give Nevada more water from the river while the Sierra Club talked about demolishing Glen Canyon Dam. For more than a century, Arizona has envied and emulated California. Now that both people and capital are leaving California and heading for Arizona, Arizonans need to ask themselves whether they want their state to be the southern California of the twenty-first century. If they do not, they had better start figuring out how to avoid what now seems inevitable. Two nonprint resources that deal with issues raised in this chapter bear mention. PBS has produced a four-part video series, entitled "Cadillac Desert: Water and the Transformation of Nature." The series focuses on the exploitation of the Colorado River, the development of central California, and water scarcity in other parts of the world. "Chinatown," a film by Roman Polanski that depicts the early years of Los Angeles's water saga, is also available in video format as part of the series. Readers may also wish to consult the home page of the University of Arizona, Water Resources Research Center at http://ag.arizona.edu/AZWATER/main.html. Their home page provides links to other water-related internet sites.

ACKNOWLEDGMENTS

I thank Tom McGuire, Bruce Dinges, and Steve Cox of the University of Arizona Press for critiques of earlier versions of this material as it appeared in *Arizona: A History* (Sheridan 1995a). Gerald Juliani of Citizens for Quality Water and Paul Wilson of the Department of Agricultural and Resource Economics of the University of Arizona graciously shared their time, knowledge, and expertise as this chapter evolved.

Water Wars in South Texas
Managing the Edwards Aquifer

John M. Donahue

Author Summary

This chapter addresses the negotiation of power relations as reflected in ideological discourse on water
management in south-central Texas. The chapter focuses on the debate and defeat of two referendums to
build a surface reservoir as an alternative source of
water to an existing underground aquifer. An analysis
follows of how proponents and opponents engaged in
the construction of a cultural reality to support their
competing agendas.

Introduction

In early western movies, Texas is often portrayed as dry, devoid of vegetation except for tumbleweed, and populated more by coyotes than
by people. Although this stereotype might fit conditions in the deserts
of West Texas, the state enjoys a wide range of environmental zones,
from the lush rice country and piney forest of the east to the desert
southwest of El Paso.

Intermediate to these two major zones, and to the south of them, is
the city of San Antonio, the third largest city in Texas after Houston
and Dallas–Fort Worth and the tenth largest city in the United States.
Given its proximity to the Mexican border, San Antonio is culturally
more like Monterrey, Mexico, than Austin, the state's capital, some
80 miles (129 kilometers) to the north. The influence of northern
Mexico can be found in San Antonio's food, music, architecture, and
people, more than half of whom can trace their origins back to Mexico.

In one important regard, however, San Antonio is unlike her

neighbor to the south and more like other cities in the United States:[1] everywhere, there are spacious lawns carpeted with water-thirsty Saint Augustine grass (*Stenotaphrum secundatum*). The grass itself, imported from tropical Africa, accounts for some 30 percent of San Antonio's annual water usage and is symbolic of the ambivalencies South Texans face in adapting to a semiarid environment. On the other side of the border, Mexicans, and the Spanish before them, long ago came to grips with living in a semiarid climate. Their homes normally front directly onto the street, obviating any need for a lawn. An inner courtyard yields a common green space for the enjoyment of all in the home, with minimal watering demands.

Adding to the cultural contrasts between northern Mexico and South Texas in the watering of landscapes is a major hydrological difference. Whereas northern Mexico depends on rainfall and riverine sources for water, San Antonio and its neighbors to the east and west sit on top of a rechargeable underground aquifer. Early settlements, both prehistoric and historic, took advantage of the springs in the eastern part of the aquifer at San Marcos and in New Braunfels, as did the first settlers of San Antonio de Bexar to their west. Water that traveled down the canals (*acequias*) from San Pedro springs to San Antonio provided ample water for the irrigated fields (*obrajes*) located between the springs and what is today the city center. The springs fed the San Antonio River, whose water was tapped for irrigation as it moved south from the city center. The Franciscans established several missions along the river and used Native American labor to build the canals and irrigate the fields. To the west of San Antonio were farmers and ranchers who drew much of their water from shallow wells, using wind-driven pumps. There seemed to be adequate water for all, humans and animals alike.

In recent years, however, the use of water from the Edwards Aquifer has become the battleground for a myriad of competing interests, geographical, government, and corporate. This chapter focuses on one event that served as a flash point in the continuing debate over management of the aquifer. The decision was whether or not to build an aboveground reservoir, the Applewhite, as an alternative source of water for the city of San Antonio. What seemed to many, especially in city hall, to be a reasonable request was voted down in popular referendums not once, but twice. For the opposition, Applewhite became a multivocal symbol that united people across the political, economic, social, and even religious spectrums. What did Applewhite signify for its proponents and opponents? What different meanings did the reservoir come to have for the interested parties? How did leaders in the debate define the value of water in the first place, and how did the different cultural meanings given to water make mediation difficult among the competing interests? In other words, how was power used in the service of one or another of the cultural definitions of water use? These are some of the questions that need to be addressed in order to understand the twice-defeated Applewhite Reservoir proposal. Indeed, the answer to these questions may shed light on possible solutions to conflicts over water use and management in South Texas and other parts of the world.

The Edwards Aquifer: A Profile

We first need to explore the several uses made of the water from the Edwards Aquifer. The semiarid region that characterizes the area between the limestone hills of central Texas and the Gulf Coast is blessed with a rechargeable underground aquifer whose waters percolate to the surface at springs in the central (Bexar County) and eastern expanses of the aquifer (Hays and Comal Counties), which, in turn, have been sites of urban population growth. With advances in pumping technology in the early twentieth century, large tracts of irrigated farmland were opened up on the western expanses of the aquifer (Medina, Uvalde, and Kinney Counties). Human adaptation to the geology of the region has created a socioeconomic landscape that concentrates the agricultural and ranching economic sector in the west, the more industrial and metropolitan sector in the center, and a major recreational and service sector in the east, around the springs in Comal and Hays Counties (see figure 10.1). To the north of the aquifer in each of the six counties lies an area of recharge where runoff from rainfall flows into the aquifer through porous limestone and sinkholes and percolates downward. Because the aquifer varies in altitude, its flow is from west to east, emerging at various springs along the way (see figure 10.2). Estimates place the capacity of the aquifer at 31–68 billion cubic meters (25–55 million acre-feet) of water—more than all the surface water in the state of Texas (Maclay 1988, 8).[2] The region's annual pumping is about 555 million cubic meters (450,000 acre-feet), or 1.0 to 2.4 percent of capacity, according to the 1988 estimate. On average, Medina and Uvalde Counties account for 38 percent of overall pumping, primarily for crop irrigation and livestock raising. Comal and Hays Counties account for 8 percent of aquifer pumping;[3] the water then flows south in the Comal and Guadalupe Rivers to petrochemical plants downstream, where industrial effluent is discharged into the rivers. The major pumpers of

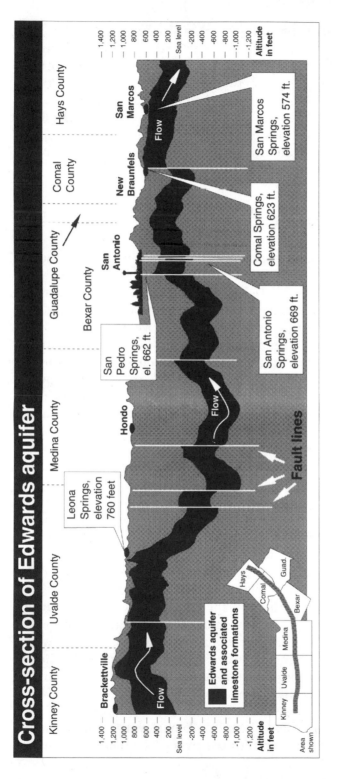

FIGURE 10.1. THE EDWARDS AQUIFER REGION

Human adaptation to the geology of the Edwards Aquifer region has created a socioeconomic landscape that concentrates the agricultural and ranching economic sector in the west, the more industrial and metropolitan sector in the center, and a major recreational and service sector in the east, around the springs in Comal and Hays Counties. To the north of the aquifer in each of the six counties lies an area of recharge where runoff from rainfall flows into the aquifer through porous limestone and sinkholes and percolates downward. Map courtesy the *San Antonio Express-News*.

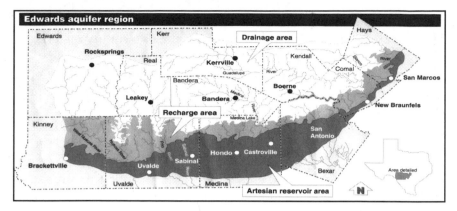

FIGURE 10.2. CROSS SECTION OF THE EDWARDS AQUIFER

Because the aquifer varies in altitude, its flow is from west to east, emerging at various springs along the way. Estimates place the capacity of the aquifer at 31–68 billion cubic meters (25–55 million acre-feet) of water—more than all the surface water in the state of Texas. Map courtesy the *San Antonio Express-News.*

aquifer water (54 percent) are the city of San Antonio and the farming communities in Bexar County.

Mention must be made of the aquatic life found in the springs at San Marcos and Comal (New Braunfels). Several species—the San Marcos salamander (*Eurycea nana*), the fountain darter (*Etheostoma fonticola*), Texas wild-rice (*Zizania texana*), and the Comal Springs salamander (*Eurycea* sp.)—are on the federal Endangered and Threatened Wildlife and Plants list and are protected by the U.S. Fish and Wildlife Service. The springs at San Marcos and Comal went dry during the record drought of 1947–1956. Fears of a new drought, combined with increased pumping from the aquifer, have led the Sierra Club and the Guadalupe-Blanco River Authority to argue for pumping limits across the region so as to maintain spring flows and protect the endangered species.

Water Use Policy in South Texas

Access to water was critical to frontier expansion during the nineteenth century in the semiarid region that characterizes the area between the limestone hills of central Texas and the Gulf Coast. Groundwater policy during the frontier period was based on the "English rule" of free capture, according to which property owners could pump water from beneath their land as long as they did not waste it.

The "rule" did nothing to resolve the conflicting interests—farming, urban, recreational, and industrial—across the five-county region supplied by the Edwards Aquifer.

A severe drought between 1947 and 1956 prompted urban and rural interests over the Edwards Aquifer to create a regional government agency under state authority. The regional agency would plan for and acquire sources of water to recharge those found in the aquifer. All parties agreed that an ample supply of water was critical to the future economic growth of the region. In 1959, after several years of intense lobbying by the San Antonio city council, the Texas legislature established, and voters approved, the creation of the Edwards Underground Water District. Each of the five counties with access to the aquifer elected three commissioners to the district. Rural interests in the Texas legislature were dominant in the district's enabling legislation. The Edwards Underground Water District was authorized "to conserve, preserve, protect and increase the recharge of and prevent the pollution of the underground water," but it was not given the authority to restrict the rights of landowners to pump underground water from their lands (Plotkin 1987, 126).

The next major change in Texas water legislation came in response to congressional passage of the national Water Quality Act in 1965. Two years later, the Texas legislature created the Texas Water Quality Board, consisting of seven governors and an executive director appointed by the governor. The board's first executive director sided with rural interests in the Edwards Underground Water District to maintain free capture and prohibit urban water interests from establishing pumping limits, as a supposed conservation measure (Plotkin 1987, 128–129).[4]

Interestingly, the first initiative for preserving the quality of the water in the Edwards Aquifer came not from the Texas Water Quality Board or the Edwards Underground Water District but from a group of citizens. A group of "land barons," headed by former governor John Connally, had initiated real estate ventures in the late 1960s and early 1970s that created the "twin development poles" of the University of Texas Health Science Center and the University of Texas at San Antonio, in northern San Antonio. Encouraged by their success, the developers proposed the construction of Ranch Town, a large suburban development over the aquifer's recharge zone designed to house 88,000 people, more than 10 percent of the city's population. Opponents, led by an urban planner at a local private university and a family with banking interests on the south side of San Antonio, began to warn citizens of the potential hazard of the development to the quality of the aquifer's water. It is important not to underestimate the importance of this early citizen action in protecting the aquifer: the relationships, shared experiences, and networks formed during this period would endure and grow into larger movements as time went on. In the meantime, the San Antonio Ranch, as it was later called, never came to fruition because of a downturn in the economy in the early 1970s. However, a core group of citizens was poised to meet the next challenge to development over the aquifer.

In 1973, La Quinta's chief executive officer, Sam Bishop, proposed construction of the Southwest's largest mall over the aquifer recharge zone. The citizen group, now organized into Citizens for a Better Environment, joined forces with a newly created community action group among working-class Mexican Americans on the west and south sides of San Antonio. Citizens Organized for Public Service (COPS), affiliated with Saul Alinsky's Industrial Areas Foundation in Chicago, and Citizens for a Better Environment brought the issue of a moratorium on development over the aquifer to a public vote. The public voted in favor of the moratorium, and the developers sued. The vote was overturned by the Texas Supreme Court, which ruled that the Texas Constitution disallowed overturning a city council zoning decision by referendum.

A new citizen group, the Aquifer Protection Association (APA), then collected 20,000 signatures calling for the county commissioners and the city council to purchase for the public trust 6,000–8,000 hectares (15,000–20,000 acres) over the aquifer recharge zone. The developer-controlled city council rejected the idea. However, in 1974, Congressman Henry B. Gonzalez was able to amend the Safe Drinking Water Act, which prohibited federal assistance to any project that might pollute urban groundwater supplies (Plotkin 1987, 137).

Applewhite Reservoir

By the late 1970s, it had become clear to developers that if the northward growth of the city over the recharge zone was to continue, an alternative to the Edwards Aquifer as the city's sole water supply had to be found. They found a ready advocate of alternative water sources in San Antonio's newly elected mayor, Henry Cisneros. He strongly promoted a city council vote on 19 July 1979 to approve a three-part water management plan that included conservation, recycling, and the construction of a surface water reservoir, called Applewhite. The council directed the water board to seek the necessary permits and environmental impact assessments. Opposition to the Applewhite Reservoir did not fully organize until nearly ten years later, when, after permits had been secured and environmental analyses had been completed, a second vote was taken on 21 July 1988. Opponents to Applewhite included those who had earlier argued for a moratorium on development over the aquifer. They feared that construction of the Applewhite Reservoir as an alternative source of water would eventually lead to increased development over the recharge zone. Others saw the reservoir as a scheme to fleece ratepayers and provide construction firms and land developers with a windfall at taxpayers' expense. They argued for a clear management plan for the aquifer that, if implemented, could satisfy the region's water needs without expensive alternative sources.

Philip Ross, a local lawyer whose land on the site of the proposed reservoir was to be seized, began a referendum petition drive to stop construction, but it fell short of the signatures needed. In July 1990, the Homeowner-Taxpayer Association of Bexar County (HTA) launched another petition drive, which picked up steam when Kay Turner, a local water activist and vice president of the HTA, took over as chair of the drive. When presented with the 79,000 signatures needed on 28 February 1991, the city council placed the proposition to stop construction of the Applewhite Reservoir on the ballot of a citywide election to be held on 4 May. Despite Philip Ross's attempt to postpone further construction until after the referendum, construction continued from January to May, with the city Water Board awarding a $37.5 million contract to a local contractor, the H. B. Zachry Company. Of the $180 million in capital costs, $104 million was to be spent on a plant to treat surface water and on a distribution system.

As the 4 May 1991 vote neared, another regional actor, the Guadalupe-Blanco River Authority (GBRA), entered the debate over management of the Edwards Aquifer. The GBRA represented the economic interests of Hays and Comal Counties, to the east of San Antonio. As mentioned earlier, the springs that feed the Comal and Guadalupe Rivers are major tourist attractions, and water from the springs, sold to downstream industrial users, is an important source of income for the GBRA. The springs are also a natural habitat of several endangered species under protection of the U.S. Fish and Wildlife Service. One month before the Applewhite elections, John Specht, general manager of the GBRA, announced that a lawsuit was ready to be filed under the Endangered Species Act.[5] Comal Springs in New Braunfels, the home of several endangered species, begins to go dry when the water level in the aquifer drops to about 190 meters (622 feet) above sea level. Although it may seem strange that the springs would go dry with so much water in the aquifer, they are at the upper end of the formation and thus are not a gauge of the quantity of water at lower depths to the west.

In 1991, fearing federally imposed pumping limits on aquifer users to protect the springs from depletion, San Antonio's mayor, Lila Cockrell, formed a political action committee called Water Now! that brought together the city's power elite, including former mayor Henry Cisneros. In the meantime, however, two water activists and Applewhite foes from San Antonio, Carol Patterson and Hans Helland, had been elected to the Edwards Underground Water District. They contended that since the aquifer held 31–68 billion cubic meters (25–55 million acre-feet) of water, it made no sense to build a reservoir that held only 59.2 million cubic meters (48,000 acre-feet)—much of which would evaporate in the hot Texas sun. Patterson and other aquifer activists argued that a more sane alternative would be to build recharge dams to ensure that more runoff returned to the aquifer. On 4 May, the voters approved an ordinance directing the city to cease construction on the Applewhite Reservoir by a vote of 63,258 to 59,833. On 10 May, a majority of the council concurred. On 19 May, a lawsuit was filed by the Lone Star chapter of the Sierra Club and the GBRA before senior U.S. judge Lucius Bunton in Midland to force the U.S. Fish and Wildlife Service to protect the endangered species in Comal Springs even if that meant limiting pumping from the aquifer in the other counties. The plaintiffs claimed that the U.S. Fish and Wildlife Service was violating the Endangered Species Act by failing to implement a plan to preserve flows at the aquifer-fed springs in New Braunfels.

Applewhite II

The issue of a surface water reservoir did not end with the vote of 4 May 1991. On 13 August 1994, voters were asked to vote again on the same issue, and they rejected it a second time by an even wider margin. By that time, however, the issue of aquifer management and control had become even more complex, with new actors and issues.

John Hall, as the state's newly appointed water commissioner, immediately began an overhaul of the Texas Water Commission (TWC), which he said had "enormous problems." Hall's arrival at the agency sparked departures of senior and mid-level managers. He brought in staff members from his previous post at the Lower Colorado River

Authority, where he had served as senior director of conservation and environmental quality.[6]

On 5 November, Texas's attorney general, Dan Morales, ruled that Section 28.011 of the Texas Water Code, which authorizes the TWC to regulate groundwater, did allow the state to delegate that authority. In a later clarifying opinion, he made clear that free capture still applied to the Edwards Aquifer. His opinion, in response to attempts to limit regional pumping from the Edwards by the Texas Natural Resource Conservation Commission, was touted as support for the state in defense against federal aquifer regulation if the Sierra Club won its suit (*San Antonio Light*, 5 November 1991).

In February 1992, TWC presented a plan for the state to manage the Edwards and other aquifers. It called for mandatory cutbacks when the aquifer drops to certain benchmark levels. Farmers would be paid for not irrigating, with the costs borne by Bexar, Comal, and Hays Counties. The plan also called for the creation of a replacement agency for the Edwards Underground Water District to implement and enforce the plan, and it retained the Applewhite Project.[7]

The City of San Antonio objected to the TWC's plan, contending that downstream users would pay nothing yet reap the benefits of the city's conservation efforts. The city called for a feasibility study of augmentation of the springs in Comal and Hays Counties, which might obviate the need for limits on pumping.

On 12 April, the TWC announced that it would be taking over management of the Edwards Aquifer. Four days later, it declared that the aquifer was really an underground river and renamed it the Edwards Underground River—which would, then, according to Texas law, be under the TWC's control.[8]

Reaction of city leaders to the TWC's action was universally negative. They placed blame on the GBRA, which had brought suit several years earlier to have the aquifer classified as a river and thus made subject to the authority of the TWC. Others noted this as another example of government bureaucracies out of control.[9]

The Texas and Southwestern Cattle Raisers Association, whose members control millions of acres of land and the water beneath it, asked a state judge in Travis County to reverse the 15 April decision on the ground that 150 years' worth of water law had been overturned without legislative due process or compensation. On 11 September, State District Judge Pete Lowry of Austin found that the Edwards Aquifer was not an underground river as the TWC had claimed, and thus the TWC had no authority to take it over.

In November, Judge Bunton announced that the Sierra Club–GBRA lawsuit would be heard before the end of the year and that the trial would be limited to four days to save money. There would be no closing arguments, and the two sides would have two weeks in which to respond with written rebuttals or points. John Hall, the state water commissioner, had asked the judge to delay his decision until the Texas legislature had had time to act on proposed legislation in its spring 1993 session. The proposed legislation called for an initial cap on pumping of 555 million cubic meters (450,000 acre-feet), with successive reductions to 493 million cubic meters (400,000 acre-feet) by 2008 and to whatever would be necessary to protect spring flow by 2012. Some board discretion was left in the bill to lift these caps.

Regional pumping was at 668 million cubic meters (542,000 acre-feet), and environmentalists had demanded 203–208 million-cubic-meter (165,000–250,000 acre-foot) pumping caps. Computer simulations performed in July 1992 by the Texas Water Development Board showed that reducing pumping to 431 million cubic meters (350,000 acre-feet) would not prevent Comal Springs from drying up (Thorkildsen and McElhaney 1992).

On 30 January 1993, Judge Bunton ruled in favor of the Sierra Club and the GBRA and urged the Texas legislature to reduce pumping from the Edwards Aquifer in times of drought by at least 60 percent (to 247 million cubic meters, or 200,000 acre-feet) to ensure the survival of endangered fish, salamanders, and plants by 31 May 1993 (the end of the legislative session).

In the aftermath of the ruling, the state legislature considered three bills that were eventually brought together in a compromise bill. The compromise called for replacing the elected Edwards Underground Water District with an appointed board called the Edwards Aquifer Authority (EAA), with three representatives from Bexar County and three each from the eastern and western counties. A larger advisory committee would bring together the various river authorities and downsteam industrial users. The authority would issue water rights permits based on historical usage and would increase or decrease pumping rights depending on spring flow rates at certain test wells. The authority would also issue a comprehensive water management plan for the region, including the development of alternative water supplies. Most of the funding for the authority's operations would come from aquifer revenues, but a small portion would come from downstream users. Only the authority could buy water rights, and landowners could sell only 50 percent of their allocations. The authority would install meters and be responsible for monitoring and protecting water quality (*San Antonio Express-News*, 28 April 1993). The compromise legislation was passed without the support of Congresswoman Karyne Conley (D-San Antonio) and Congressman Ciro Rodriguez (D-San Antonio). Both objected to the severe pumping limits placed on San Antonio and to the abolition of an elected board in favor of an appointed one (*San Antonio Express-News*, 13 May 1993). Conley and Rodriguez were prophetic in their concerns regarding the board. The Mexican American Legal Defense and Educational Fund (MALDEF) asked the Department of Justice to rule on MALDEF's contention that the appointed board violated the federal Voting Rights Act, which prohibits any retrogression of minority voting rights (*San Antonio Express-News*, 24 June 1993).

During the summer months, as the Justice Department weighed the merits of the suit, appointments to the new agency were made. As Judge Bunton's 1 September deadline for EAA pumping regulations approached, he decided to delay further action until the Justice Department made its determination on the voting rights issue. On 19 November, the Justice Department ruled that the state plan to replace the elected board with an appointed one violated Section 5 of the Voting Rights Act. This ruling put the state's aquifer agency in limbo but did not deal with the issue of pumping limits. That decision still sat in the federal court of Judge Bunton. A week later, Judge Bunton called S.R. 1477 effectively dead and declared that new legislation would be needed to meet the Justice Department's demands. Responding to a motion from the Sierra Club, he appointed Joe G. Moore, former executive director of the Texas Water Development Board, as aquifer monitor.[10] Moore's duties included oversight of pumping from the aquifer in order to ensure compliance with the Endangered Species Act (*San Antonio Express-News*, 29 December 1993).

In November 1993, one week after the Justice Department's ruling, Mayor Nelson Wolff of San Antonio named a twenty-six-member citizen committee to study city water needs through the year 2050 and, since the city would, in his opinion, face pumping limits, to suggest new sources of water, including the Applewhite Reservoir (*San Antonio Express-News*, 23 November 1993). Members of the 2050 Water Committee represented a range of city power brokers; notably absent were opponents to the Applewhite Reservoir and vocal supporters of aquifer recharge and spring augmentation. The 2050 Water Committee was charged with developing a water master plan for the city, but in effect, they were not able to take into account regional issues that impinged on city water policy (*San Antonio Express-News*, 25 October 1993).

The 2050 Water Committee held a series of meetings to develop their water master plan. At a March briefing, the president of the San Antonio Water System (SAWS), Joe Aceves, indicated that the Applewhite Reservoir would be one of his agency's recommended surface water alternatives (*San Antonio Express-News*, 10 March 1993). The SAWS master plan was unveiled to the 2050 Water Committee on 28 April, two weeks after the Sierra Club had asked Judge Bunton to declare an "aquifer emergency" and immediately restrict pumping. He had declined to do so. One week later, Mayor Wolff made a surprise visit to a meeting of the 2050 Water Committee and gave the committee two weeks in which to decide whether to recommend the Applewhite Reservoir in its report to the city council. If it did so, the council would be able to meet the 19 May deadline for calling a public referendum for August.

On 19 May, the 2050 Water Committee presented its report, which recommended the Applewhite Reservoir, to the city council. As described by its proponents, Applewhite would hold water only for discharge downstream, not for drinking. The water discharged downstream, via a diversion canal to petrochemical users in the Victoria area, would be exchanged for aquifer water captured from the Guadalupe River, stored in Canyon Lake, and brought via pipeline to San Antonio. A second pipeline would bring water to San Antonio from the Guadalupe River below Canyon Dam. The total cost of $300 million would include $76 million to complete the Applewhite Reservoir, $21.5 million for the diversion canal to deliver Applewhite water traded to petrochemical plants, $32 million for the Canyon Lake pipeline, and $130 million for a treatment plant to purify Guadalupe River water (*North Central San Antonio Sun*, 20 July 1994; *San Antonio Express-News*, 10 August 1994.) The plan also called for monies to enhance conservation measures, construction of recharge dams over the aquifer "if feasible," and reuse of wastewater for nondrinking purposes on local military bases and golf courses.

The council majority who approved the 2050 Water Plan called for a second Applewhite referendum to be held on 13 August 1994. Yet opponents on and off the council quickly noted that there were other alternatives to Applewhite. They argued that managing the aquifer more efficiently would be more cost-effective than building an expensive surface water system. In fact, opponents argued that the whole plan rested on the assumption that other river authorities would agree to sell rights to their water so it could be piped to San Antonio or traded with downstream users. And ultimately, critics argued, the building of Applewhite would do nothing to address the spring flow problem. Judge Bunton's ruling on pumping limits to protect endangered species could be met by pumping water from the aquifer and injecting it into the springs, a process called augmentation. Yet such a possibility was dismissed by Applewhite supporters, even in light of a study by the University of Texas Bureau of Economic Geology revealing that the total storage of the aquifer was 265 billion cubic meters (215 million acre-feet) of water, four times what the U.S. Geological Survey had estimated in 1978 (*San Antonio Express-News*, 13 October 1993, 22 July 1994). In other words, there seemed to be ample water in the aquifer to augment the springs in time of drought without the need to limit pumping across the entire region.

The debate entered another phase when in late July the chairman of the Catholic Archdiocese's Justice and Peace Commission argued that the Applewhite development would deface a "beautiful river valley, rather than protecting and augmenting its natural beauty. . . . [It] is a sin to misuse the Earth for our needs" (*San Antonio Express-News*, 23 July 1994). Local clergy, however, some of whom had served on the 2050 Water Committee or supported the reservoir, spoke in favor of Applewhite as a legitimate development of God-given resources.

The Justice and Peace Commission, whose anti-Applewhite statement appeared in parish bulletins the following Sunday, opposed the plan because (1) the 13 August election was hastily called and did not allow the voters to consider alternative water plans; (2) regional, state, and federal water issues—as well as legal cases—had not been resolved; (3) the 2050 Water Plan did not protect the Edwards Aquifer recharge zone from pollution and development; (4) the plan did not ensure enough flow for the New Braunfels and San Marcos Springs; and (5) the plan was too expensive (*San Antonio Express-News*, 23 July 1994).

During the final two weeks before the election, the pro-Applewhite forces drew from a $700,000 budget to buy television time to promote the 2050 Water Plan. Their "cash cows" included local businesses, including several construction and contracting firms. Cash-poor opponents turned to symbolic gestures that were carried as "news bites" on local television stations. On one occasion, a small group appeared in the offices of the San Antonio Water System with a giant blank check drawn from a fictional "Giveaway National Bank." Since no mention was made of cost in the text of the referendum as it appeared on the ballot, a vote in favor was tantamount to writing a blank check. They disputed the 2050 Water Committee's $300 million price tag for the project and predicted that construction of the reservoirs and pipelines could cost residents more than $7 billion in bonds and increased water rates. On another occasion, a group appeared at a pump in Brackenridge Park that is used to augment the flow of the San Antonio River as it makes its way through the tourist-rich downtown area. In front of the augmentation well, they discussed the possibility of augmenting spring flows at New Braunfels and San Marcos, a procedure that would protect endangered species without placing pumping limits on the wealth of water found in the aquifer. At a rally held near an early voting place on the first day of absentee voting, opponents sang a refrain set to the tune of the "Battle Hymn of the Republic" and marched to the voting booths to cast their ballots against the measure. On yet another occasion, opponents held a press conference on the downtown banks of the San Antonio River to argue that plans for the reservoir project did not address the threat of a federal takeover of the city's water supply. They argued that recharge dams and spring augmentation would be less expensive and more efficient and would protect endangered species.

On 28 July, the much-awaited University of Texas engineering study on augmentation of the Comal and San Marcos Springs was released. The study indicated that augmentation was feasible. Opponents of the Applewhite demonstrated on the steps of City Hall to argue that augmentation was a viable, cheaper alternative to the reservoir (San Antonio Express-News, 31 July 1994).

In a last-minute effort to clear up voter confusion over the use of Applewhite Reservoir water, Mayor Nelson Wolff produced a letter from the Texas Natural Resource Conservation Commission stating that the commission would look favorably on the city's request to change the permit to allow use of Applewhite water for nondrinking purposes only. On the same day, a group of twenty-two geologists, hydrologists, engineers, and academicians attached their names to a prepared press release stating that the Applewhite site had "major technical flaws and problems" from a scientific point of view (San Antonio Express-News, 12 August 1994).

More than 100,000 voters turned out on 13 August and voted down the Applewhite referendum by a margin of 55 percent to 45 percent, a greater majority than was achieved in the first referendum in 1991 (51 percent to 49 percent).

Conclusion

The causes of the double defeat of the Applewhite Reservoir referundum can be found in the history of water politics in San Antonio.

The expansion of the city northward over the recharge zone had pitted citizen environmentalists and developers against each other since the mid-1970s. However, the defeat also was due to the fact that the causes and solutions to San Antonio's water conflicts are more regional than municipal. Opponents to the reservoir pointed to regional solutions that the reservoir proposal did not address, whereas proponents argued that the reservoir would provide them with a bargaining chip in regional negotiations. Opponents countered that even if the pipeline-and-reservoir plan were feasible, the cost would fall unfairly on the ratepayers of San Antonio. In their minds, since the reservoir did nothing to alleviate the spring flow problems, San Antonians would still be faced with severe pumping limits. In sum, the debate pitted those who favored enhancing the efficient and low-cost underground storage of water against those who wished to limit access to the aquifer and substitute surface impoundments and pipelines.

The debate also revealed deeper cultural issues that separated the parties in the larger issue of management of the Edwards Aquifer. It is to these issues that we now turn.

Water is more than just a naturally occurring phenomenon; people endow water with cultural meanings. These meanings are embedded in the institutional contexts within which people interact, and in that sense, water is also a social construction. The cultural meanings ascribed to water are often shared, and the institutional contexts within which people interact often overlap. The choice to highlight one meaning to the exclusion of others in a specific social setting distinguishes one interest group from another. In the debate over the Applewhite Reservoir, the several meanings given to water were played out in distinct and often competing microcultural contexts.[11]

We can identify several microcultural contexts in the Applewhite debate in which actors had quite different cultural definitions of water. There were government agencies such as the federal judiciary and the U.S. Fish and Wildlife Service, state agencies such as the Texas Water Commission and the attorney general's office, and regional bodies such as the Edwards Underground Water District, its successor, the Edwards Aquifer Authority, and the Guadalupe-Blanco River Authority. Important nongovernmental organizations such as the Sierra Club and the University of Texas provided other layers of cultural meaning to water. Citizen groups, both quasi-official, such as the mayor's 2050 Water Committee, and unofficial, such as the Homeowner-Taxpayer Association of Bexar County and the Catholic Archdiocese's Justice and Peace Commission, brought their own cultural perspectives to the debate. Corporate interests, both construction and petrochemical, operated from their definitions.

Specifically, the debate revealed several competing definitions of water and its uses. The right of free capture of the aquifer's waters suited agricultural interests. The Sierra Club, joined by the federal judiciary and the Guadalupe-Blanco River Authority, envisioned water as an environment safe for endangered species only if pumping were limited, though it was not clearly established that such limits would ensure that the springs, the species' natural habitat, would continue flowing. The Texas Water Commission attempted to redefine the aquifer as a river, since water in that institutional context is an object of bureaucratic control. The downstream petrochemical plants saw water as a way to legally dispose of effluent from their plants. Consumers in the Homeowner-Taxpayer Association of Bexar County evaluated plans to manage water in terms of their financial impact on residential rates. Other water activists defined the aquifer as a natural resource to be managed through increased recharge in times of abundant rainfall and increased drawdowns during times of drought.

It should not be concluded that these several microcultural contexts and their corresponding cultural constructions of water are mutually exclusive. They can be made to appear so, however, when powerful actors attempt to impose their definitions on other parties and do not recognize other cultural constructs as legitimate. For example, the efforts of the Sierra Club and the Guadalupe-Blanco River Authority to impose pumping limits through the federal courts met with mixed reaction. When it was shown that pumping limits alone would not have guaranteed spring flows in a drought of record, their continued resistance to augmentation tended to undermine their position. Some taxpayers and water activists viewed the construction of surface reservoirs as an inefficient and ultimately expensive alternative to what many perceived to be a created scarcity in the first place. Hydrological estimates of aquifer capacity tended to support the position that the scarcity was an artifact created by political and corporate interests whose objective was pipeline and reservoir construction at public expense. Finally, some of the political elite characterized those who promoted management of the aquifer through augmentation as "radicals" who would "mine the aquifer" and jeopardize future growth and development in the city. The polarization of the debate led to the defeat of the Applewhite Reservoir project for a second time.

Subsequently, the Fifth Circuit Court of Appeals in New Orleans overturned Judge Bunton's ruling on pumping limitations. The Texas legislature amended its earlier legislation and made the new Edwards Aquifer Authority an elected, rather than an appointed, body. In response to the second defeat of the Applewhite project, the mayor and city council of San Antonio hired two professional mediators and asked them to bring together the parties in the Applewhite debate in an effort to fashion a water plan that would be acceptable to all. As of this writing, that group is still at work. In the meantime, the newly elected Edwards Aquifer Authority, on which sit individuals on both sides of the earlier Applewhite issue, is at work drafting plans to manage the aquifer that include licensing of all pumping from the aquifer and provision of compensation to some farmers in the western counties for not irrigating during the coming season.

Food for Thought

The Applewhite referendums and ensuing debates provide several lessons in the management of common water sources. In complex industrial societies in which water resources are shared over a wide range of geographic and microcultural contexts, one can expect that water will take on quite different cultural meanings as those contexts vary. Since governments in democratic societies are charged with the responsibility of protecting the commons, the state will be a major actor in managing such scarce resources as water. Bureaucratic control becomes, then, one cultural definition of water.

The next question is always, Control on whose behalf? The issue of power, or the ability to allocate scarce resources, arises when groups attempt to convince the state that their particular interests are part of the common interest. Major actors in the Applewhite debate were the petrochemical industries on the lower Guadalupe River. They contributed to the costs of the litigation brought by the Sierra Club and the Guadalupe-Blanco River Authority against the municipal and agricultural pumpers over the aquifer. In this case, two potentially conflicting cultural definitions of water, one as a habitat for endangered species and the other as a means of industrial production, were able to find a common ground. What is unclear from a political point of view is why the Sierra Club and the Guadalupe-Blanco River Authority were so adamantly opposed to augmentation of the spring flow to preserve the habitats. It may be due to their perception that municipal users such as the City of San Antonio were wasting water and thus, in practice, were opposed to conservation of the aquifer and its endangered species. Two consecutive defeats of an alternative surface water reservoir seem to confirm that perception.

Farmers to the west, however, as well as taxpayer groups in San Antonio, perceived the federal court's action as an attempt to assume bureaucratic control of what had been the prerogative of property owners and regional authorities. Furthermore, water activists in San Antonio had a long-term distrust of real estate developers and their surrogates on the city council. Both seemed willing to allow "development" (their common cultural ideology) over the recharge zone in spite of the danger of polluting the aquifer. The Applewhite Reservoir project seemed to many citizens to be a veiled attempt to put the aquifer further at risk. It was in this context that the water activists developed their cultural definition of the aquifer as a "gift" to be managed through augmentation and drawdowns. Yet even this group was divided into two camps. There were those environmentalists who were willing to agree to pumping limits in return for assurances that the aquifer's water quality would be protected. There were also those who believed they had a regional win-win plan in ensuring access by all parties to water during times of drought. Their plan would have entailed increased aquifer recharge and storage as well as augmentation of the springs, thus obviating the need for pumping limits.

The political process can be seen, then, as a struggle for supremacy in the public debate among several cultural definitions of water. A successful outcome lies in the ability of all parties to participate in the debate and to recognize and validate the different definitions at play. The state's role should be to ensure that such participation is broad based and well informed. As a resource, water is a hydrological given, but as a commons, it must be constructed culturally.

RESOURCES

Several World Wide Web sites offer important information about the Edwards Aquifer and about water issues in the United States at large. The *San Antonio Express-News* offers free access to a web site titled The Water Crisis at http://www.express-news.net/unauth/aquifer/aquifer.htm#b; The Edwards Aquifer Research and Data Center at Southwest Texas State University in San Marcos maintains a home page at http://www.eardc.swt.edu/localinfo/EARDC-info.html; Water Resources on the Web can be found at http://www.gslis.utexas.edu/~jsmall/water.html; and U.S. Water News Online is located at http://www.uswaternews.com.

An important contribution to the study of decentralized water management is William Blomquist's *Dividing the Waters: Governing Groundwater in*

Southern California (1992). Jay Rothman's insightful article titled "Pre-Negotiation in Water Disputes: Where Culture Is Core" appears in the fall 1995 issue of *Cultural Survival Quarterly.*

ACKNOWLEGMENTS

Of the many people who contributed their insights and knowledge, three bear special mention. The late Catherine Powell of the Department of Urban Studies at Trinity University was untiring in bringing water issues before the public for discussion. She modeled for many of us the role of citizen–academic. More recently I owe a debt of gratitude to anthropologist Marilyn J. Schlitz, whose work *Reflections on Medina Lake: 1912–1987* (San Antonio: Quadrangle Press, 1987) served as my primer in water politics in the region. She collaborated with me on a paper entitled, "Power Relations and Water Resource Management in South Texas" (1994). Finally, a special thank you to my co-editor, Barbara Rose Johnston. We organized a panel together at the 1995 annual meetings of the Society for Applied Anthropology entitled "Water Resource Development: Culture, Power, and the Environment." The idea for this volume emerged from that session.

NOTES

1. I owe this comparison to Judge James E. Barlow, "Reality of Our Water Culture Sinking In," *San Antonio Express-News,* 31 July 1996.

2. An acre-foot of water is the amount of water that could stand in one acre of land at a depth of one foot. One acre-foot is equal to 325,853 gallons and can supply a family of five for a year. In 1993, the University of Texas's Bureau of Economic Geology calculated that the aquifer holds as much as 265 billion cubic meters (215 million acre-feet) of water, four times what was estimated in 1978 (*San Antonio Express-News,* 13 October 1993, 22 July 1994).

3. Total aquifer discharge includes pumping but also spring flows. Spring flows, primarily in Comal and Hays Counties, account, on average, for 54 percent of total aquifer withdrawal.

4. Actually, pumping limits could be anticonservation if, as a result of such limits, large amounts of stored surface water are lost in evaporation (Carol Patterson, personal communication, 28 January 1997).

5. Michael Spear, regional director of the U.S. Fish and Wildlife Service's regional office in Albuquerque, told an Austin symposium on 13 April 1991 that in the case of the Endangered Species Act, federal law can supersede state laws governing wildlife and water use if the state laws do not protect a species from extinction.

6. On 1 October 1991, Hall made the surprising decision to join the Sierra Club and the Guadalupe-Blanco River Authority in their effort to have a federal judge invoke the Endangered Species Act to limit pumping from

the Edwards Aquifer. "Hall said state officials feared staying out of the lawsuit could mean federal administration of the aquifer, should the Sierra Club win the federal lawsuit" (*San Antonio Light*, 1 October 1991). Opposing the Sierra Club, the GBRA, the Cities of San Marcos and New Braunfels, and the Texas Water Commission were the City of San Antonio, a group of San Antonio industrial users such as the United Services Automobile Association, Uvalde County irrigators, and the state and federal farm bureaus (*San Antonio Light*, 2 October 1991). Shortly after Hall's decision, Judge Bunton ruled that the Texas Water Commission could not take the side of the Sierra Club and the GBRA.

7. Surprisingly, the city continued to lobby the TWC to keep alive the permit to build the Applewhite Reservoir even after voters rejected funds for its construction. The city argued that it needed the permits as leverage in negotiating for alternative sources of surface water.

8. "The Edwards aquifer is an underground river and thus, state water, and providing for the commission determination and administration of rights to the use of state water in the Edwards Underground River and related surface streams pursuant to Chapters 11 and 26 of the Texas Water Code and other applicable law" (*San Antonio Express-News*, 16 April 1992). Chapter 11 of the Water Code was approved in 1967 and created a state permit system to control the use of the state's surface waters. Chapter 26 authorizes the Texas Water Commission to protect water quality. Surface water allocation under Texas law follows the general rule of chronological priority, or "first in time, first in right." However, Texas water law also contains a series of statutory priorities for surface water usage, with top priority given to municipalities, followed by industry, irrigation, mining, hydroelectric generation, navigation, stock raising, public parks, and game preserves (*San Antonio Express-News*, 16 April 1992).

   The three-member commission had done an about-face from an interim plan, arguing that the aquifer was a river because it had well-known and defined boundaries; it had well-defined sources of water, mostly from the surface; it had a well-defined current, moving from west to east; its water had well-known destinations, in the form of natural discharge outlets at various springs; its flow was sufficient to be serviceable to those under whose land it flowed; and it provided habitat for fish and other aquatic wildlife, both within the aquifer itself and near the Comal and San Marcos Springs (*San Antonio Express-News*, 16 April 1992).

9. *San Antonio Express-News*, 16 April 1992. The Farm Bureau unsuccessfully sought a temporary restraining order in state district court to block the TWC's action. The GBRA argued against the restraining order and filed for a declaratory judgment from the court confirming the legality of the state's action. A spokesman for Texas attorney general Dan Morales said that he "was not in a position to agree or to disagree" with the TWC's decision to declare the aquifer an underground river, subject to state regulation.

10. Moore was the Sierra Club's second choice for monitor. Judge Bunton

rejected its first choice, John Specht, former manager of the GBRA, because the GBRA was a plaintiff in the suit (*San Antonio Express-News,* 29 December 1993).

11. Definitions of culture vary widely, but all tend to include both cognitive and behavioral elements closely linked to particular environments and technologies. Anthropologist David McCurdy (1997, 388) defines culture as "acquired knowledge that people use to generate and interpret experience." He goes on to note that complex societies are made up of thousands of groups that may share a common language and national culture but have specific cultures of their own. Each group may represent a microculture to the extent that its members share knowledge not common to other groups or microcultures.

Gender and Society in Bangladesh's Flood Action Plan

Suzanne Hanchett, Jesmin Akhter, and Kazi Rozana Akhter

A u t h o r S u m m a r y

This chapter discusses the integration of gender-related issues and other social constructions into a national-scale development program, Bangladesh's Flood Action Plan (FAP). The program, based on thirty different studies of flooding in Bangladesh, began in 1989 and ended in 1995. Every phase of the FAP, which was originally intended as an engineering and planning exercise, was marked by complex machinations of several economic, political, and social interest groups. In response to criticism, a Gender Study was added to one component of the FAP, the Flood Response Study, in 1991. The results of the Gender Study focused attention on the unrecognized role of women in agricultural production. Although the effects of the Gender Study on the FAP were mixed, it may serve to broaden the social perspective of future development programs.

Introduction

Foreign aid programs operate within sometimes difficult donor-recipient power relationships. Requirements to reduce government spending or otherwise change economic and social processes are common and controversial aspects of contemporary aid programs. Recipients may want aid but not want to comply with its terms and conditions, and some among the recipients may challenge the wisdom of accepting assistance at all. Such tensions, which exist to some degree in most international development projects, can produce byzantine relationships among donors and aid recipients in large projects.

In large, long-term aid programs, the interests and agendas of "insiders" and "outsiders" may come to intersect and cross, despite obvious differences among the various parties. Some foreigners may join with some local people against other coalitions of foreigners and locals, and so on. Anthropologist Sarah White describes such overlap in Bangladeshi "women and development" programs:

> To maintain that foreign aid has had a highly significant impact on the way that gender has figured in public discourse in Bangladesh is not to assume any simple opposition between outside intervention and some kind of indigenous culture. On both sides there is considerable diversity, controversy, conflict and manipulation of the issues to suit particular ends. It is not true that local gender relations are set and specifiable, as many "women and development" approaches assume. Rather, gender is a "contested image" also within Bangladesh society, and external intervention articulates and integrates with this.
> (White 1992)

This chapter discusses the integration of gender and other social considerations into a national-scale development program, Bangladesh's Flood Action Plan, here referred to as the FAP (see figure 11.1). The FAP was a program composed of thirty different studies of flood problems and issues in Bangladesh that began in 1989 and ended in 1995. It was funded by a consortium of fifteen donors, including the World Bank, which at times served as donor coordinator. The government of Bangladesh created a new unit, the Flood Plan Coordination Organization, to oversee the project. Every phase was marked by the complex machinations of several economic, political, and social interest groups. The stakes were high: successful planning efforts might result in lucrative future construction contracts, but poorly planned flood control structures might harm the delicate delta environment and human livelihoods.

The FAP began as a response to severe floods that covered nearly three-quarters of Bangladesh in 1984, 1987, and 1988. These floods disrupted the lives of residents and received significant media attention, arousing international concern for the people of Bangladesh. The final outcome of the FAP was to be a set of plans that would give Bangladeshi farmers enough protection from floods to allow them to increase food production. This improvement, it was argued, would ensure an adequate food supply for the increasing population into the next century.

The thirty FAP studies were meant to serve this common goal. Some were designated as supporting studies that would provide essential background information to five regional teams developing local

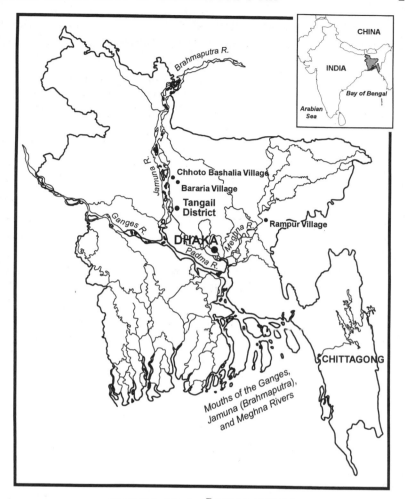

FIGURE II.I. BANGLADESH

Bangladesh's Flood Action Plan (FAP) began as a response to severe floods that covered nearly three-quarters of the country in 1984, 1987, and 1988. Indicated here are the cities and villages that were the focus of the Gender Study, a component of the Flood Response Study of the FAP. (Courtesy of Suzanne Hanchett.)

flood action plans.[1] The authors of this chapter worked on one such supporting study, the Flood Response Study, funded by the U.S. Agency for International Development, which investigated the flood experiences of 2,264 households in thirty villages throughout the floodplains (see ISPAN 1992c).[2] Another, British-funded, supporting study investigated the experiences of communities that already had flood control devices in place and compared them with the experiences of some communities that did not (see Hunting Technical Services Ltd. 1992).

Two kinds of action were planned. One was flood control—the design and construction of embankments or other structures to control water flow during the rainy season. The other was called "flood proofing"—the development of ways to help local populations survive floods with minimal disruption of work and social life. Socially defined programs were never given high priority, but they did serve to broaden the scope of some follow-up projects.

The Flood Action Plan was surrounded by controversy from its inception. Its scale and cost (more than U.S.$155 million) were grand. A coterie of Bangladeshi and foreign critics outside the FAP continually questioned whether the program represented the best use of such a large amount of money. There were numerous disputes both inside and outside the FAP about the ways in which construction planning, cost-benefit analysis, social analysis, environmental protection, and other FAP activities could or should relate to one another. Outside critics alleged that conflicts of interest pervaded the program.[3] The case against the FAP is summarized in Adnan 1991 and Haggart 1994.

One debated point was the definition of the much-discussed "flood problem," which in the FAP's view meant riverine flooding but not the cyclonic storms and tidal waves that periodically devastate coastal lands. Bangladesh, once the eastern part of the colonial Indian state of

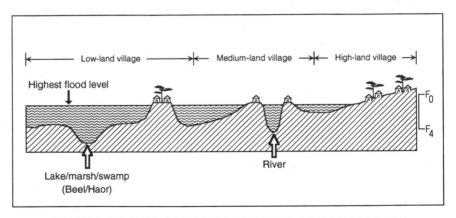

FIGURE II.2. VILLAGE TOPOGRAPHY IN BANGLADESH

During the summer monsoon season (May–October) heavy rainfall normally causes water levels to rise in the Ganges Delta. Human and animal life are more or less adapted to the delta environment. Village homes are built on high mounds. Floodplain fishes are an important part of the Bangladeshi diet, and floods provide the conditions necessary for the fish to spawn. (F-levels refer to degrees of inundation.) From Irrigation Support Project for Asia and the Near East, *Flood Response Study (FAP 14): Draft Final Report* (Dhaka, Bangladesh: Ministry of Irrigation, Water Development, and Flood Control, Flood Plan Coordination Organization, 1992).

Bengal and an independent nation since 1971, is situated on the delta of the Ganges, Brahmaputra, and Meghna Rivers (see figure 11.2). During the summer monsoon season (May–October), heavy rainfall normally causes water levels in one or more of these rivers to rise. Human and animal life is more or less adapted to the delta environment. Village homes are built on high mounds. Floodplain fishes are an important part of the Bangladeshi diet, and floods provide the conditions necessary for the fish to spawn.

Bangladesh's official language, Bengali, distinguishes normal "seasonal heavy rain and flooding" (*barsha*) from unusually deep and prolonged "severe flooding" (*banna*), which may drive people from their homes and endanger livestock or crops. In a normal year, 30 percent of Bangladesh's land surface is flooded by overbank spills during the monsoon season. But in a severe flood year, nearly all the national territory may be underwater[4] (see figure 11.3).

Monsoon season problems of greatest concern to the general public

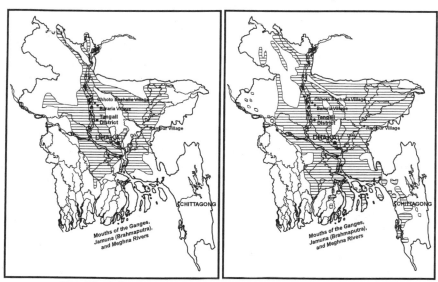

Normal flood-affected area   Flood-affected area during 1974

FIGURE 11.3. COMPARISON OF AVERAGE AND EXTREME FLOODING IN BANGLADESH

The map at left indicates the area of Bangladesh that is normally flooded during the summer monsoon season. Although this annual flooding is extensive, it is not considered out of the ordinary. The map at right shows maximum flooding in 1974. Such unusually severe floods occurred again in 1984, 1987, and 1988, arousing international concern that led to the creation of the Flood Action Plan. Adapted from Mahabub Hossain et al., *Floods in Bangladesh: Recurrent Disaster and People's Survival* (Dhaka, Bangladesh: Universities Research Center, 1987), A.T.M. Amihu Islam and Sanat Kumam Saha.

include not only unwanted water flow but also drainage congestion and waterlogging caused by railroad lines, roads, and even flood control structures themselves. Flash floods, resulting either from normal processes or from breaks in embankments, are another source of danger. Local experiences of floods and reactions to them vary from year to year and from one section of the country to another. Thus, it soon became evident that there was no single, clear "flood problem" for the FAP to solve.

Introducing a Gender Focus

Because the FAP framework, as defined by the government of Bangladesh and most donors, emphasized the mechanical aspects of flooding and its control, government officials showed little interest in the social effects of flooding. Nonetheless, several FAP studies did include social research along with mechanical studies of water dynamics, and eventually the government and like-minded donors modified their approach somewhat. Outsiders were especially critical of the early lack of attention to women's interests on the part of the government of Bangladesh and the U.S. Agency for International Development (AID).[5] In response to noisy criticism at a 1991 workshop, the U.S. government, with permission of the government of Bangladesh, added a Gender Study component (our project) to the AID-funded Flood Response Study. At first, the consideration of women's points of view made some people in both the donor and the recipient camps nervous. But outside critics were politically troublesome, and quieting them was a priority. Bangladeshi politics, services, and development schemes were (and still are) largely in the hands of men, and thus the contribution of women to agricultural production—a key goal of the FAP—was not widely acknowledged in policy-making circles.

Such biases tend to become self-perpetuating, as several generations of development researchers in Bangladesh have observed. One early report observed, "People in foreign agencies, evaluators and the elites of [Bangladesh] have no confidence in women, nor do they think that money spent on them will actually help the development of Bangladesh" (McCarthy, Abdullah, and Zeidenstein 1979, 375). The challenge facing us as FAP gender researchers was to determine whether it was necessary to include women's concerns along with men's in this significant environmental planning effort. If we found that it was, we would then have to persuade policy makers that women had standing to be included in new ways in water development projects and programs.

Interviewers for the Flood Response Study were encouraged to write case studies on subjects that interested them, and some of these focused on gender issues related to floods. These case studies helped us to understand many of the dilemmas facing women during severe floods and described some women's coping strategies. Rahima was one of the first to tell her story:[6]

Rahima

Rahima is a housewife. She is thirty-six years old and has two sons and one daughter. Her husband is a sharecropper. The family lives in Chhoto Bashalia Village in Tangail District. At flood time, Rahima's house was underwater for fifteen days. This case study describes the problems Rahima faced during the 1988 flood and how she managed to save her family from danger.

> She was very disturbed by the unclean and dangerous conditions in which they had to live during the flood. Their house was surrounded by paddy fields, and at flood time all sorts of creatures came to her house from the fields. This gave her the feeling that the place was filthy. Also, snakes came, flushed out of their underground hiding places, into the house looking for dry places. Her fear of snakes kept her awake at night. She tried to keep her children, especially the youngest one, on the bed all day so that they would not fall into the water and get leeches on them. Of course she also very much feared that her children would be bitten by snakes.
>
> During the flood time Rahima fed her children early and took them to a neighbor's house at night to sleep. She was afraid to have them sleep in the house because of the snakes. Her husband, who insisted on sleeping in the house [to prevent burglary], demanded that she keep him company. So she had to spend her nights in the flooded house without her children and in a state of fear.
>
> One night she saw a poisonous snake wrapped around the neck of the vessel (kolshi) in which she kept rice. She had that vessel on the corner of the bed, so she was terribly frightened and called to her husband. He, however, did not show any anxiety and went to sleep, but she could not sleep the whole night. Even after this frightening incident she could not leave the house at night.
>
> Her kitchen garden was only partially submerged by the flood waters. Although the fruits and vegetables she grew were not sufficient, the family was fully dependent on this source of food. Every day she had to go by herself through flood waters barefoot to the garden to gather her produce, but she felt this was very difficult and unsafe, mainly because of snakes.

For cooking purposes Rahima made a portable mud stove before the flood time, and she gathered some dried leaves and twigs, straw, and wood for fuel. She stored her fuel on a tree, and kept a bamboo ladder to climb up and get it. She did this job alone, as she is always in charge of cooking and feeding the whole family.

As her husband was quite aware of the bad effects of drinking and using flood water, Rahima had to collect water from the nearest tubewell, which was between a quarter and a half a kilometer away in Member's [that is, an elected union or arca council member's] house. This was not an easy task. Each day she walked barefoot through the water with her pitcher (*kolshi*) on her head, constantly aware of the possibility of being bitten by leeches. Because of the rules of society, which she has to obey, she had to do this job. Under no circumstances would her husband ever go and get drinking water; and because the job was so hard, she could not send her children to do it.

The division of work in the household meant Rahima had to do a lot of extra work, and she suffered from mental pressure too. Though men do some things during flood that they otherwise do not do, the burden of work falls mainly on the woman's shoulders. At times her husband became very impatient and petulant. He did not want to help her with her housework; rather, he decided to stick to traditional men's work. He took on a passive role. When he became angry she did not quarrel with him. She just accepted the situation and went on with her work.   (Hanchett, n.d.)

Rahima's was a situation like others we encountered in which the customary division of labor was only slightly modified during the severe flood crisis. Also like others, Rahima made good use of her limited resources. In her struggle to feed her family during the flood, the vegetables she had grown were of life-saving importance (see photo 11.1).

This family relied on local "patron-client" power relationships to cope with the situation, as did others we encountered. A prominent household provided Rahima's family with access to safe drinking water; other villagers also mentioned relying on local elite families for loans or food to survive the severe flood and its potentially devastating economic aftermath.

FAP Studies on Women and Floods: An Overview

FAP researchers working on at least eleven different studies, including ours, reviewed gender issues from a variety of perspectives. Nine

PHOTO 11.1. BANGLADESHI FAMILY IN FRONT OF THEIR
FLOODED HOME

People of Bangladesh do not consider flooding to be a problem until the water covers the floors of their homesteads, as in this home in Char Bhadrasan in 1993. Courtesy of Dr. Khurshida Khandakar.

studies devoted substantial attention to women's concerns, and two gave gender issues minor treatment (see note 1). From this large corpus of data and recommendations emerged some common themes relating gender to the FAP. Virtually all the studies were concerned in one way or another with women's economic position vis-à-vis men's. Another common theme was the division of labor within rural society and the ways males' and females' normal roles and responsibilities were affected by floods and their aftermath. The distinctive position of female-headed households was another gender-related topic receiving attention in more than one FAP study.

Economics, Gender, and Floods

Economic status affected people's flood experiences more than did any other factor. Wealthy people were far less disturbed by severe floods than were poor people; men were less disturbed than were women of the same socioeconomic class. Gender also affected people's capacity to cope with severe floods because of women's weaker economic position in Bangladeshi society. Key elements were women's employment, assets, and uses of credit.

The largely poor and landless Bangladeshi population experiences hunger every year during the monsoon season, when there is not enough day-labor employment to enable people to buy their daily food. The ruinous economic impact of severe floods, during which there is no day-labor work at all, on families already chronically seasonally unemployed is an intensified version of the hunger they endure every year. Some of the worst problems caused by severe floods, then, are more the result of economic inequities than the result of the floodwaters themselves. Most of the FAP studies of laboring people underscored some well-known facts of life in Bangladesh. For one, the majority of poor women not working in subsidized employment programs are employed as household servants or postharvest workers and are paid not in cash but in meals and perhaps some grain. Their husbands (if they have husbands), however, are more likely to receive daily wages for their labor. The Noakhali North Drainage and Irrigation Project (Southeast Regional) quoted upper- and middle-class farmers' wives as saying that it was difficult to find female laborers to help during the harvest because poor women were employed in subsidized Food for Work jobs with CARE. According to the women working in these subsidized jobs, the remuneration for housework was so minimal that it was not worth their while to take such jobs if they could get any others (Sir M. MacDonald and Partners Ltd. 1992).

The Land Acquisition and Resettlement Study found that despite suffering economic losses when displaced by government land acquisition for flood embankment construction projects, destitute women seeking laboring jobs in those same projects were denied these money-making opportunities (Multi-disciplinary Action Research Consultants 1992). This case represents an extreme example of unjust gender discrimination, but it is sadly typical of a general situation in which lesser economic opportunities for laboring women reduce their own and their families' capacity to recover from economic dislocation.

Differences between typically male and typically female assets affected the flood experiences of men and women. Women's hold on major economic resources, primarily land and draft animals, is weaker than is men's, and what women do have is less valuable than what men have. Their possessions (jewelry, kitchen utensils, small animals), often referred to in Bengali as "small things," are sold or mortgaged first to help their households survive.[7] This represents a rational decision on the part of the family, as women's things are not as important economically as the "big things" men tend to own, the forced sale of which is considered tragic. Despite their lesser economic significance to the family as a whole, however, the sale of a woman's possessions may leave her with no economic reserves whatsoever.

Borrowing money is one means of recovering from a flood; some of the FAP studies investigated men's and women's uses of credit. The

Northwest Regional Study found that several women had taken loans at extremely high rates of interest and sold off valuable assets in order to physically survive. This report commented that such actions could be financially ruinous to families (Overseas Development Administration 1992). Our Gender Study found that borrowing money was part of the coping and recovery strategy for two-thirds of the eighty-six women in our subsample (more than three-quarters of the landless), who had used monsoon season loans to meet basic survival needs (72 percent) or for purposes such as house repair or health care.

The flood experience of a destitute woman, Korimon, depicts a pattern of economic deprivation by now sadly familiar to most social researchers in Bangladesh.

Korimon

Korimon and her family live in Rampur Village in Brahmanbaria District. Every year, river erosion takes away a good portion of land in this village. By 1991, the village was little more than one small neighborhood with houses jammed together in its shrinking space.

> Korimon's family is from the southern neighborhood. Korimon is the second daughter of Mustafa Miah, a day laborer who lives in another village of the same Union [jurisdiction]. Poor Mustafa Miah could not give any of his children an education due to shortage of money. Korimon had to go to work at a very early age. When other children started going to school, she was collecting cow dung and also shaluk (*shapla* root) in the water. Sometimes she used to go to the field to give tobacco to her father and to help him in his work. From an early age her life was one of hardship.
>
> As she grew up her father worked hard to arrange a marriage for Korimon. So one day she got married to a man of Rampur Village. Korimon went to her husband's house with a lot of things in her mind. She wanted to make a happy family. Her husband was a very nice man. He loved her, and they were leading a happy life. Korimon was not at all unhappy in her husband's family. And she managed quite well with her husband's earnings, even though he was only a day laborer. She had her first child three years after getting married.
>
> This happiness did not last long. Within one year her family faced a terrible natural disaster. Huge flood waters destroyed her house. They became refugees and took shelter on the property of a rich man, where Korimon and her husband constructed a thatched hut. As the flood waters started receding her husband died of cholera. This time it seemed to

her that she had lost everything. This was the end of her married life, the beginning of a new chapter in her life.

Korimon had to look for a job to support herself and her baby boy. Going to other people's houses seemed to be the only option she had left. But she found it was very difficult in this village to get any sort of work, because half the year this village remains under water. At that time there is very little chance of getting any work. Only one or two months in a year could she get some work; the rest of the time she could do nothing. Finding it impossible to support herself and her boy, she had to go for begging. One or two months in a year she worked in other people's houses and the rest of the time she begged from door to door.

The toughest time for Korimon is the [monsoon] season. In reply to the question, How do you live at flood time? Korimon said, "Flood has taken everything away from me. It has taken my house, my husband, my happy family life and everything else. It has taken my only shelter place. Now, as soon as flood water comes, I go to Nasirnagar or to some other places where there is no flood water. At flood time, no one wants to give money or food to beggars." Sometimes she goes without food for the whole day; and sometimes she does not eat but still manages to feed her child.

According to Korimon poor people like her in this village do not get relief supplies. Sometimes they hear about relief, but they never get it inside the village. If they go from "door to door" [office to office] in the *upazila* (regional headquarters), then they might get some help.

Korimon still feels for this village. Once she had a house in this village, though she lost it. In the same way she lost her husband. She can not forget all those memories. She loves the people of this village. That is why she does not leave this place. She constructed a small thatched cottage in the rich man's property and lives there. This house is not waterproof. When it rains water runs inside the house. Even then, she lives there. When her husband died she could have gotten married again, but she did not. She thought about her child. She would rather spend the rest of her life with her only child. That is why without a proper house and without a husband she is still living in this Rampur Village.

Korimon's life up to the time of the interview represented many women's worst fear—a series of grievous losses driving a poor, illiterate widow to beggary. Riverbank erosion contributed greatly to the family's decline by taking their house,[8] and polluted floodwaters may well have caused her husband's fatal cholera. It is noteworthy that despite her total dependence on charity, Korimon did not receive public relief assistance during times of severe flood. Like Rahima's, her family depended heavily on a patron-client relationship to survive hard times.

Gender-Based Division of Labor

Information on the division of household labor between the sexes high-lighted the need to avoid stereotypes about the economic significance of women's agricultural work as compared with men's. Women are very much involved in agriculture in Bangladesh, if agriculture is seen as including more than just field cultivation of staple crops such as rice. In its broadest sense, agriculture includes many tasks assigned to women, such as animal husbandry, food preservation, homestead cul-tivation of fruits and vegetables, and harvest and postharvest activi-ties, as well as field crop production. But even in crop production, women's role is more significant than is usually acknowledged in gov-ernment circles. One important, but not often recognized, female re-sponsibility in crop production in Bangladesh is the storage and germi-nation of seed grain.

> In storage, rice and seed are the women's province. They watch over them to prevent loss from dampness, insects, and rats. . . . They determine how much is needed for the family (and therefore how much can be sold), when it is to be husked or milled . . . , and how much each person gets. . . . It is the responsibility of rural women to test the seed, which they have stored, for germination quality before men take it to the fields to sow.   (Abdullah and Zeidenstein 1982, 30, 24)

Our Gender Study collected detailed information on the division of household labor during floods, as did some others.[9] Nearly all routine household tasks are likely to be affected in one way or another by floods. There are various ways in which this occurs. Some tasks will of necessity cease during floods: plowing, planting, and irrigation of crops or watering of kitchen gardens, for example. Some tasks, such as open water fishing, are likely to be problematic in rough currents and monsoon storms; others, which must be performed consistently to maintain the family and its animals, become extremely difficult— sometimes impossible—during severe floods.

Men's responsibilities during floods typically are more limited than are women's. Men build rafts and platforms, purchase food, trade, and fish; they also gather some fuel and fodder. Women set up stoves and

cook, gather fuel, fetch drinking water, care for small animals, and protect and redry stored food and seed grains. Men and women cooperate
in caring for children and large livestock, building indoor platforms,
guarding the home, helping neighbors, and repairing damaged homestead mounds (*bhiti*). Men and women both care for animals during
floods.[10] In the northeastern district of Sunamganj, men and women
work together after severe floods to rebuild homestead mounds.
Women, however, do most of the routine mound repairs and mud
replastering after each monsoon.[11]

Most of the normal work of adult women—protecting granaries and
seeds, cooking, getting drinking water, and caring for animals, for example—is in the required-but-difficult category. Chores such as getting
fuel or drinking water, usually performed by children or teenagers, may
be taken over by adults during floods because they become especially
difficult or dangerous.

The 1988 flood experience of Nahar, a woman of Tangail District,
shows how one ingenious and determined woman struggled to protect
her livestock, conform to modesty standards, and perform household
chores.

Nahar

Nahar is a housewife whose husband works as a day laborer. They and
their son, a student in the ninth grade, live in the village of Chhoto
Bashalia in Tangail.

> As the water level rose Nahar became very worried and
> started preparing for a flood. She built a raft out of banana tree
> trunks, and she gathered fuel, storing it on a tree. To keep the
> bed above water level, she gathered some bricks, wading out
> into the flood water to search for them. She succeeded in
> raising the height of the bed by putting the bricks under its
> legs.
>
> In preparing food, she found that fish were easy to get but
> not easy to keep. Once she had some live fish to cook on the
> raft but as she had no place to put them, they all jumped back
> into the water while she was getting ready to cook them and
> were completely gone.
>
> She was especially anxious about the safety of her cows and
> goat, which were her only source of income. She was paying
> for her son's education by selling their milk, although her
> husband objected to her doing this. He wanted the boy to go to
> work as a day laborer like himself instead of going to school,

and he had beaten her a few times for encouraging the boy to continue his education. The public road was the only safe, dry place where she could keep her animals, so she walked about one kilometer through the water with the cows and goat and kept them there during flood time. Every day she brought straw she had stored for her cows, and when the supply was exhausted she collected water hyacinth for them. Feeding the goat was even more of a problem. The goat needed leaves. But, as many others were picking leaves for their animals too, she quarreled with her neighbors about rights to village trees. Because he got no income from the animals and they were her property, her husband was unwilling to help her with all this work. He even seemed to enjoy her trouble and spent the days gossiping in the marketplace.

When asked why her husband did not help more with household chores, she replied, "This is not the work of the male. His duty is to build and repair the house."

Nahar's bland comment accepting her husband's lack of effort masked the fact that the 1988 flood had exacerbated a marital conflict about continuing their son's education. Her husband's refusal to help care for the livestock was not typical of households we interviewed; most couples cooperated to protect animals. Nahar, however, used her animals to defy her husband's wishes, educating her son so that he would have a chance to escape the menial labor rut her husband was in.

One lesson a planner might take from this report is that spouses need to be treated as individuals because they may have different economic stakes at risk in a severe flood. Most government programs still operate on the assumption that a married couple's interests are uniform and adequately represented by the husband.

Female-Headed Households

Female-headed households account for 9 to 15 percent of all households in Bangladesh and possibly as much as 25 percent of all agricultural households. (Hamid 1992). There are several reasons for considering female-headed households separately in development planning; one of the more important ones is that such households tend to be small and economically vulnerable. But despite their handicaps, female-headed households in developing countries such as Bangladesh too often are neglected by most service providers (agricultural or veterinary extension workers, for example). It is common for agencies in Bangladesh to direct services to men on the assumption that this will benefit the women in their households. Thus, women without husbands or sons to represent their interests tend to be treated dismissively by officials conducting business in offices where women are rarely seen or, even worse, in rural markets, defined as "for men only," where women are treated rudely and insulted. Three of the FAP studies, the Flood Response Study, the Environmental Study, and the Fisheries Study (see note 1), gave special emphasis to female-headed households.[12]

The economic position of the female head of household is different from that of her counterpart senior married woman. Our study found that more women in female-headed households were employed outside the home than were women in the female sample as a whole. Another difference was found in landownership. In our total survey sample of 2,264 households, 4 percent of which were female headed, approximately the same percentage of female heads of households owned land (presumably most of it inherited from their husbands and kept in custody for their sons) as did male heads of households. This finding provided another reason to consider the special interests of female heads of households in the FAP. Because they controlled land, they had an even greater economic interest in the floods' impact on agricultural production than did other women. But their lack of male assistance put them at a greater disadvantage.

Analyzing the division of labor between the sexes, we found that female-headed households had different patterns from others. These women had responsibilities that women in other households did not. Tasks performed only by males in male-headed households, specifically by the male heads of households themselves, were performed by females in their households. These included going out into fields or marketplaces, plowing with a spade (*kodal*),[13] planting seeds, transplanting (plucking and replanting) rice seedlings, weeding, and cutting crops.[14] In the male-headed households, there were sufficient personnel to maintain more conventional divisions of labor.

Female-headed households were more vulnerable than others during severe flooding. It was clear that all or most female heads of households—contrary to the stereotype of the sheltered female—were managing, for better or worse, "on their own." If they were already poor, however, they were at risk of becoming destitute. If FAP planners wished to understand their concerns as people who own land, as agriculturalists, as wage laborers, and as people with the usual female obligations, there was no choice, we suggested, but to speak directly with them because of their typical lack of representation in the male social spheres.[15]

Mamata

Mamata is thirty-seven and has been divorced for seven years. Her husband was a rickshaw puller, and Mamata was his first wife. Since he divorced her, her husband has married three more times. Now Mamata lives with her son in Bararia Village in Tangail District. She makes money as a cigarette (biri) maker. She is paid Tk 2.50 (U.S.$.06 cents) for every 1,000 cigarette covers she makes.

> Mamata lost her house in the 1988 flood. She used to live on the bank of the Pungli River, but her house was washed away by flood waters. She then went to live on an embankment with her ten-year-old son. She built a bamboo platform there for them to live on, and they stayed on it for one month. She put a mosquito net with some paper around the platform to maintain her purdah [female seclusion]. One night it was raining, but there was no cover on the platform. So Mamata got completely wet. She just had to sit under the mosquito net and get soaked with rain water. There was no latrine, so she used to leave stool into the flood water directly from the platform, even though she was using flood water for cleaning purposes.
>
> Mamata had become sick when her house was washed away by the flood water, just at the time she had to go to the embankment to live. She was suffering from dysentery, malnutrition, and fever. She became very weak from not getting any medicine, health care, or proper food.
>
> Getting help at flood time was a big problem. She was too weak to get fresh drinking water from the nearest tubewell, and there was no one to help her. She asked one of her neighbors to get her a pot of drinking water, but she refused; so Mamata had to drink flood water. She became so sick that she was unable to take a bath for one month (the whole time she stayed on the platform), and her body and clothes smelled very bad. The only help she did get was from her eldest daughter, who was married and five months pregnant. She helped her mother prepare food on the platform. Though it was not proper food, somehow Mamata survived by eating it. Her daughter also helped her by getting medicine from the

village "quack" [paraprofessional] doctor. Because she was pregnant, the daughter found it very difficult to walk against the current of the water. Once she fell down and almost got washed away. Apart from her daughter she did not get any help from other sources. Neighbors were not at all helpful.

This is an unusually bitter report of illness, poor sanitation, embarrassment, and extreme discomfort suffered by a female head of household who was isolated from normal sources of social support. It is interesting that Mamata found her married daughter to be her only friend in this situation. Married daughters are not usually so free to help their parents because marriage shifts women's allegiance and primary responsibility to their husbands' parents.

Mamata's comment about the lack of help from neighbors was not typical of others we interviewed. In fact, friends and neighbors often helped one another as much as they could while coping with their own problems, sharing food and even providing dry spaces in which to give birth.

Neighborhoods in Bangladesh, of course, are not the same as those in Western countries, whose mobile populations easily form and break mutual assistance relationships. In a village in Bangladesh, a high value is placed on friendship, but a neighborhood (para or pratibeshi/parshi) is likely to be settled by cousins and siblings who are economically interdependent and whose reputations and relationships have as much to do with their parents and grandparents as with members of their own generation. Most rural households also are allied with local factions (samaaj) whose members provide all sorts of aid to one another in exchange for strict loyalty. Like positive bonds, familial and factional resentments and breaks also can span the generations, however. We did not question Mamata in detail about her situation, but it is possible that she was isolated because of some local conflict, perhaps one in which she had no direct role apart from being a member of a certain kin group or faction.

The Argument for Gender Balance in the Flood Action Plan

Like other crises, severe floods test people and relationships. They force difficult decisions and reveal deep "fault lines" within a community. Survival needs are social as well as physical, and mental pressures can seem intolerable. Every case of life on the raft or platform testified to women's resourcefulness and persistence in coping with adversity. None of these women, not even Korimon, took a passive approach to the problems she faced. Their stories belie official views of women's childlike dependence on male relatives.

Study findings eventually did demonstrate that women and men alike have standing to participate in programs and projects emerging out of the Flood Action Plan, though there never had been a question of including men. The most important arguments for including women were as follows:

- Women have clear interests in the impact of floods on agriculture, the main sector to benefit from the Flood Action Plan.

- Women's normal household responsibilities[16] are such that they shoulder a greater burden of household flood-coping activities than do men, most of whose normal responsibilities, except for shopping, cease during floods.

- Female household heads deserve special consideration in the FAP, because there are more female-headed households than most plan ners seem to think, and they are typically smaller, more economically vulnerable, and have unusual ways of performing household tasks when compared to male-headed households. Female heads must perform tasks that only males perform in homes with male heads. Female household heads were equally likely to own small plots of agricultural land as were the male household heads in our study sample and faced similar risks of crop damage in severe floods. However, in seeking public aid they were at a great disadvantage, as social mores make government officials typically reluctant to conduct business directly with women.

- Economic effects of severe floods on rural households are more significant than are physical effects. The physical effects are shared more or less equally by people of different socioeconomic classes, but more affluent groups are far less likely to suffer economically. Married women or female heads of household with independent economic responsibilities tend to have even less secure and lower-paying jobs than do poor men. Emergency borrowing patterns put women at greater risk than men of long-term flood-related economic loss.

The results of the FAP gender studies support the need for participatory approaches to local planning. Such approaches seem most likely to accommodate the inevitable complexity of interests—women's and poor people's included—in water management and flood control in Bangladesh.

Conclusion: Culture and Power in the Flood Action Plan

The FAP's social and gender studies stimulated much local and international discussion and debate. Conferences and workshops, which continued through 1995, at times were scenes of acrimonious disagreement about the FAP's approach (or lack of approach) to social change. Some Bangladeshi officials and donor country representatives continued to believe that it was inappropriate for the FAP or other water-oriented development programs to tackle basic social problems such as gender inequality. Others, hearing about women's and poor people's experiences during severe floods, broadened their concept of the FAP's goals and added social factors to their approaches. These debates set off powerful feelings on all sides. One Bangladeshi official took strong objection in a public forum to the social change advice of people he called "hop, skip, and jump" consultants, people who rushed in and out of Bangladesh and had no serious commitment to the country. Another official incredulously asked us in a workshop discussion about gender, "What do you want us to do, change our whole society?" Bangladeshi and foreign critics of the FAP continued to accuse government officials of taking a hard-hearted approach to their own citizens' problems. Such accusations wounded those at whom they were directed, prompting outraged public responses. On and on it went.

Arguments that it would be inappropriate for a flood planning program to attempt to reform gender relations and other societal inequalities seemed at first to have a commonsense logic. But this logic is weak in the Bangladeshi context, in which water and human society are closely interconnected. Water regime modifications, even minor ones, have profound effects on all forms of life, humans included, over large areas. Water is, after all, the dominant feature of the landscape in most regions of Bangladesh. Therefore, the capacity of civil engineering projects and programs to affect life cannot be denied.

Power relationships affected the local and international FAP process in various ways. An early debate took place among the G-7 industrial nations about whether or not floods were always disastrous in Bangladesh. Early warnings stressed the potential for flood control structures to harm the region's delicate delta environment. Even as they signed on as FAP donors, the large international powers continued to disagree among themselves about the direction the FAP should take, and throughout the life of the program they used their clout with the government of Bangladesh to tilt the research and planning agenda one way or another.

Within Bangladeshi society, the FAP studies emphasizing gender and social issues tested some existing power relationships. As our case studies and others demonstrate, in times of crisis, poor people in rural areas of Bangladesh depend on patron-client ties to locally influential people, ties still basic to peasant life worldwide. These ties, though necessary under present conditions, are maintained at a high price to the poor, who tolerate exploitative working conditions and survive at only minimal economic levels.

The most serious issue raised by our Flood Response Study was that of socioeconomic class as a key factor determining people's ability to cope with severe floods and their aftermath. The observation that economics caused more problems than floodwaters was, in its own way, a radical one. Had this observation been heeded (it was largely ignored), it would have shaken the nation's class system and the bureaucratic service delivery arrangements that reinforce it.

All the studies that included social analysis provided an opportunity for multiple rural voices to be heard in the nation's capital. But the voices were heeded by only a few elite decision makers. Nongovernmental organizations, though more important in Bangladesh than in many other developing countries, never were formally included in the FAP. Some, however, managed to create a brief political stir by organizing an anti-FAP demonstration in Tangail District in 1993.

Gender relationships—though they vary by region, class, and religious orientation—also affect flood-coping processes. The economic and social powerlessness of women relative to men handicaps them during crises such as severe floods and their aftermath. Codes of modesty make shame and humiliation inevitable when women are forced to live on rooftops, embankments, or rafts. Women's customary lack of access to public spaces and their rude treatment in queues and offices discouraged all but the most fearless from seeking certain kinds of assistance in a crisis.

Cultural values and meanings meandered in braided streams through the FAP, much as delta waters flow through the Ganges Delta. Vague and shifting ideas about the uses of the big rivers; about the dangers or benefits of floods, whether normal or severe; about proper (as opposed to actual) male and female roles and responsibilities; and about family and household organization underlay FAP discussions and disputes. Staff members of the technically oriented Ministry of

Irrigation, Water Development, and Flood Control and some donor representatives were reluctant to acknowledge their roles as powerful social change agents despite pressure to do so. More comfortable with engineering plans and diagrams or staple crop production quotas, male officials participated in sociological or environmental discussions only with resentment and impatience. The Gender Study and other socially oriented FAP projects did increase their level of comfort with sociological discussion and broadened the views of some, yet those within the system who changed their views were, we have heard, disregarded by colleagues more firmly committed to existing procedures and approaches. The dialogue had no sweeping ideological or policy effect, but it absorbed much public and private energy for a few years and produced a few programmatic shifts.

One specific result of the FAP's gender discussion is a current initiative of the Ministry of Irrigation, Water Development, and Flood Control to encourage women's participation in local water users' associations. Such efforts are faltering, but the ministry is dedicating resources to the initiatives. Another result of the general clamor about including social factors was the writing, by a Bangladeshi-led work group, of guidelines for people's participation in the planning of water regime changes (Adnan 1992). The guidelines received mixed reviews from the FAP audience, but they did represent a position to which the government of Bangladesh was officially committed. Although future FAP-inspired projects and programs may continue to spark tensions, it is clear that adding a social and gender focus to the FAP served to expand the important, multivocal Bangladesh development dialogue in ways likely to prove socially and environmentally beneficial in the long run.

Food for Thought

Most of the chapters in this book examine the impacts and implications of water management projects. Here, we consider at a very human level that which prompts large-scale water projects in the first place. Flooding in Bangladesh is part of the natural cycle of the bioregion. Life on a floodplain requires people to develop strategies that allow them to carry on the daily functions of life while floodwaters swirl around them and to exploit the opportunities provided by regular flooding. The nutrient capacity of the soil is enriched by annual floods, and aquatic ecosystems thrive in the marshy settings. When the waters recede, people carry on their productive strategies—fishing, growing rice, cultivating gardens on mounds and levees.

Although flood times are always dangerous times, some floods pose greater risk than do others. In recent years, floodwaters have claimed hundreds of lives and washed away tens of thousands of homes. Bangladesh's Flood Action Plan was formed to design strategies for minimizing the adverse impacts of annual flooding. This chapter reports on attempts to introduce an awareness of the sociocultural dimensions of flooding into the Flood Action Plan's process.

In exploring the experiences and coping strategies of families affected by flooding in Bangladesh, we begin to understand how cultural values, traditions, and behaviors structure different experiences and create different burdens for men and for women. For reasons of culture and class, women are more vulnerable than are men to the disasters created by flooding. Yet "project culture" severely inhibited the authors' ability to get this point across to policy makers and flood plan engineers. The culture and power dynamics that influenced the way the plan was designed also created tensions and barriers to modifying the plan. Future efforts might benefit from a critical examination of the culture and power dynamics that make Bangladeshi women more vulnerable than men to disaster during flood times, the strategies utilized in surviving the effects of flooding, the potential role of government in improving women's ability to recover from flood-induced disasters, and the ways in which framing of the problem directly influences the design and implementation of response strategies.

RESOURCES

The Global Water Partnership has initiated an electronic conference on gender and water. Their website is http://www.gwp.sida.se

ACKNOWLEDGMENTS

We wish to acknowledge that our study was part of a team effort under the direction of Dr. G. T. Keith Pitman and Mr. Richard Aten of ISPAN. Senior advisors to the Flood Response Study were Dr. M. Alamgir, Dr. Mustafa Alam, Dr. Murray Leaf, as well as Suzanne Hanchett. The team leader for the Environmental Study was Dr. Stanley Hirst. Gender Study interviews were conducted by Mrs. Hosne Ara Alam.

NOTES

1. The Bangladesh Flood Action Plan (FAP) was a national-scale development program, funded by a consortium of 15 donors, including the World Bank, which at times served as a donor coordinator. The FAP was a program of 30 different studies of Bangladesh flood problems and issues that were begun in 1989 and completed in 1995.

   - The Flood Control, Drainage, and Irrigation (FCD/I) Study, FAP 12, which analyzed the impacts of seventeen different projects and compiled substantial information on women's concerns (see Hunting Technical Services Ltd. 1992).

   - The Flood Response Study, FAP 14, which covered thirty villages throughout the floodplain and focused on gender-related issues in a subsample of households—emphasizing female-headed households—in seven villages (see ISPAN 1992c). The Flood Response Study presented a framework for discussion of gender in the Flood Action Plan. The authors of this chapter were responsible for the design and implementation of the Gender Study, a component of the Flood Response Study.

   - The Land Acquisition and Resettlement Study, FAP 15, which included interviews with twenty-seven women from displaced households and examined the destructive impact of the Jamuna Multipurpose Bridge project on their economic position (see Multi-disciplinary Action Research Consultants 1992).

   - The Environmental Study, FAP 16, which incorporated focus group discussions carried out with women and men in the process of conducting special studies in three subject areas. This project also included a life study (with gender analysis) of *char* people living on sandbar islands of the great rivers (see ISPAN 1992a, 1993).

   - The Fisheries Study, FAP 17, which included a "women in development" component in its socioeconomic analysis of fisheries-related activities and structures in four regions (see Overseas Development Administration 1994).

   - The Flood Proofing Study, FAP 23, which included observations and recommendations about incorporating women's needs and interests into plans to lessen the harm caused by severe floods in vulnerable locations (see ISPAN 1992b).

   Regional studies included the following:

   - The Northwest Regional Study, FAP 2, in which 100 women were interviewed and asked to rank their own needs during flooding and in the context of general development (see Overseas Development Administration 1992).

   - The North Central Regional Study, FAP 3, which, based on results of a household sample survey, compiled general comments on women's employment, household division of labor, and ways in which women's interests could be served in agricultural development planning (see BCEOM 1992).

- The Southwest Area Water Resources Management Project, FAP 4, which was limited to some general comments about women's employment patterns in the region and locally accepted stereotypic notions about the limited possibilities of expanding economic opportunities for women (see Sir William Halcrow & Partners Ltd. 1992).

- The Noakhali North Drainage and Irrigation Project (Southeast Region), FAP 5, which included a survey of ninety-eight female-headed households as well as focus group interviews. Participation data were based in part on sixteen women's group meetings, four in each zone of the area (see Sir M. MacDonald and Partners Ltd. 1992).

- The Northeast Regional Water Management Project, FAP 6, which included observations on women's roles in five case studies on locally initiated water management programs (see Shanwinigan Lavilin Inc. 1991).

All studies are available in Dhaka at the Flood Plan Coordination Organization's office or at the offices of the World Bank, Dhaka Mission.

2. The authors worked as consultants on the U.S. Agency for International Development (AID)–funded Flood Response Study (ISPAN 1992c) and Environmental Study (ISPAN 1992a, 1993) under contract with the Irrigation Support Network for Asia and the Near East (ISPAN) in Dhaka between 1991 and 1993. Rozana Akhter was responsible for the Women in Development component of the British-funded Fisheries Study from 1993 to 1995 (see ODA 1994).

3. Bangladeshis are well known for their love of debate and rhetoric, and very few members of the Dhaka elite managed to avoid discussion of the FAP during the first half of the 1990s. University professors took leave to serve as consultants to FAP studies. Others applied and were rejected. Some refused to work for the FAP and hosted regular meetings at which the program was criticized. Journalists, Bengali and European, gave running commentaries. Expatriates and Bangladeshi professionals crossed traditional boundaries and formed friendships and animosities based on their opinions about the FAP—some leaking information and others publicly accusing one another at conferences, in articles, and in newspaper editorials of all sorts of official malfeasance.

   The social walls separating FAP insiders and outsiders were not high, and internal documents were circulated more widely than some officials wished. (There was a widely resented tendency, in fact, for the government to regard all FAP reports as private communications unavailable to the public.) Relatives, friends, and colleagues disagreed about the program, which was a source of employment for large crews of otherwise unemployed or underemployed nationals. Some outsiders objected to the fact that such an extensive research program was controlled by foreigners and made efforts to form locally staffed research organizations independent of the foreign aid business.

4. Another widely discussed problem is sloughing, or erosion, of riverbanks as deltaic streams shift around, breaking down the region's typically soft soils. Besides eroding riverbanks, sloughing creates and destroys sandbar

islands, called *chars*. These processes, although studied, were of marginal significance to the FAP because no engineering strategy could affect them. The AID-funded project included a detailed survey of riverine *char* peoples and landforms in six different regions (ISPAN 1992c).

5. Opponents of the FAP formed a group with shifting affiliations. Some were professional research scientists or independent intellectuals; others were representatives of nongovernmental organizations and the press. On a couple of occasions, opponents managed to rally demonstrations against specific government decisions, but they expressed themselves mainly at conferences and in printed critiques.

6. The case studies presented here were collected by Kazi Rozana Akhter and translated by Jesmin Akhter (Hanchett, n.d.). All subjects' names have been changed to protect their privacy.

7. Women can and do own cattle and goats, which they can purchase with low-interest loans from the Grameen Bank or other credit plans. They are more likely, however, to take young animals for fattening and resale or to hold rights to the milk production of other people's cows temporarily in their care.

8. Riverbank land in erosion-prone areas is often purchased by poor families at low prices from others seeking to retreat farther inland. Such purchases are, of course, worthless investments; but a landless family may be willing to take the risk to get a chance at landownership.

9. See the Flood Response Study (ISPAN 1992c); the Flood Control, Drainage, and Irrigation (FCD/I) Study, *Project Impact Evaluation Reports* (Hunting Technical Services Ltd. 1992); and the North Central Regional Study, *Human Resources and Socio-Economics* volume (BCEOM 1992). The division of labor has also been analyzed by social researchers over the years. Two basic sources are Cain 1977 and Cain et al. 1979.

10. This information was gathered in interviews conducted by the Flood Response Study team in a village in Jamalpur District.

11. T. Abdullah, personal communication, August 1992.

12. Hamid 1992, 119. Female-headed households are usually one of two types—de jure or de facto. The former are headed mainly by widows or divorced women. De jure female heads of households have full legal responsibility for their families and property. Households in which the husband is absent, typically working elsewhere and sending back support, are de facto female-headed households; the women are married but are managing affairs of the home without their husbands' assistance.

13. In our experience, women never plowed with plows.

14. This analysis was conducted by Jesmin Akhter.

15. This suggestion was received more sympathetically than were many others we made.

16. The responsibility for a specific job must be distinguished from its actual performance, as Abdullah and Zeidenstein (1982, 22) point out: "When we describe 'women's' work, we do not mean that it is done exclusively by adult women, but rather that this work is typically and traditionally the *responsibility* of women."

PART III

The Culture and Power Dimensions of Water Scarcity

A Reversal of Tides
Drinking Water Quality
in Oaxaca de Juárez, Mexico

*M. Brian Riley, Arthur D. Murphy,
and Miguel Angel Méndez Rosado*

Author Summary

This chapter discusses the sanitation and potability of the municipal water supply in Oaxaca de Juárez, capital of the state of Oaxaca, in southeastern Mexico. The quality of drinking water in the various parts of the city corresponds to neighborhood type and socioeconomic status. Eight water-quality parameters, physical, chemical, and microbiological, were tested each week for seven months in fifteen different households from May until December 1992. Every week, residents completed a questionnaire regarding such items as how and when drinking water arrived, whether and how it was treated, and whether any household members had experienced illness and what if any treatment was taken. An inverse correlation was found between the socioeconomic status of a region and the quality of drinking water supplied by the city's system. The authors believe the reasons to be based on historical and geographic factors. No region in the city had drinking water that met the standards of the U.S. Environmental Protection Agency or the World Health Organization.

Introduction

The World Bank estimated in 1993 that almost one-third of all people in lesser-developed countries (LDCs) lack access to safe drinking water and an additional 44 percent lack sewage disposal service (World Bank 1993). Waterborne pathogens contribute to 80 percent of all disease—

more than 900 million cases of diarrhea per year and 12 million child-hood deaths per year—in the developing world (World Bank 1992b; World Resources Institute 1986, 129). Every day, some 25,000 people die from a combination of factors related to contaminated drinking water. Worldwide, a sanitary drinking water supply alone would prevent half the diarrhea and at least 90 percent of cholera cases. However, for a number of reasons, the various emerging supply and sanitary technologies have not led to a substantial improvement in the overall status of drinking water quality and supply around the world. Most people living in LDCs still do not have easy access to pure drinking water.

Mexico is the fourteenth most industrialized nation in the world (World Bank 1993), yet its water-related problems resemble those of an LDC (COPLAMAR 1985). Mexico has one of the world's highest rates of amebic dysentery; dysentery and dehydration are the leading causes of mortality for children in Mexico between birth and age five (Murphy and Stepick 1991). Mexicans from every state of the nation are continually confronted in their daily lives with poor drinking water and its related health issues. In 1990, only 51 percent of all households in Mexico had water piped in, and 19 percent did not have easy access to drinking water (INEGI 1994). Access to piped water in the home varies widely among the thirty-two Mexican states. The Federal District ranks first in access (72 percent of the homes), and the southernmost states of Guerrero, Chiapas, and Oaxaca rank lowest, with 28 percent, 25 percent, and 20 percent, respectively (INEGI 1994).

Since the 1950s, the state of Oaxaca has had the highest general mortality rate in the country, with an average life expectancy of 62.1 years, as opposed to the national average of 69.7 years (COESPO 1993). Life expectancy for women in the state stands at 64.9 years, significantly less than the national average, 75.0 years. Oaxaca and Chiapas, Oaxaca's bordering state to the east, together suffer the country's highest rate of mortality caused by intestinal infection, at 75.64 deaths per 100,000 inhabitants. In comparison, Mexico's overall average is 27.32 per 100,000 (COESPO 1993).

Water Service in the Urban Setting

The quality of services provided to urban residents in Mexico has been of concern to anthropologists since Oscar Lewis first began to study the Sanchez family in Mexico City (1961). Today, virtually everyone agrees that public services are necessary. The debate surrounding their

delivery typically centers on determining the correct mix, level of services (i.e., the size and composition of the public sector), and funding
(Rich 1982). Anthropologists studying political and social organization
in the poorer neighborhoods of cities in LDCs have noted the extent to
which political organization is tied to the struggle for regularized land
tenure and urban services (Peattie 1972; Steady 1982; Castells 1982;
Legorreta 1983; Hiernaux 1986). Radicalism gives way to conformity
and support for the establishment once minimal services are available
to a majority of the residents in a neighborhood (Vélez-Ibañez 1983;
Mangin 1973). P. Singer (1982) argues that urban social movements of
this type are a product of capitalist industrial cities in which services
are expanded in an attempt to make the city more livable. It is advan-
tageous for capitalists to support a range of social investments by local governments because this investment underwrites and socializes
many of the costs of labor reproduction and infrastructure provision
that individual businesses would otherwise have to pay (Rich 1982).

In all capitalist societies, the process of land allocation leads to residential segregation. The rich tend to live in one part of the city and the
poor in another. This segregation is a reflection not only of inherent
conditions of the landscape such as altitude, soil fertility, presence of
floodplains, and the like but also of acquired characteristics such as location relative to other activities, legality, prestige, social character,
and availability of services. Where services are concerned, their very
location is the result of political decisions that may further exacerbate
segregation (Gilbert and Ward 1988).

The primary objective of the study described in this chapter was to
test the quality of water delivered to homes in the intermediate-sized
city of Oaxaca de Juárez, Mexico, and to determine whether the socioeconomic status of geographic areas within the city affected the quality
of municipal water they received.

The State and Valley of Oaxaca

The name *Oaxaca* applies to a state, a valley, and a city. The state,
approximately the same size as Guatemala, lies within the tropics near
the seventeenth parallel north of the equator bordering the Pacific
Ocean, between the states of Guerrero and Chiapas (see figure 12.1).
High altitude gives much of the state a temperate climate. The Oaxaca
Valley, which lies in the middle of the state, ranges from 1,524 to 1,981
meters (5,000 to 6,500 feet) above sea level and is surrounded by mountain ranges of 3,048 meters (10,000 feet) or more, which create a rain

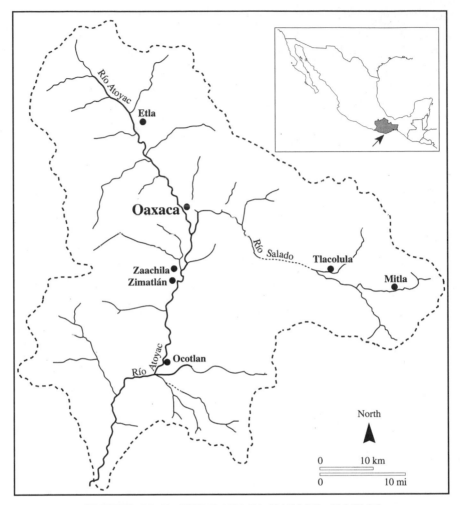

FIGURE 12.1. THE OAXACA VALLEY, MEXICO

Mexico's Oaxaca Valley is a semiarid region. The valley's watershed is cut off from externally replenished sources of surface water and underground fresh-water. The Río Atoyac, the only semipermanent supply of surface water located in the valley, begins in the foothills above the city of Etla and runs north to south through the Y-shaped valley. Map courtesy M. Brian Riley and Arthur D. Murphy.

shadow in the valley. Physical isolation and lack of water have been major factors in the development of the valley since its settlement more than 10,000 years ago (Blanton et al. 1981; Kowalewski and Finsten 1983; Lees 1989).

The Oaxaca Valley is a semiarid region (Aceves de la Mora 1976; Kirkby 1973) and suffers a pattern of severe droughts, one every four years (Dilley 1993). In essence, the valley watershed is a closed system, cut off from externally replenished sources of surface water and underground freshwater. The Río Atoyac, the valley's only semi-permanent supply of surface water, begins in the foothills above the city of Etla and runs north to south through the Y-shaped valley. Tropical hurricanes are the only occasions when the region experiences water surpluses, and much of this water is lost due to rapid runoff and flooding. An overall rainfall deficit is a critical factor in determining the quantity and quality of water Oaxacans receive.

Drinking Water Treatment and Delivery in Oaxaca de Juárez

Approximately 72 percent of the residences in Oaxaca de Juárez have access to the municipal water system. Fourteen percent have only water from wells, and another 14 percent have neither wells nor piped water. This latter group must either purchase water from neighbors or wait for a city or private water truck to fill the cistern in their community or household. Services vary greatly, depending on household location.

The first modern water facility for the city, designed to serve fewer than 40,000 individuals, was begun after an earthquake in 1931 (Aceves de la Mora 1944; Murphy and Stepick 1991). Consisting of a series of settling ponds on two mountain streams, aqueducts, and cast-iron steel pipes, this system carried water into the city from the northern village of San Felipe and from the village of Huayapan, northeast of the city (see area 5 in figure 12.2). The system provided the city with only marginally potable and reliable water.

By 1942, the city had completed work on a conventional water treatment plant, Planta Purificadora del Fortín, located in Colonia Fortín, northwest of the city center, known as the Old Center (see figure 12.2). Today, it is still the only functional conventional water plant in the city. It produces 300 liters (79.3 gallons) per second of drinking water on average, with a maximum treatment rate of 365 liters (96.4 gallons) per second. The methods used at this plant are based on the processes of sedimentation, rapid sand filtration, and disinfection with gaseous chlorine. The interval from the time the water enters the plant to the time it is discharged into municipal pipes is approximately thirty minutes. This short retention time does not allow for extensive flocculation or sedimentation of organic and inorganic materials in the water. The sand filtration system must be continually serviced for clogging by

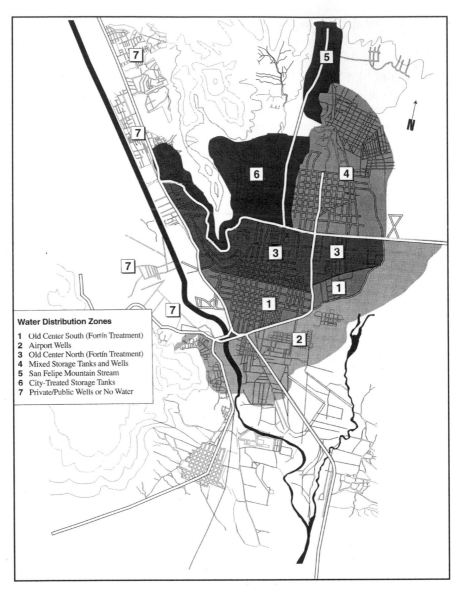

Water Distribution Zones

1 Old Center South (Fortín Treatment)
2 Airport Wells
3 Old Center North (Fortín Treatment)
4 Mixed Storage Tanks and Wells
5 San Felipe Mountain Stream
6 City-Treated Storage Tanks
7 Private/Public Wells or No Water

FIGURE 12.2. MAJOR WATER DISTRIBUTION ZONES
IN OAXACA DE JUÁREZ

The city of Oaxaca de Juárez has seven major water distribution zones. The first modern water facility for the city, designed to serve fewer than 40,000 individuals, was begun after an earthquake in 1931. By 1942, the city had completed work on a conventional water treatment plant located in Colonia Fortín, northwest of the main city center. Other water facilities exist at San Antonio de la Cal, San Felipe del Agua, Huayapan, and individual well pumping stations. Map courtesy M. Brian Riley and Arthur D. Murphy.

suspended materials. As a result, the chlorine load for raw waters is greatly increased and little of the iron and manganese found in source waters is removed. Many of the water system's problems stem from the inadequate removal of the hard-water ions of magnesium and iron, which clog pipes and cause city pumps to overheat and fail.

Other water facilities exist at San Antonio de la Cal, San Felipe del Agua, Huayapan, and individual well pumping stations. The facility at San Antonio de la Cal was initially used during the 1960s and 1970s to treat well water collected south of the city. The treatment equipment has since failed, and the plant is now used as a storage and pumping station. The San Felipe and Huayapan sources, which historically have provided a small percentage of the city's water, have been in use for approximately 420 years and 100 years, respectively. The water from both facilities originates in unprotected streams on mountain slopes north of the city.

At least forty wells supply drinking water to a large portion of the city (see area 7 in figure 12.2). The oldest wells, located next to the Río Atoyac, reach a depth of only 30 meters (98.4 feet). Many of the old well casings are broken, allowing contaminated river water to enter the water supply. Wells tapped within the past fifteen years reach 90 meters (295.2 feet) in depth and are located near Oaxaca's international airport, about seven kilometers, or a little more than four miles, southeast of the city (see area 2 in figure 12.2). The only treatment these waters receive is the addition of chlorine gas.

The village of San José Vista Hermosa, located northwest of Oaxaca de Juárez, supplies a sizable percentage of the city's raw water. From a mountain stream, the water is pumped 14 kilometers (8.7 miles) through a relatively large pipe (sixty-one centimeters, or twenty-four inches, in diameter) to the city's water treatment plant in Colonia Fortín (see area 3 in figure 12.2). Along the way, untreated raw water is diverted to at least a dozen different neighborhoods for consumption. The San José water source, with its high levels of iron and manganese, is the cause of many of the city's clogging problems.

Groundwater from the Zimatlán-Zaachila area of the Oaxaca Valley, southwest of the city (see figure 12.1), is a relatively recent addition to the municipal supply. This water is pumped in through a large-bore underground pipe over a distance of at least 12 kilometers (7.5 miles). Finally, some water is drawn from the Río Atoyac as it cuts through the city.

Technological and environmental constraints faced by the city contribute to making the water in the entire system unpotable. For numerous communities in Oaxaca de Juárez, raw water is mixed with treated water. Other neighborhoods receive inadequately treated water from heavily contaminated wells along the main river. Drinking water contamination caused by groundwater infiltration and/or back-washing is a serious and commonplace occurrence. As a direct result of varying water pressure due to city rationing, foul, shallow ground-water seeps into broken drinking water pipes. Faulty valves allow water stored on the rooftops of households to flush back into pipes as pressure drops in the water lines.

Research Methods

Sites for this study were chosen at random in stratified groups, based on previous work by anthropologist Arthur D. Murphy and sociologists Earl Morris and Mary Winter (Morris 1991; Morris et al. 1992; Murphy 1991; Winter 1991; Winter et al. 1990, 1993). Drinking water was provided by volunteer donors, whose anonymity was protected. The water was tested using the procedures described in *Standard Methods for the Examination of Water and Wastewater* (American Public Health Association 1989). Drinking water samples, strictly speaking, can represent the composition of the source only at a particular time and place. Water quality in Oaxaca de Juárez fluctuates from place to place and over time, ranging in appearance from a dark brown murkiness when water service begins to a clarity that suggests potability. Because we were limited to sampling during daylight hours, the sources tested probably had been flushed of many impurities. Thus, households are likely to be consuming water that is far more polluted than that we tested.

In all cases, drinking water samples were collected before pipe-borne water entered the household. That is, if there was sufficient water, the faucet would be allowed to flow uninterrupted for at least three minutes before sampling and analysis. This ensured that any contamination found in the water was due to contamination in the main line before the water entered the household through pipes and storage tanks.

Social Geography of Water Distribution

The neighborhoods of Oaxaca de Juárez have been categorized on the basis of age, topography, political status, land value, and general socioeconomic status of residents (see figure 12.3) (Butterworth 1973; Murphy 1987; Pacheco et al. 1991). Here, we use an eight-part classification system based on the foregoing models, supplemented with the

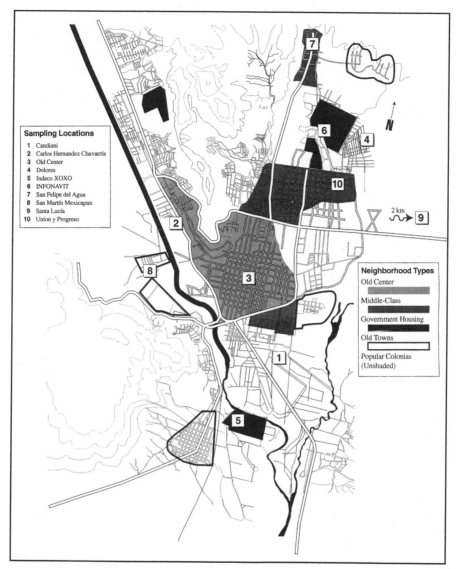

Sampling Locations

1 Candiani
2 Carlos Hernandez Chavarría
3 Old Center
4 Dolores
5 Indeco XOXO
6 INFONAVIT
7 San Felipe del Agua
8 San Martín Mexicapan
9 Santa Lucía
10 Unión y Progreso

Neighborhood Types

Old Center

Middle-Class

Government Housing

Old Towns

Popular Colonias
(Unshaded)

FIGURE 12.3. NEIGHBORHOOD TYPES AND SAMPLING
LOCATIONS IN OAXACA DE JUÁREZ

As a consequence of staggered periods of growth in Oaxaca de Juárez, different types of neighborhoods and areas of the city coincidentally receive their drinking water supplies from independent sources, each with its own independent treatment facility. With the exception of the old towns that have been incorporated into the city, most urban growth has taken place in widening circles around the city center. The areas sampled are representative of established socioeconomic divisions and neighborhood types. Map courtesy M. Brian Riley and Arthur D. Murphy.

TABLE 12.1

Water Facilities in Oaxaca de Juárez, by Neighborhood Type[a]

| Neighborhood Type | | Municipal Water Facilities | | | |
	None	Piped onto Lot	Piped into House	Piped into Kitchen	Well
Old Center	0	43	18	39	0
Popular colonias with city water	25	29	21	13	11
Popular colonias with well	6	29	20	25	21
Government housing	3	8	10	77	3
Nongovernment working class	15	41	12	9	24
Northern middle-class	1	15	16	61	7
Peripheral colonias	28	24	17	4	27
Old towns with independent water systems	21	19	27	17	17
Total Percentage for City	14%	27%	18%	26%	14%

[a]Due to rounding error, sums do not total 100 percent.

additional criteria of access to city water: Old Center, popular colonias (city districts) with city water, popular colonias with wells, government housing, nongovernment working-class neighborhoods, northern middle-class neighborhoods, peripheral colonias, and old towns with independent water systems.

As a consequence of staggered periods of growth in Oaxaca de Juárez, different types of neighborhoods and areas of the city coincidentally receive their drinking water supplies from independent sources, each with its own independent treatment facility. With the exception of the old towns that have been incorporated into the city, most urban growth has taken place in widening circles around the city center, the Old Center. This segregation of neighborhoods and their water sources makes it possible to make some general inferences about the drinking water quality of entire regions of the city. The areas sampled are representative of established socioeconomic divisions and neighborhood types (see table 12.1) (Murphy and Stepick 1991).

A majority of the homes in the relatively well off government housing and northern middle-class neighborhoods receive piped water (95 percent and 92 percent, respectively). The two poorest neighborhood types, peripheral colonias and old towns with independent water systems, had a high incidence of homes without any water (28 percent and 21 percent, respectively). This is of special interest when compared with the younger popular colonias with wells, where only 6 percent of the households had no water, indicating that the presence of a city water system does not necessarily guarantee access to water. In the working-class neighborhoods, 15 percent of the households have no water. Twenty-four percent of homes throughout the city rely on wells.

Neighborhood Types and Description of Sample Sites
The following paragraphs provide brief descriptions of neighborhood types and sample sites.

OLD CENTER
(See area 3, figure 12.3.) One hundred percent of the residences located in the Old Center receive municipal water. The heart of the city, the Old Center covers less than 20 percent of the present-day city; its boundaries correspond to the 1940 city limits of Oaxaca de Juárez (Murphy 1987). It is a place of historical monuments and colonial-style buildings. The Old Center has thousands of small businesses meeting the demands of tourists and Oaxacan citizens alike. Despite all its traffic and noise, many Oaxacans find it a desirable place to live. It has all the services offered in the city, including paved streets, sidewalks, police protection, water and sewage systems, and garbage pickup.

The Old Center is the primary water distribution area of the city. In the core of the neighborhood, drinking water is available twenty to twenty-four hours per day, seven days per week. According to a water department official, the downtown area is the first priority for receiving treated water in the city because it is the seat of the state government offices and the center of the tourist industry. This area consumes the greatest amount of the city's drinking water both because it has almost continuous water service and because it has the greatest concentration of offices, restaurants, and hotels. A few wealthy households and many hotels and restaurants supplement their drinking water with purchases from tank trucks.

The household in the Old Center tested for this study was east of Oaxaca de Juárez's downtown area, just east of the square. The residents owned an automobile and employed a domestic servant. They received drinking water twenty to twenty-four hours daily. Part of their water was stored in a rooftop storage tank and used directly for bathing and washing dishes and clothing. City water was consumed only after being boiled for at least ten minutes. This area receives its drinking water from the city's only conventional treatment plant, Planta Purificadora del Fortín.

POPULAR COLONIAS WITH CITY WATER

(See area 10, figure 12.3) With more than 200 named regions, popular colonias are Oaxaca de Juárez's most common type of neighborhood, accounting for 60 percent of the city's area. These neighborhoods range from shantytowns to well-established communities, depending largely on their age and organizational structure. With time, colonias gain legitimacy and political recognition from the local government, which may or may not lead to the provision of basic services (Murphy and Stepick 1991). The more established popular colonias with city water had the second highest incidence of homes without any water (25 percent). Popular colonias with city water tend to be older settlements and are mostly located along the Río Atoyac.

The site tested was a middle-class household in a relatively new colonia, Unión y Progreso, located northeast of the Old Center. The colonia has street curbs and many well-constructed homes but unpaved roads.

POPULAR COLONIAS WITH WELLS

(See area 5, figure 12.3.) Popular colonias with wells are located on all sides of Oaxaca de Juárez, but they are principally found near the airport, on the eastern side of the city and near the Río Atoyac.

The site sampled, INDECO XOXO, is 2 kilometers (1.2 miles) southwest of the city on the western side of the Río Atoyac. Most residents are members of the working class and commute by bus to the city. This colonia's first three-meter (9.8-foot-) well ran dry in 1983. Colonia residents deepened the well, but the water it yielded was contaminated by waste seepage. This well lasted until 1987. Finally, with the help of a federal government agency, INDECO XOXO constructed its present well (32 meters, or 105 feet, deep) farther away from the river (Prince and Murphy 1990). Untreated water from the new well is piped into homes every other night

The household we sampled stored water in a rooftop storage tank and a large concrete cistern next to the kitchen. Water from the well was used for showers and for washing clothing and was also filtered for use in kitchen cleaning. Drinking water was bought from one of the companies that delivered bottled water to the colonia.

GOVERNMENT HOUSING

(See area 6, figure 12.3.) In the early 1970s, the Mexican government created several agencies to construct housing for various sectors of the population that did not have access to housing credit.[1] These agencies built a series of duplexes and condominiums in Oaxaca de Juárez. A majority of these homes (95 pecent) receive piped drinking water. The most numerous and oldest government housing complexes are the INFONAVIT (Institute of the National Fund for Worker's Housing) communities in the northern part of the city, between the upper-middle-class Colonia Reforma and the upper-class village of San Felipe del Agua. Other government projects are found on the northwestern and southern sides of the city.

The site tested was in the third block of INFONAVIT, located north of the Old Center and east of Colonia Reforma. This subdivision received drinking water every other day from 10 P.M. to 11 A.M. Water was collected during the night, in either a ground cistern or a rooftop tank. The residents from the house we sampled bought bottled water because they knew the city water was dirty. They had not cleaned their storage tanks during the five years they had lived there.

NONGOVERNMENT WORKING-CLASS NEIGHBORHOODS

(See areas 1 and 2, figure 12.3.) This is not a specific part of the city but rather a category of people scattered about the city. This sector of the Oaxacan working class corresponds to skilled and unskilled blue-collar workers in the United States. However, one major difference exists between the working class of Oaxaca de Juárez and that of North America: these workers are much poorer. Whereas blue-collar workers in the United States can afford such luxuries as automobiles, those in Oaxaca cannot.

Colonia Carlos Hernandez Chavarría is a working-class neighborhood located beside the Río Atoyac between Oaxaca de Juarez's largest market and the Technical Institute. This community began as a squatter community in the mid-1970s and received water and political recognition in the early 1980s. The colonia receives drinking water every other day. The homeowner whose system we sampled said that in the past, he and his family drank water from their 8 meter (26.2-foot) well. When the well went dry, however, he decided to fill it in. The water here was often the most turbid in the city. The first time we sampled water from this site, a small honeybee came out of the water faucet.

Colonia Candiani was chosen as a second site from this neighborhood category. Classified as a *pueblo conurbado*, or old town, this community began receiving city water in the late 1970s. A tightly knit community, it still retains its old town flavor, with its own church, market, and patron saint's holiday. Many of the residents own and farm their land. Today, Colonia Candiani is well within the city limits. The household we sampled received water every other day, between 2 and

10 A.M. On several occasions when we came to sample, we could not obtain enough water to complete all our tests. A resident noted that when the faucet was first turned on, the water was always filled with red sediment (rust). Residents said they boiled the water for ten to fifteen minutes before drinking it. They used raw city water to wash dishes.

NORTHERN MIDDLE-CLASS NEIGHBORHOODS

(See area 7, figure 12.3.) Oaxaca de Juárez's middle-class colonias are clustered next to the government housing projects on the northern side of the city. Most households have an automobile and perhaps a domestic servant. Inside, the homes are furnished much as are middle-class homes in the United States and Canada and have two to four bedrooms. In the city's most affluent neighborhoods, most homes have running water and sewer service. Colonias San Felipe del Agua and Colonia Reforma are the two largest communities of this neighborhood type.

The household we sampled is in the city's most affluent community, San Felipe del Agua. It is located at the northern edge of the city, at the base of the Sierra de Juárez mountain range. There are a few notable mansions in this community, and many homes look as if they had been constructed in the United States. A large number of homes are constructed from traditional materials, with outer walls made of adobe, and from the outside appear to be poor. For example, the home we sampled in 1990 had sewage running in front of the house. Inside the walls, however, one could observe many signs of modest luxury, such as a large traditional Mexican patio with an American brand of washing machine and dryer in one corner. The residents stored city water in a rooftop tank. The water, however, was always quite turbid from sediment, so they did not drink it but instead used it as "gray water." For drinking water, they bought purified water or boiled the tap water for fifteen minutes before consuming it.

PERIPHERAL COLONIAS

(See area 4, figure 12.3.) Peripheral colonias are those farthest from the old center. They are on the city's least desirable land and have the greatest number of squatter residents. Because of their questionable tenure, residents face the constant possibility of eviction (Murphy 1987). The people who occupy these neighborhoods are among the poorest residents of the city.

Colonia Dolores is one the poorest communities in Oaxaca de Juárez. It is located about 7 kilometers (4.3 miles) northeast of the downtown area and about 3 kilometers (1.9 miles) east of the main INFONAVIT complex. Even though the community borders a main thoroughfare, its torn-up dirt roads are unpassable when wet. The household from which we sampled water did not have electricity and used wood as the cooking fuel. The residents drank the city water, which ran every other day, without filtering or disinfecting it.

OLD TOWNS WITH INDEPENDENT WATER SYSTEMS

(See areas 8 and 9, figure 12.3.) The final category of neighborhood includes established towns formerly outside of the city but now absorbed into it. Old towns, or *pueblos conurbados,* occupy about 11 percent of the city's land area (Murphy 1987). Several of these communities have communal wells, and many residents have private wells and own land on which they grow food staples such as corns, beans, and squash and some cash crops such as vegetables, flowers, and fruit.

Two colonias fit into the category of an old town with an independent water supply: Colonias Santa Lucía and San Martín Mexicapan. Santa Lucía is 5 kilometers (3.1 miles) east of the Old Center. Few residents there have running water; only one household in our randomly chosen block received city water. City water runs sporadically and in no apparent pattern. The household we sampled, as did many homes in Santa Lucía, used a private well for most water needs. The city water was too dirty to drink, residents said, so they drank water from their own severely contaminated private well. We were fortunate to find water at all when we came to test their home.

In San Martín Mexicapan, many households receive city water but draw on private wells instead. This area is working-class, and many residents earn less than the Mexican minimum wage (see table 12.2). San Martín is across the Río Atoyac from a market and a second-class bus station and has one of the highest population densities in the city. The services available are poor, and the dirt roads are narrow and worn. The household we sampled had a well; its water was used for washing clothes, cleaning, flushing toilets, and bathing. City water ran every other day during daylight hours. Residents drank city water without any filtering or disinfection.

Testing Parameters

We ran three types of test on the water in Oaxaca de Juárez: measures of general quality, of level of treatment, and of potability. Potability measures indicated whether the water might contain pathogens that would make it unsafe to drink.

GENERAL QUALITY

We used four parameters to measure the general quality of water: pH, biochemical oxygen demand, nitrate level, and calcium carbonate

TABLE 12.2

Neighborhood Types in Oaxaca de Juárez, by Socioeconomic Status

Socioeconomic Status	Colonia Name	Neighborhood Type	Water Source(s)
Highest	San Felipe del Agua	Northern middle-class	San Felipe Mtn. Stream
	INFONAVIT	Government housing	Fortín plant, mixed-source storage tank
	Old Center	Old Center	Fortín plant
Medium	Unión y Progreso	Popular colonia with city water	Mixed-source storage tank
	Candiani	Nongovernment working-class	City wells, private wells
	Santa Lucía	Old town with independent water system	Private wells, independent sources
	San Martín Mexicapan	Old town with independent water system	City wells, private wells
Lowest	INDECO XOXO	Popular colonia w/wells	Community well
	Carlos Hernandez Chavarría	Nongovernment working-class	City well
	Dolores	Peripheral colonia	City well

level. In general, there are no standards for these parameters. They are seen as general measures of the physical or aesthetic quality of water.

pH

Within the range of 5.0–9.0, pH has little effect in terms of toxicity (Hawkes 1979). The mean pH for Oaxaca de Juárez was 7.1 (7.0 is neutral). The Old Center had a mean pH value of 7.4, significantly higher than all other parts of the city. This is the only area of the city that consistently receives treated water. Municipal water treated at the city's only conventional water plant, Planta Purificadora del Fortín, has its pH raised in order to assist in the precipitation and flocculation of inorganic materials. INDECO XOXO had a pH significantly greater than that found in Colonia Unión y Progreso and the old town of San Martín Mexicapan. INDECO XOXO was the only tested site that used groundwater exclusively.

BOD

Biochemical oxygen demand (BOD) is an analysis of the gross amount of decaying organic material in water. As organic material breaks down, it consumes oxygen. By measuring dissolved oxygen before a sample is capped and stored in the dark, one may measure the increase in organic activity and corresponding decrease in level of dissolved oxygen. All other things being equal, organic matter itself is not toxic in water.

The United States sets no federal BOD drinking water standard. A common practice in the United States is to achieve a BOD discharge level between 20 and 30 milligrams of oxygen per liter of water before treated wastewater effluent is discharged back into a river. The mean BOD for Oaxaca de Juárez's drinking water was 55.5 milligrams per liter (mg/L). These figures are high but do not necessarily correspond with high bacterial contamination. The entire sampling area had relatively high oxygen demand, and the BOD parameter was not statistically significant for the different parts of the city. The two single greatest oxygen demands we encountered came from Colonia Candiani (156 mg/L) and the old town of San Martín Mexicapan (150 mg/L), both of which samples had been taken after rains. Surprisingly, INDECO XOXO's well water had the second lowest BOD, after the Old Center's treated drinking water. The soil there probably serves as a sandy prefilter of organic material.

Nitrates

Nitrate salts accumulate in surface water and groundwater as a result of contamination by industrial or organic waste or by chemical fertilizers. In some areas, rapid urban growth, with the accompanying intensification of agriculture and the increased utilization of ground-water, is greatly accelerating the public health danger of nitrates in drinking water. The United States has established maximum permissible limits for nitrates in drinking water at 10 mg/L or 10 parts per million (ppm). Mexican standards are even stricter, limiting nitrates to 5 mg/L.

Despite high levels of agriculture and pesticide use in the Oaxaca Valley, nitrate concentrations in drinking water do not appear to pose a serious threat in Oaxaca de Juárez. We were able to extrapolate that nitrate levels had not exceeded 15 mg/L at any one site in the city during the survey, and most samples contained only trace levels. INDECO XOXO, the sole representative of well water in the survey, had the lowest nitrate levels. This is unusual because nitrogenous compounds tend to appear in groundwater at far greater concentrations than in surface water.

Calcium Carbonates

Calcium carbonate is one of the main compounds that determine hardness of water. According to several government officials, water hardness is the most serious problem for city water in Oaxaca de Juárez. The mean value for calcium carbonate ($CaCO_3$) was 45.1 mg/L. Colonia Candiani had the highest values, with a mean of 60.0 mg/L. San Felipe del Agua's drinking water, coming directly from a mountain stream, had the smallest mean $CaCO_3$ level, with a value of 29.5 mg/L. Overall, our test results indicated a relatively low value for calcium carbonate, but two parameters we did not test for, magnesium and iron ions, greatly contribute to water's hardness in the city. For example, on examining a removed section of water main, we found thick layers of rust-colored deposits, strong evidence of iron precipitation and oxidation of the steel tubing materials.

Level of Treatment

The United States does not regulate the amount of chlorine permissible in drinking water. The important factor in determining an appropriate chlorine level is establishing the amount at which biological parameters are met—among others, total number of coliform bacteria, number of *Escherichia coli*, and number of fecal coliform bacteria. The general convention among North American drinking water plants is to discharge water with at least 2 ppm of free chlorine; free chlorine should still be present at the end of the water line.

As in most places, chlorine is the principal means of disinfecting water in Oaxaca de Juárez. With the exception of the Old Center, which receives its water from the plant at Colonia Fortín, the city's drinking water receives no filtration or primary treatment other than chlorination. For this reason, especially high concentrations of chlorine must be added and maintained in the water to ensure its cleanliness. However, our survey found that neither goal was satisfied. A chemist at the municipal water plant said that water was discharged from the plant with 2 ppm of free chlorine. On occasion, she said, the drinking water was "shocked" by adding more chlorine in order to lower bacteria counts and disinfect water lines.

Observed chlorine concentrations were not significant for the city as a whole. All ten test sites had little or no chlorine in the drinking water samples. Every site except Colonia Carlos Hernandez Chavarría and Colonia Dolores, two communities located in lower socioeconomic zones of the city, had at least one sample in which chlorine was absent. Not much of the free chlorine reaches households in the Old Center, and, as in most areas of the city, chlorine was altogether absent in the Old Center on at least one occasion. Another sample in the same location revealed one of the second highest levels of chlorine found during the entire testing period. The highest single concentration of chlorine was found at Colonia Unión y Progreso, yet Unión y Progreso also had one sample with no free chlorine present. Chlorine levels fluctuated daily at each site, with no obvious explanation other than that chlorine levels had not been monitored at the point of treatment. As expected, the well water of INDECO XOXO contained no chlorine.

Chlorates

Chlorates are a by-product of the breakdown of chlorine with organic materials. In and of themselves, chlorates do little to disinfect drinking water; they are an indicator of the former presence of free chlorine. We found no statistically significant differences in the testing area as a whole; yet, as in most of our examinations, levels in some areas differed from those in others. Colonia Candiani, with a mean of 60 mg/L, had chlorate levels significantly higher than those of Unión y Progreso and Colonia Dolores. The city does chlorinate these colonias' drinking water, but much of the free chlorine has been spent by the time it reaches homes. An interesting finding was the presence of chlorates in INDECO XOXO's well water. We believe that because this colonia is located downstream from the city, the presence of chlorates is an indicator of the enormous amounts of city water lost by seepage into the water table from city water mains. The lost chlorinated water flows downstream along the gradient of groundwater.

POTABILITY

Many microbial parameters can be used in the study of water quality. Bacterial tests, however, offer the greatest versatility because of their relative simplicity, speed, and specificity. Hence, these tests provide most standards and guidelines of water quality, which are then plotted in terms of maximum numbers of bacterial indicators of fecal pollution (total coliform bacteria, fecal coliform bacteria, and E. coli for treated water; fecal streptococci and Clostridium perfringens for untreated water) (Evison 1979; Dart and Stretton 1980).

Total Coliform Bacteria and E. coli

The total number of coliform bacteria present in a sample of water is a direct indication of bacteriological contamination and the effectiveness of disinfection measures. Coliform bacteria spores are present in soil and under other natural conditions and are ubiquitous in the natural environment. Escherichia coli is a type of coliform bacteria found only in the digestive tracts of warm-blooded animals; thus, the presence of E. coli in a water supply indicates fecal contamination.

Coliform bacteria distribution was high in the entire city of Oaxaca de Juárez. The mean MPN (most probable number) total coliform count was 2.21 (more than 5.1 bacteria per 100 mL of water), and the E. coli count was 0.79 (slightly fewer that 2.2 E. coli per 100 mL). By contrast, the U.S. Environmental Protection Agency's National Primary Drinking Water Standards and the World Health Organization's drinking water guidelines both allow fewer than 1 coliform bacterium per 100 mL of drinking water. Absolutely no E. coli is allowed. The total coliform counts in Oaxaca de Juárez were bimodal, indicating that the bacteria level tends to be either satisfactory (0 MPN) or very bad (4 or 5 MPN). San Felipe del Agua's MPN values were significantly greater than those in all other areas, with the exception of the Old Center and INDECO XOXO. Colonia Candiani showed the lowest mean of positive tests, averaging one positive per sample.

E. coli distribution was an extremely significant parameter ($p < .001$). Of the 149 samples that tested positive for coliform bacteria, 36 (24 percent) revealed the presence of E. coli, the fecal contamination indicator. Fecal contamination centered on three areas of the city. San Felipe del Agua stood out among all zones, with a mean E. coli count of

4.75 (on average, greater than 16 *E. coli* per 100 mL of water). Two other areas had average MPN counts of 1.0 or greater: Colonia Santa Lucía and the Old Center, with mean values of 1.25 and 1.0, respectively.

Conclusion

Although none of the samples in our study satisfied U.S. or World Health Organization drinking water standards, there was a wide disparity in water quality over space and time. The worst-quality water was found in the northern middle-class area, and the best-quality water was found in several of the poorer areas of the city. Thus, an inverse relationship exists between water quality and socioeconomic status (see table 12.3).

With the exception of INDECO XOXO, which operates its own shallow well near the Río Atoyac, the elite region of San Felipe del Agua had the worst water quality. The best water was found in the newer areas of the city, which get their water directly from the city's well system before it is mixed with water from municipal water tanks and mains. The most consistent water quality was found in the Old Center, which gets its water from the city's conventional water plant.

The factors that correlate most strongly with water quality appear to be the source of the raw water and the age of the water system in use. The quality of raw water is obviously important in view of the limited treatment Oaxaca de Juárez gives its drinking water. Mountain streams are polluted by raw sewage from communities and grazing animals above the city's unsecured river intakes. The city's older shallow wells along the Río Atoyac are far more polluted than the newer deep wells located to the southeast, near Oaxaca's international airport.

The systems feeding the Old Center and the wealthier neighborhoods are anywhere from sixty to ninety years old—almost archaeological in terms of functioning water systems. Those areas of the city with the most political clout today—the Old Center, San Felipe del Agua, and the INFONAVIT communities—are older, more established neighborhoods. They were the first to receive water services from the city, and their water systems are virtually the same as when they were installed. Newer developed regions in the city, including several of the communities studied—Colonias Dolores, Carlos Hernandez Chavarría, and Unión y Progreso—get their drinking water from city wells or from city storage tanks that collect water from multiple sources. The

TABLE 12.3

Neighborhoods in Oaxaca de Juárez, by Socioeconomic Status and Water Quality

Socioeconomic Status	Colonia Name	Chlorine		Bacteriological Quality		BOD (mean mg/L)
		Rank[a]	Absent (%)	Rank[b]	Total Coliform/E. coli.[c]	
Highest	San Felipe del Agua	6	50	10	16.0+	37
	INFONAVIT	7	33	7	5.1	81
	Old Center	2	25	8	8.2	21
Medium	Unión y Progreso	1	33	3	4.4	66
	Candiani	9	66	1	2.2	74
	Santa Lucía	5	55	9	5.1	68
	San Martín Mexicapan	4	25	3	4.4	66
	INDECO XOXO	10	100	6	7.2	28
	Carlos Hernandez Chavarría	3	0	2	2.9	38
Lowest	Dolores	8	0	5	5.1	93

[a]Best (1) to worst (10). Based on mean free chlorine values.
[b]Best (1) to worst (10). Based first on E. coli and then on total coliform bacteria MPN mean values (number of bacteria per 100 mL of water). Areas equal in quality receive the same rank.
[c]Calculated using mean MPN values.

multiple-source tanks receive their water from wells of different depths, some small streams, and often one of the smaller distribution plants.

Today, the old water systems are still in place and more or less functioning in the delivery of water. However, many of the municipal water lines either are broken and thus admit seepage from adjacent sewage lines or admit backwashed water from homes. With insufficient residual chlorine in the city water supply, viable pathogens are reinfecting the water even after it has been disinfected at the well or plant. Water service is rationed, and the absence of positive pressure in the pipes allows dirty water to enter; additionally, the presence of air and stationary water in steel pipes allows oxygen, iron, and other hard-water ions to react with the pipe material, resulting in rust and other types of encrustation that obstruct water flow.

Perhaps the most troubling finding has little to do with the actual quality of water delivered to homes in Oaxaca de Juárez. As mentioned earlier, next to land and housing, water availability and quality are the most politically volatile issues among the poor neighborhoods of the city. We found that municipal and state authorities consistently misrepresented the quality of water being delivered in the city. Headlines in local newspapers declared that all the water in the city system was potable even as we were obtaining results demonstrating this not to be the case. Our observation is that people are much more willing to treat their water if they receive a consistent message from the authorities. Perhaps the easiest thing that could be done in Oaxaca de Juárez to improve the quality of drinking water is simply to tell residents they are not receiving potable water because the city does not have the resources to treat it. Under such conditions and with encouragement from the authorities, many households that today do not treat their water would begin to do so.

Food for Thought

It is an assumption in the political economy of infrastructure and urban services that those areas of a city that house the most affluent populations receive the most modern and most heavily subsidized services. However, as demonstrated by this study, such an assumption is not always correct. If the case of Oaxaca de Juárez is any indication, it may often be the poorer areas, peripheral to the older, urban cores, where the newest and therefore most secure water systems are to be found. Although the poor do organize to obtain urban services (Vélez-Ibañez

1983; Castells 1982; Singer 1982), the reason why water quality in the poorer areas of Oaxaca de Juárez is better than in the Old Center and the middle-class regions is that they have newer systems, better designed and in better condition than those in the older, more affluent regions of the city.

Except for a few new residential areas, the middle class and elite in Oaxaca de Juárez, as well as in Mexico City and La Paz; Lima, Peru; and Caracas, Venezuela, tend to live near the urban center. This reflects a tradition in Latin America that defines the center as the most preferable place to live. The relatively small middle class and elite have only recently begun to occupy land outside the urban core. It is the poor who account for as much as 80 percent of the population in Latin American cities. Uncertain land tenure and the sheer numbers of the poor have made it difficult for governments to dislodge them from irregular settlements on the urban periphery. At first, political structures ignored their demands for services. However, as modern political structures emerged and the residents of the *favelas, barrios,* and *vecindades* were seen no longer as urban peasants but as potential voters (Roberts 1995), governments began looking for ways to provide what most residents wanted—water.

As sociologist Manuel Castells (1983) pointed out, the middle class and elite in Third World cities have begun to provide their own urban services because the state does not have the resources to provide them to the entire population. Thus, according to the new political discourse, it is the state's responsibility to provide minimal services to as many people as possible, and households are responsible for upgrades. In Oaxaca de Juárez, as in much of Mexico, wealthier residents can afford to pay for potable water or purification systems. High-quality services are market-driven commodities; the urban elite can afford to provide their own, whereas the middle class and urban poor must rely on the diminishing resources of the state (Topalov 1979; Lanjouw 1995). Differential distribution of urban services is both a reflection and a direct cause of accentuated stratification in cities such as Oaxaca de Juárez. What may surprise most readers is the continued insistence on the part of federal, state, and municipal authorities that municipal water is potable in the face of clear evidence to the contrary. In Mexico, the reasons for this have to do with the country's political history. What was most surprising to us was to find the same thing in projects sponsored by the United States, Japan, and the European Union in other parts of Latin America. It is not uncommon for the phrase *agua potable* (potable water) to be used to describe any system that involves a well, a pump, an elevated tank, and pipes, even if the water is not potable or there is no system to keep the water clean once it is delivered to the home. Our ethnographic experience demonstrates that in the absence of secure potable water, health would be increased significantly among the poor if they were simply told the truth. Like the rich, they are willing to purify their water if necessary. However, unlike the rich, they depend on the experts to tell them what their water is like and what they need to do to make it safe for consumption.

RESOURCES

For further discussion of these and related issues, we suggest Manuel Castells, *The City and the Grassroots* (1983); Peter Lanjouw, "Infrastructure: A Ladder for the Poor" (1995); Richard C. Rich, "The Political Economy of Public Services" (1982); Bryan R. Roberts, *The Making of Citizens* (1995); and Christian Topalov, *La urbanización capitalista* (1979).

ACKNOWLEDGMENTS

M Brian Riley is a research associate at the Center for Applied Research in Anthropology at Georgia State University; Arthur D. Murphy is chair of the Department of Anthropology at Georgia State University; and Miguel Angel Méndez Rosado is director of the microbiology laboratory at the Oaxaco Technical Institute. Our research was carried out with the assistance of a grant from the National Science Foundation. We would like to thank John Burns, Manuel Esparza, Earl Morris, Martha Rees, and Mary Winter for their assistance in preparing this chapter.

NOTES

1. The two primary agencies are INFONAVIT (Institute of the National Fund for Worker's Housing) and ISSSTE (Institute for Insurance and Social Services for Government Workers). A third agency, INDECO (National Institute for Rural Community Development and Low Income Housing), primarily subsidized land sales and community development and did not actually sell constructed homes.

Water, Power, and Environmental Health in Tourism Development

The Bay Islands, Honduras

Susan C. Stonich, Jerrel H. Sorensen, and Gus W. Salbador

━━━━━━━━━━━◆◦◀━━━━━━━━

Author Summary

This chapter examines the relationships among tourism development, water, power, and environmental health on the Bay Islands of Honduras. It examines the linkages among access to water, water quality, and environmental health for various island stakeholders and points out a number of use and user conflicts. It concludes that unregulated growth of the tourism industry, which is controlled by powerful stakeholders, and a spiraling increase in the number of tourists and ladino immigrants from the Honduran mainland have escalated the human population to a level at which the islands' land, freshwater, and marine water resources are being endangered and local communities' ability to maintain health services and other vital services is being overwhelmed. Within this framework of diminished local and national capacity, tourism is seriously affecting the health of local residents and tourists and, in turn, the sustainability of the tourist industry itself.

Introduction

Tourism has been called the "smokeless" industry, implying that it is less polluting than other kinds of industrial development. Although belching smokestacks probably are not part of the image of an ideal tourist destination for most people, the tourism industry is far from environmentally benign, and the past several decades have witnessed increased attention to its environmental consequences (e.g., Cohen 1978; Pigram 1980; Mathieson and Wall 1982, 93–132; UNEP 1984; Pearce 1989, 229–243; Hunter and Green 1995; Mieczkowski 1995; Patullo 1996, chap. 5). In recognition of the vulnerability of the environment to tourism development and the reciprocal dependence of a successful tourism industry on a healthy and enjoyable environment, a growing focus of inquiry has been the relationship between tourism and sustainable development (e.g., Nelson et al. 1993; WTO 1993). Environmental concerns have been particularly acute in two domains: threats to the fragile geography of coastal zones, especially on small islands, and degradation of critical natural resources, particularly freshwater and marine water resources (c.g., Miller and Auyong 1991; Wong 1993; IRF 1996).

Although an increasing number of studies have demonstrated linkages between the growth of tourism and degraded supplies of water, few studies have examined the differential effects of such declines on various social groups (i.e., stakeholders) in particular tourist locales. Similarly, the relationships among tourism development, water quality, and human health also have received expanded study (e.g., WHO/UNEP 1977, 1986; UNEP 1984; Archer 1985; Kocasoy 1989, 1995; Cheung et al. 1991; Hunter and Green 1995, chap. 2), but the ways in which a degraded water supply affects the environmental health of various social actors and the extent to which diverse stakeholders are able to cope with a diminished supply and quality of this critical natural resource have received far less attention. Most often, these studies have emphasized the effects of diminished water quality on the health of tourists rather than its effects on the health of various segments of the resident population. Determining the different ways in which degraded water supplies associated with the expansion of tourism influence stakeholders requires an analysis of the roles of culture and power as intermediary forces. This analysis, in turn, demands a thorough identification of diverse stakeholders who often have contesting interests and compete for access to critical water resources.

Increasing demands for water are creating scarcity and competition in many parts of the world (Gleick 1993). Generally, these competing demands are considered at the macro, intersectoral level (e.g., agriculture, industry, municipalities), and policy makers are primarily concerned with addressing competition among sectors. However, competition for water also occurs at the local level, affecting the availability and quality of water for various users within sectors. At the household level, livelihood strategies also are fundamentally dependent on water:

for drinking, washing, crop production, fishing, and food preparation, for example.

Using data collected at the local level (community, household, and individual), supplemented with interviews of key stakeholders at the national and international levels, in this chapter we examine the benefits and costs of the recent boom in tourism on the Bay Islands of Honduras. Focusing on the diverse outcomes related to access to water and environmental health for diverse island stakeholders by divisions of nationality, ethnicity, and class, we attempt to answer a number of important questions: How has tourism development affected the quantity and quality of freshwater, brackish water, and seawater in coastal zones? How have culture and power relationships affected access to and distribution and use of the water supply? Who are the relevant stakeholders who affect access, distribution, use, degradation, and conservation of water resources? In what ways are their interests complementary, competitive, and/or conflicting? What are the relationships among various stakeholders, water quality and quantity, and environmental health? And finally, what can be done to ameliorate the negative effects of tourism on the quantity and quality of water and to improve the environmental health of the human population, especially those most negatively affected?

The results presented here are based on an ongoing, interdisciplinary, and collaborative study of the interrelated human (social, economic, health, nutritional) and environmental effects of tourism development on the Bay Islands. The study uses a political ecology approach that integrates the concerns of political economy and human ecology in order to evaluate the risks and benefits of tourism development (for a discussion of the political ecology framework, see Stonich 1993, chap. 1). Ethnographic, geographic, and survey research methods were employed in three communities—Sandy Bay, West End, and Flowers Bay—situated on the western end of Roatan, the largest of the Bay Islands (see figure 13.1).

Recently, the project expanded to include a water quality and environmental health component. A critical addition was an investigation of the quality and quantity of drinking water available to island residents. Although several water quality tests had been done previously on the Bay Islands, these had concentrated on seawater near prime diving sites to determine potential risks for tourists rather than on potable water available to island residents and tourists. With the assistance of a biologist from the National Autonomous University of Honduras, a simple but reliable system for determining contamination of potable water and seawater by total coliform and fecal coliform bacteria (*Escherichia coli*) was set up at the project headquarters. More

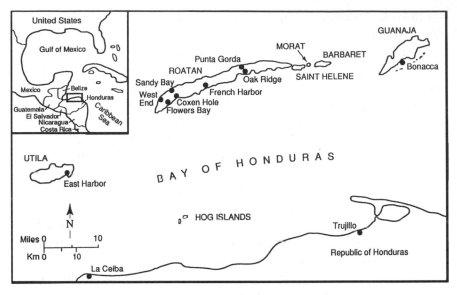

FIGURE 13.1. BAY ISLANDS, REPUBLIC OF HONDURAS

The Bay Islands are located about 50 kilometers (31 miles) off the coast of northern Honduras. They are made up of eight islands and sixty-five cays and have a total land area of approximately 238 square kilometers (92 square miles). The largest of the islands is Roatan, which covers 127 square kilometers (49 square miles) and is the site of most tourism development. Map courtesy of Susan C. Stonich

than two hundred water samples from community wells, private wells, rainwater cisterns, and points throughout the community water lines were collected and analyzed, as were samples of seawater from shoreline sites adjacent to human settlements and beach areas. Samples of "purified" bottled water were also analyzed. Medical records for one year (1993) from Roatan's only free nongovernmental medical clinic, St. Luke's Medical Mission, were examined to determine the extent to which waterborne infections (e.g., diarrhea, dysentery, enteric fever, skin and eye infections) and water-related insect vector–borne diseases (e.g., malaria and dengue fever) were affecting the local and tourist populations.

Tourism, Water, and Health

The effects of tourism on water are a major concern for a number of reasons. Water not only is necessary to sustain life and livelihoods but also is a central attraction and a vehicle for a number of primary tourist activities, such as swimming, diving, snorkeling, and fishing. Furthermore, a safe and dependable supply of water is closely related to the health of tourists and residents alike. Tourism development may affect the water supply both quantitatively, by reducing the total availability of freshwater, and qualitatively, by increasing the degree of contamination and pollution of freshwater and marine water resources. Tourism is an important user of the world's increasingly scarce water resources and often competes with other uses of water, especially in places where freshwater is sparse, such as small islands in tropical and subtropical areas (Miller and Auyong 1991). In such areas, competition is most intense during the dry season, which usually coincides with the tourist season. Several studies have shown that on a per capita basis, the demands of tourism significantly surpass domestic and municipal demands (Gajraj 1981; Grenon and Batisse 1989,156; Lvovich and White 1990). According to A. Gajraj (1981), the per capita consumption of freshwater by tourists in Barbados is six to ten times that of the local population. Shortages may also occur where freshwater is withdrawn from local aquifers to supply tourists. In some coastal regions, pumping of groundwater for beach resorts has led not only to a lowering of the groundwater tables and destruction of coastal wetlands but also to the replacement of freshwater by salt water (Oglethorpe 1982).

Tourism may also affect water quality. Unregulated and uncontrolled tourism can cause water pollution at the local level, thus jeopardizing a critical resource whose high quality is absolutely essential for the survival of the tourist industry itself. One of the most threatening concerns is contamination caused by improper disposal of human waste. Several studies have examined the linkages among tourism development, water quality, and human health (UNEP 1984; Archer 1985; Kocasoy 1989, 1995; Hunter and Green 1995, chap. 2). These studies point out the common practice of disposing of human sewage in freshwater and marine water resources, which provide an ideal medium for the spread of infectious diseases caused by bacteria, viruses, protozoa, and metazoa. Among these diseases, gastrointestinal infections caused by ingestion are the most common. Researchers also have found correlations between the level of fecal pollution of seawater, as measured by the concentration of bacterial indicators, and gastrointestinal diseases among swimmers. In addition, they have determined that although exposure to pathogenic bacteria and viruses as a result of swimming in the sea is limited, these pathogens may penetrate the respiratory system and cause eye, ear, skin, and upper respiratory infections, which at times are more common than gastrointestinal infections (Kocasoy 1989). The most common measures of pathogens in water are counts of total coliform and fecal coliform bacteria. If coliform contamination exceeds certain levels, the water is regarded as unfit for drinking or swimming. In tourist settings, high fecal coliform counts are associated with malfunction or lack of sewage and septic tank systems. To combat contamination of water by pathogens, it is essential to provide sewage treatment facilities in tourist areas. Unfortunately, even in wealthy countries, the rates of effective treatment are low. For example, along the Mediterranean coast of France, less than 50 percent of human sewage is effectively treated (Grenon and Batisse 1989, 159).

Declining water quality in tourist areas can also be caused by a number of other factors, including destruction of habitats stemming from tourism-related infrastructure (e.g., road building and hotel construction), deforestation, and erosion that lead to increased sediment loads; indiscriminate use of fertilizers and pesticides to maintain golf courses, lawns, and gardens; tourist transportation services (cruise ships, motorboats, and other vehicles) that pollute water not only with hydrocarbons but also with human waste and detergents; and the behavior of individual tourists who throw bottles, cans, and other garbage into water bodies. The economic consequences of declines in water quality are plain—tourists stop frequenting areas that are infamous for these problems. This is illustrated by the recent decline of the western Mediterranean region as a prime tourist destination and the simultaneous increase in tourism in less polluted areas such as the eastern Mediterranean and Caribbean regions, West Africa, Kenya, the Seychelles, and Mauritius (Mieczkowski 1995, 210).

Tourism Development on the Bay Islands

In response to a chronic national economic crisis and with the support and financial assistance of international donors such as the Inter-American Development Bank (IDB) and the U.S. Agency for International Development (AID), the Honduran government began aggressively promoting tourism as an economic development strategy in the early 1980s (Stonich et al. 1995). Particular emphasis was placed on the important archaeological site of Copán, the scenic beaches and historical ruins along the northern coast, and the relatively pristine reefs of the Bay Islands (Stonich, Sorensen, and Hundt 1995). By 1990, the Bay Islands were the most visited tourist destination in the country. Although politically part of Hispanic, Spanish-speaking Honduras, the

Bay Islands, with their predominantly Afro-Caribbean population, have been one of the English-speaking enclaves in the western Caribbean region (Parsons 1954). By maintaining cultural, social, and economic ties with other English-speaking enclaves, especially British Honduras (now Belize), the Cayman Islands, and the United States, and retaining the English language and Protestantism, Bay Islanders isolated themselves fairly successfully from Honduran influences even after the Wykes-Cruz Treaty returned sovereignty of the islands to Honduras in 1859. Reflecting four centuries of Anglo-Hispanic conflict in the western Caribbean region, the current effort of the Honduran government to promote tourism on the islands is the most recent attempt to integrate the islands into the mainland polity, economy, society, and culture.

The Bay Islands are located about 50 kilometers (31 miles) off the northern coast of Honduras and are easily accessible from the mainland by plane, boat, and ferry. They are made up of eight islands and sixty-five cays and have a total land area of approximately 238 square kilometers (92 square miles). The largest of the islands is Roatan, which covers 127 square kilometers (49 square miles) and is the site of most tourism development. A mountainous ridge bisects the length of the island; its steep slopes end abruptly at the coastline. Although Roatan boasts only a few palm tree–skirted, white-sand beaches (most notably West Bay Beach, Alligator Nose Beach, and Camp Bay), these beaches are spectacularly beautiful and provide ideal sites for swimming, snorkeling, and sunbathing—the major pastimes of domestic tourists and important to many international tourists as well. The islands' main international tourist attraction, however, is a fringing coral reef that scuba divers place in the same class as the Great Barrier Reef of Australia. The reef provides critical habitats for numerous marine species and protects the shores from flooding (Vega et al. 1993). Although rainfall averages at least 200 centimeters (78.7 inches) per year on all the islands, most precipitation occurs during the rainy season— the fall and early winter of the Northern Hemisphere, especially October and November. The primary tourist season is during the dry season, from January through June, during which less than 10 centimeters (3.9 inches) of precipitation falls.

In addition to the charming tropical beaches and spectacular coral reefs, reminders of the islands' rousing history are evident in remnants of prehistoric archaeological sites, pirate strongholds, English fortresses, underwater shipwrecks, and an ethnically diverse population, including English- and Creole-speaking Afro-Antilleans; Anglo-Antilleans; and North Americans; Garifuna (Black Caribs); and Spanish-speaking ladinos from the mainland. Together, these attractions make the Bay Islands ideal for several types of Central American tourism development—sun, sea, and beach tourism; adventure tourism and ecotourism; and cultural heritage tourism (Stonich, Sorensen, and Hundt 1995).

Until recently, the Bay Islands' relatively low population density, comparative isolation, and poor communications infrastructure protected them from many of the adverse social and environmental effects of tourism that have characterized much of the eastern Caribbean region. Beginning in the 1960s, a segment of small tourists made up mostly of divers and of recreational sailors began to enjoy the islands' splendid reef, clear waters, secluded harbors, and tranquil beaches. At the same time, according to most social, economic, and health measures, Bay Islanders managed to maintain a quality of life that significantly surpassed that of Honduran ladinos on the mainland (Stonich, Sorensen, and Hundt 1995).

Unfortunately, these conditions began changing radically in the 1980s in the context of the largely unregulated and uncontrolled growth of the tourism industry, which included the migration of thousands of desperately poor ladinos from the mainland seeking employment in the expanding tourism sector. In 1990, an estimated 15,000 tourists visited the Bay Islands, making the islands the most popular tourist destination in Honduras. By 1993, the number of international tourist arrivals grew to 30,000—more than the entire local population, which was estimated to be about 23,850 (BID 1994, 3). In 1994, the number of tourists climbed to 40,000, of which about 80 percent were from the United States. In addition to tourists and ladino mainlanders, the islands' population was recently augmented by a growing number of foreign-born residents, whose land purchases have provoked widespread land speculation and significant increases in the value of coastal and upland property. The influx of these newest residents was facilitated by changes in the Honduran constitution that allow ownership of coastal and frontier property by non-Hondurans.

Between 1974 and 1988, the population of the Bay Islands grew by about 110 percent, far surpassing the rise in the national population (65 percent) during the same time period. The annual population growth rate of the islands since 1988 is estimated to be more than 5.5 percent (Stonich, Sorensen, and Hundt 1995). According to data from various national censuses, the percentage of ladinos on the Bay Islands grew from 7 percent in 1970 to 12 percent in 1981 before reaching 16 percent by 1988. Community-level censuses conducted as part of this study, however, reveal a much higher percentage of ladino residents—approaching 50 percent in some communities (Stonich, Sorensen, and Hundt 1995).

Two measures of the impact of tourists usually applied at the national level are the tourist intensity ratio (TIR) and the tourist density ratio (TDR). The TIR is the ratio of tourists to local residents in a given year, and the TDR is the ratio of tourists to land area. In 1991 in the Caribbean basin (i.e., the insular Caribbean region, Mexico, Central America, and the South American countries of Colombia and Venezuela), the TIR was greatest in Belize (111.5 percent) followed by the insular Caribbean region (98.3 percent). TIRs were much lower elsewhere, with Honduras having one of the lowest in the region (3.7 percent). In terms of the TDR, the highest ratios were found in the insular Caribbean, Belize, and Costa Rica, all with TDRs greater than ten tourists per square kilometer (0.39 square mile). In contrast, Honduras had one of the lowest TDRs in the region, with 1.8 tourists per square kilometer. On the basis of these aggregate national-level data, it appears that tourists have relatively little impact in Honduras. However, when the Honduran data are spatially disaggregated, a very different picture emerges. The Bay Islands constitute only 0.2 percent of the land area in Honduras, yet in 1991 they housed more than 10 percent of the country's foreign visitors. Between 1974 and 1994, the TIR rose from 7.6 percent to 152.1 percent and the TDR increased from 4 to 168 tourists per square kilometer, with most of the increase occurring after 1988, the year the jet runway was completed on Roatan, opening up the islands to direct international flights. In the 1990s, TIR values for the Bay Islands were comparable to those in the insular Caribbean region as a whole and surpassed those in other major international tourist destinations such as Barbados and Jamaica (for comparisons with other locations, see Harrison 1992, 11–13).

Although tourists may have little impact on the country overall, they have an exceptionally high impact on the Bay Islands, surpassing the average impact in the tourist industry–dependent insular Caribbean region. Moreover, between 1988 and 1994, the total number of tourists visiting the islands increased by 167 percent. This was significantly higher than the 21 percent rise in the number of island residents, including ladino immigrants, during the same period. By the mid-1990s, the combined effects of the escalating numbers of international tourists and ladino immigrants from the mainland elevated the population to a level at which the island's freshwater supply, food supply, and other natural resources were threatened and many communities' ability to maintain health services and other vital services were overwhelmed. These conditions raise the serious question of whether population growth per se is the root cause of the environmental degradation occurring on the islands. An essentially demographic explanation is an oversimplification of reality, however, since the majority of population growth, involving tourists and ladino immigrants, is directly associated with the expansion of the tourism industry. The root cause of environmental degradation on the Bay Islands is the rapid, largely unregulated, and uncontrolled expansion of the tourism industry. Part of this expansion has included significant infrastructure development in certain domains, especially airport improvement and road construction, and a simultaneous lack of infrastructure development in other critical domains, especially water, sewage, and solid waste disposal systems. Although it is clear that escalating numbers of tourists put more pressure on the islands' environment and natural resources, the major effect of development has been to increase the number of tourist—regardless of the environmental and human costs.

We have reported elsewhere on the demographic, social, economic, ecological, nutritional, and environmental effects of the tourism industry on the Bay Islands (Stonich, Sorensen, and Hundt 1995; Stonich and Sorensen 1995). The price of tourism has included increased socioeconomic differentiation and a growing gap between rich and poor; assignment of the majority of ladinos and Islanders (Afro-Caribbeans) to low-status, low-paying, temporary jobs; reduced access by local people to the natural resources on which they depend for their livelihoods; escalating prices for food, manufactured goods, and housing; land speculation and spiraling land costs; increased outside ownership of local resources; and deterioration of the biophysical environment. Although islanders range in wealth from very rich to very poor, according to measures of economic production, income, consumption, and nutrition, ladinos generally tend to be poorer and at higher nutritional risk (see photos 13.1 and 13.2).

For ladino families, reduced access to what once were communal fishing, hunting, and gathering resources as a result of the establishment of the Sandy Bay/West End Marine Reserve has diminished their economic options further, and there is little doubt why they and their Islander counterparts are suspicious of recent efforts to designate the Bay Islands as a national marine park (Sorensen 1993). In addition, poorer island residents (both Islanders and ladinos) are indignant at being told to curtail their fishing and hunting activities by wealthier inhabitants. These owners of commercial fishing fleets, hotels, resorts, and other businesses are responsible for overfishing shrimp and lobster and are absorbed in a hotel-building spree (despite a shortage of freshwater and the absence of sewage and other waste disposal systems), unsound road building, mangrove destruction, extensive dredging of the reef, and other environmentally destructive activ-

PHOTO 13.1. HOME OF A MIDDLE-CLASS ISLANDER,
BAY ISLANDS

Islanders (Afro-Caribbeans) range in wealth from very rich to very poor, according to measures of economic production, income, consumption, and nutrition. They view government efforts to promote tourism development as part an attempt to Hispanicize the islands. Islanders are disturbed about the loss of their way of life, their values, and their language—their Afro-Caribbean ethnicity and culture. Photograph by Susan C. Stonich.

ities. Although poorer local users acknowledge that the reef and other aspects of the environment have suffered, they perceive that their own restraint will be of no benefit unless everyone can be made to cut back on fishing and other environmentally destructive activities. The discrepancy in wealth between resort owners, whose guests make the most use of the reef, and local subsistence users only furthers the attitude of poorer residents that they should not bear the burden of conservation. It is not surprising that the one private marine reserve (the Sandy Bay/West End Marine Reserve), supported by the owner of a prime diving resort, is having difficulty limiting subsistence use and has prompted escalating conflicts between Islanders and the growing numbers of ladino immigrants from the mainland.

PHOTO 13.2. LADINO GHETTO, BAY ISLANDS

In the context of the largely unregulated and uncontrolled growth of the tourism industry, thousands of desperately poor ladinos migrated from the mainland seeking employment in the expanding tourism sector. Ladinos generally tend to be poorer and at higher nutritional risk than Islanders. Photograph by Susan C. Stonich.

Environmental Concerns Affecting Freshwater and Marine Water Resources

As a result of the mismanaged growth of tourism and migration from the mainland, the islands' fragile ecosystems have suffered from severe environmental problems, most of which affect the islands' freshwater and marine water resources. Major problems stem from accelerated deforestation, erosion, and sediment discharge due to site clearing and pasture expansion; a lack of sewage, solid waste, and water treatment facilities; and an absence of hydrogeologic studies, resulting in the haphazard drilling of an escalating number of wells. The consequences of these actions include contamination of freshwater and seawater; increased salinity in underground aquifers; a declining supply of potable water; and degradation of coastal zones, including mangrove destruction, beach degradation, and coral reef damage (Vega et al. 1993).

On Roatan, both nonpoint- and point-specific erosion generate sediment deposits in coastal areas. Serious nonpoint sources of sediment include degraded watersheds in which a variety of erosion processes result in excessive sedimentation of streams during the rainy season. More than 70 percent of the island of Roatan has been cleared recently, mostly over the past ten to fifteen years (Vega et al. 1993). Deforestation has resulted primarily from expansion of pastureland for livestock by wealthier Islanders and by the spread of hillside agriculture by poor ladino immigrants from the mainlands, who are not able to find work in the tourism industry or whose low-paying jobs do not provide them with an adequate income. Elimination of the forests in the upper part of Roatan's watersheds has altered the natural hydroperiod to the extent that all but one of the island's streams dry up during the dry season, especially during April and May. Deforestation has also led to rapid runoff of rainwater that formerly filtered down into underground aquifers supplying local wells. In addition, as new wells are further drawn down the aquifer, increasing numbers of older and shallower wells are going dry.

Major point-specific sources of sediment include disturbances related to infrastructure development, such as a major highway recently completed along the length of Roatan. Clearing of land for hotel construction also has resulted in significant discharge of sediment, particularly during the rainy season, when heavy rains increase runoff to the beach and destroy coral, sea grass beds, and mangrove areas. One of the most serious sources of sediment is the unstabilized, unpaved road leading to West Bay Beach, the most popular swimming beach on Roatan (Vega et al. 1993). The road was built by the owner of one of the island's premier diving resorts, who also owns much of the property adjacent to West Bay Beach. The road was built to increase access to this area of tropical forest and premier beachfront property in order to encourage investment. An owner of one of the small hotels on West Bay Beach christened the thick red discharge that frequently flows from this road through his property and onto reefs and sea grass beds during the rainy season as "Red Clay Creek."

The lowering of the water table and the seawater intrusion that occur as water is extracted from the ground by an increasing number of wells has led to a high salt content in the water supplies of some communities. Islanders who can afford to do so now buy commercial bottled water for drinking. This water is processed on the mainland, in

San Pedro Sula, and transported to the islands by boat. Diminished access to potable water, increased salinity in the remaining supply, and increased contamination of freshwater, brackish water, and salt water are among the most significant problems and contentious issues on the islands and are likely to affect the growth and sustainability of the tourism industry.

Tourism, Water, and Environmental Health on the Bay Islands

Serious declines in the quality and quantity of potable water are the most critical environmental health risks that have emerged on the Bay Islands, and they have provoked widespread conflicts among users. Groundwater, supplemented seasonally by rainwater, is the major source of potable water on all the islands. With increasing frequency, shortages have resulted in rationing and/or an irregular supply to both domestic and commercial users. In addition, no sewage treatment system exists, so an undetermined but large amount of untreated raw sewage is piped directly into the sea. Even where latrines and septic tanks are in place, they frequently leak contaminated water into soil and groundwater. The recent growth of the cattle population, in part to meet rising tourist demand for beef, especially on Roatan, further contributes to the contamination of groundwater; it is common to see cattle grazing in fenced pastures close to wells and natural springs used for drinking water.

In response to shortages, those who can afford to do so drill wells (often several), with little forethought or knowledge as to suitable location or depth. To help alleviate the resulting problems, a non-governmental organization (NGO) on the island called the Bay Islands Development Promotion Association (APRODIB), with funding from international donor agencies, has been promoting the building and use of composting latrines, the creation of hydrogeologic maps, and the drilling of new community wells that are chlorinated and more appropriately located. To date, however, municipal agencies seem to be operating with little coordination and success. The lack of an adequate islandwide solid waste collection and disposal system provides a further source of contamination of the water supply, as well as prime breeding sites for mosquitoes and other pests.

Declining water quality and increasing water scarcity do not affect island residents and tourists equally; certain groups suffer the costs of these problems disproportionately. Patterns of access to a water supply system in rural and urban areas of Honduras are similar to those in Latin America and the Caribbean region as a whole. In Honduras, approximately 90 percent of urban households and 54 percent of rural households have access to either a house connection or a public faucet, whereas 10 percent of urban and 46 percent of rural households are without access (PAHO 1994). Data for the three Bay Islands communities that were part of this study, disaggregated by ethnicity and nationality, however, reveal patterns distinct from the aggregate Honduran data. Recently arrived foreign residents of the communities get their water from diverse sources—40 percent from private wells connected directly to their homes and 20 percent each from municipal water piped to their homes, bottled water, or some combination of these. In addition, virtually all foreign residents treat their water in some way, whether with a chlorine, ultraviolet, or membrane filtration system. In marked contrast to foreign residents, recent ladino immigrants are most likely to have water piped to their residences from municipal wells (38 percent) or obtain water from a public faucet (33 percent). Ladinos are also the only group without regular access to a water supply system—7 percent of ladino households collect water from two seeps (referred to as "springs" by local residents). No ladino household treats its water. The most diverse pattern of access and treatment is among Islander households: 57 percent of Islanders rely on municipal water connected to their homes; 6 percent have private wells with direct connections; 8 percent depend on public faucets; 3 percent use bottled water; and 21 percent draw on some combination of sources. A small percentage (11 percent) treat their water with chlorine (5 percent could not be determined).

Similar differences occur in patterns of utilization of excreta disposal facilities. The small group of relatively affluent foreign residents has greatest access to functioning toilets (80 percent) as well as septic fields or tanks (60 percent). Ladinos have the least access to such facilities (only 16 percent have functioning toilets, and only 14 percent have septic fields or tanks), and they are the most likely to live in houses with nonfunctioning toilets or latrines or no disposal facilities at all. The pattern for Islanders is intermediate between those of foreign residents and ladinos: 50 percent have functioning toilets, 35 percent have functioning latrines, 15 percent have nonfunctioning toilets or latrines, and 36 percent have septic fields or tanks.

Drinking Water Quality

Drinking water from all sources available at the community level was tested for the presence or absence of total coliform bacteria and E. coli

on the assumption that the presence of these bacteria is unacceptable
(WHO 1993). Sufficient sampling of seawater was done to calculate the
concentrations of these bacteria, using the method of most probable
number (MPN) (HACH Corporation 1993). It is extremely simple to
summarize the results of the analyses of the two hundred samples of
drinking water and of brackish water and seawater collected from
shoreline sites adjacent to human habitations and beaches. All
untreated sources of drinking water tested positively for total coliform
bacteria and E. coli. Private wells, public wells, "springs," rainwater
cisterns —all were contaminated. Even the "purified" bottled water
that had been shipped to the islands from a processing plant in San
Pedro Sula and distributed through a new franchise on Roatan was contaminated. It is impossible to measure the decline in water quality over
time or to correlate deterioration to increases in tourism because so far
as we know, no widespread community testing of potable water had
been done previously. Anecdotal evidence does exist, however. Local
residents interviewed maintained that they were more frequently ill
with diarrheal diseases than in the past. Our own personal experience
supports this. When we first visited the islands in 1981, we drank the
water everywhere with no ill effects. By 1988 (the year the jet runway
was constructed on Roatan and tourism began to skyrocket), we had
occasional gastrointestinal symptoms. In 1992, the first year we codi-
rected an Earthwatch project and supervised the fieldwork of a number
of students, only a few members of the research team became ill with
diarrhea. The following year, however, the entire team became ill on
the second day of the project, and we began chlorinating our drinking
water. In addition, several team members were diagnosed with skin
infections after conducting an underwater evaluation of the biological
health of the coral reef adjacent to the community of West End.

Uncontaminated water was found rarely and only when it had un-
dergone some treatment, as with chlorine, membrane filtration systems, or ultraviolet systems. Such systems, especially the membrane
filtration and ultraviolet systems, were found only in the homes of the
affluent island elite and foreign residents and in one high-priced diving
resort. Many middle-class owners of moderately priced hotels were
fearful of jeopardizing the health of their guests and were trying to
ensure a safe water supply by purchasing bottled water. Although
analyses question how safe such water really is, even safe water often
becomes contaminated in the process of being served to guests,
through the addition of ice made with unpurfied water or by being
poured into wet pitchers that had been washed in contaminated water,
for example. Presently, it appears that the only segments of the island

population assured of a safe water supply are the relatively affluent foreign residents, the small number of elite families, and guests in a number of upscale hotels that have water purification systems.

Brackish Water and Seawater Quality

Contamination of seawater also is of growing concern, although this concern is most often expressed in terms of the pollution's potential effects on divers and the tourism industry rather than its effects on the health of local residents. Fecal coliform analyses were conducted on seawater from diving sites and along the shorelines of swimming beaches near West Bay Beach, from the urban center of French Harbor, and from the communities of Sandy Bay, West End, and Flowers Bay. The grading system (good, acceptable, and unacceptable) was based on the criteria of the World Health Organization (WHO/UNEP 1977) for water quality. These categories are related to rates of swimming-associated gastroenteritis and skin symptoms (Cheung et al. 1991). The concentrations of fecal coliform bacteria near recreational areas of French Harbor increased from about 500 (within the acceptable range) to more than 1,000 organisms (unacceptable) per 100 milliliters of water between 1991 and 1993 (AOA 1991, 1992, 1993). By 1993, unacceptable levels also were found near drainage areas in Flowers Bay. Although precise concentrations are unspecified, unacceptable levels of total coliform bacteria and fecal coliform bacteria (*E. coli*) have also been reported in surface water and seawater collected near Roatan's other major urban centers of Coxen Hole and Oak Ridge (BID 1994). As of this writing, "good" and "acceptable" levels of contamination exist at diving sites, West Bay Beach, and most other shoreline sites; however, unregulated development, escalating populations, and the absence of water, sanitation, and waste disposal systems will very likely cause higher levels of contamination in the future.

Water Quality and Environmental Health

Current conditions on the Bay Islands have escalated the incidence of waterborne diseases such as cholera, dysentery, and hepatitis and have facilitated the transmission of water-related diseases such as malaria and dengue fever, which thrive in unsanitary conditions (BID 1994). As the only free nongovernmental medical clinic on Roatan, St. Luke's Medical Mission is the primary source of medical care for the poorest segment of the population living in Sandy Bay and nearby communities. The disproportionate use of the clinic by the poor is indicated by its relatively high number of ladino patients: although about 48 percent of the nontourist residents of Sandy Bay classify themselves as ladino, ladinos made up 70 percent of nontourist patients to St. Luke's Mission clinic. Waterborne and water-related infections and diseases are the major reasons for visits to the clinic by both Islanders and ladinos of all age groups. Acute respiratory infections, diarrhea, and parasites are the most common causes of clinic visits by both groups. Ladinos and Islanders vary most significantly in the incidence of malaria, which accounts for about 14 percent of ladino visits but only 7 percent of Islander visits. This difference is probably due to higher levels of prevalence among ladino immigrants, most of whom come from northern Honduras, where more than 70 percent of the country's malaria cases are diagnosed. Not surprisingly, barotrauma (recompression sickness) and otitis (ear infection) are the major reasons for clinic visits by tourist divers, although tourists have rates of diarrhea and skin infection comparable to those of residents. The degree to which tourists are affected by malaria is unknown, as their average stay on the islands (6.5 days) is usually too short for symptoms of the disease to appear.

Conclusion

Analyses of the relationships between tourism development and environmental health on the Bay Islands strengthen earlier findings of socioeconomic and nutritional effects, which showed that the islands' poor ladino population was reaping inadequate benefits from tourism as measured by income, patterns of consumption, and nutrition. Although all island residents and tourists currently face an increased risk of contracting diseases associated with freshwater, brackish water, and salt water, it appears that ladino immigrants confront even higher risks. Ladinos are significantly more likely than Islanders and foreigners to get their water from seeps or springs, the most highly contaminated category of water tested, and they are the most likely not to have access to functioning excreta disposal facilities. Ladinos are also the least able to protect themselves from water-related environmental health risks; for example, they are the least likely to treat their water in any way. It is not surprising that early in 1994, during the most recent outbreak of cholera on the islands, all cases were among the recent ladino immigrant population.

The environmental health of local residents has been given relatively low priority by the financially strapped government of Honduras in its efforts to promote tourism. Since 1990, government policy has stressed two interrelated efforts—economic policies aimed at expanding export earnings and stabilizing the balance of payments, and structural adjustment programs targeting the social, educational, and health sectors. Between 1989 and 1992, total public spending fell from U.S.$632 million to U.S.$239 million (in 1988 dollars). Despite this overall reduction, public investment in health increased from U.S.$.09 million in 1990 to U.S.$1.5 million in 1992, although investment in the environment and environmental sanitation fell from U.S.$12.6 million to U.S.$6 million. This pattern of spending suggests a pragmatic decision to deal with immediate health needs rather than to improve long-term health through enhanced preventive measures, such as expanded water supply and sanitation systems (PAHO 1994).

In an effort to counter declining budgets, social compensatory programs were created in the 1990s with funding from the Honduran government, international donors, nongovernmental organizations, and public–private initiatives. One of the most important of the latter has been the Honduran Social Investment Fund (FHIS), of which about 13 percent of all projects are related to health and nutrition. Among health projects, approximately 29 percent are designed to improve drinking water supplies and basic sanitation. Although the majority of FHIS projects have focused on large urban centers and poor rural communities on the mainland, a small amount of funding has gone toward improving sanitation on the Bay Islands, in collaboration with the Bay Islands Development Promotion Association (APRODIB). One such project has been to build composting latrines in a number of island communities, including Flowers Bay. Unfortunately, due to a lack of initial training and followup, few of the latrines are being used for their intended purpose; most are used as shower stalls or storage huts.

In late 1994, after conducting feasibility studies for several years, the Inter-American Development Bank (IDB) approved financing of the Bay Islands Environmental Management Project, with U.S.$19.1 million from the IDB and U.S.$4.8 million from Honduras. The IDB will work in cooperation with the relatively new Honduran Ministry of the Environment (SEDA) and Island nongovernmental organizations, including APRODIB and the Bay Islands Conservation Association (BICA). The general objective of this ambitious project is "to maintain and improve the quality of the environment on the Bay Islands as a basis for sustainable economic development" (IDB 1994). Among the specific objectives are protecting coastal and marine ecosystems through a system of integrated management; strengthening local capacity for planning, management, and administration; and improving the standard of living of residents through improvements in water supply and construction of basic sanitation facilities. To date, however, little if any evidence of project implementation and success is apparent. Despite the participatory rhetoric written into the project summary, interviews with people in the communities of Sandy Bay, West End, and Flowers Bay during the summer of 1995 revealed that few residents, apart from a small group of middle–class business owners, are aware of the project, much less involved in any way. Moreover, many residents, especially those in Flowers Bay, believe they have been intentionally excluded from benefiting from tourism development by international interests and island elite, who control the development opportunities. Many members of the island elite and middle-class business owners engage in environmentally destructive activities even as they extol the virtues of environmental conservation and support the protection of marine resources, albeit at the expense of poor ladinos and Islanders. However, without the support of these less powerful stakeholders, there is little chance that the existing marine reserves or the proposed Bay Islands National Marine Park will succeed in their conservation goals. Islanders living in Flowers Bay and other communities, however, are concerned with much more than their lack of representation and their diminished access to the natural resources on which they depend: they are equally disturbed about the loss of their way of life, their values, and their language—their Afro-Caribbean ethnicity and culture. They view government efforts to promote tourism development as part of an attempt to Hispanicize the islands. On the Bay Islands, cultural conflict is at the heart of the conflicts over tourism development and resource management.

In terms of critical natural resources, tourism development has had its greatest affect on water—freshwater to sustain lives and seawater to sustain livelihoods. Not surprisingly, conflicts over access, distribution, and degradation of natural resources also are most acute regarding water. Although it is easy to point to escalating numbers of tourists and residents as the heart of the problem, such an analysis oversimplifies a much more complex set of interrelated processes that have at their core the unregulated development of tourism within the context of the Bay Islands' history, cultures, and relationship with the mainland. Tourism development, controlled by powerful government, public, and private interests, has significantly altered relationships among various power-holding groups with interest in the islands, and with that it has changed previous patterns of use and access to freshwater and marine water resources. Whereas it is the more powerful social groups that have garnered the greatest benefits of tourism development and have been most able to protect themselves from degraded water supplies, it is the less powerful on the Islands who have borne the heaviest costs.

Food for Thought

As the international tourism industry expands, host governments argue that promoting tourism promotes national unity and economic growth. Yet many critics of tourism development in developing countries note the foreign ownership of many tourism businesses, often involving transnational corporations, and related "leakages," profits from the tourism industry leaving the country.

This chapter has raised a number of questions that are applicable to the case of the Bay Islands, but also to issues of tourism in other ecologically sensitive areas of the world.

- Is the government of Honduras justified on promoting tourism on the Bay Islands in the name of national unity and economic growth?

- How best might governments reconcile national economic interests with local ecological and sociocultural needs? On the Bay Islands, would a powerful system of laws and regulations be sufficient to ensure environmental conservation, sociocultural equity, and sustainability of the tourism sector?

- In regard to the role of local people, how might poorer Islanders and ladino immigrants overcome several hundred years of ethnic animosity and sometimes violent conflict in order to collaborate in their efforts to increase their power in affecting tourism development on the Bay Islands?

- Ecotourism is fast becoming a major industry in many tropical areas of the world. How might Bay Islanders promote sustainable ecotourism?

- Finally, how does the example of the Bay Islands affect the choice of your next vacation or diving trip?

RESOURCES

For informative historical background on current conditions on the Bay Islands, consult William Davidson's *Historical Geography of the Bay Islands* (1974). For a pair of entertaining traveler's tales of the Bay Islands, see F. Hedges and A. Mitchell's *Battles with Giant Fish* (1924) and Jane Harvey

Houlson's *Blue Blaze* (1934). For recent books on the costs of tourism in the Caribbean, consult Frank Fonda Taylor's, *To Hell with Paradise* (1993) and Polly Patullo's *Last Resorts* (1996). A worthwhile World Wide Web site on tourism and the environment in Latin America and the Caribbean, with links to many other sites, can be found at http://www.planeta.com.

ACKNOWLEDGMENTS

Research for this chapter was made possible by grants from the University of California Research Expedition Program, Earthwatch, and the University of California Academic Senate. Special thanks are due Dr. George Haseman and Dr. Gloria Lara of the Honduran Institute of Anthropology and History; Dr. Becky Myton of the National Autonomous University of Honduras and the Honduran Ministry of the Environment; Dr. Jackie Woods, Director of the Roatan Hospital; St. Luke's Medical Mission; and Cheryl Galindo and the staff of the Bay Islands Conservation Association for their support. We also would like to thank the hundreds of Bay Islanders who participated in our study, the many U.S. and Honduran student and project volunteers, students in Dr. Stonich's seminar on tourism, and Matthea Cremers for their efforts in collecting and analyzing the data.

CHAPTER 14

Culture, Power, and the Hydrological Cycle
Creating and Responding to Water Scarcity on St. Thomas, Virgin Islands

Barbara Rose Johnston

Author Summary

This chapter reemphasizes the centrality of culture and power in instigating and responding to what many perceive to be a "natural" disaster. Land use patterns and precipitation and stream flow data from St. Thomas, Virgin Islands, are used to illustrate the role of culture in creating a condition of permanent drought. Social responses to declining water quality and availability over a 100-year period are reviewed, and the political, economic, cultural, and environmental implications of response are assessed. Institutional mechanisms for managing water are seen to restrict access in various ways, with this restriction playing a critical role in the commodification process.

Introduction

St. Thomas, one of the Virgin Islands of the United States, is located eighteen degrees north of the equator, sixty-four degrees west of Greenwich, 64.4 kilometers (40 miles) east of Puerto Rico, and some 1,609 kilometers (1,000 miles) southeast of Miami, Florida. Rising from sea level to a height of 474 meters (1,556 feet), the island encompasses 73.17 square kilometers, or 28.25 square miles. It is a mountainous island, part of a volcanic chain of some 100 islands and cays. There are no rivers, although historically two streams flowed year-round. There are a number of intermittent streams and springs and a large aquifer in the central part of the island (see figure 14.1). More

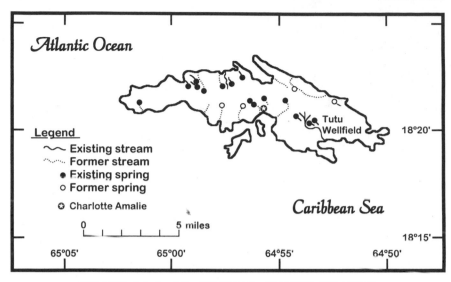

FIGURE 14.1. ST. THOMAS, VIRGIN ISLANDS

The island of St. Thomas is located 64.4 kilometers (40 miles) east of Puerto Rico and some 1,609 kilometers (1,000 miles) southeast of Miami, Florida. Rising from sea level to a height of 474 meters (1,556 feet), the island encompasses 73.17 square kilometers, or 28.25 square miles. It is a mountainous island, part of a volcanic chain of some 100 islands and cays. Map courtesy Barbara Rose Johnston.

than 102 centimeters (40 inches) of rain falls on the island each year, most of it during the hurricane season, from July to November. The weather is mild, and the trade winds provide a constant breeze.

Some 55,000 people call St. Thomas home, and another million or more tourists visit its shores each year. On some days, the island's population exceeds 130,000 people, all struggling to get around on an island 22.5 kilometers (14 miles) long and 4.8 kilometers (3 miles) wide. Tourism has driven up land prices to the point that few can afford to farm. Much of the island's food is imported on barges or flown in from Puerto Rico, the United States, Mexico, and Europe. Tourism has also attracted immigrants from up and down the West Indian chain (typically working as laborers and service workers), from the continental United States (entrepreneurs opening restaurants, shops, and other businesses), and from the yachting capitals of the world (sailors from Australia, South Africa, Europe, and the United States working in the charter-yacht sector). Although St. Thomas's political structure is dominated by black native Virgin Islanders (in terms of both elected offices and government employment), the economy is largely controlled by white residents. Native Virgin Islanders (people whose families date back to the pre-1917 era of Danish control) are now a minority.

For those employed in the government and business sectors, economic well-being is tied to the tourist dollar and thus depends on the financial health of foreign countries, where good fortune translates into expendable income and recreational tourism, as well as the price of oil, which affects the cost of transporting people and goods to an otherwise isolated location. For the 25 percent of the population living at or below the federal poverty level, survival means access to welfare, food stamps, subsidized housing, and other federal and local government entitlements. For all residents, life has been fundamentally transformed by a series of hurricanes that hammered the island in 1989 (Hugo), 1995 (Luis and Marilyn), and 1996 (Bertha). Repair of infrastructure and recovery of the tourism industry after Hurricane Hugo took many years, only to be ripped to shreds by the winds of Hurricane Marilyn, during which 85 percent of the island's structures were severely damaged or destroyed. Survival has meant reliance on assistance from the Red Cross and the Federal Emergency Management Agency (FEMA) and other forms of disaster relief; it has meant learning how to live for months on end with no electricity, no running water, no telephone service, schools closed or in double session, the loud noise of generators, and the incredible despair of seeing a rebuilt island destroyed again in the next year's hurricane.

This chapter examines one of the enduring yet ever-changing problems of life on St. Thomas: the problem of water scarcity. Because perception of, incidence of, and response to water scarcity are shaped by sociocultural and political economic factors as well as environmental conditions, the chapter begins with a historical overview.

The Past

For at least three thousand years, people have made the Caribbean island of St. Thomas their home. The earliest Virgin Islanders lived in coastal villages. They trapped reef fish, collected shellfish, and hunted turtles and manatees. They harvested native fruits, tubers, and other plants. And they used wood, stone, and shell to fashion the material necessities of life. Later peoples lived in coastal and inland villages, near streams and springs but also on hilltops affording a down-island view (and thus a lookout point for traders or invaders). They fished, farmed, and wove cloth from cotton. They carved furniture, statues, weapons, and canoes, using hardwoods from the island's forests. They used nets to capture schools of fish and deposited their catch in the shallows, where stone walls kept out sharks and kept in a fresh supply of food. They stored water, juices, manioc, corn, and other goods in pottery and baskets. They lived in open-air houses with palm-thatched roofs, slept in hammocks (a Carib Indian word), and stewed their food in "pepper pots" (seasoned with West Indian chilis). They traded honey and colorful bird feathers, lengths of cotton cloth, stone jewelry, and tools. All that was needed in life—food, medicine, water, shelter, clothing, transportation—was fashioned from the immediate surroundings. Thus, survival in pre-Columbian times required an intimate knowledge of the environment (Johnston 1982; Johnston and Lundberg 1985).

In 1671, when Denmark established the first permanent European settlement on St. Thomas, the island was apparently uninhabited. Some of the indigenous inhabitants may have been captured to work as slaves in Puerto Rico. Most likely the majority of indigenous islanders died from European-introduced plagues that had swept up and down the island chain—smallpox, measles, chicken pox, influenza, and the common cold. Some may have fled in their boats to other islands in the West Indies, joining the Carib Indian populations on St. Vincent and Dominique. As was the case on other Caribbean islands, initial decimation of the indigenous population through slavery, disease, and warfare was followed by the establishment of European agricultural settlements. The early Danish settlers set the forests afire and planted cotton, indigo, and tobacco. By the 1690s, plantations worked by African slaves were producing sugar cane. The plantations flourished on St. Thomas until the mid-1700s, when crop yields declined because of increasing water scarcity and decreasing soil fertility. Other Caribbean colonies had become the primary producers of such commodities as cotton, tobacco, sugar, rum, molasses, coffee, and spices.

Agriculture declined, but the economy of St. Thomas grew. With its excellent harbor, its location between the Greater and Lesser Antilles, and its politically neutral status (Denmark remained neutral during the numerous European wars of the seventeenth and eighteenth centuries), St. Thomas became the marketplace of the Caribbean.[1] By 1780, the majority of the island's population lived in town and worked in the shipping and commerce industries (Dookhan 1974; Knox 1852; Lewis 1968).

The West Indian colonies were dependent economies. During the plantation period, they relied on a continuous supply of labor from

Africa, access to European and American markets for trade of their luxury goods for staples, and capital investments from Europe and the United States to support the plantation infrastructure. The decline of the slave trade and emancipation of slaves, the establishment of competitive plantations in India, Africa, and the Pacific, a decline in sugar prices, and changes in shipping technology all played a role in the decline of Caribbean island economies (Mintz 1977, 1985).

In 1847, laws were passed in Denmark that allowed for the gradual emancipation of slaves over a twelve-year period. A revolt on St. Croix on 2 July 1848 spread rapidly to St. Thomas, and after successfully taking over the town, slaves were declared free. In 1854, it was estimated that 25 percent of the effective working force was lost through emigration in the six years following emancipation (Dookhan 1974, 240). Trade continued to run the St. Thomian economy, but a series of disasters over the next thirty years caused shipping companies to move elsewhere. In 1853, 100 people died of malaria; in 1853–1854, cholera killed 1,865; and in 1866–1867, another cholera epidemic killed 1,200 to 1,300 people. In an attempt to improve the circulation of water in the overcrowded and polluted harbor, a second channel was cut in 1867. Shortly after this, a hurricane struck, followed by an earthquake and a tidal wave, and every ship in the previously protected "hurricane hole" was sunk. In 1871, two hurricanes hit the island. The Royal Mail Steam Packet transferred its West Indies headquarters to Barbados, and other businesses soon followed suit (Dookhan 1974, 220).

Agricultural production for the export market had ceased by the end of the nineteenth century. In 1908, there was only one sugar mill on the island, and it was not in operation (Westergaard 1917, 255). In 1917, when Denmark sold the Virgin Islands to the United States for $25 million, the islands were $3.75 million in debt to Copenhagen and operating at a loss of $190,000 per year (Evans 1944, 36–37). In the sixty years following emancipation, the economy had declined, and islanders were pretty much left alone to carry on as best they could.

To some degree, and for some people, survival in the Danish era hinged on the political relations and economic well-being of European and American nations. For the majority of island residents, however, survival during this period required many of the skills and knowledge used by pre-Columbian islanders; indeed, archaeological sites from the historical and pre-Columbian periods show marked similarities (Johnston and Lundberg 1985).[2] People settled in the same locations, usually near streams or springs. They harvested and consumed a similar assemblage of shellfish, reef fish, turtles, and manatees; they grew food for their households using a similar system of slash-and-burn shifting cultivation; and they stored their goods in locally made pots (shaped and fired in a similar fashion) and baskets.

In 1917, when the United States acquired the Virgin Islands, there were few economic differences between the Virgin Islands and other West Indian colonies. The majority of the people were of African ancestry and were involved in the production of household provisions, with limited participation in wage-labor systems. The sugar cane industry on St. Croix was all but defunct, as was the bay rum industry on St. John. Limited wage-labor opportunities were available on St. Thomas, where port facilities in the harbor of Charlotte Amalie supplied coal and provisions for steamships. Landowners and other local elite were Danes, European Jews, or of mixed European-African ancestry (U.S. Bureau of the Census 1917). A sizable French colony had also been established on St. Thomas, populated by Acadian farmers and fishers with family ties to the islands of St. Barts (St. Barthélemy) and Guadeloupe. The remaining population, the majority, consisted of emancipated slaves and descendants of slaves originally taken from their homes in West Africa.

For most folks, life in the first few years of American rule differed very little from that in the Danish era. Between 1825 and 1925, the island's population fluctuated between 10,000 and 14,000 people, with a steady 2,000 living in the rural regions and the remainder concentrated in the town of Charlotte Amalie (Johnston 1981, 72). For urban residents, wage labor was an irregular source of income, often tied to the arrival of ships, and survival meant harvesting shellfish, keeping fish traps, cutting wood and making charcoal, and keeping a "ground" in the country (growing food for the table on abandoned or unused land). For rural residents, environmental knowledge was all the more crucial. Until the mid–1900s, rural residents produced their own food and transported goods to market by sailboat or donkey.[3] Their homes lacked electricity, and their villages lacked sewer systems. Survival meant knowledge of the locations of springs; the ability to harvest wild plants for food; the skills to weave baskets, ropes, seines, and fish traps; and knowledge of soils, weather patterns, plant propagation, and animal husbandry. Survival also meant having an extensive network of social relationships, by which an excess catch was shared or a specialist's knowledge of midwifery was repaid with gifts of food, cloth, or a day's labor in rethatching a roof. An intimate knowledge of the characteristics, values, and uses of local environmental features allowed a subsistence-level lifestyle to flourish (Johnston 1987; Olwig 1985, 1996).

Developing a Tourist Industry

The purchase of the islands by the United States was followed by a period of military rule (1917–1931), with the islands receiving very little federal attention or funding. Application of United States Coastwise Laws, which prohibited foreign carriers from transporting passengers or liquor into and out of United States ports, undermined an already weak shipping economy (Governor of the Virgin Islands 1933), though the production of rum and the incidence of smuggling continued (O'Neill 1972).[4]

In 1931, President Herbert Hoover visited the islands and drew national attention to the conditions of extreme poverty there: 90 percent of the population fell below the federal poverty level, and unemployment rates exceeded 60 percent (Governor of the Virgin Islands 1934). President Hoover's visit and his widely publicized remarks prompted support for congressional funding of New Deal development programs designed by the United States Bureau of Efficiency in 1929. These programs included the creation, management, and funding of cooperative agricultural and industrial organizations such as the Virgin Islands Company (VICO), later the Virgin Islands Corporation (VICORP), with federal funds. On St. Thomas, VICO initiated efforts to foster and promote the growth of tourism. The federal government purchased and renovated a hotel, which was managed for several years by the federal government and then leased to a private sector operator. VICO also initiated a series of infrastructure improvements, including the construction of catchment basins and storage facilities for drinking water in and around the town of Charlotte Amalie.

The onset of World War II and the threat of German submarines in the Caribbean resulted in a renewed U.S. military interest in St. Thomas in the late 1930s. At this time, the naval base was enlarged, an airstrip was constructed, deepwater docking facilities for submarines were built, and thousands of naval personnel were stationed on the island. These actions created a base infrastructure that allowed for postwar expansion of the tourism industry. Airplanes could land, and cruise ships could dock in existing facilities on St. Thomas. The military presence on St. Thomas also introduced thousands of residents of the continental United States to the island, broadening American awareness and creating a large class of potential tourists.

In 1954, the territorial government's ability to improve the island's infrastructure and attract investors for the tourism industry was significantly enhanced by a reorganization of the Virgin Islands Constitution. Included in this reorganization were provisions that required the return to the territorial treasury of all federal income taxes collected on the Virgin Islands and all taxes collected in the United States on liquor bottled on the islands. This change brought a considerable amount of money into local government hands. The constitutional reorganization also gave the territorial government increased autonomy in negotiating economic inducements for U.S. investments in the Virgin Islands, including waivers of property and income taxes on major U.S. and foreign investments for as long as twenty-five years.

The Cuban revolution of 1959, and the U.S. reaction to that event, was a final factor stimulating the tourist economy in the Virgin Islands. Before the revolution, Cuba had received the greatest number of tourists in the Caribbean region and the largest share of the U.S. tourism market. After the revolution, Cuba nationalized businesses owned by U.S. citizens, including hotels and resorts. The U.S. government refused to recognize Cuba's new government. As tourists and tourism investors sought other markets and destinations, St. Thomas, with its military-constructed infrastructure, tax breaks, and "safe" political climate, became the new "American paradise" (*International Tourism Reports* 1986, 71–72).

By the 1960s, the Virgin Islands were markedly different from other West Indian colonies. Waivers of property and income tax and other economic incentives led to the installation of oil and aluminum refineries on St. Croix. Tourism development on St. Thomas and the creation of a United States National Park on St. John attracted 300,000 tourists in 1962, representing a 300 percent increase in tourism over a seven-year period. This economic growth was in direct contrast to the still existing peasant economy of much of the English-speaking Caribbean region. The Virgin Islands became a magnet for the underemployed, and thousands of people moved to the islands to work at the refineries, in construction, and in the hotel and service industries.

By 1985, tourism accounted for 49 percent of all private sector employment on the Virgin Islands. The government, which was directly and indirectly funded by tourism, accounted for an additional 33 percent of employment. With a tourism-based economy, the Virgin Islands generated a per capita gross national product higher than that of any other country in the Caribbean region. However, this phenomenal transformation did not occur without some cost (Johnston 1987). Resources were redefined; patterns of critical resource access, use, and control were changed; and environmental degradation (erosion, pollution) was intensified. In numerous ways, people became further and further divorced from their island setting and at the same time increasingly dependent on the United States for federal funding, investment, tourists, technology, food, medicine, and education (Johnston 1990, 1994). Dependence and alienation created distinct sociocultural as well as biophysical repercussions, changes that are reflected in the story of water scarcity.

Water, Agriculture, and Public Health

Water resources in the early plantation period were described in terms of stream flow, springs, and rainfall. In the first thirty or so years following initial deforestation, plant cover was replaced first by cotton, indigo, and tobacco and shortly afterward by sugar cane. Deforestation and the changes in vegetative cover caused considerable degeneration of the island's ecosystem. Erosion was intense,[5] and the loss of the forest cover probably had a severe effect on filtration and absorption of rainfall, altering local microclimates as well as the rate at which subsurface aquifers were replenished (Jordan 1972; Jordan and Fisher 1977; Johnston 1981).

Perception of water resources and response to water scarcity during the plantation period were described by C. G. A. Oldendorf, a Danish Moravian missionary living on the Virgin Islands in 1767–1769:

> There are indeed sources and springs to be found in these islands; their waters, however, are not entirely sweet, but nevertheless drinkable. The only real fresh water is rainwater, which is collected with great care. It is collected in gutters which are attached to the roofs of houses on all sides, and it is then drained off by means of pipes, either into barrels or into a cistern. Enough water is collected in this manner after a couple of heavy rainfalls to supply a plantation for a quarter of a year or longer; indeed, some of it can even be given to the Negroes and the livestock. In particular, a good supply of it is laid in at that time in casks. . . . Whenever there occurs an exceptionally long-lasting drought, the price of rainwater rises sharply, and this is paid gladly, if in fact it is to be had. In those periods, one must pay a quarter to three-quarters of a piece of eight for a tub of water, which is about the amount that a [Negro] can carry on his head. In April 1758, such a quantity of water was sold in Bassin for an entire piece of eight. . . . Even that rainwater which had been left standing in the cracks of the rocks was drunk at such times. After a while, it becomes covered with a bluish film; care must be taken not to

remove any more of this film than is necessary while dipping water out, because it covers and preserves the water against the heat of the sun.

(Oldendorf [1770] 1987, 53)

In those times, water resources were defined in terms of agricultural needs and potable supplies. Oldendorf's account, like many other diaries and histories of the 1700s and 1800s, gave considerable attention to weather events and climate conditions (see also Knox 1852), as these conditions not only affected crop yields but also played a key role in public health:

> The sudden changes in the weather in October (1766) and the persistent rain in November caused the customary onset of epidemic diseases. . . . The period from June to September 1767 was also a time of starvation and sickness for (the Negros). But their hardships were intensified even more on account of a shortage of drinking water, which manifested itself in April and May 1768. On account of the hot and dry weather, the sugarcane began to dry up appreciably toward the middle of May 1768, and it had to be harvested with the utmost speed. The hot, foul fever that suddenly afflicted many Blacks and Whites alike in the last two months of that year and which killed a number of them, had its roots for the most part in the conditions brought about by six months of heat and drought previously mentioned, followed by extended, persistent rainfall. For the Negroes the problem was intensified by the lack of good food.
>
> (Oldendorf [1770] 1987, 568)

As noted earlier, the plantation economy was relatively short-lived; by the early 1800s, many plantations had been abandoned and economic activity centered on the town of Charlotte Amalie, where the majority of islanders lived. By 1835, there were 14,000 people on the island, with some 2,500 of them cultivating plantations (Westergaard 1917). Water resources became defined even more in terms of rainfall. The Danes built a large catchment on the edge of town, a cistern to store 3,785 cubic meter (1 million gallons) of rainwater, and a system of clay pipes that delivered freshwater to fountains and some houses in town. A number of public wells were built in and around town, and drainages were paved, allowing storm runoff to flow directly into the harbor. Recognizing the connection between garbage disposal and public health, town residents were under regulation to "sweep before their doors, and place the matter with house refuse by their dwellings for removal in public carts to the leeward of the town" (Knox 1852, 202).

When the United States took possession of the Virgin Islands, there had been no infrastructure development in recent memory. Between 1911 and 1917, nearly one-third of the infants born each year died by their first birthday—320 per 1,000 live births, about three times the infant mortality rate then prevailing in the continental United States. Malaria was endemic, and cholera was a frequent killer. Also common were elephantiasis, diphtheria, leprosy, and typhoid (O'Neill 1972, 80). In an effort to improve sanitation, a night-soil removal service was introduced shortly after the United States assumed control, and soon after that a saltwater flushing system was put in place. The saltwater flushing system included a pumping station and a network of pipes laid in the streets of the town, providing water to flush toilets and drain sewage back into the harbor (Dookhan 1974, 267).

A series of droughts in 1924 brought the issue of water supply to a crisis point, and following testimony to the United States Congress, funds were allocated through VICO to build a number of concrete reservoirs (cisterns), each fed by a paved catchment on the hills of St. Thomas surrounding the town of Charlotte Amalie. Other efforts to improve the water supply included drilling wells for the few remaining plantation owners who were, with the aid of the federal government, attempting to build a cattle export industry. In later years, a series of small earthen dams was built to enhance agricultural water supply, following testimony before Congress in 1948 by the governor of the Virgin Islands, William Hastie, who argued: "We have no permanent streams, and no underground water, but we hope with the efforts of the Soil Conservation Service and our own we will be able to hold the run-off in the hills and force more of it underground and thereby . . . make the most of our meager water supply" (Boyer 1983, 210).

Water and Power

Tourism development efforts in the 1950s included clearing out the slums and shanties in town and building cement-block housing for the island's poor, using largely unmodified designs for public housing projects in cities like New York and Chicago; building a first-class hotel; and providing the water-intensive amenities that first-class tourists were accustomed to—mainly flush toilets, showers, swimming pools, and ice for evening cocktails. Historian William Boyer notes that in

1957, Governor Walter A. Gordon's "most difficult problem was the persisting water shortage, particularly on St. Thomas. When drought occurred, the problem became severe, and demand for water steadily increased as housing projects, new schools, hotels, and hospitals were brought into operation. After firing his commissioner of public works, Gordon finally resorted to barging water into St. Thomas from Puerto Rico, which did not really alter the shortage" (Boyer 1983, 234).

Following the Cuban revolution and the shutdown of Cuba's American tourism industry, considerable investment interest was focused on the Virgin Islands, and the federal government gave infrastructure development a high priority for funding. Inhibiting tourism on St. Thomas and industry on St. Croix were the problems of unreliable water supplies and power facilities. For the first time, these two resources were seen by governing authorities to be critically linked.[6] Soon after President John F. Kennedy's appointment of Ralph Paiewonsky as governor of the Virgin Islands (1961–1968),[7] VICORP purchased the islands' first seawater desalination plant, which opened on St. Thomas in 1962.[8] Three more plants were built shortly thereafter, generating electrical power while producing potable water. These facilities were built with federal funds and were initially operated by the federal government. In 1965, the facilities were sold to the territorial government, to be managed by the newly created Water and Power Authority (WAPA) (See Photo 14.1) (Boyer 1983, 258).[9]

Water was now linked with power. At the same time, the political management of water supply was separated from that of sewage and other wastewater disposal, an action that eventually affected water quality. In February 1969, hours before he left office, Governor Paiewonsky signed into law an act establishing the Virgin Islands Port Authority, an act approved by Secretary of the Interior Stewart Udall four days before he left office. This legislation created an authority whose purpose was "to establish, acquire, construct, develop and improve, own, operate, and manage any and all types of air terminals, marine terminals, and industrial, commercial, residential, and recreational developments," including warehouses, quarries, cement-block plants, parking areas, resale outlets, hotels, motels, apartment complexes, guest houses, restaurants, and office buildings as well as related facilities such as sewage disposal plants and public refuse dumps. Shortly after the end of his term, Paiewonsky was appointed to the Port Authority's board of directors and then elected as its chairman (O'Neill 1972, 102–103).

The island's economy and population boomed from the 1960s through the 1980s, creating an increased demand for water and power

PHOTO 14.1. WATER AND POWER AUTHORITY (WAPA)
DESALINATION FACILITY, ST. THOMAS

The federally funded Virgin Islands Corporation (VICORP) purchased the islands' first seawater desalination plant, which opened on St. Thomas in 1962. Three more plants were built shortly thereafter, generating electrical power while producing potable water. In 1965, the facilities were sold to the territorial government, to be managed by the newly created Water and Power Authority (WAPA). Photograph by Barbara Rose Johnston.

and placing an increased strain on waste disposal systems. Improvements to sewage disposal facilities and the public dump were quite low on the Port Authority's list of priorities. There was more money to be made in building airports, marinas, hotels, and other facilities to attract tourists. Problems with sewage disposal, marine pollution, and contamination of the water distribution system were often ignored or denied by the Port Authority as well as by subsequent agencies created to monitor and protect natural resources.[10]

In 1975, after being informed that the territory must meet the requirements of the federal Safe Drinking Water Act, the territorial government passed the Virgin Islands Safe Drinking Water Act. In 1977, drinking water standards were established, and in 1978, the Department of Natural Resources (DNR, merged in the mid-1980s with the Virgin Islands Planning Office to form the Department of Planning and Natural Resources) began monitoring water quality in public water supplies. Tests were conducted, including counts of total coliform bacteria and measures of turbidity, for contaminants that represented a significant health hazard. In establishing its testing program, the DNR argued that monitoring for certain substances was inappropriate, contending that radionuclides and organic chemicals were problems that affected the continental United States but not the Virgin Islands and thus were not likely to be found in the public water supply system: "Since the Virgin Islands does not have any surface drinking water suppliers of this type (i.e., lakes, rivers, etc.) this problem should not affect the Virgin Islands, and . . . none of the regulated compounds have ever been detected in past samples collected from cisterns, wells, ponds and guts [small creeks] of all three islands and analyzed under other programs" (DNR 1984, 8).

Because the Virgin Islands Safe Drinking Water Act was essentially a replication of the federal act, conditions specific to the islands' water supply were not incorporated into the original language of the act. Thus, DNR monitoring was carried out only in selected portions of the public water supply system. "Noncommunity water systems," such as schools, hospitals, day-care centers, Head Start centers, restaurants, hotels, guest houses, shopping centers, transient marinas, campgrounds, recreation centers, bars, fast-food outlets, and other very small systems serving transient consumers, were not monitored. Nor were private water supplies (rainwater stored in cisterns), bottled water, or industrial, commercial, and agricultural water supplies. This lack of a comprehensive program for monitoring all aspects of the public water supply and testing for a wider variety of contaminants played a key role in later crises, as indicated later in the discussion of the Tutu Wellfield.

Whereas the DNR was responsible for monitoring the quality of certain sources of the water supply, WAPA was responsible for ensuring an adequate supply of potable water. Water scarcity problems were recognized by WAPA, but strategies employed were typically limited to those that offered the greatest income-generating potential, especially in terms of lucrative contracts for construction and material supplies. From the start, desalination did not produce enough water to meet local needs, and water continued to be periodically barged from Puerto Rico. While a number of government-funded studies noted that desalination was "too costly a method to be practical as a major source of potable water," WAPA ignored their recommendations for dealing with water shortages (Boyer 1983, 341–342; cf. Peebles et al. 1979). Corrosion and equipment failure forced all four desalination plants on St. Thomas to shut down for several weeks in 1977, causing a loss of millions of dollars in perishable goods, putting a halt to industrial activity, and resulting in a subsequent loss of significant tax revenues. As described by William Boyer:

Chief among WAPA's ills in the 1970s were heavy corrosion of plants, little or no preventative maintenance, six executive directors in four years, poorly trained personnel and middle management, lack of expertise, inadequate record keeping and billing, and scandalous waste. An estimated one-half of all potable water pumped into the islands' pipe system could not be accounted for, according to a "revelation" by the new Public Works Commissioner in mid-1979. A 1976 audit found that the expenses of potable water supply and distribution exceeded income by 74 percent.

(Boyer 1983, 342)

Despite the mechanical problems of operating desalination plants in a warm, moist island setting and a complete dependence on oil to power the plants, water generated through desalination was seen as a limitless, though admittedly expensive, resource.[11] WAPA's response to water supply problems was a decision to build more desalination plants. Plant closures for days, weeks, and even months at a time continued throughout the 1980s, and they continue to the present.

People no longer looked to the skies in times of drought; instead, they turned to WAPA. The system of hillside catchments and public water supply cisterns built by the Danes and expanded by the United States government was abandoned. The notion of drought itself changed from a water shortage brought on by lack of rainfall to a water shortage brought on by mechanical failure. Laws requiring the construction of rooftop catchments and basement cisterns adequate to meet the water needs of a building's residents were on the books but were rarely enforced, as it was assumed that WAPA desalination water would meet needs for potable water.[12] Thus, hotels, public housing projects, schools, hospitals, and the numerous government buildings housing the sizable territorial government workforce built from the 1960s through the 1980s rarely had sufficient rainwater supplies. There was simply too much money to be made in ignoring and denying the problem of water scarcity.

The Present

Tourism development has radically transformed land use patterns on St. Thomas. Resorts, condominiums, and time-shares have been built in rural areas, and housing projects and residential developments have been carved into the many hills, valleys, and ridgetops outside town. For the first time since the early plantation days, more people live "in the country" than live in town. WAPA power lines run up and down the length of the island. Water and sewer services are, for the most part, limited to town; in the country, people generally rely on rooftop catchments and basement cisterns to store "sweetwater" and use septic tanks with leach fields to dispose of sewage. Repeated break-downs of WAPA facilities in the 1970s and early 1980s prompted many hotels and businesses to acquire backup generators, and a number of hotels have built their own desalination plants. WAPA's main cus-tomer is the government, which buys, though rarely pays for, water for its offices, schools, and housing projects. Audits of the system con-tinue to reveal that more than half the water pumped and processed is lost, mostly through aging, leaky pipes, and illegal hookups. Further-more, the water distribution and supply system is often contami-nated—old clay pipes have broken or been inadequately repaired, cis-tern inflow filters are often lacking, and maintenance is rare.

For the past thirty years, private water delivery trucks have hauled water to replenish empty cisterns in the country, and in the past decade the number of private delivery companies has grown (see photo 14.2). Traditionally, these businesses provided water for cus-tomers outside the WAPA delivery system (the majority of people who live outside Charlotte Amalie). Since Hurricane Hugo (1989), how-ever, the private water supply and delivery industry has mushroomed. Hurricane Luis (1995) loosened up the island's structures, and a week later Hurricane Marilyn tore roofs, rain gutters, and catchment sys-tems from 85 percent of the buildings. Ten months later, Hurricane Bertha (1996) tore away the blue FEMA tarps covering many roofs, pulled apart newly replaced roofs, and ripped away many of the re-maining rain gutters. As a result, water delivery companies now pro-vide much of, and in many cases all, the water for household con-sumption in rural areas. As of June 1996, St. Thomas had nineteen different water delivery companies, each with its own fleet of trucks hauling water around the island, and seven water quality and supply companies drilling wells, analyzing water quality samples, treating cistern water, and selling reverse osmosis and other water purification equipment. An additional four companies were producing and bot-tling "purified" water, three of them obtaining their water from wells and running it through charcoal filters and reverse osmosis and ultra-violet water purifiers and the fourth obtaining and then purifying water from WAPA.

For obvious reasons, the population of St. Thomas has become keenly aware of how critical a resource water is. Obtaining water is no

PHOTO 14.2. PRIVATE DELIVERY TRUCKS FILLING
THEIR TANKS WITH DESALINATED WATER, ST. THOMAS

People no longer looked to the skies in times of drought; instead, they turned to the Water and Power Authority (WAPA). The notion of drought itself changed from a water shortage brought on by lack of rainfall to a water shortage brought on by mechanical failure. It was assumed that WAPA desalination water would meet needs for potable water. Photograph by Carolyn Davis.

longer seen as simply a matter of harvesting rainfall or converting salt water. In 1995, following Hurricane Marilyn, the WAPA plant was shut down for six weeks, and because of downed poles, some people went without power for more than three months. No power meant no energy to work the pumps that draw cistern water up through the pipes and into the toilets, so people hauled buckets of water into their homes for household needs. The price of bottled water jumped (from $1.04 to $1.39 per gallon in the weeks following the hurricane), as did the price of ice. No power also meant no refrigeration. (At a local bar, a cold six-pack of Old Milwaukee beer was reportedly sold for some ten times its normal selling price.)

For a number of reasons, Hurricane Marilyn resulted in increased contamination in the water production, storage, and distribution system. Sewage plants were off-line and coastal waters were polluted, so contamination entered the system through the marine inflow pipe. WAPA's plant and storage and distribution facilities were damaged, and contamination occurred throughout its system. Finally, hurricane winds deposited debris and other contaminants in private cisterns. Contamination notices for WAPA supplies and for a host of public and private water sources, including restaurants, hotels, hospitals, and schools, were posted in the local newspaper in the weeks and months following the hurricane. (Although notices of excessive coliform counts in the public housing water supply had been published for years, the increased federal presence in the territory following the hurricane meant an increase in the monitoring and testing of water supplies.) In the months following Hurricane Marilyn, the *Virgin Islands Daily News* published numerous announcements about water quality, advertisements for water delivery services, and news stories examining just about every aspect of water supply. Readers were given tips on cistern maintenance, told how to chlorinate their cisterns,[13] and advised that although time and intense sunlight causes the blue FEMA tarps to deteriorate, possibly causing carcinogenic chemicals to be leached into rainwater harvest systems, short-term use should be safe.

Water became a critical issue of public concern. Not only was access to potable water limited, but safe, "pure" water was in scarce supply, as suggested by the following remarks by Virgin Islander Carolyn Cook, published in an opinion piece in the local newspaper:

> OK, folks, I've about had it. Is it just me, or is anyone else wondering? Is there any way to recycle candle wax? Am I crazy jumping out my car to run behind 60 men, women and children to get two bags of ice? Is this really me hauling buckets of water up three flights of stairs to empty toilets? . . . I was wondering. . . . Exactly how many different types of bacteria, funguses, insects and/or reptiles are now residing in my cistern? Where, exactly, did this proliferation of "pure" bottled water come from? How "pure" is "pure"?
>
> (*Virgin Islands Daily News*, 6 October 1995, 18)

Destroying the Islands Main Aquifer

Public concern over water quality intensified in early 1996 with reports of a multimillion-dollar settlement in a lawsuit over culpability in polluting the Tutu Wellfield, a subsurface aquifer in an intensely populated region of the island (see figure 14.1).[14] A keyed-up and water-stressed public received the news that cancer-causing chemicals were polluting the island's main aquifer—the aquifer that supplied the full-time needs of 1,600 residents and had been used for many years by water delivery services to fill cisterns all over the island. An estimated 11,000 people may have been exposed for a period of approximately twenty years to the chemical compounds in Tutu water (Davis 1996,

19; Bollentini 1996, 5). Water from this aquifer was used to mix the sodas sold at the island's movie theater complex, to make ice and provide water for several popular restaurants, to clean clothes at local laundromats (few can afford to use cistern water to wash their clothes),[15] and to clean the ever-present grime from the island's dirt roads off cars at a popular car wash. The U.S. Environmental Protection Agency (EPA) warned island residents at public hearings and in reports available for public review and comment (described and reported in a series of *Daily News* articles) to avoid drinking the water, purchasing water from delivery trucks that might originate in the Tutu Wellfield, touching contaminated soil, showering with contaminated water, and coming into contact with water while washing cars. Individuals who drank or used water from the Tutu Wellfield were strongly encouraged to get regular medical checkups.

Adding insult to injury, the *Daily News* reported on a chain of events indicating that government officials knew of the problem as early as 1983, when the Department of Natural Resources received a report of contamination from a private consulting firm.[16] In 1987, the owner of Tillet Gardens (the site of an old sugar plantation housing tourist shops, silk-screening and other craft workshops, and a bottled water operation) noticed that the water from his well smelled like gasoline and informed the EPA. An investigation conducted by the Virgin Islands Department of Planning and Natural Resources (DPNR) between 1987 and 1990 (reported in the U.S. EPA's narrative summary of sitz history) indicated that volatile organic compounds, including tetrachloroethylene, benzene, 1, 2-dichloroethylene, and trichloroethylene, were contaminating some twenty-two commercial, residential, and public wells.[17] Water from some of these wells had been transported by water delivery trucks throughout the island. Potentially responsible parties identified by the EPA included gasoline stations, automobile repair shops, a dry cleaner, and a silk–screening operation (Esso, Texaco, Laga Industries, O'Henri Dry Cleaners, Ramsay Motors, Tillet Gardens, the Virgin Islands Housing Authority, the Virgin Islands Education Department, Antilles Auto, Four Winds Plaza Development Corporation, and Western Auto), with Esso identified as the most likely primary contributor. Possible sources of contamination included underground storage tanks containing petroleum and waste oil, drum storage areas, contaminated catch basins, oil separators, floor drains, a sump holding tank, a leaching pit, aboveground storage tanks, and an evaporation pit. These operations also used various toxic materials, including solvent-based auto flushes, dry-cleaning fluids, dye strippers, ammonium hydroxide, and mineral spirits.

Between 1987 and 1991, the EPA relied on the DPNR to monitor the site and inform the public. Many people continued to use the aquifer, typically to fill water delivery trucks. In 1987, the DPNR closed down Tillet Well, three private wells, and thirteen commercial wells. The EPA followed this action by using emergency funds to decontaminate five residential cisterns and providing an alternative water supply to those residences as monitoring of the remaining wells continued. In 1990, under an EPA order, Esso Standard Oil Company, Texaco Caribbean Inc., and O'Henri Dry Cleaner took over the monitoring program and continued to provide an alternative water supply to residences affected by groundwater contamination.

In July 1989, the major landowners in the area, the Harthman family and the Four Winds Plaza Development Corporation, filed suit against Esso. Esso denied culpability and filed suit against other companies identified by the EPA (Texaco, Laga Industries, O'Henri Dry Cleaners, Ramsay Motors, and Western Auto). These companies filed a countersuit against Esso. At the same time, Esso hired Soil Test Inc. to study the area, violating EPA and DPNR laws that require public notice before testing soil and water for contamination. Soil Test's results indicated that Esso was the major source of contamination. Esso filed the report in an office in Puerto Rico and failed to disclose the document as lawsuits proceeded, thus forcing the other companies involved in litigation to conduct their own series of expensive tests.

On 31 December 1991, the EPA requested funds for community relations efforts, and in April 1992 it submitted an application to include the Tutu Wellfield on the CERCLIS National Priorities List of Superfund sites (the site was finally listed as "preremedial" in 1995). In 1994, concern over the Tutu Wellfield's water quality was the subject of an article by biologist Olassee Davis (1996) in the *Virgin Islands Daily News*. Public hearings on the extent of contamination of the Tutu Wellfield and the associated public health risks were held in early 1996, following the highly publicized settlement of court cases. In 1995, Esso paid $2.7 million to Texaco, following disclosure of the buried report. In January 1996, the landowners won a $7 million settlement from Esso and Danny Bayard, owner of the Esso Service Station. In April 1996, the Puerto Rican law firm of Golman, Antonetti, Cordova, and Axtmayer and subsidiaries of the Esso Corporation were fined more than $1 million for withholding evidence and obstructing litigation; two of the four lawyers were barred from practicing before the U.S. District Court in the Virgin Islands for three years, another for one year. In remarks following the decision in this case, U.S. District Court Judge Stanley Brotman said, "During the past 20 years as a US District Judge, I cannot recall being involved with a more disturbing proceeding" (Rake 1996, 3). A final round of legal action remains as the EPA and the Virgin Islands government move to recover costs associated with cleaning up the aquifer, conservatively estimated at $15 million.[18]

Conclusion

> I think they have been careless. We need to be checking our water supplies on a regular basis. Look who was getting the water—the innocent housing people.
>
> (Janice Hodge, Kmart cashier, quoted in Bollentini and Hodge 1996)

> There was too much politics involved and the agencies were passing the buck. I'm especially worried about the small kids who were exposed. These chemicals are bad even when you touch them or breathe them. I am concerned that mixing them with soap can make it worse because contaminants will mix with lye and bleach in soap and form new compounds.
>
> (Felipe Ayala Sr., retired teacher, quoted in Bollentini and Hodge 1996)

> It is a coverup because no one has done anything and this water has been polluted for years. The government has just been going through the motions.
>
> (Roy Raimer, retired firefighter, quoted in Bollentini and Hodge 1996)

> From Tutu to Mariendal, residents owe it to themselves and their children to learn of the potential for exposure. In addition, all local health professionals are obligated to understand the causes and subsequences of exposure so that they may adequately serve those who are at risk.
>
> (Helen Gjessing, 1996, 14)

On one level, some may interpret the story of how the Tutu Wellfield ended up on the CERCLIS National Priorities List as a story of ignorance; fundamental errors in the territorial government's water quality monitoring programs (sampling only some of the water supply and testing for only certain types of contaminants); denial (on the part of government, users, and polluters); greed (placing government funds and energies in a continual pursuit of economic development activities rather than environmental protection activities); and a fear of expensive lawsuits.

On another level, the destruction of St. Thomas's primary subsurface aquifer can be tied to a much larger process of development, alienation, and dependence. The loss of a subsistence-oriented lifestyle, though accompanied by an improvement in certain standards of living, also meant loss of access to and control over natural resources. People had fewer and fewer opportunities to interact with the natural environment and fewer reasons to maintain an interest in or knowledge about their natural surroundings. At the same time, dependence on outside technology and expertise (to produce water, for example), on the continental United States (in various political and economic ways), and on the tourism dollar contributed to a dysfunctional governance. The response to emerging crises was often denial prompted by fear: Fear that a media focus on island crises would cause tourists to change their travel plans. Fear that public outcry would bring on a political backlash and subsequent loss of office for elected officials, as well as loss of jobs for the many relatives and friends who enter public service on the coattails of a politician. And fear that an investigation of problems would uncover the more illicit aspects of the development process.

The population of St. Thomas has changed markedly over time, with a great number of cultural groups trying to survive and thrive on a relatively small rock in the middle of the Caribbean. The island's limited water resources have supported subsistence lifestyles for thousands of years, export agricultural economies for a hundred years, a shipping and market economy for another hundred years, and, most recently, a tourism economy for the past fifty years. Water scarcity and quality were persistent problems throughout the pretourism era, problems exacerbated by human action and inaction. Technology and development prompted a temporary shift in the political and social perception of water: drinking water was seen to be a perpetual resource, thanks to desalination, and water quality concerns were perceived as an issue for other people and other places. Pollution was rarely defined as a significant factor influencing life on the Virgin Islands.

Hurricanes smashed the illusion of technosupremacy. As islanders struggled to adjust to posthurricane conditions, news of the Tutu Wellfield contamination was in some ways just one more on a long list of disasters. However, the resulting series of news articles (both about the Tutu Wellfield and about water quality issues in general), public hearings, radio shows, and letters to the editor all suggest that a significant education process is now under way, a process that is influencing the cultural perception of water. Today, residents of St. Thomas are keenly aware that water quality problems include much more than the natural by-products of too many people living on a warm, moist tropical island. The specter of cancer and other health problems looming over a large cross section of the population is causing St. Thomians to look again at the ground, the air, and the water around them as critical and essential resources on which their lives and future depend.

Food for Thought

This chapter suggests that recent disasters—hurricanes and the pollution of the island's main subsurface aquifer—have forced St. Thomians to rethink their notions of the meaning and value of water. Whether simple awareness of the public health risks associated with water quality and supply problems will be enough to stimulate substantive change in the overall quality of life on St. Thomas remains to be seen. Dependence and the dysfunctionalism that dependent relationships create permeate every aspect of life on the islands. In countless ways, people are conditioned to turn to the United States for economic and technical assistance in resolving local problems.

Although defining water scarcity in ways that emphasize the connection between supply and quality is a crucial step toward regaining local control of critical resources, it is merely one part of a much more complicated and involved process of change that must take place if island life is to regain some semblance of sustainability. What is needed? This chapter suggests the need for the following:

- A transformation of the cultural definition and value of critical resources in ways that emphasize biophysical conditions as well as sociocultural needs.

- A transformation of local patterns of resource access and use in ways that reflect both biophysical parameters and sociocultural needs.

- A restructuring of the resource-related decision-making system to prioritize a holistic approach to human and environmental concerns.

These changes imply an economy that recognizes biophysical constraints and sociocultural needs; social and educational structures that foster and encourage environmental interaction and value environmental knowledge; and political structures and strategies that not only are capable of responding to emerging crises in effective ways but also are proactive—that protect people and their island setting in ways that prevent new crises from developing.

ACKNOWLEDGMENTS

I gratefully acknowledge the comments, observations, and water quality data provided by scientist and planners working for the Virgin Islands Department of Planning and Natural Resources (1981–1996). Their contributions remain, at their request, anonymous. Special thanks are owed to archaeologist Emily Lundberg, who provided information, corrections, and review comments on an earlier version of this chapter. For their hurricane stories, copies of newspaper accounts, and efforts to capture "water-system" images, I owe a debt of gratitude to Carolyn and Charlie Davis.

NOTES

1. Some historians argue that a significant component of the St. Thomian market was the import and resale of African slaves. Historian Sven Green-Pedersen estimates that between 1733 and 1802, a total of 123,000 slaves were imported to the Danish colonies and about 70,000 of these were exported for resale (Boyer 1983, 5).

2. A survey of pre-Columbian sites in the early 1980s found that some 25 percent had been misidentified and were actually plantation period sites. The confusion arose because of the similar assemblages of shell, bone, and locally made pottery found at both pre-Columbian and plantation period sites and the practice of dating sites solely on ceramic characteristics.

3. For example, according to the Record of Deeds in St. Thomas, in 1899, Jeremia Hatchett purchased 2.6 hectares (6.5 acres) of land at Water Bay, near the eastern end of the island, for DKr$6 in 1899. In August 1944, the local newspaper published an article about Hatchett, noting that "Jeremia Hatchett celebrates his 100th birthday at his home in Estate Baker. . . . Born in Jost Van Dyke, Mr. Hatchett came to St. Thomas six years after emancipation . . . for 20 years he has not been in town" (*Virgin Islands Daily News*, 16 August 1944, 1). This statement suggests that food, clothing, medical needs, and so forth were all met within the community or with the help of other community members. Interviews with St. Thomian's about living conditions in rural areas in the 1930s through the 1960s support this contention (Johnston 1987).

4. In 1980–1981, I mapped a series of Prohibition-era rum production sites located in isolated bays on St. Thomas and nearby cays (with the copper works and mounds of rum bottles in abundant evidence). In August 1982, I interviewed two fishermen on St. Croix who had worked in the late 1920s and early 1930s making rum and selling their product to smugglers for $5 per case.

5. In 1980, I surveyed a small, sheltered cove on the northern side of St. Thomas where the slopes are steep and rainfall is plentiful. A recent storm surge had cut deeply into the valley floor, leaving layers of archaeological material exposed and eroding in the berm. From the surface down, recent material was deposited in a few feet of sand and soil. Plantation-period ceramics, glass, and other debris were deposited in the next level. A sterile layer of soil 48–69 centimeters (18–24 inches) deep followed. The lowest level consisted of late–prehistoric-period material (B. R. Johnston and E. R. Lundberg, archaeological field notes, December 1980).

   Erosion on the steep slopes is by no means a problem of the past. In 1981, I drove my Jeep down a recently graded unpaved road to a beach on the northern side of the Island. I returned a few months later to find that the road had deteriorated to a foot trail, with banks 1.2 to 1.8 meters (4 to 6 feet) high where the old surface had been. The beach at the bottom of the hill was strewn with boulders and mud. Rocks in the nearshore waters were covered with a slippery film of algae, as were the nearshore coral reefs. Overdevelopment in the coastal zone, leakage from septic tanks, and runoff from the network of unpaved roads on the island's steep slopes have severely impacted the health of island reefs and reef fisheries (see De Graf and Moore 1987; Moore 1989).

6. In all fairness, water and power were linked during the plantation period. In 1715, there were thirty-two windmills providing energy to pump water from wells and assist oxen or slaves in turning millstones and processing sugar cane.

7. According to journalist/author Edward O'Neill, Paiewonsky's appointment was the result of political–economic ties forged by Prohibition–era activity. Paiewonsky's father, Isaac, operated a liquor business, trading shiploads of Virgin Islands rum for supplies of White Horse Scotch when Joe Kennedy "needed it" (1972, 68). When Paeiwonsky was appointed, he was president of his family's company, A. H. Riise Distillery.

8. Later purchases of desalination plants caused considerable controversy. In 1978, Robert Grimshaw of Connecticut was appointed executive director of the Water and Power Authority (WAPA). After visiting Israel to inspect desalination plants manufactured by the Israeli Desalination Engineering Company (IDE), Grimshaw recommended, and WAPA's board of directors approved, IDE's bid to build three plants in the Virgin Islands "even though their bid was $4 million higher than the bid of Aqua-Chem, the Wisconsin-based firm responsible for building the first plant on St. Thomas" (Boyer 1983, 344).

9. "While the Tennessee Valley Authority was still largely a paper organization, a grant of $1 million by the Public Works Administration set up the not-dissimilar Virgin Islands Company (VICO) and put the U.S. government into the businesses of sugar growing and refining, rum distilling, water supply, and power production, with a work force that eventually reached about 2,000 full- and part-time employees" (O'Neill 1972, 53).

10. In June 1996, when I last visited the island, smoke from the public dump

could be seen from miles away. For the past ten years, subsurface methane fires have periodically flared up there, sending plumes of toxic ash all over the southwestern side of the island. The hospital's biohazardous and radioactive waste (from its X-ray and oncology units), chemicals from the Island's one-hour photofinishing labs, debris left by several recent hurricanes, abandoned cars, and other assorted by-products of island living have been dumped, compressed, and left to rot at the Bovoni Dump, which is situated on and in the island's main mangrove lagoon. Media coverage, government inquiries, federal fines, and other actions have taken place over the years, yet the problems remain.

11. In a comment typical of many government reports, Esmond Devas of the Caribbean Research and Development Center wrote: "Water does not present a practical constraint sufficiently serious to prevent further tourist development, although it is certainly an expensive item (derived from desalination plants) which reduces the profitability of investment, and in this sense represents a financial constraint" (1982, 21). This comment was found in the proceedings of a conference; precisely the same wording later appeared in the 1985 *Virgin Islands 2000* planning document released by the chamber of commerce's Office of Planning, Policy, and Research.

12. This assumption was common as recently as 1991. At that time, I was hired to prepare an environmental impact assessment for one of the Virgin Islands Housing Finance Authority projects. When my review of plans for the federally subsidized low-income condominium development found inadequate rooftop catchment space for the estimated water needs of building residents (and thus a failure to comply with local building codes), I was told by the project supervisor and the private developer that there was no need for concern, as WAPA would be trucking in all the water needed to make up the shortfall. I managed to get the plans modified to include slightly larger catchment space, low-flow toilets, filters for cistern entry and outflow pipes, and residential unit-specific water meters. These water conservation requirements in the building specifications were a first for public housing on St. Thomas.

13. Multiply cistern length by width, and then multiply that by the depth of the water in the cistern. Multiply that by 7.5 to obtain an estimate of the amount of water held in the cistern. Add 6 ounces of chlorine bleach for each 1,000 gallons of water.

14. Sources for this section, in addition to those cited in the text, include articles, editorials, and letters to the editor published by the *Virgin Islands Daily News* from January through July 1996, interviews with island residents and members of local environmental groups in July 1996, and interviews recorded in earlier ethnographic fieldwork. Informants included biologists who were testing the water supply in 1980–1981, planners and other government officials responsible for water management policy in 1984–1986, interviews in 1984 with the owner of a "pure spring water" bottling company that drew water from the Tutu Wellfield, and periodic

interviews from 1982 through 1987 with the owner of a restaurant that drew all its water from the contaminated fields. In every case, people were aware that the water supply system had its problems, but most of the informants expressed no concern over the possibility of contamination and apparently were unaware of the risks associated with the use of contaminated water.

The EPA's record of activity for the Tutu Wellfield can be found on the World Wide Web. Sources for this overview of EPA activity include the EPA's web site for Region 2 (http://www.epa.gov/region02/superfun/ site_sum/0202749c.htm) and the Right-to-Know Network's (http://www. rtk.net) copy of the EPA's CERCLIS (Superfund) database for the Tutu Wellfield, Virgin Islands, EPA Region 2, EPA ID# VID982272569.

15. For ten years, I washed my family's clothes at island laundromats. Over time, I learned to avoid facilities that left our laundry reeking of gasoline-like fumes. Laundromat workers, however, were unaware of any problem with their water. I once had the opportunity to meet with an owner of a chain of island laundromats, who insisted that the odor came from his WAPA-powered dryers, not the water.

16. Interviews with informants in 1981 and 1982 indicated that problems with water quality in the Tutu Wellfield were known and, indeed, expressed in some publications. For example, a report prepared by the Virgin Islands Water Resources Center, published in June 1979, noted:

> The Virgin Islands have severe quality problems due to waste contamination of ground water and problems with supply. Much ground water is of poor quality because of the intensive development of areas where rainfall and occasional streamflow replenish (recharge) the ground water reservoir. . . . Storm run-off, containing among other contaminants oils and lead from leaded gasoline, recharges ground water in the shallow small aquifers in urbanized areas. Turpentine Run (Tutu) on St. Thomas exemplifies these problems.
>
> (Peebles et al. 1979, 21)

17. The U.S. EPA Superfund National Priorities List entry for Tutu Wellfield lists the following hazardous contaminants in the water and, in most cases, in the soil:

> 1,1,2–TRICHLOROETHANE; 1,2–DICHLOROETHYLENE; ANTIMONY; ARSENIC; BENZENE; BERYLLIUM; BROMODICHLOROMETHANE; CADMIUM; LEAD; MANGANESE; MERCURY, METALLIC (in the soil only); METHYL-T-BUTYL ETHER; TETRACHLOROETHYLENE; THALLIUM; TRICHLOROETHYLENE; VANADIUM; VINYL CHLORIDE. Hazardous materials are contained in a 108-acre plume. A stream leading to Turpentine Run (the major drainage in the area that runs three miles to the Mangrove Lagoon) lies a few hundred feet from the edge of the

plume. The plume is moving southeast. (U.S. EPA Superfund National Priorities List, site summary for Tutu Wellfield (http://www.epa.gov/region02/superfun/site_sum/0202749c.htm))

18. The site was first discovered in 1983, and culpable polluters were first identified by the EPA and the DPNR in 1987. Lawsuits were filed in 1991, but the first settlements were not reached until 1995. I believe two factors were significant in bringing this case of environmental crime to court. First, the election of Bill Clinton to the presidency in 1992 brought a reorganization of government, and for the first time in three presidential terms, the EPA received significant increases in funding and staff. The environmental policy mandate established by the Clinton administration was one of enforcement in all arms of the executive branch, including the U.S. Department of Justice. Second, in 1994, the Virgin Islands territorial court took over jurisdiction of all criminal cases except those involving federal law. This allowed federal prosecutors to set aside their previous caseload of rapes, robberies, and other crimes and focus on environmental lawbreakers, white-collar criminals, and international drug dealers.

Water Between Arabs and Israelis
Researching Twice-Promised Resources

Rosina Hassoun

Author Summary

Understanding the resource-related issues involved in
the Arab-Israeli conflict requires confronting the
myths and paradigms held by the principal parties and
by researchers. Maintaining the fragile peace in place
today between Palestinians, Israel, and their Arab
neighbors turns on finding compromises and new solutions among old players. The current and historical
uses of water in the region and the social, economic,
and ecological repercussions of the use of water as a
weapon reverberate in today's peace negotiations. This
chapter explores the development of cultural attitudes
toward water, historical waters, changes in the flows
and uses of water, regional ecology, and the depth of
the current water crisis in the context of a search for
solutions.

Introduction

"Today in the Middle East, a joint Arab and Israeli ecoterrorist group
blew up the main Negev water pipeline. Farmers in the Negev are
without water, and extensive flooding has occurred at the site of the
blast. The ecoterrorist group claims the pipeline is an unecological
waste of precious resources that threatens the very survival of future
generations of Arabs and Israelis," states a headline news story. Fortu-
nately, in the 1990s, at least, this story is science fiction. Current
newspaper accounts do not provide a clear picture of the role of water
resources in the Arab–Israeli conflict. Arguments about the role of

water vary widely, ranging from those that present water as a core issue to those that frame it as a marginal problem that can be solved by a "technofix."

One element that appears to be missing from the debate over the role of water is the degree to which culture, including normative attitudes and behaviors, is woven into the conflict. The debate has centered on the hydropolitics of the region, with a central focus on the power relationships among the different parties. However, it is not just issues of distribution, availability, and access that are critical to the water debate. Water use patterns correlate with cultural attitudes and lifestyles.

An examination of the differences in access to and availability of water, water use patterns, and lifestyles of Palestinians, Israelis, and citizens of the front-line states illustrates the interrelatedness of power, water, and culture in the current situation. An overview of water use practices and water resource management in the Arab–Israeli conflict is critical to understanding the seriousness of current water problems. Just as peace negotiations appear to be progressing, problems with water quality and quantity may beleaguer any headway being made toward a lasting peace.

Although water appears to be a limiting factor in the economic development of the region and in the quality of life of the people living there, was water always central to the conflict? If not, was there a historical turning point at which water became more significant? The dominant thesis presented here is that cultural differences between Arabs and Israelis play a critical role in water use and access. Cultures are not stagnant; therefore, cultural changes in attitudes and behaviors related to water resources are relevant to the debate over the importance of water in the Arab–Israeli conflict.

A Brief Review of the Water Debate

The debate over the role of water in the Arab–Israeli conflict is almost as old as the conflict itself. To date, at least three schools of thought exist. One school of thought can be classified as a resource scarcity viewpoint, with water as the key factor in the conflict. Some proponents of this viewpoint predict increasing conflict in the Middle East as water demand from increasing populations outstrips supply (Kelly and Homer-Dixon 1996, 20; Wolf and Ross 1992). Projections of Israeli water supply falling below demands have been in the literature for some time, with some articles predicting an imminent severe water crisis (Meyers 1986). That impending crisis is seen as the reason for the precipitation of violent conflicts in the region.

Another side of this argument is the assertion that major food production problems are forthcoming in the region as a result of population growth (Jensen 1990). A proposed solution to the food production problem, in the face of shortages of water for irrigation, is an increase in rain-fed agriculture over the short term (Jensen 1990).

The second viewpoint portrays water as a contributing factor rather than a causal agent in the conflict. For example, a desire for the water of the Litani River in Lebanon may be a reason for continued Israeli presence in southern Lebanon but was not the reason for the initial occupation. The third school of thought, espoused by a substantial number of engineers and economists, presents water as a marginal problem that can be resolved with technology.

Some critics claim that there is an element of exaggeration in predictions of immediate danger of violent confrontations over water (Rogers and Lyndon 1994, xix). In 1992, at a symposium held at Harvard University, a number of experts on water in the Arab world discussed water supply and demand, problems of water delivery, the economics of water, the hydropolitics of the region, the problem of transboundary water and shared water resources, and proposed solutions (Rogers and Lyndon 1994). Among the solutions set forth were repairing leaking and aging water infrastructure, improving agricultural practices, increasing data collection and monitoring of water resources, and carrying out more strategic planning and better water policy in Arab countries (Rogers and Lyndon 1994, xiii–xix). Desalination plants were discussed as an unlikely technological solution for the near future because of the associated costs (Dabbagh et al. 1994). The experts addressed the problems from a pragmatic point of view, and many of their solutions appear sound—if countries in the Middle East will adopt these practices. The problem not addressed was how to achieve their adoption in the context of the region's other problems and its differing cultures.

The water debate must also be placed in the context of other regional economic and resource-related problems. Portraying the parties as inherently violent or the situation as ancient and intractable does the people of the region, both Arabs and Jews, a great disservice. Problems in the Middle East are similar to problems plaguing other developing regions of the world, especially regions that have experienced long periods of colonialism and resource extraction.

Comparative Analysis of Cultures: Predominant Myths and Lifestyles

The ultimate irony of the conflict between Palestinians and Israelis is that they do share one deeply felt religious concept—that the land and all its resources have been endowed to them by God. This gives rise to the problem of a twice-promised land with twice-promised resources. This problem is complicated by differences in beliefs and practices. Since practices vary according to locality and nationality, the overview of cultural differences presented here is restricted to generalizations about Islamic and Jewish beliefs concerning water—beliefs specific to attitudes of Palestinians and Israelis. Attitudes in the rest of the Arab region may vary but are based on similar Islamic beliefs.

Although there is a sizable minority population among Palestinians of Christians, Druze, and other non-Muslims, Islamic practice and belief have dominated in the region for approximately the past 1,500 years. Prior to the Western colonial period, Islamic law regulated water practice in the region of Palestine. Islamic law, the *shari'ah*, dictates land and water usage and rights and reflects principles laid down in the Quran (the Muslim holy book) and by the *hadith* (accepted sayings and stories of the prophet Mohammed).

An in-depth analysis of Islamic water concepts is beyond the scope of this chapter; however, Islamic scholars (e.g., Dutton 1992) contend that one of the most basic premises of Islam is the concept of water as cleansing and pure. Muslims are obliged to perform ritual cleansing (ablutions) before prayer. Another important principle concerning water is the right of all to access to water.

In Islam, punishment is reserved for those who deny access to water, pollute water, and damage the productivity of the land. Rewards are merited by those who plant trees, care for animals properly, and maintain the land. Deeply held communal concepts and tenets of sharing (Dutton 1992, 51–52) govern land and water use law and practice. Islamic law is pragmatic about determining water and land usage based on individual cases.

The concept that development of the land endows ownership is inherent in Islamic law. This is one of the basic arguments put forth by Palestinians for ownership of the land and water, based on their present and prior (pre-1948) land and water usage. The communal aspect of land and water use by Palestinians has been a source of conflict between Palestinians and Israelis. Village communal land and open communal land used for grazing is classified as undeveloped (*mawat*), but this land can also be considered part of a religious trust (Dutton 1992, 51–52). The Israeli government holds that the *mawat* and *waqf* (undeveloped land and land set aside for the poor or for the mosque) are unowned lands available for Israeli settlement. This has resulted in bitter conflict over land confiscation.

Further complicating the situation is the fact that in Islamic law, water rights are often ascribed according to historical calculations of the amount of water needed to produce certain crops. However, modern lifestyles and agriculture require higher allocations of water than the historical allocations. In Islam, large rivers and deep wells are considered communal property and a sacred trust (Dutton 1992), yet even with such beliefs, practice varies widely. Problems of water allocation, access, and pollution beleaguer the entire region.

The images the two peoples have of the land and its resources influence their land and water practices. Palestinians and Israelis have fundamentally different views of the land and their place on it. Some of these differences may stem from their lifestyles prior to 1948, when Arabs constituted the majority population of Palestine and 70 percent of the Arab population was agrarian (Khalidi 1984, 236–237; Anglo-American Committee of Inquiry [1945–1946] 1991). In contrast, most of Israel's current majority Jewish population came from urban backgrounds in European and American cities.

One goal of negotiations leading to real and lasting peace between these parties would be the reconciliation of their different paradigms toward the land and its resources. Neither the Israelis nor the Palestinians are monolithic in their outlook, but an examination of some of their ideological and literary works can reveal some general trends.

Old Testament views give humans dominion over the land and animals: the land is said to have been given to the people to utilize for human needs. A recurring image in Judaism is the building of a temple; construction and sanctification of place are an important element of Jewish belief and play a prominent role in the philosophy of political Zionism and development of the land. Israeli concepts can be traced in the writings of major Zionist leaders such as Theodor Herzl, Vladimir Jabotinsky, David Ben-Gurion, and Itzhak Ben-Zvi. In addition, an entire genre of Israeli poets has chronicled the pioneering idealism (*chalutzuff*) or *kibbutzim* movement (the collective farms) (Sachar 1996).

In order to encourage Jewish immigration to Palestine, the early Zionist movement promoted the slogan "A land without a people for a people without a land" (Prittie 1967). Behind the scenes, however, they knew that this land was inhabited by a majority of Arabs. However, the slogan succeeded in sparking the imagination of the international Jewish community. It became one of the enduring myths of the pre-1948 immigration movement. Today, the reality of the Arab Palestinian population is too well known for this myth to be widely accepted.

A more persistent theme in Zionist literature recalls Jewish scripture and the concept of a promised land exclusively for the Jews. This concept was institutionalized into Israeli land laws and the policies of the Jewish Agency. From its inception, the Jewish Agency collected funds for land in Palestine with the stipulation that such land should never be sold or transferred to non-Jews. This attitude, held by many modern Israeli settlers, makes it difficult for the Israeli government to trade land for peace. Closely tied to the Jewish concept of a promised land is the concept of *aliya*, the return. Deeply ingrained in the mainstream of Zionist thought is the idea of the right of Jews everywhere to "return" to the homeland. This concept fails to acknowledge the land's limited carrying capacity.

When Jews began migrating en masse to Palestine just prior to the creation of the Jewish state, they saw the land and its resources as opportunities. To them, the land was a wasteland to be tamed. They brought with them images of European and American lifestyles based on monocropping, modern agricultural practices, swimming pools, and manicured lawns. Because they had no knowledge of the ancient regional patterns of agriculture, settlers of the *kibbutzim* adopted European agricultural models. Therefore, the paradigms of the Jewish and Arab peoples vary greatly.

Israeli water use policy is still in the formative stages. Israel is a new country, established in 1948. Thus, Jewish religious concepts of land-ownership and water rights have not been institutionalized over centuries, as with Islamic law. The early Zionist movement contained a strong element of collectivism (in the *kibbutzim*) and active socialist and communist parties. In practice, Israeli law contains both religious and secular concepts. One of the first acts of the Israeli government in 1948 was to nationalize all the water properties of the state and place them under the administration of the Merkerot Water Company (Kliot 1994). The water distribution system for the region was completely redesigned to favor Israeli development.

Israeli water laws regulating pollution were unable to keep pace with the rapid development of the state and still tend to favor development over protection. The pesticides found in fish from the Sea of

Galilee (Wynne 1986) and recent epidemics of waterborne diseases from fecal contamination of wells (Simchen et al. 1991; Tulchinsky et al. 1988) are only a few examples of pollution problems. Although monitoring has focused primarily on protecting Jewish settlements, *kibbutzim*, and cities, some of the most severe water pollution exists in Gaza, where levels of water salinity greater than 400 parts per million (ppm) have been recorded (Shawwa 1993, 29) and bacterial contamination of the aquifer is already causing serious illness in the Arab population (Bellissari 1994, 52–63). Dysentery, kidney disease, and cardiovascular disease are just some of the health problems resulting from this contamination (Bellissari 1994).

Israeli water laws have created a large inequality between Palestinians and Israelis in access to water. Israelis of the Jewish faith have virtually unlimited access to water, whereas Palestinian Arabs, whether citizens of Israel or residents of the occupied territories, live with more than 2,000 restrictive laws that limit their access to land and water (Shehadeh 1988). The approximately 1.5 million Palestinians in the West Bank have been restricted to the 1976 water allocations or 25 percent (75–80 million cubic meters, or 60,803–64,857 acre-feet) of the shared resources of the aquifer that underlies the West Bank (Benvenisti 1984). In contrast, the 100,000 or more Israeli settlers in the West Bank have virtually unlimited access to water (see Libiszewski 1995).

Israelis' response to questions of why they have treated the Palestinians in this fashion is necessity—the necessity of providing security for Jewish citizens and of avoiding the threat of terrorism. The Zionist concept of an independent Jewish state in which Jewish culture and lifestyles may flourish without the threat of non-Jewish intervention and possible persecution, is a dream come true. The magnitude of longing for this utopian state in the Israelis, who carry a deep sense of historical persecution, should not be underestimated.

The approximately 2 million or more Palestinian Arabs living in Israel and the occupied territories are seen as spoilers of this dream. Many Israelis perceive themselves as living in a garrison state under conditions of constant siege (Frankel 1996, 23). This is the heart of the deep tragedy of these two peoples, who are irrevocably tied to each other through their connection with this one land and its resources.

Palestinian literary and poetic works are not directly comparable to Israeli literature and poetry in that they lack an ideology equivalent to Zionism. Palestinian philosophies show considerable diversity. However, certain themes are evident in Palestinian nationalistic writings and poetry. The writings of Edward Said and the poetry of Kamal Nassar, Mahmoud Darwish, and Fawaz Turki were used to determine the Palestinian paradigms.

Palestinians claim descendancy from all the previous inhabitants of the land, including Arabs and ancient Canaanites and Philistines. Muslims believe that they, not the Israelis, are the rightful inheritors of the land—also by God-given right. The Quran, the Muslim holy book, makes no mention of any prophecy giving the land to the Jewish people.

A recurring theme in Palestinian poetry is a reference to the land as mother. Over the centuries, Palestinians living on the land developed a strong concept of the motherland, as opposed to some cultures' perception of a fatherland. Ingrained in this image of mother are concepts of fertility. This type of analogy is also found in much of the literature of indigenous peoples such as Native Americans. Palestinians do not consider their land to be a desert. Generations of Palestinians speak about the abundance of produce, fruit, olives, and grain brought forth from their land. Stories of the land of Palestine producing oranges as large as grapefruits abound among Palestinian refugees (Sayigh 1979). There is an idyllic quality to the accounts of Palestine as a land of abundance—a sort of paradise lost.

Paradise lost to the Palestinians was not paradise found to the Israelis. For the Israelis, if a paradise exists in Palestine, it is a paradise they have to carve out of a desert wilderness. It is the labor of the pioneers to transform the land and "make the desert bloom." Palestinians strongly oppose this concept. Although they admit that there are desert areas in the Negev and near the Dead Sea, they view Palestine as a historically beautiful and fruitful land and see Israeli attempts to transform it as deforming and destructive (Interviews 1995).[1]

At the same time, younger Palestinians long for a lifestyle similar to that of their Israeli counterparts. The current generation of Palestinians is more educated than were previous generations, and increasingly fewer and fewer of them are entering into traditional agriculture. The backbreaking work associated with tilling the soil is no longer popular with many Palestinian youths. The Israeli *kibbutzim* movement has also suffered from a lack of young immigrants who are willing to accept the hardships of the traditional collective farm.

The majority of Palestinians, both Muslim and Christian, also believe that a homeland in Palestine is their God-given right. There is a strong sense among Palestinians of having been cheated and forcibly evicted from their native land, and like the Israelis, they have a concept of the right to return to their former land and houses. This right has not been acknowledged by the Israelis.

The distinctions between the paradigms of these two peoples are startling. A reconciliation of such disparaging viewpoints will not come easily. A spirit of cooperation and trust must be fostered between these parties for there to be a possibility of achieving a lasting peace.

An Asymmetry of Power

One of the popular myths regarding Israel is that of a little David (Israel) confronting the giant Goliath (the entire Arab world). The reality of the situation in the Middle East, however, is very different. Israeli military might exceeds that of all the countries in the region (Libiszewski 1995, 31). Since the Gulf War in 1990, with direct military intervention by the United States and many of the former European colonial powers in the Middle East, the Arab world has lost considerable power. The Gulf War widened previously existing differences among Arab countries. Negotiations between Israel and the neighboring Arab states are not bilateral talks between Israel and a united Arab world. The talks have broken down into a series of multilateral talks, illustrating the relatively weaker position of the Arabs.

Israel remains the sixth largest military might in the world. Its nuclear capability has been confirmed, but since Israel refuses to sign nuclear nonproliferation agreements or allow international inspection of its nuclear facilities, its exact capabilities are unknown. For the residents of the West Bank and the Gaza Strip and all Palestinians living in the Israeli state, Israel is the controlling power over their lives. The goal of current Arab–Palestinian peace talks is to give the Palestinians a modicum of control over their daily lives in exchange for peace for neighboring Israeli settlements.

At present, the power to make decisions regarding allocation of resources for both Palestinians and Israelis lies totally in Israeli hands. Even though Palestinians may not be making wise allocations of natural resources, as discussed on the following pages, any inequalities in distribution are the ultimate responsibility of the Israelis by virtue of their power. Much of the resignation and resentment felt by Arabs stems from the development of Israeli legal hegemony over the region's resources.

Regarding land and property laws, the Absentee Land Laws of 1948–1953 gave the Israeli government the power to confiscate property from Arab landowners if they were deemed not to be currently occupying the property (Shehadeh 1988). This legalized the taking of the houses, fields, and property of the hundreds of thousands of Palestinian refugees created in 1948. Theoretically, Arabs who are merely away on vacation could have their property confiscated. This law has been continuously applied to Palestinians, and the confiscations continue.

In the case of agricultural land, the Absentee Land Laws mean that Palestinian farmers inside Israel and in the West Bank and the Gaza Strip must farm their land continuously every season or the land will be subject to confiscation. This law has effectively done away with the traditional fallow periods that allowed the soils to recover.

Palestinian farmers are becoming more and more dependent on expensive fertilizers and chemicals in an attempt to maintain yields (Interview with Palestinian farmer 1994).[2] Over time, loss of soil fertility occurs, accompanied by increasing soil erosion. Palestinian farmers are aware of the ecological damage but are helpless to prevent it, as they must continue to farm intensively in order to maintain their land and feed their families. Such laws are forcing the Palestinians into ecocide—the destruction of their own environment. The inequality in power relationships in the region is also reflected in the region's water history.

Water Policy and Practice in and Around the Jordan Valley

One method for determining the role of water in the current Arab–Israeli conflict is to examine water policy and practice in the region over time. Some authors address only violent conflicts that have a blatant water component. Yet, conflicts are not restricted to outbursts of violence; they can smolder as "cold wars" for long periods of time. Water use and attitudes can be long-standing sources of aggravation and friction between neighboring countries.

In the Middle East, where true water scarcity exists (the usable amount of available water exceeds demand), the relative importance that governments (power brokers) place on water is determined by the degree to which water is calculated into national security policy and long-term strategic plans. One question to be determined is how the Arabs' and Israelis' cultural differences in attitudes toward water and land are reflected in their respective policies.

A Brief Ecological History of the Region from Ancient Times

The water history of the region of Palestine is an ancient story. One way to place the situation in perspective is to examine an ecological and anthropological time line of the region. Although both the Palestinians and the Israelis claim to be the descendants of early owners of the land (the ancient Canaanites and the Hebrews, respectively), the first inhabitants were the early *Homo sapiens* who migrated from Africa to this land. These earliest inhabitants may be the ancestors of all modern populations in the region, along with people who arrived during subsequent invasions.

The region of Palestine has been inhabited for centuries by a diverse population, and this continued human presence has had lasting effects on the land. Resource extraction has been ongoing and has intensified during subsequent invasions. During the time of the first semisettled and settled peoples, the Natufians and the Canaanites, the ancient agricultural practices of rock terracing, scratch-plow tilling, and multi-cropping developed (Khalidi 1984). With each introduction of peoples, advances in agriculture were added to this basic matrix of agricultural practices. Over the centuries, agricultural methods and lifestyles have shifted with the different influxes and influences of peoples.

By the twelfth century, the predominantly Arabic-speaking population of Palestine was described by travelers as producing an abundance of crops, including wheat, vegetables, citrus fruit, and olives (Khalidi 1984, 28). The Palestinian Arabs had developed a village agricultural system. For defense, villages were normally located on the tops of hills and surrounded by steep slopes, which were unsuited for agriculture. At the heart of each Muslim or Christian village was a mosque or church. Houses radiated from the center and were surrounded by individual household gardens, where vegetables and fruits were raised.

The surrounding steeper areas were rock terraced and planted with citrus and/or olive trees. Animals grazed beneath the trees. In the valleys below the villages, grains such as wheat and barley and other crops were grown on collective village lands. Individual plots of various quality were tilled by individuals and rotated on a five-year basis to ensure fair distribution of land.

Some parcels of land were *mushaa* (public lands) and *waqf* (religious lands); they were tilled for the village and mosque and their produce was distributed to the needy. In addition, the crop rotation system allowed for fallow periods to allow the land to rest. Trade took place between the agricultural villages and the cities. In the cities, crafts flourished, which were sold and traded for agricultural produce. The cities were centers for the marketing of goods as well as for education, culture, and learning. This system of collective village farming was disrupted, however, by Turkish and British colonial tax schemes, which created some of the first landless peasants in the early 1900s (for a more complete explanation, see Hassoun 1993 and Khalidi 1984).

Historically, much of the region's coastal areas and mountains were covered with Mediterranean scrub forest that included native plant species such as olive trees (which have been cultivated for centuries) and the famous cedars of Lebanon. However, much of the region was deforested by ancient Roman and Greek armies in order to build ships and roads, and the native scrub forest was replaced with arboriculture. Unlike North Africa, where overgrazing has been a serious problem leading to extensive desertification, much of the fertile crescent was preserved by native Arab agricultural practices, although localized problems with overgrazing existed. Today, the remaining Mediterranean scrub forest is endangered by the expansion of modern populations.

For centuries, every square inch of arable land in most parts of the region has been pressed into service. Patterns of irrigation, crop rotation and fallow, rock terracing, intercropping, and grazing have painstakingly been practiced. The image of the Arab as farmer is more representative than the prevalent stereotype of the Arab as rich sheik or terrorist.

Water History from 1900 to 1948

The roots of the dispute over water resources in the Jordan Valley predate the creation of the state of Israel.

During the colonial period, especially during the period of British mandate in the early 1900s, the valley's countryside and cities were integrated into the international market system. A system of cash crops, supplanting the informal trade system of the previous century, began to alter traditional relationships between the cities and rural areas as goods were diverted to foreign markets and more cash crops were produced. As early as 1945, the Anglo American Committee of Inquiry recommended legislation to restrict digging any further wells in the coastal aquifer near Haifa, Tel Aviv, and Lydda (Anglo American Inquiry 1945–46 vol. 1: 395). The Anglo American survey provides the earliest documented reference to signs of saltwater intrusion due to overpumping in coastal Palestine. Unfortunately, the recommendations were not heeded and today there is widespread and severe saltwater intrusion into the coastal groundwater.

As early as the turn of the twentieth century, the World Zionist Organization had undertaken an assessment of the water resources of Palestine and devised a plan for utilization of the Jordan-Yarmūk river system in preparation for settling thousands of Jews in Palestine (Wolf 1995, Libiszewski 1995). Therefore, for the Israelis, water has always been an integral component of strategic planning and of their perception of the conflict with the Arabs of the region. For the Palestinians and those in neighboring Arab countries, an awareness of water came only after the influx of Jewish settlers, after the creation of the Jewish state, and after the displacement of hundreds of thousands of Palestinians had created a crisis on the ground.

By 1947, the eve of the United Nations vote to partition Palestine, the Jewish population of Palestine owned 6 to 7 percent of the land (Khalidi 1984; Anglo-American Committee of Inquiry [1945–1946] 1991). As a result of international political pressure, the United Nations voted to partition Palestine into Jewish and Arab states, giving more than half the country's traditional land area to the Jews. Jerusalem was to become an international city. Although Jews the world over rejoiced at the creation of the Jewish state, the Arab world viewed it as unfair to the Arab population of Palestine—an imposition of a European settler state in the heart of the Arab world.

Water History from 1949 to 1967

One of the first undertakings of the new Israeli government in 1948 was to initiate a massive restructuring of the country's surface water resouces in order to create a national water network (see figure 15.1). The project was designed to divert water from the Galilee region in the north to the agricultural areas in the Negev (Naqab) Desert. In 1959, the government of Israel nationalized all the country's water resources. This nationalization annulled all private ownership of water resources and expropriated them to the Ministry of Agriculture, under the purview of a water commissioner (Darr, Feldman, and Keman 1976).

Israeli's Mekerot Water Company was given the right to construct the Kinneret-Negev Conduit, a massive pipeline 15.24 centimeters (6 inches) in diameter with four pumping stations using 30,000 horsepower, designed to carry water almost the entire length of the country. The original pipeline began at the Yarkon River (fed by springs just

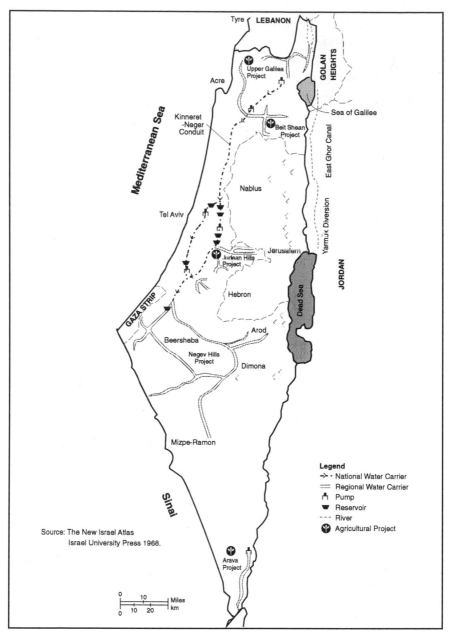

FIGURE 15.1. ISRAELI WATER PROJECTS (1977)

One of the first undertakings of the new Israeli government in 1948 was to initiate a massive restructuring of the country's surface water resources in order to create a national water network. The water project was designed to divert water from the northern Galilee region to the agricultural areas in the Negev Desert. Map courtesy Rosina Hassoun.

south of Tel Aviv) and stretched 96.6 kilometers (60 miles) to Beer-sheba, where the water was used in agricultural projects in the Negev region (Hassoun 1989). By the 1980s, the conduit, reaching from the Sea of Galilee (also known as Lake Kinneret or Lake Tiberias) to the Negev Desert, was carrying 420–450 million cubic meters (340,489–364,819 acre-feet) of water per year (Kliot 1994, 214).

In addition to the Kinneret-Negev Conduit, the Israelis undertook a huge project to drain Lake Huleh (Hula) and the marshes in the northern Galilee region. Palestine had been bestowed with three bodies of open water in close proximity—Lake Huleh, the Sea of Galilee, and the Dead Sea. Because of biblical references to it, the Sea of Galilee is one of the best-known freshwater bodies in the world. Lake Huleh, also a freshwater lake, was the lesser known of the three bodies of water.

Annual snowmelt on Mount Hermon in Syria fed the springs of the Golan Heights and the Banias Springs and Banias River in Lebanon. These are the headwaters of the Jordan River. Water flowed into the marshes of the Galilee region, which lay within the migratory routes of African, Asian, and European wildlife; thus, the wetlands were populated with wildfowl from three continents. The marshes of the Galilee region were one of the world's most unusual wetlands (Howells 1956). In 1947, British naturalist Victor Howells was the last scientist to catalog the wildlife of Palestine prior to the creation of the Jewish state.

The Arabs who traditionally inhabited this marshland area used its water grasses, papyrus, and reeds to make unique baskets. Historically, this area, the Safad subdistrict, contained some seventy-eight villages. In December 1948, its population was 87 percent Arabic and 13 percent Jewish (Khalidi, 1984). It became the scene of heavy fighting in 1948 and of a massive exodus of Arabs as a result of Israeli military operations. By 1957, the marshes had been drained and Lake Huleh was a dry lake bed. Israel had "reclaimed" some 6,070 hectares (15,000 acres) of wetland for intensive cultivation and settlement.

Today, this region is one of Israel's model agricultural areas. The population is predominantly Jewish, and the names of the majority of the Arab villages that once existed there no longer appear on most maps (Khalidi 1992). The refugee camps in Lebanon are filled with Palestinian Arabs from the Galilee region (Sayigh 1979, 75–97), even though according to the United Nations partition plan (originally rejected by the Arabs), the region was to have remained part of the Palestinian state. The change in population in the region resulted in a change of lifestyle, opening the way for future utilization and diversion of water there.

The intensity of Israeli efforts to capture this area during the war in 1948 and the water diversion projects that were implemented almost immediately thereafter indicate the strategic importance of the Galilee region's water resources to the emerging Jewish state. Soon after occupation of the region in 1948, plans were made for the Rutenberg Project, designed to transform the Sea of Galilee into a reservoir by adding control works at its lower end. As a result, the Sea of Galilee is now Israel's largest reservoir, with some 500–600 million cubic meters (405,354–486,425 acre-feet) of water storage (Shuval 1980). Water from the Sea of Galilee flows via control structures into the Jordan River, where it is diverted just below the Yarmūk River to provide water for Jewish cities and settlements.

As a result of the drawdown of water from the Sea of Galilee and the removal of the marshes, which acted as a natural filter for the surface waters, the lake now suffers from severe eutrophication. Twice a year its surface becomes reddish brown from the brown alga *Peridium cinctim* (Shuval 1980). The lake has also suffered increased salination, and chemical pollution, including nitrogen and pesticide runoff from nearby agricultural projects, eventually enters its waters.

Some Israeli researchers deny that the sudden eutrophication and increased salination are a result of Israeli water management practices (Shuval 1980). However, Palestinians familiar with the region claim that the draining of the marshes and the water diversion are the cause of the ecological troubles of the Sea of Galilee (Hassoun 1989). Native fishes such as the musht (*Tilapia galilaea*, or Saint Peter's fish) are decreasing in number with the deoxygenation of the lake's waters (Hassoun 1989). Over time, increasing salination of the water, algal blooms, and pollution of the lake have become the subject of intense investigation (Libiszewski 1995).

As to the Jordan River, the Israelis diverted the majority of the water flow from the river and its tributaries for Jewish use. The kingdom of Jordan planned a large agricultural development in the Ghor Valley, with dams on the tributaries of the Jordan River. With the aid of American engineers, Jordan devised a plan to expand irrigation on the Jordanian side of the Jordan Valley in 1959 (Libiszewski 1995) and began a project to dam the Yarmūk River, a tributary of the Jordan.

In 1964, Israel bombed the water structures built by Jordan (Waterbury 1994, 45). This act was the first direct military confrontation in the Arab–Israeli conflict over the region's water. Jordan has since expanded the East Ghor Canal (now called the King Abdullah Canal), but many of the Jordanian plans for water development were scuttled by Israel's diversion of water and use of force (Libiszewski 1995). Jordan currently has one of the lowest water utilization rates in the region due to insufficient supplies and water losses caused by an aging infrastructure (Libiszewski 1995).

The massive changes in the water resources of the Galilee region and the Jordan River made by the Israelis severely affected the entire region. The draining of the Galilee region had a "sponge" effect, drying out the surrounding Arab regions of Lebanon, Jordan, and the Golan Heights in Syria. Those countries all had plans for the use of these waters. The situation has kept Israel at odds with its Arab neighbors since the creation of the Israeli state.

Water History from 1967 to the Present

Prior to 1967, the Israelis were utilizing their full surface water capacity. With their subsequent capture of the West Bank and the Golan Heights and invasion and occupation of southern Lebanon, they now control almost the entire headwaters of the Jordan River and its flow to the Sea of Galilee. With every armed conflict, the Israelis have increased their control of the region's water.

In 1967, when Israel seized the West Bank and the Gaza Strip, one of the first acts of Israeli authorities was to freeze the water allotments of the Palestinians at set levels until the year 2010 (Military Order No. 158, 1 October 1967). Since then, Palestinians have been required to seek permits to drill new wells. In all but a handful of cases (some five exceptions, for minor wells), their requests have been denied (Mc-Dowall 1994). Palestinian water use for agriculture is restricted, monitored by gauges, and heavily taxed.

Although Palestinian water use has been restricted, Jewish use is virtually limitless. Average domestic consumption by urban Arab Palestinians in the occupied territories is 60 liters (15.8 gallons) per day, compared with 137 liters (36.2 gallons) in Jordan and some seven times more for Jewish Israelis (McDowall 1994, 140). In some Palestinian cities, especially during the summer months, water is delivered only two days per week. In some cases, water allotments drop to less than 35 liters (9.2 gallons) per day—what the United Nations considers the minimum healthy allotment for human beings.

One of the more recent environmental consequences of the diversion of water from the Jordan River and the Galilee region to the Negev Desert is the biological death of the Dead Sea. With the cutting off of freshwater inflow to the Dead Sea, the upper layers of the sea became increasingly saline (Gat and Stilker 1981). When the salinity of the upper water layers exceeded that of the lower layers, the Dead Sea experienced a turnover, which killed the brine shrimp and bacteria, effectively sterilizing the sea. The Dead Sea, which had been a stable body of water for 10,000 years, has lost 21 percent of its area since completion of the Israeli water network in 1952 (Steinhorn and Gat 1983, 84). Even though Israel's potash works mine significant areas of the Dead Sea, the drying out of this body of water represents a cultural as well as a financial loss for the region.

The Current Water Crisis

Arab populations in the region are increasing at an estimated 3 percent per year (Libiszewski 1995, 67–68), and countries in the region have placed an inordinate emphasis on agricultural production, pushing land use to the limit. Food security is imperative for each country struggling to reach self-sufficiency, whereas reliance on foreign food imports creates greater food dependence.

Even with its farming efforts and use of the latest agricultural techniques, the modern state of Israel is not agriculturally self-sufficient—nor does it have that capacity. Indeed, Israel imports the greatest amount of foreign foodstuffs of any country in the region (Beaumont and Mclachlan 1985). Water use, as described earlier, is at its maximum, and sustainable levels of consumption have been exceeded in the Gaza Strip and on the coastal plain. By every estimate, the population of Israel has already surpassed the carrying capacity of the land.

Contrary to popular media concepts of the Arab world, most of the countries bordering Israel are not wealthy oil-producing states. Bread riots occurred in Jordan in 1995, and during the Gulf War in 1990 King Hussein of Jordan made one of the first direct threats relating to water, stating that water was the only reason Jordan would enter the fighting (see Libiszewski 1995). The growing population of Israelis utilizing the water Jordan desperately needs may be a source of constant concern to the people of Jordan.

The Question of Settlements
One of the most volatile areas of contention between Arabs and Israelis is the issue of Israeli settlements in the occupied territories and Jerusalem. The Arab nations contend that these settlements constitute a violation of international law, and the United Nations has

supported this interpretation. According to the Fourth Geneva Convention, occupiers are not allowed to settle permanently on lands taken by force. Israel, however, contends that these international laws do not apply to Israeli actions.

Even in the midst of peace talks, Israel announced plans to continue to settle more than 100,000 Jewish immigrants in the occupied territories. More than 30,000 Israeli settlers now live in the Gaza Strip, and more than 300,000 Jewish settlers live in the West Bank (Libiszewski 1995). Jerusalem, claimed by both the Arab and the Jewish peoples as their capital city, has experienced an enormous boom of Israeli settlements, which now ring the entire city. When the peace negotiations required a halt to the building of new settlements, the Israeli government considered the area around Jerusalem to be exempt from the restrictions. As a result, more than sixty-two new units have been built in and around Jerusalem alone since the start of the peace talks (*Settlement Watch* 1996). The settlements have created a de facto alteration of conditions on the ground since the talks began, making a final compromise to the status of Jerusalem increasingly more difficult to obtain. More troublesome yet are the long-term environmental consequences of the settlements.

A cycle of environmental destruction takes place each time an Israeli settlement is built. Typically, the cycle begins when land is confiscated from Arab inhabitants. The land is cleared, and some soil erosion begins. The construction of houses, roads, parking lots, and sidewalks prevents reabsorption of rainwater into the aquifers below, and the runoff is polluted with petroleum and other chemicals—consequences of modern settlement wherever it occurs. Early in the process of building the settlement, modern drilling equipment is brought in and a deep well is created to supply the new settlement with water. As previously discussed, this lowers the water table, diminishing water quantity and quality for the surrounding Arab population. These deep wells and their almost unlimited use for Israeli monoculture, gardens, and swimming pools place a heavy burden on the water resources of the region.

Nearby Arab villages experience first a loss of land and then increased crowding. With reduced access to waste disposal services and proper sanitation, the crowding causes increased disease rates in many Palestinian villages. Moreover, the drawdown of water in the wells concentrates any contaminants present. In attempts to compensate for the loss of confiscated agricultural lands, Palestinian farmers further push the production capacity of what land is left. This cycle of environmental degradation is initiated by each new settlement.

Another aspect of the settlement issue is the resentment created by the confiscation of land from the Palestinians by lifestyle incongruities between Palestinians and Israeli settlers. Palestinians living in areas under Israeli occupation have been subject to curfews during which they are confined to their houses and thus are unable to tend their fields or go to work, sometimes for months at a time (Shehadeh 1988). Settlers, on the other hand, have almost complete freedom of movement and are subject to few government restrictions.

Palestinians under Israeli occupation have been subject to several other forms of mass punishment. The Palestine Human Rights Information Center in Jerusalem reports that between 1987 and 1992, the Israeli authorities uprooted and destroyed more than 140,000 trees under the pretext of building new settlements or as mass punishment. The majority of these trees were fruit-bearing olive and citrus trees that were vital to the Palestinians' economy. The loss of these trees promotes desertification, forcing more and more Palestinians to leave the land (Libiszewski 1995, 21). In the West Bank and the Gaza Strip, the cycle of settlement building and ecological disruption is a continuing source of friction, often causing violent confrontations between Palestinians and Israelis.

Many Israeli settlers, especially those who are highly religious, view the settlements as an essential part of the Israeli experience and integral to Zionism. A religious fervor informs their actions. They hold a strong belief that once the land is "liberated" from non-Jews, it will be Jewish land in perpetuity. Such beliefs on the part of some make it difficult for more moderate Jewish elements to exchange land for peace or to slow or halt the building of settlements.

Other Water Problems: Salinity and Chemical Contamination

The water difficulties facing Arabs and Israelis are not limited to problems of quantity and supply. Increasing salination of the Sea of Galilee and saline infiltration of the coastal aquifer represent serious problems. Salinities in some areas of Israel are six times what they were before 1948 (Shuval 1980). Although experimentation with plants that can be grown in brackish water is a possibility, once soil salinities exceed certain levels, there is no solution to the salt problem. Today, an area of southern Iraq, where the ancient city of Sumer once flourished, is a human-made desert; overirrigation by Sumerians and Babylonians caused soil damage that even modern technology cannot reverse (Beaumont and Mclachlan 1985).

Water quality problems are also involved in the regional conflict. The issue of chemical and fertilizer use is a critical environmental problem in Israel. According to Israeli sources (Darr, Feldman, and Kamen 1976), many of the coastal wells in Israel are contaminated with high levels of nitrogen-containing compounds (known carcinogens) from fertilizers. The Israeli government's program for agricultural development took such precedence that when the nitrogen levels in the wells exceeded allowable limits, the limits were simply raised. What effect this has had on the health of Jews and Arabs in these areas is not known.

A disturbing element of the conflict between these two peoples emerges in the case of pesticides. Palestinian farmers in the Gaza Strip and the West Bank are becoming increasingly dependent on chemical pesticides (interview with a Palestinian farmer 1994).[3] One problem they face involves the types of chemicals available, their cost, and their proper use. All over the Third World, chemical companies are selling highly toxic chemicals to farmers who lack knowledge about their dangers and training in their proper use (Weir and Shapiro 1981; Carson 1962).

Palestinian farmers in the occupied territories currently use a huge arsenal of chemicals, among them some thirty that have been banned or restricted in most developed countries (Safi and El-Nahal 1991; Hassoun 1993). Among these chemicals are DDT, 2,4,5-T (a component of agent orange, used as a herbicide), phosval (an extremely toxic chemical responsible for neural damage in exposed victims), and a sobering list of other potentially hazardous agents. The Israeli government is responsible for allowing the use of these chemicals and for supplying them to the farmers.

Most of these chemicals are not accompanied by labels or instructions in Arabic, and the farmers receive little or no safety equipment or instruction. Compounding the problem is the worldwide practice by poor people in the Third World countries of storing foodstuffs and drinking water in empty chemical containers. Jewish Israeli farmers apparently are not using the worst of these offending chemicals, leading some Palestinians to cry foul play and discrimination (Safi and El-Nahal 1991). There is a definite need for education of the Palestinian farmers about these chemicals and provision of safety equipment and safer alternatives.

In the Gaza Strip, where there exist open sewers and lack of sewage treatment, the groundwater is polluted with human waste, which has the potential for combining with chemical runoff from the fields to form new and potentially more dangerous chemicals. Such a chemical soup may be an ecological time bomb set to go off as these chemicals concentrate in the food chain.

Palestinian researchers (Safi and El-Nahal 1991) note a rise in cancer rates in the Gaza Strip but do not have the resources to determine the connections and causal agents. The potential chemical contamination of the little fresh groundwater left in the coastal aquifer poses a serious threat to human health. In the meantime, farmers are concerned more about having enough water to maintain their yields than about possible chemical contamination.

Conclusion

Whether it is the quantity of water in an aquifer, the degree of pesticide contamination, or the number of Palestinians living in the Gaza Strip, researchers of the Arab–Israeli conflict are faced with a constant dilemma as authors and sources disagree about the data. For example, Israeli sources estimate the Arab population of the Gaza Strip to be close to 700,000, whereas the Palestinian Authority estimates the number to be more than 800,000. Since the Palestinian Authority now controls the Gaza Strip, and given the problems Israel had in subduing the area, the Palestinian estimate may be more accurate, or so such logic would dictate.

All available data concerning the water supply in the region are, at best, just rough estimates, since the more accurate estimates are state secrets. Most of the water data concerning Palestinians and Israelis come from Israeli sources. In many cases, accurate surveys of resources have never been made. Thus, the probability of bias exists on all sides.

Researchers have their own biases. Those trained in ecology and resource management place water at the heart of the conflict in the Middle East. By their definition, water scarcity and an increasing population lead to conflict. For engineers, the issues are water delivery and infrastructure problems; their solutions lie in technology. For anthropologists, the problem is culture.

The cultures of the peoples involved cannot be ignored in finding solutions to the water problem. The Arab–Israeli conflict did not begin over water: it began as a struggle between two national identities and cultures claiming the same land, and that remains its essence. Rooted in the clashes of culture are ideologies and philosophies that involve water. Thus, water, culture, and the politics of power in the Middle East appear to be inseparable components of the conflict.

The political Zionism on which Israel was founded depicts Israel as a safe haven for all the Jews of the world. Israeli policy allows any Jewish person from anywhere in the world to come to Israel and be granted citizenship, without limitation. When immigrants arrive, it is expected that the state will accommodate them and their dreams. Israel is being built on a Western industrial lifestyle, as evidenced by its agricultural methods, water use, production of municipal waste, and infrastructure development. Water has always been a strategic aspect of Israeli policy and planning. If the water crisis were suddenly to become so severe that Israel had to curb or stop immigration of Jews to Israel, it would have a far-reaching impact on Israeli culture and Zionist philosophy.

On the other hand, all land has a carrying capacity, and Israel, with its current boundaries, must eventually face that fact. The principle of exchanging land for peace has been established as an integral element of the Arab–Israeli peace negotiations. Part of the backlash in Israeli society against the current peace talks may be a recognition of the scarcity of land and resources available for Jewish immigration.

The Palestinians base their arguments on historical possession of the region's land and water resources. The Palestinian Authority is asking for equitable access to the West Bank's aquifers to compensate for severe limitation of access to water over the past twenty years (Palestine Environmental Protection Authority 1994). As mentioned earlier, in Islam, denial of access to water is a grievous sin. This belief gives rise to some of the resentment the Palestinian population bears for Israel's occupation of the West Bank and the Gaza Strip. The Palestinians are asking for more than double their current water allotment at a time when Israel, by all accounts, is using 100 percent of the available surface water and is overexploiting many of the underground water resources, such as the coastal aquifer.

Will Jewish Israelis be willing to make substantial changes in their lifestyle in order to provide more water for the Palestinians and neighboring Jordanians, whom they view as enemies? Will they sacrifice their swimming pools, gardens, high agricultural yields, economic development, and financial gains for a fragile peace with the Palestinians and neighboring Arab countries? Will they ever relinquish control of the Golan Heights, which contains the headwaters of the Jordan River and contributes to their water security?

In the Gaza Strip, the quality of life continues to deteriorate, perhaps more so under Palestinian control (Kelly and Homer-Dixon 1996, 18).

The Palestinian Authority appears to have neither the will nor the resources to provide real relief in terms of freshwater and economic development. Dissatisfaction appears inevitable, increasing the threat of Islamic revitalization or an upsurge of "fundamentalism." Political scientists Kimberly Kelly and Thomas Homer-Dixon (1996) argue that the Palestinians, in accepting the Oslo agreement and voting overwhelmingly in recent elections for the more moderate Fatah faction of the Palestine Liberation Organization (PLO), have rejected a fundamentalist point of view. They conclude that as long as real progress occurs, the possibility of a fundamental Islamic uprising is low. Although fundamentalism is growing in the Gaza Strip and in some parts of the West Bank, a high percentage of Palestinians are highly educated and disinclined to adopt a more fundamentalist outlook.

From another perspective, the Arab countries and the Palestinians have had to sacrifice quality of life, agricultural improvements, and economic development to Israel's current water utilization regime and security interests. One could also argue that development in the Arab world has been slowed by large expenditures for the arms race in the region. It might also be said that economic development in the Middle East has been held captive by the maintenance of a status quo in order to supply cheap oil to Western countries. Will Western countries be willing to make sacrifices to secure clean water supplies for the Arab world? Who will finance expensive solutions such as massive water diversions from Turkey or the Nile River or large desalination plants? Desalination plants have life spans of only thirty or more years (see Dabbagh et al. 1994 for a costs-benefit analysis) and are economically feasible only for the richer oil-producing states. The oil revenues of the Middle East do not accrue to the states that neighbor Israel. Deep divisions in the Arab world and overwhelming infrastructure problems prevent Arabian oil from being a panacea to solve all the region's problems.

Quick solutions are not arrived at easily. On the other hand, the progress made in recent peace talks that allowed for the withdrawal of Israeli troops from Hebron is encouraging. Israel's prime minister, Benjamin Netanyahu, compromised on the Hebron redeployment of troops and the leader of the PLO, Yasser Arafat, compromised on allowing continued Israeli presence in Hebron, with Israeli troops protecting Jewish settlers inside the city.

In spite of such progress, the water problems in the Middle East appear to be reaching a crisis level.[4] Since the turn of the century, water has unilaterally been a major factor in Israeli planning. Arabs and Palestinians had no clearly articulated long-term water strategy in the early 1900s because under European colonialism, most Arabs did not have control over their resources. Palestine and the surrounding states were focused on securing their national homelands, with the emphasis on land rights. Only after the creation of Israel, when water supply and demand problems became critical, did water figure centrally in Arab demands and strategies.

The conflict over water had been going on well before the Israeli bombing of Jordanian water structures in 1964, and progress toward regional water solutions has been slow. Some of the proposed solutions, such as increasing the use of wastewater in the region, may not be sound, in part because of the problem of polluting shallow aquifers but also because they are culturally unacceptable to many Muslims. In research examining health issues among Arabs in the United States, the concept of bodily fluid contamination as being *haram*, or unclean, surfaced repeatedly with Muslim subjects (Hassoun 1995). Thus, solutions to the water problem must be both culturally and environmentally sound.

Whether or not the dire predictions of imminent water conflict in the Middle East have merit, a clear path to reducing tensions lies in finding culturally, financially, and environmentally sound solutions to the region's water supply and water quality problems. The role of the United States in extraction of resources from the region and as peace broker means that both the Arabs and the Israelis are looking to the United States for help in solving their problems.

Lasting peace in the Middle East will arrive when trust is established between the parties, yet trust cannot develop so long as one party controls all the region's water resources. Arrangements for sharing resources and for sharing responsibility for the region's well-being will have to be developed. Cultural modifications, lifestyle changes, and rearrangement of expectations will have to be part of the solution—all of which are difficult to achieve.

The water, resource, and population problems facing the Middle East present the greatest challenge to the survival of the cultures and nations of the region. Nowhere in the world is the industrialized lifestyle more seriously challenged than in the fragile environment of the Middle East. Although a predominant myth about the Middle East is that its lands and cultures have endured unchanged for thousands of years, the reality is that change has been brisk in the past few decades. Cultural change, whether adaptive or maladaptive, is a component of both Israeli and Arab life. In surviving over the centuries, both Arab and Israeli cultures have demonstrated an inherent willingness to overcome difficulties and challenges. Whether or not they will be able to overcome the water challenge will have a profound effect on global peace and security in a world of growing population and limited resources.

RESOURCES

Readers may wish to consult the home page of the Applied Research Institute—Jerusalem: The Water Research Unit at http://www.arij.org/water/ for ongoing analysis of water use and management issues in Palestine. The Israeli government site on the internet is found at http://www.israel.org/index.html. Stephen Libiszewski's electronic book (1995) *Water Disputes in the Jordan Basin Region and Their Role in the Resolution of the Arab-Israeli Conflict* can be found at the web site of the center for Security Policy and Conflict Research at the Swiss Research Foundation, http://www.fsk.ethz.ch/encop/13/en13. htm. Finally, the work of Thomas Homer-Dixon on environment and security issues has special relevance for the Arab–Israeli case and other peoples facing resource scarcity.

NOTES

1. Interviews were conducted in 1994 and 1995 among several Palestinians who were associated with water and agricultural projects. Names are withheld to protect anonymity.
2. Ibid.
3. Ibid.
4. John Waterbury (1994, 45) predicts that there will be no direct confrontation over water in the next twenty years and contends that water is a strategic rather than a causal agent in the conflict. His analysis is based on water supply and demand and on interpretation of the hydropolitics of the conflict. His historical analysis of the water conflict pinpoints 1964 as the turning point when water became part of the direct conflict. However, that analysis fails to include the role of water in Zionist political ideology and the deep-rooted concept of access to water inherent in Islamic thought.

Conclusion

John M. Donahue and Barbara Rose Johnston

The contributors to this volume have presented a number of cases in which various parties have struggled for control over water, a resource held in common but in most cases a resource of diminishing quantity and quality. All parties in these conflicts perceived this resource as critical to their way of life in one way or another. What different cultural meanings does water have for the contending parties, and how do these meanings complicate mediation among the various interests? How are some social actors able to impose their definition of water on other social actors with different but equally legitimate definitions? In other words, how is power used in the service of one or another of the cultural definitions of water? These are some of the questions that the case studies have raised and that need to be addressed in order to reach an understanding of the cultural bases of water conflicts. Indeed, the answers to these questions may bring to light potential solutions to conflicts over water use and management in the twenty-first century.

In the introduction to this book, we spoke of the crisis of water scarcity. As the Chinese characters for *crisis* might suggest, this scarcity can represent both great danger and great opportunity. Water conflicts are not new to the human community. In fact, conflicts allow us to see in full light the contending values. As anthropologist Eric Wolf reminds us, "the arrangements of a society become most visible when they are challenged by crisis" (1990, 593). What *is* new to the human community is the global scope of socioeconomic relationships, which can connect even the most remote human communities to all others.

Yet these communities are organized quite differently from one another. In the cases presented here, we have seen three kinds of social organization. Some communities, such as those of the Cree, the Hopi, and the Lummi, are organized along kinship lines and share strong cultural definitions of water. To date, the Lummi have been the most successful of these groups in protecting their rights to water, the lifeblood of their cultural identity. Other local groups, though not organized by kinship, may share many of the same concerns for sustainability of local water resources. As in the case of the opponents to the Applewhite Reservoir in South Texas, they may form coalitions that cut across class, ethnic, political, and religious lines to protect a water resource that they define as necessary for the continuation of local social and biological life.

A second form of social organization is what Wolf calls tributary organization. Government bureaucracies represent a form of tributary system in which moneys are collected to finance public works, such as the Tennessee-Tombigbee Waterway and the El Cajón Dam. Just as water in a tributary stream flows into a larger river or lake, wealth in the form of taxes or interest payments on loans flows to the sponsoring agency in tributary organizations. There, the projects for water management are formulated and funded. These plans are often shaped by bureaucratic managers and technocrats who must ensure not only that the funds are spent but also that they are spent according to plan. As in the case of the Lake Biwa project in Japan, several government agencies may have separate policy objectives regarding water and thus have separate cultural definitions. Bureaucratic institutions in the tributary mode frequently maintain their power through the funding of water projects and therefore may develop what James Nickum and Daniel Greenstadt felicitously call project culture. Since these projects sustain their founding institutions as well as manage water resources, the first objective may often take precedence over the second—an irony illustrated at the completion of the Central Arizona Project when water finally arrived in Tucson and the citizens voted not to allow it for drinking.

The third way in which humans organize themselves is the marketplace. Herein, water is defined as a commodity to be bought and sold. The process of modernization or development, as the expansion of the marketplace is often called, usually demands resource enclosure, through which water ceases to be a commons (a kinship use of water) and becomes state property (a tributary use of water) or private property (a market use of water). Wolf (1990, 593) notes that

> the three modes of categorizing social actors . . . imply quite different relations to "nature" and the cosmos. When one mode enters into conflict with another, it also challenges the fundamental categories that empower its dynamics. Power will then be invoked to assault rival categorical claims. Power

is thus never external to signification—it inhabits meaning and is its champion in stabilization and defense.

Thus, water resource conflicts are not simply a matter of "good guys" versus "bad guys." At stake in these conflicts between, for example, the Hopi and Peabody Coal or Honduran Bay Islanders and the international tourism industry are different modes of social organization with attendant cultural meanings of water. The danger is that in the conflict, local or kinship values of water may be overwhelmed, given the superior bureaucratic and economic resources of the other social actors.

These case histories lay out the dangers for those who lose out in water conflicts. Although the cases focus on the short-term losers, there is another, more fundamental, issue of what Nickum and Greenstadt call the "conflict between human institutions and complex ecological processes." In other words, if water scarcity is not addressed in a sustainable fashion at each local level, all humankind could be the loser in the long run. Thus, the short-term losers may be the local prophets of a coming global aquatic Armageddon. The tragedy of an island overwhelmed by ecological disaster is also a warning to a finite world made up of "complex ecological processes" that are not yet fully understood in themselves, let alone understood in terms of whether or not they are amenable to tributary or market-based management. How can we know? How can we make social actors in each venue—kinship group, tributary organization, and marketplace—view the legitimate concerns and cultural values of the others?

The contributors to this volume suggest that the point of departure must be the local ecosystem, where biological and cultural life are daily reproduced and nurtured. In the case of water, the global is also local. The cultural conflicts surrounding water originate and are played out in local ecosystems, and the solutions to those conflicts can be found there as well. It is to those conflicts and solutions that we now turn by examining the central themes unifying this collection of case studies.

Conflicts over rights and resources represents a dominant theme in this book. A number of authors explore ways in which the rights of people organized in local kinship groups are often subordinated to the demands of larger political and economic organizations. This is more than a story of "how the natives were robbed." Subsistence-oriented groups, such as the Hopi, the Lummi, and the Cree define, shape, and utilize biophysical resources in ways that maximize their social and ecological capacity for cultural and biological reproduction. Although private or public corporate use of water resources may differ from that of local kinship groups, sustainability is critical. We have much to learn from social actors as the Hopi, the Lummi, and the Cree, whose notions of resource sustainability are intrinsically linked to social, cultural, economic, and biophysical health.

Unfortunately, as illustrated in William Derman's analysis of hydropolitics in Zimbabwe, water resource development and management strategies often ignore traditional resource land use patterns and deny the credibility of local resource knowledge. Defining and shaping water access and use rights to encourage the growth of export agriculture means also denying the traditional communal rights to access and use of water resources. The Zimbabwe case is by no means unique. When a government policy or commercial enterprise threatens either the existence of the resource or the people dependent on it, everyone loses. Sustainability refers to biological and human community integrity. Sustainability is not negotiable.

A second dominant theme in this volume is the effort to examine hydropolitics with the goal of mapping out the meaning and dynamics of "project culture." Thus, a number of cases explore the tributary mode of the social organization of water. Kinship and local coalitions are still present in the analysis, but the focus is more on government activity in water management and specifically on several cases of project culture. Kreg Ettenger reports that when the government of Quebec announced its plans to carry out the James Bay Hydroelectric Project, the people in the region who would be most affected by the project, the Cree Indians, had not been consulted. However, the Cree were subsequently able to negotiate their own study, which included a social impact assessment. He notes the difference between this study, defined and shaped by the community, and previous studies, defined and shaped by government and industry scientists. Both share similar empirical observations on the impacts of change, but the interpretations of these changes are vastly different. To a Cree, a reservoir is a body of water that drowns out the past, disrupts the present, and inhibits the meaning and reality of a culturally viable future. A reservoir takes away the opportunity to use critical resources and to pass along knowledge (history, beliefs, lifeways)—it creates psychosocial as well as cultural, economic, and biological impacts. To a Hydro-Quebec scientist, however, a reservoir is viewed in terms of biomass productivity and other ecosystemic frames of reference.

This case illustrates an important characteristic of project culture. Often, development projects, whether public or private, involve the distancing of bureaucratic institutions from human and ecological systems. This distancing can even take the form of denial of existing threats to human health and safety, as in the Mexican city of Oaxaca de Juárez, where public officials deny that the municipal water supply is contaminated, in spite of scientific evidence to the contrary. Similarly, international donors have often redefined the meaning of having potable water to mean merely having a well.

The centralization of authority and capital in water management often increases the distance between those who decide and those who experience the consequence of the decision. One solution to the negative effects of project culture is to reconnect planners and people, as illustrated in Kreg Ettenger's and John Donahue's chapters. The Cree study, for example, became the basis for a Canadian court decision not to expand further the James Bay Hydroelectric Project. Similarly, as described in Donahue's chapter about the Edwards Aquifer in South Texas, after two defeats of a resolution to build a surface reservoir in San Antonio, the city council hired two professional mediators who brought together a coalition of opponents to discuss the issue with proponents and planners.

Another aspect of project culture is that hydrodevelopment includes dreams and promises as well as political and economic opportunities. The chapters by William Loker and Kreg Ettenger describe how those dreams and promises might not include the people affected. Furthermore, Thomas Sheridan and Claudia Rogers suggest in their chapters that the political and economic opportunities of a project may become more important than the outcome. In other words, the project may take on a life and meaning of its own, with much money to be made in the battle over funding and in the process of building. Whether or not the dream materializes may be insignificant.

A significant aspect of project culture is bureaucratic inertia. Bureaucracies are structured and defined by past events and agendas and carry with them a legacy of outdated goals and interests. Suzanne Hanchette, Jesmin Akhter, and Kazi Rozana Akhter's discussion of Bangladesh's Flood Action Plan illustrates this point quite well. The plan was an attempt to design strategies to minimize the adverse effects of annual flooding. The authors note that for reasons of culture and class, women in Bangladesh are more vulnerable than are men to the disasters created by flooding. Yet project culture severely inhibited the authors' ability to get this point across to policy makers and flood plan engineers. The culture and power dynamics that influenced the way the plan was designed also created tensions and barriers to modifying the plan. Gender became a "disconnect" between project planners and those who were most severely affected by the flooding.

Finally, Nickum and Greenstadt provide an important caveat in their discussion of bureaucratic management of water and project culture in the Lake Biwa project in Japan. Their definition of project culture is tied to the observation that "where water rights are held by the government, they become the property of specific agencies, *each with its own bureaucratic culture* [emphasis added]. The mobility and multiple uses of water inevitably mean that numerous government bodies will claim rights over it at one point or another in the hydrological cycle." Typically, issues of resource rights are discussed in terms of government, industry, and other stakeholders—social groups with historical claims to the contested resource—implying a context of inequity, with government and industry winning out over the less powerful. Yet especially in developed countries, enclosure of the commons has historically been undertaken in the name of the public. A lengthy history of resource management has produced elaborate, fragmented, and thus cumbersome sets of bureaucracies. Conflicts over rights to resources, as illustrated by the Lake Biwa example, are often conflicts among government agencies (the left hand promoting resource integrity, the right hand promoting economic development).

A third dominant theme of this volume is the effort to explore the tension between hydrodevelopment and local efforts to sustain biological and cultural life. Perhaps the most common issue raised in the various chapters is the significance of popular participation in decisions regarding water management. For example, the key to the success of the Lummi in recapturing some control over their resource base was the existence of a treaty assigning them water rights. The very threat of a lawsuit prevented further development and forced compliance with the intent of the treaty. The treaty made the Lummi's voice equal to that of their opponents in the debate. Clearly, solutions to water-related conflicts will not be found until all stakeholders enjoy some parity in the political process. As Rosina Hassoun's discussion of the Arab-Israeli conflict suggests, asymmetrical power relations spell disaster for negotiating access to a commons. By contrast, the Lake Biwa project in Japan illustrates how stakeholders can evolve a policy over time when all have a part in the decision-making process.

A further lesson regarding the political process emerges from these chapters. Sheridan, like Nickum and Greenstadt, notes the transient nature of the coalitions "that form and dissolve depending on the issue at hand." Donahue found that in South Texas, "a core group of citizens" formed in the 1960s and 1970s to protect the quality of water in the Edwards Aquifer. "The relationships, shared experiences, and networks formed during this period," he notes, "would endure and grow into larger movements as time went on." The formation of social movements to protect water resources requires the emergence of new leaders and the forging of new political alliances. As in the case of the Applewhite Reservoir, the relative power of political and corporate interests allows them to fashion and refashion projects until their objectives are met. By contrast, citizen coalitions may be fragile because of the specific ties that bind them to a particular place and case. Nevertheless, future coalitions are drawn from networks formed, leadership developed, and skills honed in past battles.

And finally, a fourth significant theme emerging from this collection of cases is the demonstration that crises involving water scarcity and water quality are as much a product of cultural values, social contexts, economic activities, and power relationships as they are a result of biophysical forces and conditions. The majority of cases presented here demonstrate the links between enclosure (and thus the loss of critical resource rights); alienation from water resources (and, at a more fundamental level, from the opportunity to interact with, know, and value water resources); degenerative change in human and biological systems; and, in some places and cases, the incidence of violent conflict. This is the "great danger" dimension of current water crises. Governments or industries that exploit water resources for short-term profit with little or no accountability to local communities can quickly turn fragile ecosystems into economic enclaves that depend entirely on external infusions of tourist dollars or on the uncertainties of international commodity markets. In the case of the Bay Islands of Honduras, for example, efforts to build tourism may indeed bring about the deaths of both tourism and the island ecosystem. Similarly, the transformation of St. Thomas, Virgin Islands, from a subsistence-based economy to a market economy involved a transfer of control over water and its management from local residents to social actors who represent dependence on external, highly technological water systems. This techodependence, and the environmental alienation that accompanied it, led to the destruction of the largest source of subsurface water on the island.

In a sense, the Hopi and Arab-Israeli cases with which this volume begins and ends encapsulate many of the issues discussed in the other chapters and point the way to possible solutions. Accountability in the political process of water allocation is fundamental, especially when the lifeways of entire peoples are at stake. Sustainability of water both as a resource and as a cultural marker is best served when all stakeholders are at the table. As in the case of the air we breathe, so with the water we drink: there cannot be winners and losers. Either we all win or we all lose.

ACKNOWLEDGMENTS

The authors acknowledge their debt to Eric Wolf (1982, 1990) in their analysis of kinship, tributary, and capitalist uses of water.

References

Abdullah, T. A., and S. A. Zeidenstein. 1982. *Village Women of Bangladesh: Prospects for Change.* Elmsford, N.Y.: Pergamon Press.

Abramovitz, J. N. 1995. "Freshwater Failures: The Crises on Five Continents." *World Watch* (September–October) 27–35.

Abya Yala News. 1996. "Confronting Cultural Extinction, Indigenous Cultures Continue to Vanish from the Americas." *Abya Yala News* 10, no. 2 (summer): 2. Oakland, Calif.: South and Meso American Indian Rights Center.

Aceves de la Mora, J. L. 1944. *El agua en la ciudad de Oaxaca: Monografía histórica.* Oaxaca: Publicaciónes del Gobierno del Estado de Oaxaca.

———. 1976. *Climatología del estado de Oaxaca.* Oaxaca: INDECO-OAXACA.

Adams, W. M. 1992. *Wasting the Rain: Rivers, People, and Planning in Africa.* Minneapolis: University of Minnesota Press.

Adnan, S., et al. 1991. *Floods, People, and the Environment: Institutional Aspects of Flood Protection Programmes in Bangladesh, 1990.* Dhaka: Research and Advisory Services (House 27, Road 6, Dhanmondi R/A, Dhaka-1205).

———. 1992. *People's Participation: NGOs and the Flood Action Plan, An Independent Review.* Dhaka: Research and Advisory Services (House 27, Road 6, Dhanmondi R/A, Dhaka-1205).

Akiyama, M., and M. Nakamura. 1994. "Water Resource Management in a Metropolitan Region Downstream of a Large Lake: Osaka, Japan." In *Metropolitan Water Use Conflicts in Asia and the Pacific,* edited by J. E. Nickum and K. W. Easter. Boulder, Colo.: Westview Press.

Altman, J. A. 1994. "Toward a Stakeholder-Based Policy Process: An Application of the Social Marketing Perspective to Environmental Policy Development." *Policy Sciences* 27, no. 1:37–51.

Alvard, M. 1993. "Testing the 'Ecologically Noble Savage' Hypothesis: Interspecific Prey Choice by Piro Hunters of Amazonian Peru." *Human Ecology* 21, no. 4:355–387.

American Public Health Association. 1989. *Standard Methods for the Examination of Water and Wastewater.* 17th ed. Washington, D.C.: American Public Health Association.

Anglo-American Committee of Inquiry. [1945–1946] 1991. *A Survey of Palestine.,* Vols. 1 and 2. Reprint, Washington, D.C.: Institute for Palestine Studies.

AOA (Aquarium of the Americas). 1991. "Bacterial Contamination in Waters in and Around Roatán, Islas de la Bahía, Honduras, Central America." Mimeo. New Orleans: Aquarium of the Americas.

———. 1992. "Bacterial Contamination in Waters in and Around Roatán, Islas de la Bahía, Honduras, Central America." Mimeo. New Orleans: Aquarium of the Americas.

———. 1993. "Bacterial Contamination in Waters in and Around Roatán, Islas de la Bahía, Honduras, Central America." Mimeo. New Orleans: Aquarium of the Americas.

Archer, E. 1985. "Emerging Environmental Problems in a Tourist Zone: The Case of Barbados." *Caribbean Geography* 45–55.

Ashworth, W. 1986. *The Late Great Lakes: An Environmental History.* New York: Knopf.

Basso, K. 1996. *Wisdom Sits in Places:* Landscape and Language among the Western Apache. Albuquerque: University of New Mexico Press.

BBC Television. 1995. *The Hopi Way.* Under the Sun series. Manchester, England: BBC Television.

BCEOM (Compagnie Nationale du Rhone Euroconsult, Mott MacDonald International, and Satec Development in association with Desh Upodesh Ltd. and BETS Ltd.). 1992. *Human Resources and Socio-Economics Study (FAP 3): Supporting Report.* Dhaka: Ministry of Irrigation, Water Development, and Flood Control, Flood Plan Coordination Organization.

Beaumont, P., and K. Mclachlan. 1985. *Agricultural Development in the Middle East.* New York: Wiley.

Bellissari, A. 1996. "Public Health and the Water Crisis in the Occupied Territories." *Journal of Palestine Studies* 23, no. 2:52–63.

Benvenisti, M. 1984. *The West Bank Data Project.* Washington, D.C.: American Enterprise Institute for Public Policy.

Berger, T. R. 1977. *Northern Frontier, Northern Homeland: The Report of the Mackenzie Valley Pipeline Inquiry.* Ottawa: Supply and Services Canada.

———. 1981. "Some Environmental and Social Impacts of the James Bay Hydroelectric Project, Canada." *Journal of Environmental Management* 12:157–172.

———. 1988. "The Intrinsic Difficulty of Predicting Impacts: Lessons from the James Bay Project." *Environmental Impact Assessment Review* 8:201–220.

Berkes, F. 1988. "Environmental Philosophy of the Chisasibi Cree Peoples of James Bay." pp 7–21 in *Traditional Knowledge and Renewable Resource Management in Northern Regions,* edited by M. M. R. Freeman and L. N. Carbyn. Edmonton, Alberta: Boreal Institute for Northern Studies, Occasional Publications, no. 23.

Berkman, R. L., and W. K. Viscusi. 1973. *Damming the West: Ralph Nader's Study Group Report on the Bureau of Reclamation.* New York: Grossman.

BID (Interamericano de Desarrollo). 1994. "Programa de manejo ambiental de las Islas de la Bahía." Manuscript, 21 September.

Blanton, R. E., et al. 1981. *Ancient Mesoamerica: A Comparison of Change in Three Regions.* Cambridge: Cambridge University Press.

Blomquist, William. 1992. *Dividing the Waters: Governing Groundwater in Southern California.* San Francisco: Island Press.

Bodley, John H. 1990. *Victims of Progress.* 3rd ed. Mountain View, Calif.: Mayfield.

Bolding, A. 1996. "Caught in the Catchment: Past, Present, and Future of Nyanyadzi Water Management." In *University of Zimbabwe and ZIMWESI Water for Agriculture: Current Practices and Future Prospects.* Proceedings of workshop held in Harare 11–13 March. Mimeo.

Bollentini, N. 1996. "EPA to Lay Out Cleanup Options for Contaminated Tutu Aquifer." *Virgin Islands Daily News,* 2 March, p. 5.

Bollentini, N., and H. Hodge. 1996. "Views on the News: Do You Think the Government Effectively Handled the Tutu Wells Contamination?" *Virgin Islands Daily News,* 16 February, p. 14.

Bordewich, F. M. 1996. *Killing the White Man's Indian: Reinventing Native Americans at the End of the Twentieth Century.* New York: Doubleday.

Bourassa, R. 1985. *Power from the North.* Scarborough, Ontario: Prentice-Hall of Canada.

Boyer, W. A. 1983. *America's Virgin Islands: A History of Human Rights and Wrongs.* Durham, N.C.: Carolina Academic Press.

Bracken, Paul J. 1979. Arizona Tomorrow: A Precursor of Post-Industrial America. Croton-on-Hudson, NY: Hudson Institute.

Bradfield, R. 1995. *An Interpretation of Hopi Culture.* Derby, England: Privately printed. (Originally published in 1973 as *A Natural History of Associations,* Vol. 2. London: Duckworth.)

Braidotti, R., et al. 1994. *Women, the Environment, and Sustainable Development: Towards a Theoretical Synthesis.* London and Atlantic City, N.J.: Zed.

Bratton, M. 1994. "Land Redistribution, 1980–1990." In *Zimbabwe's Agricultural Revolution,* edited by M. Rukuni and C. Eicher. Harare: University of Zimbabwe Press.

Brew, J. 1979. "Hopi Prehistory and History to 1850." In *Handbook of North American Indians,* vol. 9, *The Southwest,* edited by A. Ortiz. Washington, D.C.: Government Printing Office.

Brightman, R. 1993. *Grateful Prey: Rock Cree Human-Animal Relationships.* Berkeley: University of California Press.

Brody, H. 1981. *Maps and Dreams.* New York: Pantheon Books.

Brush, S., and D. Stabinsky, eds. 1996. "Tribal Rights." pp. 25–40 in *Valuing Local Knowledge.* Washington, D.C.: Island Press.

Buege, D. 1996. "The Ecologically Noble Savage Revisited." *Environmental Ethics* 18, no. 1:71–88.

Bullock, A. 1995. "Hydrological Studies for Policy Formulation in Zimbabwe's Communal Lands." Pp. 69–82 in *Dambo Farming in Zimbabwe: Water Management, Cropping, and Soil Potentials for Smallholder*

Farming in the Wetlands, edited by R. Owen et al. Harare: University of Zimbabwe Press.

Burton, L. 1991. *American Indian Water Rights and the Limits of the Law.* Lawrence: University Press of Kansas.

Bush, D., and W. Martin. 1986. "Potential Costs and Benefits to Arizona Agriculture of the Central Arizona Project." In *Arizona Agricultural Experiment Station Technical Bulletin 254.* Tucson: University of Arizona, College of Agriculture.

Butterworth, D. S. 1973. "Squatters or Suburbanites? The Growth of Shantytowns in Oaxaca, Mexico." Pp. 208–232 in *Latin American Modernization Problems,* edited by R. E. Scott. Champaign: University of Illinois Press.

Cain, M. 1977. "The Economic Activities of Children in a Village in Bangladesh." *Population and Development Review* 3, no. 3:201–227.

Cain M., et al. 1979. "Class, Patriarchy, and Women's Work in Bangladesh." *Population and Development Review* 5, no. 3:405–438.

Caldwell, L., ed. 1988. *Perspectives on Ecosystem Management for the Great Lakes.* Albany: State University of New York Press.

Callicott, J. B. 1982. "Traditional American Indian and Western European Attitudes Toward the Environment: An Overview." *Environmental Ethics* 4, no. 4:293–318.

———. 1996. "American Indian Land Ethics." *Environmental Ethics* 18, no. 1:438.

Caribbean Tourism Research and Development Centre. 1985. *Caribbean Tourism Statistical Report.* Christchurch, Barbados: Caribbean Tourism Research and Development Centre.

Carson, R. 1962. *Silent Spring.* New York: Fawcett Books.

Castells, M. 1982. "Squatters and Politics in Latin America: A Comparative Analysis of Urban Social Movements in Chile, Peru, and Mexico." In *Towards a Political Economy of Urbanization in Third World Countries,* edited by H. I. Safa. Delhi: Oxford University Press.

———. 1983. *The City and the Grassroots: A Cross-Cultural Theory of Urban Social Movements.* Berkeley: University of California Press.

Cato Institute. 1996. *How Corporate Welfare Won.* Policy Analysis No. 254, 15 May. Washington, D.C.: Cato Institute.

Cernea, M. 1988. *Involuntary Resettlement in Development Projects: Policy Guidelines in World Bank–Financed Projects.* World Bank Technical Paper No. 80. Washington, D.C.: World Bank.

Cernea, M., and S. Guggenheim. 1993. *Anthropological Approaches to Involuntary Resettlement: Policy, Practice, and Theory.* Boulder, Colo.: Westview Press.

Chance, N., ed. 1968. *Conflicts in Culture: Problems of Developmental Change Among the Cree.* Ottawa: Canadian Research Centre for Anthropology.

Chen, M. A. 1986. *A Quiet Revolution: Women in Transition in Rural*

Bangladesh. Dhaka: BRAC Prokashana (also Cambridge, MA: Schenkman Publishing, 1983).

Cheung, W. H. S., et al. 1991. "Epidemiological Study of Beach Water Pollution and Health Related Bathing Water Standards in Hong Kong." *Water, Science, and Technology* 23:243–252.

CHTISB (Cree Hunters and Trappers Income Security Board). 1995. *Annual Report, 1993–94.* Quebec: Cree Hunters and Trappers Income Security Board.

Clark, R. 1993. *Water: The International Crisis.* Cambridge, Mass.: MIT Press.

Clemmer, R. 1984. "The Effects of the Energy Economy on Pueblo Peoples." In *Native Americans and Energy Development,* vol. 2, edited by J. Jorgenson. Boston: Anthropology Resource Center and the Seventh Generation Fund.

———. 1978. *Black Mesa and the Hopi.* In *Native Americans and Energy Development,* edited by J. Jorgenson. Boston: Anthropology Resource Center.

———. 1984. *Pueblo Indian Water Rights: Struggle for a Precious Resource.* Tucson: University of Arizona Press.

Coate, C. 1995. "The Biggest Water Fight in American History: Stewart Udall and the Central Arizona Project." *Journal of the Southwest* 37, no. 1:79–101.

COESPO (Consejo Estatal de Población de Oaxaca). 1993. *Oaxaca Demografico.* Oaxaca: Consejo Estatal de Población de Oaxaca.

Cohen, E. 1978. "The Impact of Tourism on the Physical Environment." *Annals of Tourism Research* 5:215–237.

Cohen, J. 1995. *How Many People Can the Earth Support?* New York: Norton.

Collins, D. 1995. "Capitalism, Environmentalism, and Mediating Structures: From Adam Smith to Stakeholder Panels." *Environmental Ethics* 17, no. 3:227–244.

Colson, E. 1960. *Social Organization of the Gwembe Tonga.* Manchester, England: Manchester University Press.

———. 1971. *The Social Consequences of Resettlement.* Manchester, England: Manchester University Press.

Cook, C. 1995. Opinion piece. *Virgin Islands Daily News,* 6 October, p. 18.

Cooley, M., et al. 1969. *Regional Hydrogeology of the Navajo and Hopi Indian Reservations, Arizona, New Mexico, and Utah.* U.S. Geological Survey Professional Paper, No. 521-A. Washington, D.C.: Government Printing Office.

Coordinación General de Plan Nacional de Zohas Deprimidas y Grupos Marqinados (COPLAMAR). 1985. *Salud.* Vol. 4 of *Necesidades esenciales en México.* 3rd ed. Federal District, Mexico: Siglo Veintiuno Editores.

Cordell, L. 1984. Prehistory of the Southwest. New York: Academic Press.

———. 1989. "Hopi Prehistory: Overview and Issues." In *Seasons of the Kachina,* edited by L. Bean. Proceedings of the Conference on the Western Pueblos 1987–88, California State University, Hayward. Ballena Press.

Cordell, L., and G. Gumerman, eds. 1989. *Dynamics of Southwest Prehistory.* Washington, D.C.: Smithsonian Institution Press.

Corona, R., et al. 1982. *La mortalidad en México*. Federal District, Mexico: Instituto de Investigaciónes Sociales, Universidad Nacional Autónoma de México.

Cultural Survival Quarterly. 1996. "Paavaha and Paanaquu: The Wellsprings of Life and the Slurry of Death." *Cultural Survival Quarterly* 19, no. 4:40–45.

Curtis, S. A. 1992. "Cultural Relativism and Risk-Assessment Strategies for Federal Projects." *Human Organization* 51, no. 1:65–70.

Czaya, E. 1981. *Rivers of the World*. New York: Van Nostrand Reinhold.

Dabbagh, T., et al. 1994. "Desalination: An Emergent Option." Pp. 203–241 in *Water in the Arab World: Perspectives and Prognoses*, edited by P. Rogers and P. Lyndon. Cambridge, Mass.: Harvard University Press.

Darr, P., S. L. Feldman, and C. Kamen. 1976. *The Demand for Urban Water*. Leiden: Nijhoff.

Dart, R. K., and R. J. Stretton. 1980. *Microbiological Aspects of Pollution Control*. 2nd ed. Amsterdam: Elsevier.

Davidson, W. 1974. *Historical Geography of the Bay Islands: Anglo-Hispanic Conflict in the Western Caribbean*. Birmingham, Ala.: Southern University Press.

Davis, O. 1996. "Tutu Well Contamination Shows Need for Regulation." *Virgin Islands Daily News*, 23 February, p. 19.

De Graf, J., and D. Moore. 1987. *Proceedings of the Conference on Fisheries in Crisis*. Charlotte Amalie, St. Thomas: U.S. Virgin Islands Department of Planning and Natural Resources, Division of Fish and Wildlife.

Denevan, W. 1992. "The Pristine Myth: The Landscape of the Americas in 1492." *Annals of the Association of American Geographers* 82:369–385.

Derman, B. 1990. "The Unsettling of the Zambezi Valley: An Examination of the Mid-Zambezi Rural Development Project." Working Paper, September. Harare: Centre for Applied Social Sciences.

Derman, B., and J. Murombedzi. 1994. "Democracy, Development, and Human Rights in Zimbabwe: A Contradictory Terrain." *African Rural and Urban Studies* 1, no. 2:119–144.

———. 1996. *Changing Land-Use in the Eastern Zambezi Valley: Socio-Economic Considerations*. Harare: World Wide Fund for Nature–Zimbabwe and Centre for Applied Social Sciences.

———. 1997a. "Nature, Culture, and Development in the Zambezi Valley." Pp. 73–96 in *Life and Death Matters*, edited by B. Johnston. Thousand Oaks, Calif.: Altamira Press.

Devas, E. 1982. "The Future of Tourism in the U.S. Virgin Islands." Christchurch, Barbados: Caribbean Tourism Research and Development Centre.

Dilley, F. B. 1993. "Climate Change and Agricultural Transformation in the Oaxaca Valley, Mexico." Ph.D. diss., Pennsylvania State University, Philadelphia.

Donahue, J. M., and M. J. Schlitz. 1994. "Power Relations and Water Resource Management in South Texas." Paper presented at the annual meetings of the Society for Applied Anthropology, Cantun, Quintana Roo, Mexico, April 13–17, 1994.

Dookhan, I. 1974. *A History of the Virgin Islands of the United States.* Charlotte Amalie, St. Thomas: Caribbean University Press.

DPNR (Department of Planning and Natural Resources). 1984. *Water Quality.* Report summarizing the first five years of implementation of the Virgin Islands Drinking Water Act, prepared for the Department of Conservation and Cultural Affairs. Charlotte Amalie, St. Thomas: U.S. Virgin Islands Department of Planning and Natural Resources.

Dumars, C. 1984. *Pueblo Indian Water Rights: Struggle for a Precious Resource.* Tucson: University of Arizona Press.

Dunbar, R. G. 1983. *Forging New Rights in Western Waters.* Lincoln: University of Nebraska Press.

Dutton, Y. 1992. "Natural Resources in Islam." Pp. 59–67 in *Islam and Ecology,* edited by F. M. Khalid and J. O'Brien. London: Cassell.

Eastman, S. 1996. "The Annual Review of Waterway Events." *Waterways Journal* 110, no. 38:8.

Echeverria, J. D., et al. 1989. *Rivers at Risk: The Concerned Citizen's Guide to Hydropower.* Washington, D.C.: Island Press.

The Ecologist. 1993. *Whose Common Future? Reclaiming the Commons.* Philadelphia: New Society Publishers.

Eggan, F. 1950. *Social Organization of the Western Pueblos.* Chicago: University of Chicago Press.

Evison, Lilian, M. 1979. Microbial Parameters of Raw Water. *Biological Indicators of Water Quality.* A. James and Lilian Evison, editors. John Wiley & Sons: Chichester, Great Britain.

ENEE (Empresa Nacional de Energía Electrica). 1991. *Estudio de factibilidad, Proyecto Hidroeléctrico Remolino y Sico II.* Tegucigalpa, Honduras: Empresa Nacional de Energía Electrica.

Enge, Kjell, and Scott Whiteford. 1989. *The Keepers of Water and Earth: Mexican Rural Social Organization and Irrigation.* Austin. University of Texas Press.

Evans, L. H. 1944. *The Virgin Islands: From Naval Base to New Deal.* Ann Arbor, Mich.: J. W. Edwards.

Feit, H. A. 1989. "James Bay Cree Self-Government and Land Management." Pp. 68–98 in *We Are Here: Politics of Aboriginal Land Tenure,* edited by E. Wilmsen. Berkeley: University of California Press.

Fewkes, J. 1900. "Tusayan Migration Traditions." Pp. 573–633 in *Nineteenth Annual Report of the Bureau of American Ethnology, Smithsonian Institution (1897–98).* Washington, D.C.: Government Printing Office.

———. 1906. Hopi Shrines Near the East Mesa, Arizona. American Anthropologist. 8:346–375.

Fiske, S. J., and R. M. Wulff, eds. 1987. *Anthropological Praxis: Translating Knowledge into Action.* Boulder, Colo.: Westview Press.

Flannery, R. 1995. *Ellen Smallboy: Glimpses of a Cree Woman's Life.* Montreal: McGill-Queen's University Press.

Fradkin, P. 1984. *A River No More: The Colorado River and the West.* New York: Knopf, 1981. Reprint, Tucson: University of Arizona Press.

Frankel, G. 1996. *Beyond the Promised Land: Jews and Arabs on the Hard Road to a New Israel.* New York: Simon & Schuster.

Gajraj, A. 1981. "Threats to the Terrestrial Resources of the Caribbean." *Ambio* 10, no. 6:307–311.

Galdis, A. V. 1985. *Tennessee-Tombigbee Corridor Study Main Report.* Mobile, Ala.: U.S. Army Corps of Engineers, Mobile District.

Gallup (New Mexico) Independent. 1993. "Coal Mining May Threaten Hopi Water, Culture." 20 December.

Garncr, P., and M. Holmcs. 1995. *An Analysis of the Annual Economic Impact of the Tennessee-Tombigbee Waterway.* Report prepared for the Tennessee-Tombigbee Waterway Development Authority. Livingston: University of West Alabama.

Gat, J., and M. Stilles. 1981. "La Mer Morte." *La Recherche* 12, no. 126:1084–1092.

Gedicks, A. 1993. *The New Resource Wars: Native and Environmental Struggles Against Multinational Corporations.* Boston: South End Press.

Geertz, A. W. 1984. "A Reed Pierced the Sky: Hopi Indian Cosmography on Third Mesa, Arizona." *Numen* 31, no. 2:216–241.

Gilbert, A., and P. M. Ward. 1988. "Land for the Rich, Land for the Poor." Pp. 129–137 in *The Urbanization of the Third World,* edited by J. Gugler. New York: Oxford University Press.

Gjessing, H. 1996. Letter to the editor. *Virgin Islands Daily News,* 14 February, p. 14.

Gleick, P., ed. 1993. *Water in Crisis: A Guide to the World's Fresh Water Resources.* New York: Oxford University Press.

Goff, J. 1973. *George W. P. Hunt and His Arizona.* Pasadena, Calif.: Socio-Technical Publications.

Goldsmith, E., and N. Hildyard. 1986. *The Social and Environmental Effects of Large Dams.* San Francisco: Sierra Club Books.

Golley, F. 1993. *A History of the Ecosystem Concept in Ecology: More Than the Sum of the Parts.* New Haven, Conn.: Yale University Press.

Goodland, R. J. 1978. *Environmental Assessment of the Tuccuri Hydroproject, Rio Toncantins, Amazonia, Brazil.* Brazilia: Electronorte, S.A.

Gottlieb, R. 1988. *A Life of Its Own: The Politics and Power of Water.* New York: Harcourt Brace Jovanovich.

Governor of the Virgin Islands. 1933. *Annual Report of the Governor of the Virgin Islands to the Secretary of the Department of the Interior.* Washington, D.C.: Government Printing Office.

———. 1934. *Annual Report of the Governor of the Virgin Islands to the Secretary of the Department of the Interior.* Washington, D.C.: Government Printing Office.

Greaves, T. 1993. "The Indians Are Winning." Paper presented at the annual meeting of the Society for Applied Anthropology, San Antonio, Texas, March 1993. (Available from the author at TGreaves@Bucknell.edu.)

———. 1995. Cultural Rights and Ethnography. *General Anthropology* 1, no. 2:1, 3–6.

———. 1996. "Tribal Rights." Pp. 25–40 in *Valuing Local Knowledge: Indigenous People and Intellectual Property Rights,* edited by S. Brush and D. Stabinsky. Washington, D.C.: Island Press.

Green, S. R. 1985. *The Tennessee-Tombigbee Waterway: An Overview.* Mobile, Ala.: U.S. Army Corps of Engineers, Mobile District, Public Affairs Office.

Greenstadt, D. T. 1993. "Environment and Development at Lake Biwa." Pp. 31–49 in *Policy Making Process Case Studies.* University of California, San Diego: Graduate School of International Relations and Pacific Studies.

Gregory, H. 1916. *The Navajo Country: A Geographic and Hydrographic Reconnaissance of Parts of Arizona, New Mexico, and Utah.* U.S. Geological Survey Water Supply Paper. Washington, D.C.: Government Printing Office.

Grenon, M., and M. Batisse, eds. 1989. *Futures for the Mediterranean Basin: The Blue Plan.* Oxford: Oxford University Press.

Guerrero, M. 1992. "American Indian Water Rights: The Blood of Life in Native North America." In *The State of Native America: Genocide, Colonization, and Resistance,* edited by M. A. Jaimes. Boston: South End Press.

HACH Corporation. 1993. *HACH Analytical Procedures: Coliform Procedures.* Loveland, Colo.: HACH Corporation.

Hack, J. T. 1942. "The Changing Physical Environment of the Hopi Indians of Arizona." *Papers of the Peabody Museum of American Archaeology and Ethnology* 36:1.

Haggart, K., ed. 1994. *Rivers of Life.* Dhaka: Bangladesh Centre for Advanced Studies (House 620, Road 10/A, Dhanmondi R/A, Dhaka-1209).

Hall, G. E., and C. M. Slater, eds. 1992. *County and City Extra: Annual Metro, City, and County Data Book.* Lanham, Md.: Bernan Press.

Hamid, S. 1992. "Female-Headed Households." Pp. 118–131 in *Rethinking Rural Poverty: A Case for Bangladesh,* edited by H. Z. Rahman and M. Hossain. Dhaka: Bangladesh Institute of Development Studies.

Hanchett, S. n.d. *Women's Empowerment and the Development Research Agenda: Feminist Issues.* In press.

———. n.d. Unpublished Field Notes. Irrigation Support Project for Asia and the Near East Study/ISPAN, Flood Response Study (FAPK). RPSH Consulting Services, 5119 SE 44th Street, Portland, OR 97206.

Hansen, A., and A. Oliver-Smith. 1982. *Involuntary Migration and Resettlement: The Problems and Responses of Dislocated People.* Boulder, Colo.: Westview Press.

Hanson Annual Report. 1996. Hanson Industries. 581 Main St. Woodbridge, NJ 07095.

Harcourt, W., ed. 1994. *Feminist Perspectives on Development.* London and Atlantic City, N.J.: Zed.

Harrison, D. 1992. "International Tourism and the Less Developed Countries:

The Background." Pp. 1–18 in *Tourism and the Less Developed Countries*, edited by D. Harrison. New York: Halsted Press.

Hassoun, R. 1989. "The Arab-Israeli Conflict from the Viewpoint of Ecological Anthropology: Peasants, Blood, and Water." *Florida Journal of Anthropology* 14:39–50.

———. 1993. "Save the Musht." *The Link: Americans for Middle East Understanding* 26:4.

———. 1995. "A Bioanthropological Perspective of Hypertension in Arab-Americans in the Metropolitan Detroit Area." Ph.D. diss., University of Florida.

Hawken, P. 1993. *The Ecology of Commerce: A Declaration of Sustainability.* New York: HarperCollins.

Hawkes, H. A. 1979. "Invertebrates as Indicators of River Water Quality." In *Biological Indicators of Water Quality*, edited by A. James and L. Evison. Chichester, England: Wiley.

Hays, S. 1975. *Conservation and the Gospel of Efficiency.* New York: Atheneum.

Hedges, F., and A. Mitchell. 1924. *Battles with Giant Fish.* Boston: Small, Maynard.

Hiernaux, D. 1986. *Urbanización autoconstrucción de vivienda en Tijuana.* Federal District, Mexico: Centro de Ecodesarrollo.

Homer-Dixon, T. 1996. "Project on Environment, Population, and Security: Key Findings." *Environmental Change and Security Project Report*, no. 2 (spring): 45–48.

Homer-Dixon, T., et al. 1994. "Environmental Change and Violent Conflict." Pp. 391–400 in *Beyond the Numbers: A Reader on Population, Consumption, and the Environment*, edited by L. A. Mazur. Washington, D.C.: Island Press.

Hossain, M., et al. 1987. *Floods in Bangladesh: Recurrent Disasters and People's Survival.* Dhaka: Universities Research Centre.

Hough, W. 1906. "Sacred Springs of the Southwest." *Records of the Past* 5, no. 6:163–169.

Houlson, J. H. 1934. *Blue Blaze: Danger and Delight in Strange Islands of Honduras.* London: Duckworth.

Hourani, A. 1991. *A History of the Arab Peoples.* Cambridge, Mass.: Belknap Press.

Howells, V. 1956. *A Naturalist in Palestine.* London: Andrew Melrose. Pp. 160–165.

Hu, H., and N. K. Kim. 1993. "Drinking-Water Pollution and Human Health." Pp. 31–42 in *Critical Condition: Human Health and the Environment*, edited by E. Chivian et al. Cambridge, Mass.: MIT Press.

Hundley, N. 1975. *Water and the West: The Colorado River Compact and the Politics of Water in the American West.* Berkeley: University of California Press.

Hunter, C., and H. Green. 1995. *Tourism and the Environment: A Sustainable Relationship?* London: Routledge.

Hunting Technical Services Ltd. in association with Bangladesh Institute of Development Studies. 1992. *FCD/I Agricultural Study (FAP 12): Final Report.* Dhaka: Ministry of Irrigation, Water Development, and Flood Control, Flood Plan Coordination Organization.

Hydro-Quebec. 1993. *Grand-Baleine Project Feasibility Study.* 30 vol. Montreal: Hydro-Quebec.

IDB (Inter-American Development Bank). 1994. *Bay Islands Environmental Management Project: Project Summary.* Washington, D.C.: Inter-American Development Bank.

INA (Instituto Nacional Agraria). 1979. "Informe sobre el levantimiento catastral, avaluo y promoción realizada en el Proyecto Hidroeléctrico El Cajón." Unpublished report.

INEGI (Instituto Nacional de Estadística, Geografía, e Informatica). 1994. *Anuario estadístico de los Estados Unidos Méxicanos.* Federal District, Mexico: Instituto Nacional de Estadística, Geografía, e Informatica.

Intergovernmental Report on Global Climate Change. 1995. New York: Cambridge University Press.

International Tourism Reports. 1986. "Cuba." National Report No. 116. *International Tourism Reports* 2:69–79.

IRF (Island Resources Foundation). 1996. *Tourism and Coastal Degradation: Costs and Benefits of Caribbean Coastal Tourism.* Report prepared for the United Nations Environment Programme. Charlotte Amalie, St. Thomas: Island Resources Foundation. Internet address: http://www.irf.org/irunep.html.

ISPAN (Irrigation Support Project for Asia and the Near East). 1992a. *FAP 16 Environmental Study: Environmental Impact Assessment Case Study, Surma- Kushiyara Project.* Dhaka: Ministry of Irrigation, Water Development, and Flood Control, Flood Plan Coordination Organization.

———. 1992b. *FAP 23 Flood Proofing Study: Draft Issues Report.* Dhaka: Ministry of Irrigation, Water Development, and Flood Control, Flood Plan Coordination Organization.

———. 1992c. *Flood Response Study (FAP 14): Draft Final Report.* Dhaka: Ministry of Irrigation, Water Development, and Flood Control, Flood Plan Coordination Organization.

———. 1993. *Environmental Impact Assessment Case Study, Bhelumia-Bheduria Project: FAP 16 Environmental Study and FAP 19 Geographic Information System.* Dhaka: Ministry of Irrigation, Water Development, and Flood Control, Flood Plan Coordination Organization.

Israel, Government of. 1991. *Background: Water, Israel, and the Middle East.* Israeli Foreign Ministry, Information Division. Berne, Switzerland: Israeli Embassy. Mimeo.

Jensen, M. E. 1990. "Arid Lands: Impending Water-Population Crisis." Pp. 14–19 in *Hydraulics/Hydrology of Arid Lands.* New York: American Society of Civil Engineers.

Johansson, B., et al. 1995. "Assessment of Surface Water Resources in the

Manyame Catchment—Zimbabwe." In *Swedish Meteorological and Hydrological Institute,* Technical Report no. 60.

Johnson, R. 1977. *The Central Arizona Project, 1918–1968.* Tucson: University of Arizona Press.

Johnston, B. R. 1981. "The Problem of Water in St. Thomas, U.S.V.I.: A Cultural Ecological Study." Master's thesis, San Jose State University.

———. 1982. "Paleoecological Research in the U.S. Virgin Islands." *National Park Service Science News Bulletin* (fall).

———. 1987. "The Political Ecology of Development: The Impacts of Tourism in St. Thomas, Virgin Islands. Ph.D. diss., University of Massachusetts, Amherst.

———. 1990. "Save Our Beach Dem, and Our Land, Too." *Cultural Survival Quarterly* 16:2.

———. 1994. "Environmental Alienation and Resource Management: Virgin Islands Experiences." Pp. 194–205 in *Who Pays the Price? The Sociocultural Context of Environmental Crisis,* edited by B. R. Johnston. Washington, D.C.: Island Press.

———. 1997. *Life and Death Matters: Human Rights and the Environment at the End of the Millenium.* Bellevue, CA: Alta Mira Press.

Johnston, B. R., and E. R. Lundberg. 1985. "Archaeological Survey in the U.S.V.I.: A Preliminary Report." In *Proceedings from the 10th International Congress for the Study of Caribbean Archaeology.* Quebec: University of Montreal Press.

Jordan, D. G. 1972. *Land-Use Effect on the Water Regimen of the U.S.V.I.* U.S. Geological Survey Professional Paper No. 800-D. Washington, D.C.: Government Printing Office.

Jordan, D. G., and D. W. Fisher. 1977. *Relation of Bulk Precipitation and Evapotranspiration to Water Quality and Water Resources, St. Thomas, Virgin Islands.* U.S. Geological Survey Water Supply Paper No. 1663-1. Washington, D.C.: Government Printing Office.

Juliani, G. 1996. Telephone interview, 24 September.

Kada, Y., and A. Furukawa. 1984. "Mizu to Mura (Water and Village)." In Hiroyuki Torigue and Yukiko Kada, editors, Mizu to *Hito ho Kankyoo Shi (The Environmental History of the Water People).* Tokyo: Ochanomizu Shoten.

Kally, E. 1993. *Water and Peace: Water Resources and the Arab-Israeli Peace Process.* New York: Praeger.

KCM, Inc. Ca. 1993. "Developing a Long-Term Plan to Address Flood Problems." *Whatcom County, Lower Nooksack River Comprehensive Flood Hazard Management Plan.* Seattle, Wash.: KCM, Inc.

Kelly, K., and T. Homer-Dixon. 1996. *Environmental Scarcity and Violent Conflict: The Case of Gaza.* Washington, D.C.: American Association for the Advancement of Science; Toronto: University College.

Kelso, M., W. Martin, and L. Mack. 1973. *Water Supplies and Economic Growth in an Arid Environment.* Tucson: University of Arizona Press.

Khalidi, W. 1984. *Before Their Diaspora: A Photographic History of the Palestinians 1876–1948.* Washington, D.C.: Institute for Palestine Studies.

————. ed. 1992. *All That Remains: The Palestinian Villages Occupied and Depopulated by Israel in 1948.* Washington, D.C.: Institute for Palestine Studies.

Kirkby, A. V. T. 1973. "The Use of Land and Water Resources in the Past and Present Valley of Oaxaca, Mexico." In *Memoirs of the Museum of Anthropology, University of Michigan,* vol. 1, *Prehistory and Human Ecology of the Valley of Oaxaca,* edited by K. V. Flannery. Ann Arbor: University of Michigan Press.

Kliot, N. 1994. *Water Resources and Conflict in the Middle East.* London: Routledge.

Knox, J. P. 1852. *An Historical Account of St. Thomas, West Indies.* New York: Scribner.

Kocasoy, G. 1989. "The Relationship Between Coastal Tourism, Sea Pollution, and Public Health: A Case from Turkey." *Environmentalist* 9, no. 4:245–251.

————. 1995. "Effects of Tourist Population Pressure on Pollution of Coastal Seas." *Environmental Management* 19, no. 1:75–79.

Kowalewski, S. A., and L. Finsten. 1983. "The Economic Systems of Ancient Oaxaca: A Regional Perspective." *Current Anthropology* 24:4.

Lanjouw, G. J. 1995. *International Trade Institutions.* New York: Longman.

Lanjouw, P. 1995. "Infrastructure: A Ladder for the Poor." *Finance and Development* 32, no. 1:33–35.

Lanz, K. 1995. *The Greenpeace Book of Water.* New York: Sterling.

La Rusic, I. 1991. *Managing Mishtuk: The Experience of Waswanipi Band in Developing and Managing a Forestry Company.* Lethbridge, Alberta: University of Lethbridge, Centre for Aboriginal Management Education and Training.

Lee, D., and A. Dinar. 1995. *Review of Integrated Approaches to River Basin Planning, Development, and Management.* World Bank Policy Research Working Paper No. 1446. Washington, D.C.: World Bank.

Lees, S. 1995. "Water Shortage as an Ecopolitical Ploy." Paper presented at the annual meeting of the American Anthropological Association, Washington, D.C.

Lees, S. H. 1989. "Oaxaca's Spiraling Race for Water." In *Applying Anthropology,* edited by A. Podefsky and P. Brown. Mountain View, Calif.: Mayfield.

Legorreta, J. 1983. *El processo de urbanización en ciudades Petroleras.* Federal District, Mexico: Centro de Ecodesarrollo.

Le Moigne, G., et al., eds. 1994. *A Guide to the Formulation of Water Resources Strategy.* World Bank Technical Paper No. 263. Washington, D.C.: World Bank.

Lewis, G. K. 1968. *The Virgin Islands: A Caribbean Lilliput.* Evanston, Ill.: Northwestern University Press.

Lewis, O. 1961. *The Children of Sanchez: Autobiography of a Mexican Family.* New York: Random House.

Libiszewski, S. 1995. *Water Disputes in the Jordan Basin Region and Their Role in the Resolution of the Arab-Israeli Conflict.* ENCOP Occasional Paper No. 13. Zurich: Center for Security Policy and Conflict Research/ Swiss Research Foundation. Internet version: http://www.fsk.ethz.ch/encop/13/en13_ch 4.htm.

Loker, W. 1986. "Agricultural Ecology and Prehistoric Settlement in the El Cajón Region of Honduras." Ph.D. diss., University of Colorado, Boulder.

————. 1989. "Contemporary Land Use and Prehistoric Settlement: An Eth-noarchaeological Approach." Pp. 136–186 in *Archaeological Research in the El Cajón Region,* vol. 1, edited by K. Hirth, G. Lara Pinto, and G. Hase-mann. University of Pittsburgh Memoirs in Archaeology No. 1. Pitts-burgh, Pa.: University of Pittsburgh.

————. 1995. "Dam Development: The Social, Ecological, and Financial Effects of the El Cajón Dam." Paper presented at the annual meeting of the Society for Applied Anthropology, 30 March, Albuquerque, New Mexico.

Lowi, M. 1996. "Political and Institutional Responses to Transboundary Water Disputes in the Middle East." *Environmental Change and Security Project Report,* no. 2 (spring): 5 8.

Lowi, M. R. 1993. *Water and Power: The Politics of a Scarce Resource in the Jordan River Basin.* New York: Cambridge University Press.

Luckingham, B. 1989. *Phoenix: The History of a Southwestern Metropolis.* Tucson: University of Arizona Press.

Lukes, S. 1993. "Five Fables About Human Rights." *Dissent* (fall): 427–437.

Lvovich, M., and G. White. 1990. "Use and Transformation of Terrestrial Water Systems." Pp. 235–250 in *The Earth as Transformed by Human Action: Global and Regional Changes in the Biosphere over the Past 300 Years,* edited by B. L. Turner et al. Cambridge: Cambridge University Press.

McCarthy, F. 1977. "Bengali Village Women as Mediators of Social Change." *Human Organization* 36, no. 4:363–370.

McCarthy, F. E., T. Abdullah, and S. Zeidenstein. 1979. "Program Assessment and the Development of Women's Programs: The Views of Action Workers." Pp. 355–378 in *Women and Development: Perspectives from South and Southeast Asia,* edited by R. Jahan and H. Papanek. Dhaka: Bangladesh Institute of Law and International Affairs.

McCully, P. 1996. *Silenced Rivers: The Ecology and Politics of Large Dams.* London and Atlantic City, N.J.: Zed.

McCurdy, David W. 1997. "Using Anthropology." Pp. 383–394 in *Conformity and Conflict: Readings in Cultural Anthropology,* Ninth edition, edited by James Spradley and David W. McCurdy. New York: Addison Wesley Longhan.

McCutcheon, S. 1991. *Electric Rivers: The Story of the James Bay Project.* Montreal: Black Rose Books.

McDowall, D. 1994. *The Palestinians: The Road to Nationhood.* London: Minority Rights Publishing Group.

McEachern, A. 1991. "Reasons for Judgement: *Delgamuukw vs. A. G. Smithers* Registry" (B.C.). No. 0843.

McFarlane, M. J. 1995. "Dambo Gullying in Parts of Zimbabwe and Malawi." In *Dambo Farming in Zimbabwe: Water Management, Cropping, and Soil Potentials for Smallholder Farming in the Wetlands,* edited by R. Owen et al. Harare: University of Zimbabwe Press.

MacGregor, R. 1989. *Chief: The Fearless Vision of Billy Diamond.* Toronto: Penguin Books Canada.

McGuire, T. R., et al. 1993. *Indian Water in the New West.* Tucson: University of Arizona Press.

Maclay, R. W. 1988. "Statigraphic Subdivisions, Fault Barriers, and Characteristics of the Edwards Aquifer, South Central Texas." Pp. 6–11 in *Aquifer Resources Conference Proceedings: Geological and Managerial Considerations Relating to the Edwards Aquifer of South Central Texas.* San Antonio: Trinity University, Division of Science, Mathematics, and Engineering; and South Texas Geological Society.

McNamee, G. 1994. *Gila: The Life and Death of an American River.* New York: Orion Books.

Magadlela, D. 1996. "Whose Water Right Is Right? A Look at Irrigators and Catchment Farmers' Watered Relations." In *University of Zimbabwe and ZIMWESI Water for Agriculture: Current Practices and Future Prospects.* Proceedings of workshop held in Harare 11–13 March. Mimeo.

Mangin, W. 1973. "Sociological, Cultural, and Political Characteristics of Some Urban Migrants in Peru." Pp. 315–350 in *Urban Anthropology: Cross-Cultural Studies of Urbanization,* edited by A. Southall. Oxford: Oxford University Press.

Manzungu, E. 1995. "Engineering or Domineering? The Politics of Water Control in Mutambara Irrigation Scheme, Zimbabwe." *Zambezia: The Journal of the University of Zimbabwe* 22, no. 2:115–136.

Martin, C. 1978. *Keepers of the Game: Indian-Animal Relationships in the Fur Trade.* Berkeley: University of California Press.

Masayesva, V. 1995. *The Hopi Way.* Under the Sun Series. Manchester, England: BBC Television.

Mathieson, A., and G. Wall. 1982. *Tourism: Economic, Physical, and Social Impacts.* London: Longman.

Matiza, G. 1996. "Drought Relief and Irrigation." Pp. 1–9 in *University of Zimbabwe and ZIMWESI in Water for Agriculture: Current Practices and Future Prospects.* Proceedings of workshop held in Harare 11–13 March. Mimeo.

Matiza, T. 1992. "The Utilization and Status of Dambos in Southern Africa: A Zimbabwean Case Study." In *Wetlands Conservation Conference for Southern Africa: Proceedings of the SADCC Wetlands Conference,* edited by T. Matiza and H. N. Chabwela. Gland, Switzerland: IUCN.

Meyers, N. 1986. "Down to the Very Last Drop." *Nature* 322, no. 6081:677.

————, ed. 1993. *Gaia: An Atlas of Planet Management.* New York: Anchor Books.

Middleton, N., et al. 1994. *Tears of the Crocodile: From Rio to Reality in the Developing World.* Boulder, Colo.: Westview Press.

Mieczkowski, Z. 1995. *Environmental Issues of Tourism and Recreation.* Lanham, Md.: University Press of America.

Mies, M., and V. Shiva. 1993. *Ecofeminism.* London and Atlantic City, N.J.: Zed.

Miller, M. L., and J. Auyong, eds. 1991. *Proceedings of the 1990 Congress on Coastal and Marine Tourism* (25–31 May 1990, Honolulu). Vol. 1 and 2. Newport, Rhode Island: National Coastal Resources Research and Development Institute.

Milton, K., ed. 1993. *Environmentalism: The View from Anthropology.* New York: Routledge.

Mindeleff, V. 1891. "A Study of Pueblo Architecture: Tusayan and Cibola." Pp. 3–228 in *Eighth Annual Report of the Bureau of American Ethnology, Smithsonian Institution (for 1886–7).* Washington, D.C.: Government Printing Office.

Mintz, S. 1977. *Caribbean Transformations.* Baltimore: Johns Hopkins University Press.

————. 1985. *Sweetness and Power: The Place of Sugar in Modern History.* New York: Viking.

Momaday, N. S. 1974. "Native American Attitudes to the Environment." Pp. 79–85 in *Seeing with a Native Eye: Essays on Native American Religion,* edited by W. Capps. New York: Harper & Row.

Monet, D., and Skanu'u (A. Wilson). 1992. *Colonialism on Trail: Indigenous Land Rights and the Gitksan and Wef'sunet'en Sovereighty case.* Philadelphia: New Society Publishers.

Moore, D. 1989. "The U.S. Virgin Islands Faces a Resource Crisis." White Paper, 20 March. Charlotte Amalie, St. Thomas: U.S. Virgin Islands Department of Planning and Natural Resources, Division of Fish and Wildlife.

Morris, E. W. 1991. "Household, Kin, and Nonkin Sources of Assistance in Home Building: The Case of the City of Oaxaca." *Urban Anthropology* 20, no. 1:49–66.

Morris, E. W., et al. 1992. "Households and Their Housing in Oaxaca, Mexico: The View from the Bottom." Pp. 195–208 in *Housing in the Third World: Analyses and Solutions,* edited by L. Kilmartin and H. Singh. New Delhi: Concept.

Motor Columbus (Consulting Engineers). 1976. *El Cajón Project: Update of Feasibility Study.* Report on file at the Empresa Nacional de Energía Electrica, Tegucigalpa, Honduras.

Moyo, S. 1995. *The Land Question in Zimbabwe.* Harare: SAPES Books.

Multi-disciplinary Action Research Consultants. 1992. *Land Acquisition Study (FAP 15): Draft Final Report.* Dhaka: Ministry of Irrigation, Water Development, and Flood Control, Flood Plan Coordination Organization.

Murphy, A. D. 1987. "Studying Housing Areas in a Developing Nation: Lessons from Oaxaca City, Mexico." *Housing and Society* 14:143–160.

———. 1991. "City and Crisis: Introduction and Overview." *Urban Anthropology* 20, no. 1:1–14.

Murphy, A. D., and A. Stepick. 1991. *Social Inequality in Oaxaca: A History of Resistance and Change.* Philadelphia: Temple University Press.

Nakamura, M. 1995. "Lake Biwa: Have Sustainable Development Objectives Been Met?" *Lakes and Reservoirs: Research and Management* 1:3–29.

Nakashima, D., and M. Roué. 1994. *Great Whale Environmental Assessment Community Consultation: Final Report for Whapmagoostui and Chisasibi.* 4 vols. Report prepared for the Grand Council of the Crees (of Quebec) and the Cree Regional Authority under contract with Hydro-Quebec.

Nakashima, M. 1993. "Water Allocation Methods and Water Rights in Japan." *World Bank Technical Paper* No. 198:45–68, Washington, D.C.: World Bank.

Nelson, J. G., R. Butler, and G. Wall, eds. 1993. *Tourism and Sustainable Development: Monitoring, Planning, Managing.* Heritage Resources Centre Joint Publication No. 1. Waterloo, Ontario: University of Waterloo.

Nelson, R. 1993. "Searching for the Lost Arrow: Physical and Spiritual Ecology in the Hunter's World." Pp. 201–228 in *The Biophilia Hypothesis,* edited by R. Kellert and E. O. Wilson.

Nequatewa, E. 1936. *Truth of a Hopi: Stories Relating to the Origin, Myths, and Clan Histories of the Hopi.* Flagstaff, Ariz.: Northland Press.

Newton, J. 1995. "An Assessment of Coping with Environmental Hazards in Northern Aboriginal Communities." *Canadian Geographer* 39, no. 2: 112–120.

Nichols, W. D. (Western Region Ground Water Specialist, U.S. Geological Survey). 1993. Letter to William M. Alley, Chief, Office of Ground Water, Water Resources Division, U.S. Geological Survey, 28 October.

Niezen, R. 1993. "Power and Dignity: The Social Consequences of Hydroelectric Development for the James Bay Cree." *Canadian Review of Sociology and Anthropology* 30, no. 4:510–520.

Norgaard, R. 1994. *Development Betrayed: The End of Progress and a Co-Evolutionary Envisioning of the Future.* London and New York: Routledge.

OAS (Organization of American States). 1992. *Honduras: Projecto de Manejo de los Recursos Materiales Renovables de la Cuenca del Embalse El Cajón.* Estudio de Factibilidad. Departemento de Desarrollo Regional y Medio Ambiente. Washington, D.C.: Organization of American States.

Oglethorpe, M. 1982. "Recent Developments in Maltese Water Supply." *Geography* 67:62–64.

Ohlsson, L., ed. 1995. *Hydropolitics: Conflicts over Water as a Development Constraint.* London: and Atlantic City, N.J.: Zed.

Okura, E. 1990. *Omi shonin no keifu* (A genealogy of the Omi merchants). Tokyo: Shakai Shiso Sha.

Oldendorf, C. G. A. [1770] 1987. *A Caribbean Mission*, edited by J. J. Bossard, translated by A. R. Highfield and V. Barac. Ann Arbor, Mich.: Karoma.

Olwig, K. F. 1985. *Cultural Adaptation and Resistance on St. John: Three Centuries of Afro-Caribbean Life.* Gainesville: University of Florida Press.

———. 1996 "Commons as Symbolic and Lived Place: The Virgin Islands National Park and West Indian Family Land." Paper presented at the annual meeting of the American Anthropological Association, 20–24 November, San Francisco.

O'Neill, E. A. 1972. *The Rape of the American Virgins.* New York: Praeger.

Orlove, B., and S. B. Brush 1996. "Anthropology and the Conservation of Biodiversity." *Annual Review of Anthropology* 25:32–52.

Orni, E., and E. Efrat. 1980. *Geography of Israel.* 4th ed. Jerusalem: Israel University Press.

Orr, D. W. 1994. *Earth in Mind: On Education, Environment, and the Human Prospect.* Washington, D.C.: Island Press.

Ortiz, A. 1979. *Handbook of North American Indians*, vol. 9, *The Southwest.* Washington, D.C.: Government Printing Office.

Outwater, A. 1996. *Water: A Natural History.* New York: Basic Books.

Overseas Development Administration, U.K., and Japan International Cooperation Agency. 1992. *Social Impacts Study (FAP 2): Draft Final Report.* Dhaka: Ministry of Irrigation, Water Development, and Flood Control, Flood Plan Coordination Organization.

Overseas Development Administration. 1994. "Flood Action Plan/FAP 17 Fisheries Studies and Pilot Project." *Final Report (Draft)*, Main Volume. Report funded by ODA (Overseas Development Administration, U.K.) in conjunction with the Government of Bangladesh. (Available at Flood Plan Coordination Organization office in Dhaka.)

Pacheco, P. D., et al. 1991. "Neighborhood Type and Housing Characteristics in Oaxaca." *Urban Anthropology* 20, no. 1:31–48.

PAHO (Pan American Health Organization). 1994. "Honduras." Pp. 252–265 in *Health Conditions in the Americas*, vol. 2. Washington, D.C.: Pan American Health Organization.

Palestine Environmental Protection Authority. 1994. *Gaza Environmental Profile. Part One: Inventory of Resources, Gaza.* Gaza: Palestine Environmental Protection Authority.

Palmer, R. 1977a. "The Agricultural History of Rhodesia." In *The Roots of Rural Poverty in Central and Southern Africa*, edited by R. Palmer and N. Parsons. London: Heinemann.

———. 1977b. *Land and Racial Domination in Rhodesia.* Berkeley: University of California Press.

Palmer, T. 1994. *Lifelines: The Case for River Conservation.* Washington, D.C.: Island Press.

Parsons, J. 1954. "English-Speaking Settlements of the Western Caribbean." *Yearbook* (Association of Pacific Coast Geographers), 16:3–16.

Parsons, M. 1947. "The Colorado River in Arizona Politics." Master's thesis, University of Arizona, Tucson.

Partridge, W. 1993. "Successful Involuntary Resettlement: Lessons from the Costa Rican Arenal Hydroelectric Project." Pp. 351–374 in *Anthropological Approaches to Resettlement: Policy, Practice, and Theory*, edited by M. Cernea and S. Guggenheim. Boulder, Colo.: Westview Press.

Partridge, W. L., A. Brown, and J. Nugent. 1982. "The Papaloapan Dam and Resettlement Project: Human Ecology and Health Impacts." Pp. 245–263 in *Involuntary Migration and Resettlement: The Problems and Responses of Dislocated People*, edited by A. Hansen and A. Oliver-Smith. Boulder, Colo.: Westview Press.

Patullo, P. 1996. *Last Resorts: The Cost of Tourism in the Caribbean*. London: Cassell.

Pearce, D. G. 1989. *Tourism Developmc.* 2nd ed. Harlow, England: Longman Scientific & Technical.

Peattie, L. R. 1972. *The View from the Barrio*. Ann Arbor: University of Michigan Press.

Peebles, R. W., et al. 1979. *Waterplan: A Comprehensive Water Management Framework for the U.S. Virgin Islands*. Technical Report No. 2, June. Charlotte Amalie, St. Thomas: U.S. Virgin Islands Water Resources Research Center.

"Perspective: Nibbling Around the Edges." 1996. *Investors Business Daily*, 4 June.

Peters, P. 1994. *Dividing the Commons: Politics, Policy, and Culture in Botswana*. Charlottesville: University of Virginia Press.

Petts, G. E. 1988. "Water Management: The Case of Lake Biwa, Japan." *Geographical Journal* 154:367–376.

Pigram, J. J. 1980. "Environmental Implications of Tourism Development." *Annals of Tourism Research* 7:554–583.

Pisani, D. 1989. "The Irrigation District and the Federal Relationship." Pp. 257–292 in *The Twentieth Century West: Historical Interpretations*, edited by G. Nash and R. Etulain. Albuquerque: University of New Mexico Press.

Plotkin, S. 1987. *Keep Out: The Struggle for Land Use Control*. Berkeley: University of California Press.

Posluns, M. 1993. *Voices from the Odeyak*. Toronto: NC Press.

Postel, S. 1992. *Last Oasis: Facing Water Scarcity*. New York: Norton.

———. 1993. "Water Scarcity Spreading." P. 106 in *Vital Signs 1993*, edited by L. Brown, H. Kane, and E. Ayres. New York: Norton.

Postel, S., et al. 1996. "Human Appropriation of Renewable Fresh Water." *Science* 271 (February):785–788.

Preister, K. 1987. "Issue-Centered Social Impact Assessment." Pp. 39–55 in *Anthropological Praxis: Translating Knowledge into Action*, edited by S. J. Fiske and R. M. Wulff. Boulder, Colo.: Westview Press.

President's Council on Sustainable Development. 1996. *Sustainable America:*

A New Consensus. Washington, D.C.: Government Printing Office. E-mail address: pcsd@igc.apc.org.

Prince, Z., and A. D. Murphy. 1990. "Generative and Regulative Organization in Site and Service Housing Projects: A Case Study from Oaxaca, Mexico." *City and Society* 4:2.

Prittie, T. 1967. *Israel: Miracle in the Desert.* New York: Penguin.

Private Eye. February 1996.

Rake, L. 1996. "Sanctions Hit $1M in Tutu Wells Case." *Virgin Islands Daily News,* 25 April, p. 3.

Rashid, H. E. 1991. *Geography of Bangladesh.* 2nd ed. Dhaka: University Press.

Redford, K. 1991. *The Ecologically Noble Savage.* New York: Orion Books.

Reed, R. 1990. "Cultivating the Tropical Forest." Pp. 139–149 in *Conformity and Conflict,* edited by J. Spradley and D. McCurdy. New York: Harper-Collins.

Reisner, M. 1986. *Cadillac Desert: The American West and Its Disappearing Water.* New York: Viking Penguin.

Republic of South Africa. Department of Water Affairs and Forestry. 1995. "You and Your Water Rights." Booklet. Internet version: http://www.polity.org.za/za/wtrights.html.

Rhodesia, Government of. 1976. *The Water Act.* Harare: The Government Printers.

Rich, R. C. 1982. "The Political Economy of Public Services." In *Urban Policy Under Capitalism,* edited by N. Fainstein and S. Fainstein. Pp. 191–212. Vol. 22, *Urban Affairs Annual Review.* Beverly Hills, Calif.: Sage.

Richards, A., and J. Waterbury. 1996. *A Political Economy of the Middle East.* Boulder, Co.: Waterview Press.

Richardson, B. 1991. *Strangers Devour the Land.* New York: Knopf, 1976. Reprint, Post Mills, Vt.: Chelsea Green.

Roberts, B. R. 1995. *The Making of Citizens: Cities of Peasants Revisited.* London: Arnold.

Rogers, C. M. 1985. *Guide to Waterfront Development Activities Within the Tennessee-Tombigbee Corridor.* Mobile, Ala.: U.S. Army Corps of Engineers, Mobile District.

Rogers, P., and P. Lyndon, eds. 1994. *Water in the Arab World: Perspectives and Prognoses.* Cambridge, Mass.: Harvard University Press.

Rogers, P., et al. 1989. *Eastern Waters Study: Strategies to Manage Flood and Drought in the Ganges-Brahmaputra Basin.* Arlington, Va.: Irrigation Support Project for Asia and the Near East (ISPAN, 1611 N. Kent St.).

———. 1994. *Water and Development in Bangladesh: A Retrospective on the Flood Action Plan.* Arlington, Va.: Irrigation Support Project for Asia and the Near East (ISPAN, 1611 N. Kent St.).

Rogge, A. E., et al. 1995. *Raising Arizona's Dams: Daily Life, Danger, and Discrimination in the Dam Construction Camps of Central Arizona, 1890s–1940s.* Tucson: University of Arizona Press.

Rusinek, W. 1984. "Against the Compact: The Critical Opposition of George W. P. Hunt." *Journal of Arizona History* 25:155–170.

Sachar, H. M. 1996. *A History of Israel from the Rise of Zionism to Our Time.* 2nd ed. New York: Knopf.

Sachs, W. 1996. "Neo-Development: Global Ecological Management." Pp. 239–252 in *The Case Against the Global Economy and for a Turn Toward the Local,* edited by G. Mander and E. Goldsmith. San Francisco: Sierra Club Books.

Safi, J. M., and Y. Z. El-Nahhal. 1991. *Mutagenic and Carcinogenic Chemicals in the Gaza Strip Agricultural Environment.* Report by the Arab Consultants Group. West Bank, Israel: Hebron University, Faculty of Agriculture.

Said, E. 1980. *The Question of Palestine.* New York: Vintage Books.

Salisbury, R. F. 1986. *A Homeland for the Cree: Regional Development in James Bay, 1971–1981.* Toronto: University of Toronto Press.

Sam-Cromarty, M. 1992. *James Bay Memoirs: A Cree Woman's Ode to Her Homeland.* Lakefield, Ontario: Waapoone.

Sanbongi, K. 1988. *Mizu to shakai to kankyoo to* (Water, society, and the environment). Tokyo: Sankaido.

SARDC (Southern African Research and Documentation Centre), in collaboration with IUCN and SADC (Southern African Development Community). 1994. *State of the Environment in Southern Africa.* Harare: South African Research and Documentation Centre.

Sardik, A., and S. Barhouti. 1994. "The Water Problems of the Arab World: Management of Scarce Resources." Pp. 1–37 in *Water in the Arab World: Perspectives and Prognoses,* edited by P. Rogers and P. Lyndon. Cambridge, Mass.: Harvard University Press.

Sayigh, R. 1979. *Palestinians: From Peasants to Revolutionaries.* London and Atlantic City, N.J.: Zed.

Schlitz, M. J. 1987. Reflections on Medina Lake: 1912–1987. San Antonio: Quandrangle Press.

Schorr, T. S., ed. 1984a. *Las represas y sus efectos sobre la salud.* Federal District, Mexico: Organización Panamericana de Salud.

———. 1984b. "Reubicación de poblaciónes afectadas por represas: Observaciónes y linamientos prácticos." Pp. 221–293 in *Las represas y sus efectos sobre la salud,* edited by T. S. Schorr. Federal District, Mexico: Organización Panamericana de Salud.

Scott, C. 1993. "Custom, Tradition, and the Politics of Culture: Aboriginal Self-Government in Canada." Pp. 311–333 in *Anthropology, Public Policy, and Native Peoples in Canada,* edited by N. Dyck and J. Waldram. Montreal: McGill-Queen's University Press.

Scott, C., and K. Ettenger. 1994. *Great Whale Environmental Assessment Community Consultation: Final Report for Wemindji and Eastmain.* 2 vols. Report prepared for the Grand Council of the Crees (of Quebec) and the Cree Regional Authority under contract with Hydro-Quebec. Montreal: Hydro-Quebec.

Scudder, T. 1962. *The Ecology of the Gwembe Tonga.* Manchester, England: Manchester University Press.

———. 1973. "Resettlement." Pp. 707–719 in *Man-Made Lakes: Their Problems and Environmental Effects,* edited by W. C. Ackerman, G. F. White, and E. B. Worthington. Washington, D.C.: American Geophysical Union.

Scudder, T., and E. Colson. 1982. "From Welfare to Development: A Conceptual Framework for the Analysis of Dislocated People." Pp. 267–287 in *Involuntary Migration and Resettlement: The Problems and Responses of Dislocated People,* edited by A. Hansen and A. Oliver-Smith. Boulder, Colo.: Westview Press.

———. n.d. "Long-Term Research in Gwembe Valley, Zambia." In *Long-Term Field Research in Social Anthropology,* edited by R. V. Kemper. In press.

Selby, H. A., et al. 1990. *The Mexican Urban Household: Organizing for Self-Defense.* Austin: University of Texas Press.

Settlement Watch. 1996. Periodic Reports Published by law. The Palestinian Society for the Protection of Human Rights. P.O. Box 20873, Jerusalem.

Shanwinigan Lavalin Inc., Northwest Hydraulic Consultants, in association with Engineering and Planning Consultants Ltd., Bangladesh Engineering and Technological Services, Institute for Development Education and Action, and Nature Conservation Movement. 1991. *Northwest Regional Water Management Project (FAP 6): Work Plan (Draft).* Dhaka: Ministry of Irrigation, Water Development, and Flood Control, Flood Plan Coordination Organization.

———. 1993. *Local Initiatives and People's Participation in the Management of Water Resources.* Report prepared by the Northeast Regional Water Management Project (FAP 6). Dhaka: Ministry of Irrigation, Water Development, and Flood Control, Flood Plan Coordination Organization.

Sharma, N., et al. 1996. *African Water Resources: Challenges and Opportunities for Sustainable Development.* World Bank Technical Paper No. 331. Washington, D.C.: World Bank.

Shaw, R. 1989. "Living with Floods in Bangladesh." *Anthropology Today/ Royal Anthropological Institute Newsletter* 5, no. 1:11–13.

Shawwa, I. R. 1993. "The Water Situation in Gaza." Pp. 37–84 in *Water: Conflict or Cooperation? Israel/Palestine: Issues in Conflict, Issues for Cooperation.* 2nd ed. Vol. 2, no. 2. Jerusalem: Israel/Palestine Center for Research and Information.

Shehadeh, R. 1988. "Occupier's Law: Israel and the West Bank." Washington, D.C.: Institute for Policy Studies.

Sheridan, T. 1986. "The Anglo Settlement of Arizona." Pp. 218–247 in *Arizona: The Land and the People,* edited by T. Miller. Tucson: University of Arizona Press.

———. 1995a. *Arizona: A History.* Tucson: University of Arizona Press.

———. 1995b. "Arizona: The Political Ecology of a Desert State." *Journal of Political Ecology* 2:41–57.

Shiga Ken (Shiga Prefecture). 1983. *Biwa-Ko soogoo kaihatsu 100 mon* (100 questions on the comprehensive development of Lake Biwa). Otsu, Japan: Shiga Ken Keikaku Bu Suisei Shitsu.

———. 1996. *Biwa-Ko no soogoteki hozen no tame no katai to kongo no torikumi* (Critical questions on the comprehensive preservation of Lake Biwa and coming challenges). Otsu, Japan: Shiga Ken Keikaku Bu Suisei Shitsu.

Shkilnyk, A. 1985. *A Poison Stronger Than Love: The Destruction of an Ojibwa Community.* New Haven, Conn.: Yale University Press.

Shue, H. 1980. *Basic Rights: Subsistence, Affluence, and U.S. Foreign Policy.* Princeton: Princeton University Press.

Shuval, H. 1980. *Water Quality Management Under Conditions of Scarcity: Israel, a Case Study.* New York: Academic Press.

Simchen, E., et al. 1991. "An Epidemic of Waterborne Shigella Gastroenteritis in Kibbutzim of Western Galilee in Israel." *International Journal of Epidemiology* 20, no. 4:1081–1088.

Simmons, P. 1995. *Words Into Action: Basic Rights and the Campaign Against World Poverty.* Oxford: OXFAM

Singer, P. 1982. "Neighborhood Movements in São Paulo." In *Towards a Political Economy of Urbanization in Third World Countries,* edited by H. I. Safa. Delhi: Oxford University Press.

Sir M. MacDonald and Partners Ltd., UK, in association with Nippon Koei Company Ltd., Resources Development Consultants Ltd., House of Consultants Ltd., and Desh Upodesh Ltd. 1992. *South East Region Water Resources Development Programme BGD/86/037 (FAP 5): Regional Plan Report, Volume I, Part 1 (Draft).* Dhaka: United Nations Development Programme, World Bank, and Bangladesh Ministry of Irrigation, Water Development, and Flood Control, Flood Plan Coordination Organization.

———. 1993. *South East Region Water Resources Development Programme BGD/86/037: Noakhali North Drainage and Irrigation Project Feasibility Study, Volume 6—Annex G, Sociology and Public Participation (Draft).* Dhaka: United Nations Development Programme, World Bank, and Bangladesh Ministry of Irrigation, Water Development, and Flood Control, Flood Plan Coordination Organization.

Sir William Halcrow & Partners Ltd. in association with Danish Hydraulic Institute. 1992. *Southwest Area Water Resources Management Project (FAP 4): Inception Report.* Dhaka: Ministry of Irrigation, Water Development, and Flood Control, Flood Plan Coordination Organization.

Slater, C. M., and G. E. Hall. 1992. *County and City Extra: Annual Metro, City, and County Data Book.* Lanham, Md.: Bernan Press.

Smith, K. 1986. *The Magnificent Experiment: Building the Salt River Reclamation Project, 1890–1917.* Tucson: University of Arizona Press.

Smith, T. 1980. "Lewis Douglas, Arizona Politics, and the Colorado River Controversy." *Arizona and the West* 22:125–162.

Smith, Z.A. 1985. *Interest Group Interaction and Groundwater Policy Formation in the Southwest.* Lanham, Md.: University Press of America.

————. (ed). 1989. *Water and the Future of the Southwest.* Albuquerque: University of New Mexico Press.

Sorensen, J. C. 1993. *A Plan to Establish, Develop, and Manage the Bay Islands National Marine Park.* Report prepared for the Government of Honduras, the United Nations Development Programme of Honduras, and the Environmental Programs section of the Inter-American Development Bank. Gainesville, Fla.: Tropical Research and Development, Inc.

Spierenburg, M. 1995. *The Role of the Mhondoro Cult in the Struggle for Control over Land in Dande (Northern Zimbabwe): Social Commentaries and the Influence of Adherents.* Occasional paper, NRM Series. Harare: Centre for Applied Social Sciences.

Steady, F. 1982. "Urban Malnutrition in West Africa: A Consequence of Abnormal Urbanization and Underdevelopment." In *Towards a Political Economy of Urbanization in Third World Countries,* edited by H. I. Safa. Delhi: Oxford University Press.

Stevens, J. 1988. *Hoover Dam: An American Adventure.* Norman: University of Oklahoma Press.

Stine, J. K. 1993. *Mixing the Waters: Environment: Politics, and the Building of the Tennessee-Tombigbee Waterway.* Akron, Ohio: University of Akron Press.

Stonich, S. C. 1993. *I Am Destroying the Land! The Political Ecology of Poverty and Environmental Destruction in Honduras.* Boulder, Colo.: Westview Press.

Stonich, S. C., and J. H. Sorensen. 1995. "The Political Ecology of Tourism Development in the Bay Islands, Honduras: Aspects of Nutritional Status and Environmental Health." Paper presented at the annual meeting of the Society for Applied Anthropology, 29 March–2 April, Albuquerque, New Mexico.

Stonich, S. C., J. H. Sorensen, and A. Hundt. 1995. "Ethnicity, Class, and Gender in Tourism Development: The Case of the Bay Islands. Honduras." *Journal of Sustainable Tourism* 3, no. 1:1–28.

Tanner, A. 1979. *Bringing Home Animals: Religious Ideology and Mode of Production of the Mistassini Cree Hunters.* New York: St. Martin's Press.

Tansill, C. C. 1932. *The Purchase of the Danish West Indies.* Baltimore: Johns Hopkins University Press.

Taylor, F. F. 1993. *To Hell with Paradise: A History of the Jamaican Tourist Industry.* Pittsburgh, Pa.: University of Pittsburgh Press.

Tennessee-Tombigbee Waterway Development Authority. 1995. *List of Industries in the Tenn-Tom Waterway Corridor.* Columbus, Miss.: Tennessee-Tombigbee Waterway Development Authority.

Texas Water Commission. 1990. *Watermaster: Local Monitoring of the Use and Allocation of Texas Waters.* Austin: Texas Water Commission.

Thorkildsen, D., and P. D. McElhaney. 1992. *Model Refinement and Applications for the Edwards (Balcones Fault Zone) Aquifer in the San Antonio Region, Texas.* Report No. 340, July 1992. Austin: Texas Water Development Board.

Tulchinsky, T. H., et al. 1988. "Waterborne Enteric Disease Outbreaks in Israel 1976–1985." *Israel Journal of Medical Sciences* 24, no. 11:644–651.

Topalov, C. 1979. *La urbanización capitalista.* Mexico, DF: Edicol.

Torori, C., et al. 1996. "Land Tenure and Water Resources." In *Land We Trust: Environment, Private Property, and Constitutional Changes,* edited by C. Jama and J. B. Ojwang. London and Atlantic City, N.J.: Zed.

Turner, A. C. 1987. "Activating Community Participation in a Southern Paiute Reservation Development Program." Pp. 118–132 in *Anthropological Praxis: Translating Knowledge into Action,* edited by S. J. Fiske and R. M. Wulff. Boulder, Colo.: Westview Press.

Turner, T. S. 1992. "The Role of Indigenous Peoples in the Environmental Crisis: The Example of the Kayapo of the Brazilian Amazon." *Perspectives in Biology and Medicine* (autumn): 526–545.

UNEP (United Nations Environment Programme). 1984. "Tourism and the Environment" (Special Issue). *Industry and the Environment* 7, no. 1.

Upham, S. 1982. *Politics and Power: An Economic and Political History of the Western Pueblo.* New York: Academic Press.

U.S. Army Corps of Engineers. 1992. *Project Maps.* Mobile, Ala.: U.S. Army Corps of Engineers, Mobile District.

———. 1995. *Waterborne Commerce Statistics, Fiscal Years 1985–1994.* New Orleans: Waterborne Commerce Statistics Center.

———. 1996. *Tennessee-Tombigbee Tonnage Reports.* Mobile, Ala.: U.S. Army Corps of Engineers, Mobile District.

———. n.d. "Economic Impact Forecasting System." Computerized database covering every county in the United States. Champaign: University of Illinois Press.

U.S. Bureau of the Census. 1917. *Census of the United States Virgin Islands.* Washington, D.C.: Government Printing Office.

———. 1995. *Statistical Abstract of the United States: 1995.* 115th ed. Washington, D. C.: Government Printing Office.

U.S. Department of the Interior. 1990. *Proposed Permit Application, Black Mesa-Kayenta Mine, Navajo and Hopi Indian Reservations, Arizona: Final Environmental Impact Statement OSM-EIS-25.* 2 vols. Denver: Office of Surface Mining Reclamation and Enforcement.

U.S. Geological Survey. 1995. *Results of Ground-Water, Surface-Water, and Water-Quality Monitoring, Black Mesa Area, Northeastern Arizona 1992–93.* Water Resources Investigations Report No. 95-4156. Tucson: U.S. Geological Survey, Western Regional Office.

Usher, P. J. 1993. "Northern Development, Impact Assessment, and Social Change." Pp. 98–130 in *Anthropology, Public Policy, and Native Peoples in Canada,* edited by N. Dyck and J. Waldram. Montreal: McGill-Queen's University Press.

Van Dyke, J. C. 1901. *The Desert: Further Studies in Natural Appearances.* New York: Scribner.

Vecsey, C. 1980. "American Indian Environmental Religions." Pp. 1–37 in *American Indian Environments: Ecological Issues in Native American*

History, edited by C. Vecsay and R. W. Venable. Syracuse, N.Y.: Syracuse University Press.

———. 1987. "Grassy Narrows Reserve: Mercury Pollution, Social Disruption, and Natural Resources: A Question of Autonomy." *American Indian Quarterly* 11, no. 4:287–314.

Vega, A. et al. 1993. *Watersheds, Wildlands, and Wildlife of the Bay Islands, Honduras: A Conservation Strategy*. Report prepared for the United States Agency for International Development. Gainesville, Fla.: Tropical Research and Development, Inc.

Vijfhuizen, C. 1996. "Rainmaking, Political Conflicts, and Gender Images: A Case from Mtema Chieftaincy." Pp. 1–17 in *University of Zimbabwe and ZIMWESI Water for Agriculture: Current Practices and Future Prospects*. Proceedings of workshop held in Harare 11–13 March, 1996. Mimeo.

Vélez-Ibañez, C. E. 1983. *Rituals of Marginality: Politics, Process, and Culture Change in Central Urban Mexico, 1969–1974*. Berkeley: University of California Press.

Villarreal, D. R., and V. Castaqeda. 1986. *Urbanización y autoconstrucción de vivienda en Monterrey*. Federal District, Mexico: Centro de Ecodesarrollo Editorial Claves Latinoamericas.

Volante, E. 1992. "Ex-UA Professor Predicted CAP Crisis in 1967." *Arizona Daily Star*, 2 December.

Voth, H.R. 1905a. *Hopi Proper Names*. Publication No. 100, Anthropological Series 6, no. 1:63–113. Chicago: Field Columbian Museum.

———. 1905b. *The Traditions of the Hopi*. Publication No. 96, Anthropological Series 8. Chicago: Field Columbian Museum.

Waldram, J. B. 1988. *As Long as the Rivers Run: Hydroelectric Development and Native Communities in Western Canada*. Winnipeg: University of Manitoba Press.

Walther, A. 1994. *Regulating the Edwards Aquifer: A Status Report*. Austin: Texas House of Representatives, House Research Organization.

Waterbury, J. 1994. "Transboundary Water and the Challenge of International Cooperation in the Middle East." Pp. 39–64 in *Water in the Arab World: Perspectives and Prognoses*, edited by P. Rogers and P. Lyndon. Cambridge, Mass.: Harvard University Press.

Waters, F. 1963. *Book of the Hopi*. New York: Viking.

Weir, D., and M. Shapiro. 1981. *Circle of Poison: Pesticides and People in a Hungry World*. San Francisco: Institute for Food and Development Policy.

Welch, J., and P. Stekler. 1994. *Killing Custer*. New York: Penguin.

Welsh, F. 1985. *How to Create a Water Crisis*. Boulder, Colo.: Johnson.

Westergaard, W. 1917. *The Danish West Indies 1791–1917*. New York: Macmillan.

White, R. 1984. "Native Americans and the Environment." Pp. 179–204 in *Scholars and the Indian Experience*, edited by W. R. Swagerty. Bloomington: Indiana University Press.

———. 1995. *The Organic Machine: The Remaking of the Columbia River.* New York: Hill & Wang.

White, S. C. 1992. *Arguing with the Crocodile: Gender and Class in Bangladesh.* Dhaka: University Press; London and Atlantic City, N.J.: Zed.

Whiteley, P. 1988a. *Bacavi: Journey to Reed Springs.* Flagstaff, Ariz.: Northland Press.

———. 1988b. *Deliberate Acts: Changing Hopi Culture Through the Oraibi Split.* Tucson: University of Arizona Press.

———. 1992. *Hopitutungwni: "Hopi Names" as Literature.* In *On the Translation of Native American Literatures,* edited by B. Swann. Washington, D.C.: Smithsonian Institution Press.

———. n.d. *Hopi Topoi: Negotiations with Ethnography.* Washington, D.C.: Smithsonian Institution Press. In press.

WHO (World Health Organization). 1977.

———. 1993. *Guidelines for Drinking-Water Quality: Recommendations.* 2nd ed. Vol. 1. Geneva: World Health Organization.

WHO/UNEP (World Health Organization/United Nations Environment Programme). 1977. *Health Criteria and Epidemiological Studies Related to Coastal Water Pollution.* Copenhagen: World Health Organization, Regional Office for Europe.

———. 1986. *Correlation Between Coastal Water Quality and Health Effects.* Copenhagen: World Health Organization, Regional Office for Europe.

Wiley, P., and R. Gottlieb. 1982. *Empires in the Sun: The Rise of the New American West.* New York: Putnam.

Wilkinson, C. F. 1996. "Home Dance, the Hopi, and Black Mesa Coal: Conquest and Endurance in the American Southwest." *Brigham Young University Law Review,* 2.

Wilson, P. 1992. *An Economic Assessment of Central Arizona Project Agriculture.* Report prepared for the Office of the Governor and the Arizona Department of Water Resources. Tucson: University of Arizona, Department of Agricultural and Resource Economics, College of Agriculture.

———. n.d. *Economic Discovery in Federally Supported Irrigation Districts: A Tribute to William E. Martin and Friends.* In press.

Winpenny, J. 1994. *Managing Water as an Economic Resource.* London: Routledge.

Winter, M. 1991. "Interhousehold Exchange of Goods and Services in the City of Oaxaca." *Urban Anthropology* 20 no. 1:67–86.

Winter, M., et al. 1990. "Planning and Implementation in the Informal Sector: Evidence from Oaxaca, Mexico." *City and Society* 4 no. 2:131–143.

———. 1993. "The Health Status of Women in Oaxaca: Determinants and Consequences." *Social Science and Medicine* 37:1351–1358.

Wittfogel, K. 1957. *Oriental Despotism: A Comparative Study of Total Power.* New Haven, Conn.: Yale University Press.

Wolf, A., and J. Ross. 1992. "The Impact of Scarce Water Resources on the Arab-Israeli Conflict." *Natural Resource Journal* 32, no. 4:919–958.

Wolf, A. T. 1995. *Hydropolitics Along the Jordan River: Scarce Water and Its Impact on the Arab-Israeli Conflict.* Tokyo: United Nations Press.

Wolf, E. 1982. *Europe and the People Without History.* Berkeley: University of California Press.

———. 1990. "Distinguished Lecture: Facing Power—Old Insights, New Questions." *American Anthropologist* 92:586–596.

———. 1992.

Wollock, J. 1993. "James Bay: A Review of Strategies." *Akwe:kon Journal* 10, no. 3:30–41.

Wong, P. P., ed. 1993. *Tourism vs. Environment: The Case for Coastal Areas.* Dordrecht, Netherlands: Kluwer.

Woodall, B. 1996. *Japan Under Construction.* Berkeley: University of California Press.

World Bank. 1989. *Bangladesh: Action Plan for Flood Control.* Washington, D.C.: World Bank, Asia Region, Country Department 1.

———. 1990. *Flood Control in Bangladesh: A Plan for Action.* World Bank Technical Paper No. 119. Washington, D.C.: World Bank, Asia Region, Technical Department.

———. 1992a. Morazan Dam Emergency Project. Staff Report. Washington, D.C.: World Bank.

———. 1992b. *World Development Report 1992.* New York: Oxford University Press.

———. 1993. *World Development Report 1993: Investing in Health.* New York: Oxford University Press.

World Resources Institute. 1986. *World Resources 1986.* Washington, D.C.: World Resources Institute.

Worster, D. 1985. *Rivers of Empire: Water, Aridity, and the Growth of the American West.* New York: Pantheon Books.

WTO (World Tourism Organization). 1993. *Sustainable Tourism Development: Guide for Local Planners.* Madrid: World Tourism Organization.

Wynne, D. 1986. "Potential Impact of Pesticides on the Kinneret and Its Watershed over the Period 1980–1984." *Environmental Pollution* (Series A) 42, no. 4:373–386.

Young, R., and W. Martin. 1967. "The Economics of Arizona's Water Problem." *Arizona Review.* Tucson: University of Arizona, College of Business and Public Administration.

Yukiko, K., and F. Akira. 1984. "Mizu to mura (Water and village)." Pp. 25–46 in *Mizu to hito no Kankyoo Shi* (The environmental history of water and people), edited by T. Hiroyuki and K. Yukiko.

Zaag, P. van der. 1996. "Water Allocation Principles in Catchment Areas: Some Notes on Constraints and Opportunities." In *University of Zimbabwe and ZIMWESI Water for Agriculture: Current Practices and Future Prospects.* Proceedings of workshop held in Harare 11–13 March. Mimeo.

Zimbabwe, Government of. 1994. *Report of the Commission of Inquiry into Appropriate Agricultural Land Tenure Systems Under the Chairmanship of Professor Mandivamba Rukuni.* 3 vols. Harare: The Government Printer.

————. 1996. *Land Acquisition Act. Revision of Act 3/1992.* Harare: The Government Printer.

Contributors

Jesmin Akhter has bachelor of social science (honors) and master of social science degrees in anthropology from Jahangirnagar University, Dhaka, Bangladesh. She worked as a research associate on two Flood Action Plan studies: the Flood Response Study (FAP No. 14) and the Environmental Study (FAP No. 16). Mrs. Akhter has done consulting assignments on gender, health, and sanitation for the United Nations Children's Fund (UNICEF) and other development agencies. She lives in Dhaka.

Kazi Rozana Akhter has an M.Sc. in demography and an M.S. in philosophy from Dhaka University. Her research in Bangladesh includes work with women in development, fisheries, and social survey design and implementation. She worked as a research associate with the Flood Action Plan (Flood Response and Environment studies) from 1991 to 1994, and is currently a W.I.D. consultant to the Inland Fisheries project of the Government of Bangladesh—World Food Program's Integrated Food Assisted Development Project in Bangladesh.

Bill Derman is professor of anthropology and associate director of research of the African Studies Center at Michigan State University. His research experience includes work on natural resource management issues in the Gambia River Basin (1984); rural development and resettlement in the eastern Zambezi Valley in Zimbabwe in collaboration with the Center for Applied Social Sciences (CASS) at the University of Zimbabwe (1987 to the present); research on fishing communities and fishing policy in Malawi (1991–1993); and an analysis of two pilot water catchment authorities that divide Zimbabwe's waters between a large-scale commercial farming sector and small-holders under the conditions of structural adjustment as mandated by the International Monetary Fund.

John M. Donahue is professor and chair of the Department of Sociology and Anthropology at Trinity University in San Antonio, Texas. He has done field research in Colombia and Peru on internal migrations and in Bolivia and Nicaragua in the area of primary health care. His publications include *Health in the Andes* (with Joseph Bastien, American Anthropological Association, 1981) and *The Nicaraguan Revolution in Health: From Somoza to the Sandinistas* (Bergin and Garvey, 1986). His interest in water issues stems from his work in public health and to the fact that San Antonio is located over the Edwards Aquifer, whose management is the focus of continuing debate among local, county, state, and federal actors.

Kreg Ettenger is a Ph.D. candidate and teaching associate in the Department of Anthropology at Syracuse University. He has conducted research on indigenous knowledge systems of the eastern James Bay Cree, and on environmental and social issues in the United States and India. His work with the Cree community of Eastmain has focused on issues of cultural identity and wildlife management, leading to his interest in how water and other natural resources are managed and perceived by various parties in the James Bay region.

Tom Greaves is professor of anthropology at Bucknell University in Pennsylvania. He is editor of *Intellectual Property Rights for Indigenous Peoples, a Source Book* (Society for Applied Anthropology, 1994), a former president of the Society for Applied Anthropology, and serves currently as chair of the Committee for Human Rights of the American Anthropological Association. Since 1989 Tom Greaves has written extensively on aspects of contemporary indigenous struggle in North America, and on its ethical and practical consequences for anthropology.

Daniel Greenstadt is senior analyst for Environmental Business International, Inc., in San Diego, California. In 1992 he received a master's in Pacific international affairs from the Graduate School of International Relations and Pacific Studies at the University of California, San Diego. With support from the East–West Center, the University of California, and the Lake Biwa Research Institute he carried out studies in the Lake Biwa region.

Suzanne Hanchett is a social anthropologist who received her doctorate from Columbia University (1970) and is the CEO of RPSH Consulting Services, Portland, Oregon. She has worked in United States urban poverty areas, South Asia, and the Middle East in program planning and evaluation, organizational development, child welfare, women's health, gender analysis, and participatory approaches to environmental planning. She was a senior advisor to the Bangladesh Flood Action Plan (USAID-funded Flood Response Study and Environment Study) from 1991 to 1993, and returned to Bangladesh in 1997 to do applied research in potable water services.

Rosina Hassoun received her Ph.D. in anthropology from the University of Florida, Gainesville, in 1995 where she studied the interaction of culture, the environment, and human biology with an area specialization in the Middle East. Among her publications is "The Arab–Israeli Conflict from the Viewpoint of Ecological Anthropology: Peasants, Blood, and Water," which appeared in the *Florida Journal of Anthropology* (1989). Dr. Hassoun is currently employed with Genesys Health System in Flint, Michigan, as a biological/medical anthropologist and teaches as adjunct professor at Michigan State University.

Barbara Rose Johnston in an anthropologist and senior research fellow at the Center for Political Ecology in Santa Cruz, California. She has developed and coordinated global research projects in human rights and the environment, tourism, and cultural survival, and conducted fieldwork projects in the Caribbean, United States, and Canada. She is editor and principal author of *Who Pays the Price? The Sociocultural Context of Environmental Crisis* (Island Press 1994) and editor of *Life and Death Matters: Human Rights and the Environment at the End of the Millennium* (Alta Mira 1997).

William M. Loker is assistant professor of anthropology at California State University, Chico. He received his doctorate in anthropology from the University of Colorado in 1986. His doctoral research was carried out in the El Cajón region of Honduras in 1983–84, and he returned to the region in 1994 and 1997 to assess the El Cajón dam as a development strategy and to study its social and ecological effects. Loker has also carried out field research elsewhere in Central America and in the Peruvian Amazon (1987–89), studying social and environmental aspects of tropical forest colonization and development.

Vernon Masayesva is a member of Isngyam, the Coyote clan, at the Third Mesa Hopi village of Hotvela. As one of the first Hopi to attend college, he received a B.A. in political science from Arizona State University and a M.A. in education administration from Central Michigan University. In 1984, he was elected to the Hopi Tribal Council, and elected to serve as Chairman of the Hopi Tribe from 1989 to 1993. He has worked to protect Hopi land and natural resources and has been actively involved in the defense of aquifer water since the early 1980s. He is currently writing a book on the Hopi water crisis.

Miguel Angel Méndez Rosado received his master's degree in microbiology from the Instituto Politécnico in Mexico City. He is currently director of the microbiology laboratory at the center for post graduate studies at the Instituto Tecnológico de Oaxaca. The laboratory specializes in testing and certifying various locally produced goods such as *mezcal* and cheese. Professor Méndez specializes in the uses of appropriate indigenous fermentation technologies in the production of commercially viable consumer products.

Arthur D. Murphy is chair and professor of anthropology at Georgia State University in Atlanta, Georgia. He has done fieldwork in Mexico, Panama, and the United States on housing, household organization, and migration. His interest in water and urban infrastructure issues stems from his work in urban community development and the chronic shortages of water in Oaxaca, which are a focus of continuing conflict between competing interests and elites.

James Nickum, an economist, is on leave from the Program for the Environment at the East–West Center in Honolulu, Hawaii. In 1996–97 he was visiting professor in the Department of Economics, Keio University, Tokyo, and is currently visiting professor in the Department of Social and International Relations at the University of Tokyo. He has written extensively on water use and management issues in China and the Pacific Rim.

M. Brian Riley is a research associate at the Center for Applied Research in Anthropology at Georgia State University. He received his master's degree in applied anthropology from Georgia State University and a B.A. in environmental studies from Baylor University in Waco, Texas. He has conducted research on water quality and the political economy of water distribution in Mexico and South America.

Claudia M. Rogers worked with the U.S. Army Corps of Engineers, Mobile District, for fifteen years. Among her duties was coordinating economic development analyses for the Tennessee-Tombigbee Corridor Study. She recently accepted a position with the Department of the Interior's Minerals Management Service in the Gulf of Mexico Regional Office. She will manage social impact assessments for all projects relating to oil and gas exploration and extraction on the outer continental shelf, as required by the National Environmental Policy Act. She received her doctorate in applied anthropology from Columbia University in 1976.

Dr. Gus Salbador is director of St. Luke's Medical Mission in Roatan, Bay Islands, Honduras. After retiring from his private practice in Montana, he became an Episcopal priest and assumed the director's position in the Bay Islands. He has become increasingly interested in waterborne and water-related diseases as the primary causes of morbidity and mortality of the poor.

Thomas E. Sheridan is the curator of ethnohistory at the Arizona State Museum of the University of Arizona. Dr. Sheridan specializes in the ethnology, ethnohistory, and political ecology of the southwestern United States and northern Mexico. He has written or edited eight other books and monographs, including *Los Tucsonenses: The Mexican Community of Tucson, 1854–1941* (University of Arizona Press, 1986), *Arizona: A History* (University of Arizona Press, 1995), and *Paths of Life: American Indians of the Southwest and Northern Mexico* (with Nancy Parezo; University of Arizona Press, 1996).

Jerrel H. Sorensen currently is country director in Tajikistan for Relief International where he is overseeing a number of public health projects in the capital, Dushanbe, and in refugee areas. He received his M.A. in anthropology from Western Michigan University. He has done fieldwork in Mexico, Central America, Armenia, and Zaire.

Susan C. Stonich is associate professor of anthropology and environmental studies at the University of California, Santa Barbara. She received her Ph.D. in anthropology from the University of Kentucky in 1986. She has carried out fieldwork in Appalachia, California, and Central America, where she focused on problems related to the human and environmental impacts of economic development. Currently, her research interests center on development conflicts in coastal zones, including those related to the growth of tourism.

Peter Whiteley is professor and chair of the Department of Anthropology at Sarah Lawrence College, Bronxville, New York. Peter Whiteley has conducted ethnographic research at Hopi since 1980, serving as consultant and expert witness to the Hopi Tribe in federal litigation since 1988, and as field consultant to BBC Television for the film "The Hopi Way," which discusses contemporary Hopi society and the water problem. He has published two books on Hopi social history, *Deliberate Acts: Changing Hopi Culture through the Oraibi Split* (University of Arizona Press, 1988) and *Bacavi: Journey to Reed Springs* (Northland Press, 1988); *Hopi Topoi*, a collection of essays, is forthcoming from Smithsonian Institution Press.

Index

Abdullah, T. A., 214, 221, 234
Abramovitz, J. N., 3
Abya Yala News, 46
Access to a water supply, 276–77, 302, 319, 329
Aceves de la Mora, J. L., 240, 241
Adams, W. M., 74, 75, 91
Adan, S., 212, 230
Africa, 73–75
  see also Zimbabwe
Agency for International Development, U.S. (AID), 211, 214, 268
Agriculture:
  Arabs and Israelis, water between, 318, 320, 322–24, 330, 333
  catchment farmers, 86, 87
  commercial farmers, 78, 80, 89
  El Cajón Dam (Honduras), 111–13
  fertilizers, 101, 111, 112
  herbicides, 101, 111, 112
  Honduras, 100–102
  irrigation, 84–85, 87, 89, 183, 315
  St. Thomas (Virgin Islands), 293–95
  weeding, 101
  Zimbabwe, 78–80
Akhter, J., 234, 377
Akhter, K. R., 234, 377
Akiyama, M., 161
Alabama and Tennessee-Tombigbee Waterway, 133–35
  see also Tennessee-Tombigbee Waterway
Alienation, environmental, 345
Alinsky, Saul, 193
Alvard, M., 32
Anthropological Approaches to Involuntary Resettlement: Policy, Practice, and Theory (Cernea & Guggenheim), 117
Anthropological Praxis (Fiske & Wulff), 138
Anthropologists in southern Africa, 74
Applewhite reservoir (TX), 193–95
  see also Texas, water wars in South
Aquifers, use and abuse of:
  Arabs and Israelis, water between, 319
  coal mines and slurries, 18–26

Hopi society and environmental adaptation, 10–13
  springs/water/rain in Hopi secular and religious philosophy, 13–18
  St. Thomas (Virgin Islands), 302–5
  stakeholders and shareholders, opposing interests of, 27–30
  see also Texas, water wars in South
Arabs and Israelis, water between:
  comparative analysis of cultures, 316–21
  conclusions, 334–38
  ecological history of the region, 323–24
  potential scenario, 313
  power, an asymmetry of, 321–22
  resources, informational, 338
  settlements, question of Israeli, 330–32
  three schools of thought, 314–15
  1900 to 1948, 324–25
  1949 to 1967, 325–29
  1967 to present, 329–30
  water quality, 332–34
Archer, E., 264, 267
A Reed Pierced the Sky (Geertz), 31
Arizona, *see* Central Arizona Project (CAP)
Arizona: A History (Sheridan), 166, 186
Arizona Tomorrow, 185
Arms race in Middle East, 336
Ashurst, Henry, 171
Ashworth, W., 91
Aspinall, Wayne, 176–77
Auyong, J., 264, 267
Availability of clean water for natural/human purposes, 76

Bacterial tests, 256–57
Bahnimptewa, Stanley, 27–28
Bangladesh's Flood Action Plan (FAP):
  conclusions, 230–31
  controversies, 212–14
  culture and power, 228–30
  economics/gender and floods, 217–21
  female-headed households, 223–26
  Korimon, 219–21
  labor, gender-based division of household, 221–23

Mamata, 225–26
Nahar, 222–23
Rahima, 215–17
studies used to produce, 210–11
women's concerns, including, 214–17,
    226–28
Barbados, 271
*Basic Rights: Subsistence, Affluence, and
    U.S. Foreign Policy* (Shue), 96
Batisse, M., 267, 268
Battles with Giant Fish (Hedges &
    Mitchell), 283
Bayard, Danny, 304
Bay Islands (Honduras):
    brackish water and seawater quality,
        279
    conclusions, 280–83
    drinking water quality, 277–79
    health, tourism and environmental,
        276–77, 279–80
    resources, informational, 283–84
    tourism development on the, 268–74
Beaumont, P., 330, 332
Bellingham Herald, 43–46
Bellingham (WA), 38–40
Bellissari, A., 319
Ben-Gurion, David, 317
Benzene, 303
Ben-Zvi, Itzhak, 317
Berger, T. R., 66
Berkes, F., 69
Berkman, R. L., 176, 177
Biochemical oxygen demand (BOD), 253
Bishop, Sam, 193
Black Mesa (AZ), 10
Black Mesa-Kayenta Mine (AZ), 19, 28
Blake, Harry, 173
Blanton, R. E., 240
Blomquist, W., 205
Blue Blaze (Houlson), 283
Bodley, J., 42
Bolding, A., 83, 86, 92
Bollentini, N., 303
Book of the Hopi (Water), 31
Borders, geopolitical, 2
Bordewich, F., 42–43
Bourassa, R., 68
Boyer, W. A., 295, 296, 298–99, 308, 309
Bracken, P. J., 185
Braidotti, R., 90
Bratton, M., 78
Brightman, R., 32
Bringing Home Animals (Tanner), 68
Britain, 324
Broadleaf tropical forest, 111

Brody, H., 32
Brotman, Stanley, 304–5
Brower, David, 176
Brown, A., 105
Brush, S. B., 32
Buege, D., 32
Bullock, A., 80
Bunton, Lucius, 195–98
Bureaucratic inertia, 343
Bush, D., 181
Butterworth, D. S., 244

*Cadillac Desert. The American West and
    Its Disappearing Water* (Reisner),
    137, 180–81
*Cadillac Desert: Water and the
    Transformation of Nature* (TV
    show), 186
Cain, M., 234
Calcium carbonates, 254
Caldwell, L., 91
California, *see* Central Arizona Project
    (CAP)
Callicott, J. B., 32
Canada, *see* James Bay Hydroelectric
    Project (Canada)
CAP, *see* Central Arizona Project
Capitalism and small-scale subsistence
    economies, 27–30
Caribbean basin, *see* St. Thomas (Virgin
    Islands)
Carpenter, Delph, 169–70
Carson, R., 333
Carson, W. H., 19, 22, 25, 34
Carter, Jimmy, 173, 180–81
Cash indemnification and El Cajón Dam
    (Honduras), 108–9
Castells, M., 239, 260, 261
Catchment farmers, 86, 87
Cattle ranching, 111
Central Arizona Project (CAP):
    Arizona v. California, 175–76
    Colorado River Compact and anticom-
        pact crusade, 169–72
    conclusions, 183–86
    envious of California, Arizona, 166–67
    history behind, 163, 172–75
    Imperial Valley (CA), 167–69
    local populations and resource users in
        management decisions, 177–80
    political side of water ecology, 164–66,
        176–77
Centralization of authority and capital in
    water management, 343
Cernea, M., 105, 114

Chaffey, George, 167–68
Chandler, Harry, 170
Chemical oxygen demand (COD), 155
Cheung, W. H., 264, 279
Chief (MacGregor), 68
Chlorates, 255–56
Chlorine, 243, 254–55
Cisneros, Henry, 193
City and the Grassroots, The (Castells), 261
Civil Engineering, 117
Clarke, R., 76
Climate change, global, 29
Clinton, Bill, 29
Coal mines and slurries, 18–26, 29–30
Cockrell, Lila, 195
Cohen, E., 77, 264
Coliform bacteria, 256–57, 265–66, 277–78
Collectivism, 316–18
Colonialism, 78–81, 288–89, 315, 324
Colorado, 169–70
    see also Central Arizona Project (CAP)
Colson, E., 90, 105
Colter, Fred T., 174
Communal aspect of land and water use, 78–80, 86, 316–18
Concerned Citizen's Guide to Hydropower, 138
Conflicts over rights and resources, 341–42
Conley, Karyne, 198
Connally, John, 192
Cooley, M., 32
Cordell, L., 32
Corporate welfare, 136
Cree Indians, 48, 51
    Abraham W., 65
    Alice M., 61, 62, 64
    Charlie M., 58
    Daisy C., 54, 58, 61, 62, 64
    Daniel M., 60, 67
    Dennis C., 64
    Edward G., 60
    Florrie M., 59
    Luke T., 62
    Minnie C., 58, 61
    Minnie G., 62
    resources on, informational, 68–69
    Rose D., 65
    Willie M., 54
    Winnie S., 54, 65
    see also James Bay Hydroelectric Project (Canada)
Cuba, 292, 296

Cultural Survival Quarterly, 34, 206
Culture and water:
    Arabs and Israelis, water between, 316–21
    Bangladesh's Flood Action Plan (FAP), 228–30
    Bay Islands (Honduras), 282–83
    Cree Indians, 68
    local ecosystems, 341
    Lummi Nation, 41
    Middle East, 314, *see also* Arabs and Israelis, water between
    power relationships, 3–5, 209–10
    project culture, 343
    Texas, water wars in South, 202–3, 205
    see also various subject headings
Curtis, S. A., 53
Cyclonic storms, 212–14
Czaya, E., 1

Dabbagh, T., 315
Dams:
    (Africa), 74–75
    (Africa) Zambezi Valley, 84
    opposition to, worldwide, 77
    (U.S.) All-American Canal, 168, 169
    (U.S.) Cliff, 180
    (U.S.) Hoover, 168, 169, 172
    (U.S.) Laguna, 174
    (U.S.) Orme, 177–80
    (U.S.) Parker, 172
    (U.S.) Roosevelt, 164, 180
    (U.S.) Stewart Mountain, 180
    see also El Cajón Dam (Honduras); James Bay Hydroelectric Project (Canada)
Darr, P., 325, 333
Darter, fountain, 191
Darwish, Mahmoud, 320
Davidson, W., 283
Davis, Arthur, 168–69, 173
Davis, O., 302, 304
Dead Sea (Middle East), 329–30
Decentralization of water allocation, 86–87
Decision-making process, 29
    see also Local populations and resource users in management decisions
Deforestation, 274, 275, 293, 324, 332
De Graf, J., 309
Democracy and representation, issues of, 88
Denevan, W., 32
Denmark, 288, 289
Deprivation of people's subsistence rights, 97–98, 114–17

Derman, B., 84, 92, 93, 377
Desert, The (Van Dyke), 185
Desertification, 75
1, 2–Dichloroethylene, 303
Dilley, F. B., 241
Disease and water quality, 237–38,
    267–68, 278, 295, 319
*Dividing the Waters: Governing
    Groundwater in Southern California*
    (Blomquist), 205–6
Dominy, Floyd, 176
Donahue, J. M., 377
Donor-recipient power relationships,
    209–10
Dookhan, I., 288, 289, 295
Douglas, Lewis, 170–71
Droughts:
    Africa, 75, 82
    Lake Biwa (Japan), 157
    St. Thomas (Virgin Islands), 295,
    296
    Texas, 192
Dutton, Y., 316, 317

East Ghor Canal (Jordan), 328
Eastman, S., 136
Ecologist, 3
*Ecology of Commerce: A Declaration of
    Sustainability* (Hawken), 138
Economic Impact Forecasting System,
    132
Economics and flooding, 217–21
Edwards Aquifer (TX), 188–92, 204
    see also Texas, water wars in South
El Cajón Dam (Honduras), 95
    cash indemnification, 108–9
    as development strategy, 102–4
    land use patterns, changing, 111–13
    local residents impacted by, 109–11
    overview of El Cajón region, 98–102
    resettlement, 106–7
    resources on, informational, 117
    social and ecological impacts, 104–5
    subsistence rights, 96–98, 113–17
Electrical generation, 165–66
    see also James Bay Hydroelectric
    Project (Canada)
Electric Rivers (McCutcheon), 68
*Ellen Smallboy: Glimpses of a Cree
    Woman's Life* (Flannery), 68
El-Nahal, Y. Z., 333, 334
Employment rates and Tennessee-
    Tombigbee Waterway, 128, 133–35
Endangered species, 178, 191, 194–95
Energy Group PLC, 19

Enge, K., 89
English water law, 78
Environmental alienation, 345
Environmental Protection Agency (EPA),
    21–22, 27
Erosion, soil, 274, 275, 293, 322
Escherichia coli, 256–57, 265–66, 277–78
Esso Standard Oil Company, 303, 304
Ethiopian droughts, 75
Ethnic/racial diversity and Tennessee-
    Tombigbee Waterway, 128
Ettenger, K., 378
Eutrophication, 155
Evans, L. H., 289
Excreta disposal facilities, 277

Famines, 75
Fecal coliform bacteria, 265–66, 279
Federal agencies responsible for managing
    water resources, 123–24
    see also Organizations, government
Feit, H., 69
Feldman, S. L., 325, 333
Female-headed households in Bangladesh,
    223–26
Feminist anthropologists, 74
Fertilizers, 101, 111, 112, 333–34
Feudal warlord model, 166
Fewkes, J. W., 15, 32
Finsten, L., 240
Fisher, D. W., 293
Fishing, 39, 59–63, 157
Fiske, S. J., 138
Flannery, R., 68
Flooding, *see* Bangladesh's Flood Action
    Plan (FAP)
Food, reliance on store-bought, 63
Food for thought:
    aquifers, use and abuse of, 27–30
    Bangladesh's Flood Action Plan (FAP),
    230–31
    Bay Islands (Honduras), 283
    Central Arizona Project (CAP), 184–86
    El Cajón Dam (Honduras), 116–17
    James Bay Hydroelectric Project
    (Canada), 68
    Lake Biwa Comprehensive
    Development Plan (Japan), 159–61
    Lummi Nation, 42
    Oaxaca de Juárez (Mexico), drinking
    water quality in, 259–61
    St. Thomas (Virgin Islands), 307–8
    Tennessee-Tombigbee Waterway,
    137–39
    Texas, water wars in South, 204–5

Zimbabwe, 89–90
Foreign aid programs, 209–10
Four Winds Plaza Development
    Corporation, 303, 304
Fradkin, P., 91, 169, 170, 172–77
Frankel, G., 319
Furukawa, A., 146
Future implications, see Food for thought

Gajraj, A., 267
Galdis, A. V., 130, 131
Galilee region (Middle East), 327–29
    see also Arabs and Israelis, water
        between
Garcia, William, 24
Gat, J., 330
Gaza Strip (Middle East), see Arabs and
    Israelis, water between
Gender-specific analysis, 74
    see also Bangladesh's Flood Action
        Plan (FAP)
Geneva Convention, Fourth, 330–31
Geological Survey, U.S. (USGS), 22
Gilbert, A., 239
Gjessing, H., 305
Glaciers, 1
Gleick, P., 2, 77, 91, 264
Goff, J., 170
Golley, F., 91
Gonzalez, Henry B., 193
Goodland, R. J., 105
Gordon, Walter A., 296
Gottlieb, R., 177, 179–81
Government and opposing interests of
    stakeholders/shareholders, 27–30
    see also Organizations, government
Great Whale River Hydroelectric Project
    (Canada), 47, 51, 52–53
Greaves, T., 46, 378
Greeks, 324
Green, H., 264
Green, S. R., 126
Greenstadt, D., 378
Gregory, Herbert, 11–12
Grenon, M., 267, 268
Guggenheim, S., 114
Gulf War in 1990, 321, 330

Habitability, 42
Haggart, K., 212
Halcrow, W., 233
Hall, John, 197
Hamid, S., 223
Hanchett, S., 216, 378
Hansen, A., 105

Hanson, Lord, 19
Hanson Industries, 19, 28
Harcourt, W., 90
Harding, Warren, 173–74
Harquahala Irrigation District (U.S.), 183
Harrison, D., 271
Harvey, J., 283
Hassoun, R., 324, 327, 328, 333, 337, 378
Hastie, William, 295
Hawken, P., 138
Hayden, Carl, 171, 175, 177
Hays, S., 164
Health and water quality:
    Arabs and Israelis, water between, 319
    Bay Islands (Honduras), 267–68, 276–80
    lesser-developed countries, 237–38
    St. Thomas (Virgin Islands), 294–95
    see also Oaxaca de Juárez (Mexico),
        drinking water quality in
Hedges, F., 283
Helland, Hans, 195
Herbicides, 101, 111, 112
Herzl, Theodor, 317
Hiernaux, D., 239
Historical Geography of the Bay Islands
    (Davidson), 283
Homeland for the Cree (Salisbury), 68
Homelands, habitable, 42
Homer-Dixon, T., 2, 5, 314, 335, 336
Honduras, see Bay Islands (Honduras); El
    Cajón Dam (Honduras)
Hoover, Herbert, 170, 171–72, 291
Hopi Indians, 9
    environmental adaptation, 10–13
    moral philosophy, 26
    Peabody Western Coal Company,
        18–25
    religious system, 12–13, 25
    resources useful for study of water
        rights issues, 30–31
    springs/water/rain in secular and reli-
        gious philosophy, 13–18
    see also Aquifers, use and abuse of
Hough, W., 15, 16
Houlson, J. H., 283
Household labor and gender-based
    division of labor, 221–23
Howells, Victor, 327
Hu, H., 2
Human Organization, 138
Hundley, N., 169–73, 175, 176
Hundt, A., 268, 270, 272
Hunt, George W., 170
Hunter, C., 264
Hurricanes, 287, 289, 300, 301

Hussein, King (Jordan), 330
Hydraulic hypothesis, 164

Ice conditions and river conversion, 57
Impact Assessment, 138
Imperial Valley (CA), 163, 167–69
Indigenous societies:
    Canaanites (Middle East), 323
    Central Arizona Project (CAP), 163
    Choctaw Tribe (MS), 128
    Gitksan (Canada), 67
    motherland, reference to land as the,
        320
    Munqapi Indians (AZ), 18–19
    Natufians (Middle East), 323
    Navaho Nation (AZ), 9, 25, 28, *see also*
        Aquifers, use and abuse of
    Paiute Indians (AZ), 138
    Wet'suwet'en (Canada), 67
    Yavapai Indians (AZ), 178–79
    see also Aquifers, use and abuse of;
        Cree Indians; Hopi Indians; James
        Bay Hydroelectric Project (Canada);
        Lummi Nation (Pacific Northwest
Ingram, Helen, 182
Inter-American Development Bank (IDB),
    100, 268, 281
International law and Israeli settlements,
    330–31
Investment, Tennessee-Tombigbee
    Waterway and local, 133–35
Iron, 243
Irrigation, 84–85, 87, 89, 183, 315
Islamic law, 316–17
    see also Arabs and Israelis, water
        between
Israel, *see* Arabs and Israelis, water
        between

Jabotinsky, Vladimir, 317
Jackson, Henry, 176, 177
Jamaica, 271
James Bay Hydroelectric Project (Canada):
    conclusions, 68
    Eastmain river then and now, 53–54
    fishing, 59–63
    Great Whale River Hydroelectric
        Project, objections to, 51–53
    physical changes and river travel,
        54–58
    psychological impacts of development,
        63–66
    vast complex, 49–50
    water quality, 58–59
James Bay Memoirs (Sam-Cromarty), 68

Japan, *see* Lake Biwa *listings*
Jensen, M. E., 315
Jerusalem, 331
Johansson, B., 92
Johnson, Lyndon B., 177, 178
Johnson, R., 175–77
Johnson, Verne, Jr., 40
Johnston, B. R., 288–90, 292, 293, 308,
    309, 378–79
Jordan, 328–30
Jordan, D. G., 293
Judaism, 317
    see also Arabs and Israelis, water
        between
Juliani, G., 184

Kada, Y., 146
Kamen, C., 333
Keepers of the Game (Martin), 32
Kelly, K., 314, 335, 336
Kelso, M., 181
Keman, C., 325
Kennedy, John F., 296
Kentucky and Tennessee-Tombigbee
    Waterway, 133 35
    see also Tennessee-Tombigbee
        Waterway
Khalidi, W., 317, 323–25, 327
Kibbutzim movement, 317, 318, 320
Killing Custer (Stekler & Welch), 42
*Killing the White Man's Indian:
    Reinventing Native Americans at
    the End of the Twentieth Century*
    (Bordewich), 42–43
Kim, N. K., 2
King Abdullah Canal (Jordan), 328
Kinneret-Negev Conduit (Israel), 325–27
Kinship lines, social organization along,
    339–40
Kirkby, A. V., 240
Kliot, N., 318
Knox, J. P., 288, 294, 295
Kocasoy, G., 264, 267, 268
Kowalewski, S. A., 240
Kyoto (Japan), *see* Lake Biwa *listings*

Labor, gender-based division of
    household, 221–23
Ladinos, Spanish-speaking (Bay Islands in
    Honduras), 269, 272–74, 277, 279–80
Laga Industries, 303, 304
Lake Biwa Comprehensive Development
    Plan (Japan):
    after the, 157–59
    conclusions, 159–61

phase one: 1972–1982, 154
phases two/three: 1982–1997, 156–57
resources on, informational, 161
rules governing lake's development, 153–54
Special Measures Act of 1972, 153, 158
Lake Biwa (Japan):
conclusions, 159–61
cutoff plan, 149
doughnut plans, 150–51
flood control structure to water source, 147–48
history behind, 145–47
Otsu shore, development along the, 152
overview of, 141–45
pipeline plan, 149–50
submerged dam plan, 150
Lake Huleh (Middle East), 327
Land as a living organism, 16
Land availability and El Cajón Dam (Honduras), 110–11
Land tenure, 73, 78, 81–82
see also Zimbabwe
Land use patterns and El Cajón Dam (Honduras), 111–13
Lanjouw, P., 261
La Rusic, I., 69
Last Resorts (Patullo), 284
Lawns, 188
Lebanon, 327, 329
Lees, S. H., 4, 240
Legislation:
(Honduras) Wykes Cruz Treaty of 1859, 269
(Japan) New Lake Biwa Environmental Preservation Measures Act of 1980, 155
(Japan) Revised Basic Law for Pollution Control Measures of 1970, 155
(Japan) River Law of 1896, 146–47
(Japan) Special Measures Act of 1972, 153, 158
Rhodesia's Water Act of 1947, 78
(U.S.) Boulder Canyon Project Act of 1928, 171
(U.S.) Colorado River Basin Project Act of 1968, 177
(U.S.) Colorado River Compact, 163, 169–72
(U.S.) Endangered Species Act, 195, 198
(U.S.) Point Elliott Treaty of 1855, 41
(U.S.) Public Works Bill of Fiscal Year 1971, 126
(U.S.) Safe Drinking Water Act, 193

(U.S.) Voting Rights Act, 198
(U.S.) Water Quality Act in 1965, 192
(Virgin Islands) Safe Drinking Water Act, 297, 298
(Zimbabwe) Land Acquisition Act of 1992/1996, 81
(Zimbabwe) Streambank Protection Regulation of 1952, 80
(Zimbabwe) Water Act of 1927, 80
(Zimbabwe) Water Act of 1976, 78
(Zimbabwe) Water Act of 1996, 82–83
Legorreta, J., 239
Le Moigne, G., 93
Lesser-developed countries (LDCs), 237–38, 333
Lewis, G. K., 288
Lewis, O., 238
Libiszewski, S., 319, 321, 325, 328, 330–32, 338
Livestock, 111
Local populations and resource users in management decisions:
Central Arizona Project (CAP), 177–80
climate change, global, 29
cultural definitions of water, 205
Edwards Aquifer (TX), 192–93
El Cajón Dam (Honduras), 115–16
Great Whale River Hydroelectric Project (Canada), 51–53
James Bay Hydroelectric Project (Canada), 66–67
tension between hydrodevelopment and sustaining biological/cultural life, 344–45
traditional water resource and management strategies, 342
see also Culture and water; Power and culture
Loker, W. M., 118, 379nn
Lomayestiwa, 26
Lowi, M. R., 2
Lowry, Pete, 196
Luckingham, B., 165
Lukes, S., 96
Lummi Nation (Pacific Northwest):
Bellingham and Whatcom County (WA), 38–39
conclusions, 42
cultural rights, water rights as, 41
freshwater important to, 39–41
Nooksack River watershed (WA), 37–38
overview of, 36
Lundberg, E. R., 288, 289, 309

Lvovich, M., 267
Lynam, T., 85
Lyndon, P., 315

MacDonald, M., 218, 233
MacGregor, R., 68
Mack, L., 181
Maclay, R. W., 189
Magadlela, D., 86
Magnesium, 243
Making of Citizens, The (Roberts), 261
Mangin, W., 239
Manzungu, E., 86
Maquiladora textile industries in
    Honduras, 104
Marketplace, social organization along
    the, 340
Martin, W., 181
Martin, William, 181
Masayesva, Rebekah, 29
Masayesva, V., 16, 23, 27, 379
Mathieson, A., 264
Matinenga, E. T., 80, 82
Matiza, G., 80, 81, 92
Maxwell, George, 173
McCarthy, F. E., 214
McCracken County (KY) and Tennessee-
    Tombigbee Waterway, 133
McCully, P., 2, 91
McCurdy, D., 208
McCutcheon, S., 68
McFarland, Ernest, 175
McFarlane, M. J., 92
Mclachlan, K., 330, 332
McNair County (TN) and Tennessee-
    Tombigbee Waterway, 133
McNamee, G., 167
Meiji Restoration (1868) in Japan, 146
Mekerot Water Company (Israel), 318,
    325
Mercury contamination, 62
Mesa-top-villages (AZ), 10, 31–32
Mexico:
    cultural differences between southern
        Texas and northern, 187–88
    health issues, water-related, 238
    mortality rates, 238
    Planta Purificadora del Fortin, 241
    San José Vista Hermosa, 243
    services provided to, quality of, 238–39
    see also Oaxaca de Juárez (Mexico),
        drinking water quality in; Texas,
        water wars in South
Meyers, N., 1, 2, 315
Middle East, 2

see also Arabs and Israelis, water
    between
Middleton, N., 1
Mieczkowski, Z., 264, 268
Mies, M., 90
Miller, M. L., 264, 267
Milton, K., 32
Mindeleff, V., 32
Mining, multinational, *see* Aquifers, use
    and abuse of
Mintz, S., 289
Mishongnovi village (AZ), 24
Mississippi and Tennessee-Tombigbee
    Waterway, 133–35
    see also Tennessee-Tombigbee
    Waterway
Mitchell, A., 283
*Mixing the Waters: Environment,
    Politics, and the Building of the
    Tennessee-Tombigbee Waterway*
    (Stine), 137
Moenkopi Wash (AZ), 18–19
Moeur, Benjamin, 172
Momaday, N. S., 32
Monet, D., 67
Monsoons, 212–14
Montezuma, Carlos, 179
Moore, D., 309
Morales, Dan, 196
Morris, E., 244
Moyo, S., 78
Mugabe, Robert, 81
Mugabe, Robert G., 86
Mulholland, William, 171
Murombedzi, J., 93
Murphy, A. D., 238, 241, 244, 246, 251
Muslims, *see* Arabs and Israelis, water
    between

Nakamura, M., 161
Nakashima, M., 147
Nassar, Kamal, 320
Nelson, R., 264
Netanyahu, Benjamin, 336
Nevada, 169–70
    see also Central Arizona Project (CAP)
New Mexico, 169–70
    see also Central Arizona Project (CAP)
Nichols, W. D., 22
Niezen, R., 43
Nitrates, 253–54
Nitrogen, 155, 333
Nixon, Richard, 126
Nobunaga, Oda, 145
Norgaard, R., 91

Northwestern Coast cultural area,
36
see also Lummi Nation (Pacific
Northwest)
Norviel, W. S., 173
Nugent, J., 105

Oak-pine forest, mixed, 111
Oaxaca de Juárez (Mexico), drinking
water quality in, 237
conclusions, 257–61
neighborhood types and sample sites,
247–52
research methods, 244
resources, informational, 261
social geography of water distribution,
244–47
state and valley of Oaxaca, 239–41
testing parameters, 251, 253–57
treatment and delivery, 241–44
Oglethorpe, M., 267
O'Henri Dry Cleaners, 303, 304
Ohlsson, L., 2
Oil, Arabian, 336
Okura, E., 145
Oldendorf, C. G., 293–94
Oliver-Smith, A., 105
Olwig, K. F., 290
O'Neill, E. A., 295, 296, 309
Organizations, government:
(Africa) Southern African Development
Community (SADC), 86
(Bangladesh) Ministry of Irrigation,
Water Development, and Flood
Control, 229–30
(Canada) Berger Inquiry, 66
(Canada) Hydro-Quebec, 51–53
(Canada) Mackenzie Valley Pipeline
Inquiry, 66
(Honduras) Ministry of the
Environment, 281
(Honduras) National Autonomous
University, 265
(Honduras) National Electrical Energy
Company (ENEE), 104, 106–9
(Japan) Ministry of Agriculture, 151,
160–61
(Japan) Ministry of Construction
(MOC), 147, 149–52, 158, 160
(Middle East) Anglo American
Committee of Inquiry, 324–25
(Middle East) Israeli Ministry of
Agriculture, 325
(Middle East) Palestine Human Rights
Information Center, 332

(Middle East) Palestine Liberation
Organization (PLO), 336
(Middle East) Palestinian Authority,
335–36
(U.S.) Army Corps of Engineers, 127,
130, 132
(U.S.) Bureau of Efficiency, 291
(U.S.) Bureau of Reclamation, 180, 183
(U.S.) Central Arizona Water
Conservancy District, 181
(U.S.) CERCLIS National Priorities List
of Superfund sites, 304, 305
(U.S.) Edwards Aquifer Authority (TX),
197–98, 202
(U.S.) Edwards Underground Water
District in Arizona, 192, 195, 202
(U.S.) Environmental Protection
Agency (EPA), 303
(U.S.) Federal Emergency Management
Agency (FEMA), 287, 300
(U.S.) Fish and Wildlife Service, U.S.,
195, 202
(U.S.) Guadalupe-Blanco River
Authority (TX), 194–97, 202, 203
(U.S.) Housing and Urban
Development, U.S. Department, 138
(U.S.) Office of Management and
Budget, 181
(U.S.) Office of Surface Mining
Reclamation and Enforcement
(OSMRE), 20–22, 27–29
(U.S.) Reclamation Service, 168
(U.S.) San Antonio Water System, 199
(U.S.) Texas Water Commission,
195–96, 203
(U.S.) Texas Water Quality Board, 192
(U.S.) 2050 Water Committee (TX),
198–99
(U.S.) Washington's Department of
Ecology, 40
(Virgin Islands) Department of Natural
Resources, 297–98
(Virgin Islands) Department of
Planning and Natural Resources,
297, 303
(Virgin Islands) Virgin Islands
Company, 291, 295
(Virgin Islands) Virgin Islands
Corporation, 291, 296, 297
(Virgin Islands) Virgin Islands Port
Authority, 296
(Virgin Islands) Water and Power
Authority, 297–301
(Zimbabwe) Administrative Court, 78,
80

(Zimbabwe) Agricultural and Rural Development Authority, 81, 83
(Zimbabwe) CAMPFIRE, 85
(Zimbabwe) Mid-Zambezi Valley Rural Development Project (MZP), 84, 85
(Zimbabwe) Ministry of Local Government and Rural and Urban Development, 79
(Zimbabwe) Ministry of Rural Resources and Water Development, 89
(Zimbabwe) National Water Authority, 83, 87
(Zimbabwe) Water Resources Management Strategy, 83
Organizations, private:
(Honduras) Bay Islands Conservation Association, 281
(Honduras) Bay Islands Development Promotion Association, 276, 281
(Honduras) Honduran Social Investment Fund, 281
(Middle East) World Zionist Organization, 325
(U.S.) Aquifer Protection Association (TX), 193
(U.S.) Arizona Highline Reclamation Association, 174
(U.S.) California Development Company, 167–68
(U.S.) Citizens Concerned About the CAP Project, 178
(U.S.) Citizens for a Better Environment (TX), 193
(U.S.) Citizens Organized for Public Service (TX), 193
(U.S.) Homeowner-Taxpayer Association of Bexar County (TX), 194
(U.S.) Justice and Peace Commission (TX), 200, 202–3
(U.S.) Maricopa Audubon Society, 178
(U.S.) Mexican American Legal Defense and Educational Fund, 198
(U.S.) National Reclamation Association, 173
(U.S.) National Resources Defense Council, 29
(U.S.) Rio Salado Project, 180
(U.S.) Texas and Southwestern Cattle Raisers Association, 196
Orlove, B., 32
Orr, D., 73, 90
Oslo agreement (Middle East), 336

Paalölöqangw (Hopi deity), 15, 26
Pacheco, P. D., 244
Pacific Northwest, see Lummi Nation (Pacific Northwest)
Paiewonsky, Ralph, 296
Palestinian Arabs, 319–20
see also Arabs and Israelis, water between
Palmer, R., 78
Parsons, J., 269
Parsons, M., 170
Partridge, W. L., 105, 114
Patterson, Carol, 195
Patullo, P., 264, 284
Peabody Western Coal Company, 9, 18–26
see also Aquifers, use and abuse of
Pearce, D. G., 264
Peattie, L. R., 239
Peebles, R. W., 311
Pesticides, 333–34
Peters, P., 90
Petts, G. E., 161
pH, 253
Pharaonic projects, 77
Phosphorus, 155–56
Pigram, J. J., 264
Pisani, O., 166
Plotkin, S., 192, 193
Polar ice caps, 1
Political side of water ecology:
accountability in water allocation, 345
Central Arizona Project (CAP), 164–66, 176–80
indigenous cultures and their political struggles, 42–43
Japan, 143, 145
Tennessee-Tombigbee Waterway, 136
Zimbabwe, 88–90
see also various subject headings
Population:
Bay Islands (Honduras), 270, 271–72
El Cajón region (Honduras), 98–99
Japan, 156
Lake Biwa (Japan), 149
St. Thomas (Virgin Islands), 286, 290, 291
Whatcom County (WA), 38–39
Poslun, M., 68
Postel, S., 1, 2, 76
Poverty:
Bangladesh, 217–19
Bay Islands (Honduras), 272–74, 279–80
flooding, 217–21

St. Thomas (Virgin Islands), 287
Power and culture:
  Bangladesh's Flood Action Plan (FAP),
    228–30
  Bay Islands (Honduras), 282–83
  donor-recipient relationships, 209–10
  Middle East, 314, 321–22, see also
    Arabs and Israelis, water between
  overview of, 3–5
  project culture, 343
  social organization, 340–41
  St. Thomas (Virgin Islands), 295–99
  see also various subject headings
Power from the North (Bourassa), 68
Practicing Anthropology, 138
President's Council on Sustainable
    Development, 138
Prittie, T., 317
Project culture, 342–44
Property rights, 78, 88, 159–60, 321–22
Psychological impacts of development,
    63–66

Quality of water, see Water quality
Quebec (Canada), see James Bay
    Hydroelectric Project (Canada)
Quran, the, 320

Racial/ethnic diversity and Tennessee-
    Tombigbee Waterway, 128
Racism and Central Arizona Project
    (CAP), 170, 173–74
Rake, L., 305
Ramsay Motors, 303, 304
Red Cross, 287
Redford, K., 32
Red tide of a flagellate plankton, 155
Reed, R., 46
Reflections on Medina Lake: 1912–1987
    (Schlitz), 206
Reisner, M., 2, 137, 169, 174–83
Religion and Arab–Israeli water disputes,
    316–18, 320–21, 332, 335
Resettlement and El Cajón Dam
    (Honduras), 106–7
Resources, informational:
  Arabs and Israelis, water between,
    338
  Bay Islands (Honduras), 283–84
  Cree Indians, 68–69
  El Cajón Dam (Honduras), 117
  gender and water, 231
  Hopi/Native American water rights
    issues, 30–31

indigenous cultures and their political
    struggles, 42–43
Lake Biwa Comprehensive
    Development Plan (Japan), 161
Oaxaca de Juárez (Mexico), drinking
    water quality in, 261
Texas, water wars in South, 205–6
Rhodesia, land and water in, 77–81
  see also Zimbabwe
Rice, Texas wild-, 191
Rich, R. C., 239, 261
Richardson, B., 68
Rifkind, Simon, 176
Rights, universal human, 95–96
Riparian principle, 78
Rivers:
  (Africa) Nile, 74
  (Africa) Shire, 74
  (Africa) Zambezi, 74, 77
  (Bangladesh) Brahmaputra, 213
  (Bangladesh) Ganges, 213
  (Bangladesh) Meghna, 213
  bottom lands, 100–101
  (Canada) Eastmain, 47–48, see also
    James Bay Hydroelectric Project
    (Canada)
  (Canada) Fraser, 37
  current, loss of, 55
  effluent discharges into, 58
  (Honduras) Humuya, 100
  (Japan) Lake Biwa, see Lake Biwa
    listings
  (Japan) Seta River, 142, 147–48
  (Japan) Uji, 142
  (Lebanon) Banias, 327
  (Mexico) Río Atoyac, 241, 243
  (Middle East) Jordan, 327–29
  (Middle East) Litani, 315
  as natural systems, 77
  (South America) Amazon, 1
  (U.S. & Mexico) Colorado, see Central
    Arizona Project (CAP)
  (U.S. & Mexico) Gila, 174
  (U.S.) Comal, 189
  (U.S.) Guadalupe, 189, 199
  (U.S.) Nooksack, 37–41
  (U.S.) Salt, 180
  (U.S.) Tennessee, see Tennessee-
    Tombigbee Waterway
  (U.S.) Tombigbee, see Tennessee-
    Tombigbee Waterway
  (Zimbabwe) Manyame, 86
Rivers at Risk, 137
Rivers of Empire: Water, Aridity, and the

Growth of the American West
   (Worster), 163
Roads and sediment deposits, 275
Roberts, B. R., 261
Rockwood, Charles, 167–68
Rodriguez, Ciro, 198
Rogers, C. M., 132
Rogers, P., 315
Rogge, A. E., 164
Roman-Dutch water law, 78
Romans, 324
Ross, J., 314
Ross, Philip, 194
Rothman, J., 206
Rum industry, 290
Rusinek, W., 170, 171

Sachar, H. M., 317
Sachs, W., 74, 90
Safi, J. M., 333, 334
Sahelian drought and famine of
   1969–1974, 75
Said, Edward, 320
Salamander, Comal Springs/San Marcos,
   191
Salinity:
   Arabs and Israelis, water between, 319,
      329–30, 332, 336
   Bay Islands (Honduras), 275–76
   Eastmain River (Canada), 58, 61
   St. Thomas (Virgin Islands), 296,
      298–99
Salisbury, R., 68
Salmon, 39
Salt River Valley (AZ), 164
Sam-Cromarty, M., 68
San Antonio Express-News, 206–8
San Antonio (TX), 187–88
   see also Texas, water wars in South
Sanbongi, K., 149
Sand filtration systems, 241–42
Sayigh, R., 320, 327
Scarcity of freshwater supply:
   conflicts over rights and resources,
      341–42
   dominant motif in contemporary con-
      sideration of water, 76–77
   project culture, 342–44
   social organization, 339–41
   spreading worldwide, 35–36
   technodependence, 345
   tension between hydrodevelopment
      and sustaining biological/cultural
      life, 344–45
   types of scarcity, three, 5

United Nations, 1–2
   see also various topic headings
Schlitz, M. J., 206
Schorr, T. S., 105–8
Scudder, T., 90, 105
Sea of Galilee (Middle East), 327–29
Secakuku, Ferrell, 19
Sediment deposits in coastal areas, 274,
   275
Shapiro, M., 333
Shareholders and stakeholders, opposing
   interests of, 27–30, 87
Sharma, N., 75
Shawwa, I. R., 319
Shehedeh, R., 319, 322
Sheridan, T., 89, 164–67, 186, 380
Shiga Prefecture (Japan), *see* Lake Biwa
   listings
Shiva, V., 90
Shkilnyk, A., 48
Shue, H., 118
Shuval, H., 328
Sibert, William L., 175
Sierra Club, 176, 195, 196–97, 202, 203
Simchen, E., 319
Singer, P., 239, 260
Skanu'u, 67
Slavery, 288, 289
Slurry, coal transportation by, 18–26,
   29–30
Smith, G. E., 173
Smith, K., 164
Smith, T., 171
Social impact assessment and local
   knowledge, 66–67
Social organization, 339–41
Sorensen, J. H., 268, 270, 272
Southern Pacific Railroad, 168
Specht, John, 194
Spierenburg, M., 92
Springs/water/rain in Hopi secular and
   religious philosophy, 13–18
St. Croix (Virgin Islands), 292, 296
St. Thomas (Virgin Islands):
   agriculture and public health, 293–95
   aquifer, main, 302–5
   conclusions, 305–8
   geographic description, 285–86
   past, the, 287–90
   political/economic structure, 286–87
   power and water, 295–99
   present, the, 299–302
   tourist industry, developing a, 291–93
Stakeholders and shareholders, opposing
   interests of, 27–30, 87

Statistical Abstract of the United States,
  134
Steady, F., 239
Stekler, P., 42
Stepick, A., 238, 241, 246
Stevens, J., 167–69, 172
Stiger, Sam, 183
Stine, J., 137
Stonich, S. C., 113, 268, 270, 272
Strangers Devour the Land (Richardson),
  68
Subsistence rights, 96–98, 105, 113–17
Sugar cane, 290
Superfund, 304, 305
Sustainability of water as resource and
  cultural marker, 345–46
Sustainable America: A New Consensus,
  138
Sustainable development, 29, 138
Syria, 329
Systemic deprivation, 97, 114–17

Tanner, A., 51, 68
Taylor, F. F., 284
Technodependence, 345
Tennessee-Tombigbee Waterway:
  benefits and project economics, 126–
    30
  conception of, 124–25
  conclusions, 136–39
  construction of, 125–26
  current effects, 132–35
  engineering feat, 123
  history behind, 126
  Tennessee-Tombigbee Corridor Study,
    128–31
Tetrachloroethylene, 303
Tewa, Dennis, 9
Texaco Caribbean Inc., 303, 304
Texas, water wars in South:
  Applewhite II, 195–201
  Applewhite reservoir, 193–95
  conclusions, 201–5
  cultural contrasts between northern
    Mexico and southern Texas, 187–88
  Edwards Aquifer, 189–91
  resources, informational, 205–6
  water use policy, 191–93
To Hell with Paradise (Taylor), 284
Toilets, 277
Tokugawa Period (1603–1867) in Japan,
  145–46
Topalov, C., 261
Tourism:
  environmental impact of, 263–68

St. Thomas (Virgin Islands), 286–87,
  291–93
  tourist density/intensity ratio, 271
  see also Bay Islands (Honduras)
Traditions of the Hopi (Voth), 31
Transportation, waterway, 54–57, 124,
  128
Tributary organization, 340
Trichloroethylene, 303
Truth of a Hopi (Nequatewa), 31
Tsakwani'yma, 26
Tulchinsky, T. H., 319
Turkey, 324
Turki, Fawaz, 320
Turner, A. C., 138
Turner, T., 42–43
Tutu Wellfield (St. Thomas-Virgin
  Islands), 303

Udall, Morris, 173
Udall, Stewart, 176, 296
United Nations, 1–2, 325, 330
University of Texas, 200–202
Upham, S., 32
Urbanización Capitalista (Topalov), 261
Usher, P. J., 66
Utah, 169–70
  see also Central Arizona Project (CAP)

Van Dyke, J. C., 185
Vecsey, C., 48
Vega, A., 269, 275
Victims of Progress (Bodley), 42
Vilez-Ibañez, C. E., 239, 259
Virgin Islands, 289–90
  see also St. Thomas (Virgin Islands)
Virgin Islands Daily News, 302, 303, 308,
  310
Virú Valley (Peru), 35
Viscusi, W. K., 176, 177
Voices from the Odeyak (Posluns), 68
Voth, H. R., 9, 18

Wages and El Cajón Dam (Honduras), 110
Waldram, J. B., 48
Wall, G., 264
Walter, Jesse, 15
Ward, P. M., 239
Water: The International Crisis (Clarke),
  76
*Water Disputes in the Jordan Basin
  Region and Their Role in the
  Resolution of the Arab–Israeli
  Conflict* (Libiszewski), 338

Water quality:
  Arabs and Israelis, water between,
    318–19, 332–34
  Central Arizona Project (CAP), 184
  fish and aquatic environments threat-
    ened, 76–77
  James Bay Hydroelectric Project
    (Canada), 58–59
  Lake Biwa (Japan), 154–57
  lesser-developed countries, 237–38
  tourism, 263–68, see also Bay Islands
    (Honduras)
  see also Health and water quality;
    Oaxaca de Juárez (Mexico), drinking
    water quality i
Weeding, 101
Weir, D., 333
Welch, J., 42
Welfare burden, corporate, 136
Welsh, F., 175–81
West Bank (Middle East), see Arabs and
    Israelis, water between
Westergaard, W., 289
Western Auto, 303, 304
Whatcom County (WA), 38–40
White, G., 267
White, R., 32, 91
White, S., 210
Whiteford, S., 89
Whiteley, P., 32
Wiley, P., 177, 179–81
Wilkinson, C., 33
Williams, Susan, 40
Wilson, P., 177, 182, 183
Winter, M., 244
Wittfogel, K., 90
Wolf, A., 314
Wolf, E., 339, 340, 346

Wolff, Nelson, 198, 199, 201
Wong, P. P., 264
Words into Action: Basic Rights and the
    Campaign Against World Poverty,
    117
World Bank, 75, 76, 87, 100, 105, 237–38
World Health Organization (WHO), 279
World War II, 291
Worster, D., 163, 164, 166
Worthlessness, sense of, 64
Wozencraft, Oliver, 167
Wulff, R. M., 138
Wynne, D., 319
Wyoming, 169–70
  see also Central Arizona Project (CAP)
Wyoming v. Colorado in 1922 (prior ap-
    propriation), 169

Young, Robert, 181

Zaag, P. van der, 92
Zambezi Valley (Zimbabwe), law and
    water rights/discourse and, 83–88
Zeidenstein, S. A., 214, 221, 234
Zimbabwe:
  conclusions, 87–90
  exploring different
    uses/understandings of water, 75
  Land Acquisition Act of 1992/1996, 81
  land division, 81
  private/public water, 78, 88
  Rhodesia, land and water in, 77–81
  Water Act of 1996, revising the, 82–83
  Zambezi Valley, law and water
    rights/discourse and, 83–88
Zionism, 317–18, 332, 335
  see also Arabs and Israelis, water
    between

Island Press Board of Directors